THE ROUGH GUIDE TO

Naples
& the Amalfi Coast

D1121013

This third edition written and researched by

Martin Dunford

with additional contributions by

Natasha Foges

ROUGH GUIDES

roughguides.com

Contents

Introduction to
Naples and the Amalfi Coast

Italy's third largest city after Rome and Milan, Naples couldn't be more different from its northern counterparts; it's quite unlike anywhere else in Italy, or indeed the world – a chaotic, mesmerising metropolis that will soon have you under its spell. Not only that, the city's prime location on the Bay of Naples, within easy reach of some of Europe's greatest archeological sites, the fabled islands of the bay itself, not to mention Italy's most jaw-dropping stretch of coast, are big draws as well.

Naples and its region are undeniably appealing, with a huge variety of things to see and do, but the city comes with a lot of baggage. Plenty of Italians have never been here, and swear that they never will. Internationally, too, its reputation has never been strong, and has only worsened as the ongoing and well-publicized struggle against organized crime plumbs new depths. You may feel the same, and quite honestly it's easy to visit Pompeii and Herculaneum, the islands and the Amalfi Coast and barely set foot in the city. But to do that would be to miss somewhere unique, a city that just two centuries ago was one of the largest cities in Europe and a must-visit for any self-respecting Grand Tourist. With Italian Unification its power waned, and its fortunes over the last century have mirrored those of the wider Italian south, marred by poverty, corruption and stuttering economic growth. But with caution, and good information, Naples is as accessible – and no more dangerous – than anywhere else in Italy. The city also provides a vibrant and fascinating base for seeing many of the nearby attractions, with an integrated transport network around the Bay of Naples that makes it a perfect half of a two-centre holiday. Spend time here before heading off for the more bucolic delights of the islands or coast – it's arguably one of Europe's most undiscovered tourist cities.

ABOVE BEACH UMBRELLAS, POSITANO

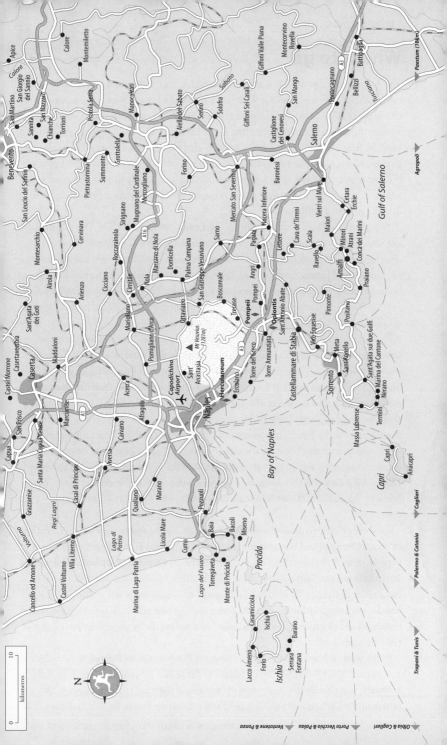

Where to go

The diversity of attractions in Naples and its region means that – time permitting – you can pack a lot into your holiday. With just a weekend to spare, Naples makes a great city-break option, giving you the right amount of time to cover the main sights and wander the atmospheric ancient centre; if you have a week at your disposal, you could also take in some of the bay's famous archeological sights, as well as spend a couple of days island-hopping – or bypass the city altogether and take the dramatic coast road to the towns around Amalfi. Any longer than this and you can explore the city, coast and islands at your leisure, with great public transport connections cutting travelling (and driving) time to a minimum.

If Naples is your base, head straight for the **Centro Storico**, a UNESCO world heritage site whose dead-straight streets follow the grid of the ancient Greek and Roman settlements the city was founded on. This area is Naples' spiritual heart, home to an array of churches and palaces, and a street-level commerce that couldn't be further from the homogenized centres of many of Europe's major cities. The big museums and attractions are elsewhere, but if you experience only one thing in the city, it should be this. Beyond the old centre, **Via Toledo** is the modern hub of Naples, a busy shopping street that leads up from a cluster of portside attractions – the **Palazzo Reale**, **Teatro di San Carlo** and **Castel Nuovo**, among others – to the **Museo Archeologico Nazionale**, one of the great museums of Europe, home to the best of the region's ancient Roman finds. West of Via Toledo, the jungle of congested streets that make up the notorious **Quartieri Spagnoli** neighbourhood rubs shoulders with the elegant boulevards of **Chiaia**, a haven of designer shopping and high-end dining that is quite at odds with much of the rest of the city. Up above, reachable by funicular, **Vomero** is similarly well-heeled, a nineteenth-century residential quarter that boasts heart-stopping views and some of the city's most historic museums, most notably in the **Certosa di San Martino**. Northeast of here, on another of Naples' hills, **Capodimonte** harbours a former residence of the Neapolitan royals, now home to the excellent **Museo Nazionale di Capodimonte**, one of Italy's finest art collections.

But there's plenty to draw you out of the city too. To the **south**, the evocative remains of ancient **Pompeii** and **Herculaneum** need little introduction, but Roman ruins have been unearthed all along the coast, and the less famous remains of **Oplontis**, **Stabiea** and **Boscoreale** are also worth a visit, along with an ascent of Vesuvius, which dominates the coast south of the city. Beyond here, the sprawl of Naples peters out and you're into holiday territory, concluding with the resort town of **Sorrento** – an appealing mixture of earthiness and elegance that is a good base for sampling the many and varied delights of the whole peninsula.

To the **west** of Naples lie the fabled Phlegrean Fields or **Campi Flegrei**, so named for the volcanic activity that has been a feature of the region for centuries. The remarkable **Solfatara**, just outside the main town of **Pozzuoli**, is the most visible instance of this: an otherworldly landscape of bubbling mud and sulphurous fumaroles. Pozzuoli itself is

home to a number of sights dating back to a time when it was the principal port of ancient Rome – remains which provide a taster of the ruined cities of **Baia** and **Cumae** beyond. North of Naples lie more ancient sites, principally in **Capua** and in the provincial capital of **Benevento**, but the area's real draw is the vast royal palace at **Caserta**, an eighteenth-century pile which dominates the town.

The **islands** of the Bay of Naples – **Capri**, **Ischia** and **Procida** – are a massive draw, and many people arrive at Naples' train station or port and ship right out again on the first ferry. Of the three islands, **Ischia** has perhaps the broadest appeal, much larger than its neighbours and with an assortment of attractions that make it suitable for everything from a day-trip to a fortnight's holiday: climb to the top of its extinct volcano, relax in its healing spa waters, or just eat and laze the days away in one of its small-scale resorts. **Capri** is smaller and more scenically spectacular, but it can be heaving in high season – and its high prices reflect its popularity. The dazzling landscape and sharp Mediterranean light make it truly special, however, and it would be a pity to come to Naples and not visit at all – though it's best out of season or after the day-tripping masses have gone home. Tiny **Procida** is an alternative – largely unknown except to the locals, and out of season at least a sleepy haven of fishing villages and picturesque beaches.

The **Amalfi Coast** draws crowds of admiring visitors, and no wonder: its crags and cliffs, girdled by a spectacular coastal road, are as mind-blowing as you are given to expect. If you avoid the tourist hotspots, and travel outside the peak months of July and August, you'll find it bearably busy, and with a range of rewards in the shape of stunning coastal towns like **Amalfi**, **Ravello** and **Atrani**.

When to go

Like the rest of Southern Italy, Naples enjoys a mild Mediterranean **climate**, with warm summers and mild winters. The hottest months are June through to August, although temperatures are rarely uncomfortably high, and the islands and coast usually enjoy the benefit of a cooling breeze. The wettest period tends to be the autumn and early winter, when the region is prone to thunderstorms and downpours, particularly in October. January and February can also be wet and cold, but conditions usually improve by March and April. The **best times to visit** are May, June and September, when the weather is usually warm and sunny, and also the months of the year when you're most likely to catch a festival (see p.30). The soaring temperatures of August, and the fact that this is when the Italians take their annual holiday, make this the month to avoid, especially in Naples, when everything is closed, and the coastal resorts, when everything is crowded and expensive.

AVERAGE TEMPERATURES AND RAINFALL

	Jan	Feb	Mar	Apr	May	Jun	Jul	Aug	Sep	Oct	Nov	Dec
Max/Min (°C)	13/5	13/5	16/7	18/9	23/12	26/16	30/19	30/19	27/16	22/13	17/8	13/6
Rainfall (mm)	80	100	80	100	60	30	30	30	80	130	140	100

Author picks

Martin Dunford has travelled every inch of the Naples region and loves it in all its different aspects, but there are certain places and activities that for him make visiting truly special.

Beaches Procida (p.181) has plenty of attractive beaches to choose from, and Ischia's long, sandy beaches make the island the ideal choice for a break with the kids (p.166).

Budget options Your holiday budget will go a long way in Naples, which has plenty of inexpensive accommodation, and makes a good base for day-trips. But there also some great budget choices on the islands and on the Amalfi Coast (pp.82–84, pp.177–178, p.184, p.208, pp.218–219 & p.224).

Culture The impressive collections of the Museo Archeologico Nazionale (p.67), Museo Nazionale di Capodimonte (p.71) and MADRE (p.57) make Naples an obvious base for a cultural break.

Death cults Death is a recurring motif in Naples – in its weird cemeteries full of skulls (p.71), underground catacombs (p.71) and death cult churches (p.51) – and an interesting way to understand the city.

Food Naples is arguably Italy's greatest foodie location – unpretentious home-style restaurants serve up great pasta and freshly caught fish and seafood. It's also the home of pizza and if you love *gelato*, you're in for a treat. Up in the hills and along the Amalfi Coast, you'll also find very special restaurants (p.145 & p.87).

Nature Hike into the hinterland of the Sorrentine peninsula to escape the crowds and experience the region's beauty in its most primal form (p.129).

Pampering The thermal spas of Ischia are perfect for easing away aches and pains (p.177).

Romance The stupendous backdrop of the Amalfi Coast makes the swanky hotels of hilltop Ravello the ultimate romantic hideaway (p.220).

Seaside Sorrento is the quintessential coastal resort, with a lovely old town, good restaurants and appealing hotels at all prices (p.132).

> Our author recommendations don't end here. We've flagged up our favourite places – a perfectly sited hotel, an atmospheric café, a special restaurant – throughout the guide, highlighted with the ★ symbol.

FROM TOP GELATO; PASTA AND PRAWNS; COASTAL HIKE

17

things not to miss

It's not possible to see everything that Naples and the Amalfi Coast have to offer in one trip – and we don't suggest you try. What follows, in no particular order, is a selective taste of the region's highlights, from clifftop towns and heavyweight museums to active volcanoes and unforgettable Roman ruins. All highlights have a page reference to take you straight into the Guide, where you can find out more. Coloured numbers refer to chapters in the Guide section.

1 PAESTUM
Page 230

This series of Hellenistic temples, set among the flatlands to the south of Salerno, constitute one of Italy's most haunting and evocative ancient sites.

2 MUSEO NAZIONALE DI CAPODIMONTE
Page 71

A vast palace above the city centre holding one of the best collections of Renaissance art in Italy.

3 CUMAE
Page 107

A visit to the cave of the Cumean Sibyl was a must in ancient times, and the site as a whole remains one of the region's most atmospheric and compelling places.

4 RAVELLO
Page 220

The fabulous views from Ravello have graced a thousand postcards. A true retreat.

 CENTRO STORICO, NAPLES
Page 43

There's nowhere like it, in Italy or the world, and wandering around these ancient streets and soaking up the atmosphere is an essential Naples experience.

 AMALFI
Page 214

Piled up on a cliffside, this ancient maritime republic makes an appealing base for the entire Amalfi Coast. At the central piazza, precipitous steps climb to the town's Duomo.

 VESUVIUS
Page 118

Climbing to the summit of mainland Europe's only active volcano is something you should definitely not miss.

 NAPOLI SOTTERRANEA
Page 50

If there's one thing that's more spectacular than strolling the streets of Naples' old centre, it's poking about the streets underneath it by candlelight.

 LA MORTELLA
Page 172

A Mediterranean garden as beautiful as you'll find anywhere in the world.

PIZZA
Pages 85–90

Where better to eat pizza than in the city where it was invented? Neapolitan-style pizza has a soft and chewy base and simple toppings, baked quickly in a scorching oven.

Itineraries

Naples and its region have so much to offer that it's sometimes hard to know where to start, especially if your time is limited. Below we've listed a number of suggested itineraries that take in the best of what the region has to offer, based on time and specific interests. There's no need to follow them slavishly – they're ideas that fit together both geographically and thematically, no more – but we hope they give you an easily digested taste of the huge richness and diversity of Naples and the Amalfi Coast.

A LONG WEEKEND IN NAPLES AND BEYOND

We reckon Naples is one of the most underrated destinations for a weekend break that there is; not only is there loads to see in the city itself, but the multitude of attractions nearby is easily accessible.

❶ Centro Storico, Naples Wherever you stay in Naples, a stroll through the historic centre should be your first activity. **See p.43**

❷ Museo Archeologico Nazionale, Naples You'd be mad to come to Naples and not visit what is perhaps the greatest collection of Roman finds anywhere. **See p.67**

❸ Herculaneum Smaller and easier to assimilate than Pompeii, Herculaneum is also close to the city and combines well on a day-trip with Vesuvius. **See p.112**

❹ Vesuvius You can't ignore the glowering hulk of Vesuvius wherever you are in the city; excursions to its crater are a must. **See p.118**

❺ Pompeii It's obvious, but do you really want to go home and say you didn't bother? **See p.122**

❻ Sorrento Were there ever two resorts more sybaritic than Sorrento and its near neighbour Capri? Of the two, Sorrento is the more

down-to-earth and enjoyable, plus it's the best jumping off point for Capri. **See p.132**

❼ Capri It would be a shame to come to Naples and not see Capri – scenically it's stunning, and on a day-trip you can easily escape the crowds by walking the coast or jumping on a bus. **See p.151**

THE COAST AND ISLANDS

The great thing about Naples is its proximity to some of the most storied and spectacular resort destinations in Italy. With a full two weeks, you could cover it all, and get to know Naples well; if you have less time, pick from the stops below, skipping over an island or speeding through the Amalfi Coast to Paestum.

❶ Centro Storico, Naples The Centro Storico is Naples' beating heart, and you can easily discover it on a day's stroll, taking in some of the key sights along the way – notably the churches of Santa Chiara and San Domenico Maggiore, the Gesù Nuovo and the amazing Cappella Sansevero. **See p.43**

❷ Chiaia and Santa Lucia, Naples Believe it or not, it's possible to come to Naples and barely aware of the city's seaside location. Don't make that mistake by ensuring you wander the streets of these two upscale neighbourhoods close to the waterfront. **See p.73 and p.75**

ABOVE POSITANO

❸ **Naples' Museums** The Museo Archeologico Nazionale houses the greatest collection of ancient Roman artefacts in Italy, perhaps the world. If archeology isn't your thing, you could head to Museo Nazionale di Capodimonte for fine art, or MADRE for contemporary works. See p.57, p.67 & p.71

❹ **Vomero, Naples** Ride the funiculars up to Vomero – an appealing place, with plentiful shops and restaurants, and home to a variety of sights – best of which is the Certosa di San Martino – plus stunning views over the city and beyond. See p.79

❺ **Procida** The smallest of the three bay islands has a relaxed, unpretentious feel. See p.181

❻ **Ischia** The largest and most diverse of the bay islands, with lots of activities if you only have a couple of days: walking to the summit of the island; exploring La Mortella (a must); and, of course, just lazing on the beach. See p.166

❼ **Capri** It's the most obvious choice among the islands, but also the one most easily explored in a day or so; try to stay overnight to really get the best out of it. See p.151

❽ **Sorrento** One of the most appealing of all Italian seaside resorts; not to be missed if you want a spot of indolent indulgence. See p.132

❾ **Amalfi** Perhaps the best base for visiting the Amalfi Coast, it's just a bus ride away from everything and has a great old town and plenty of places to stay and eat. See p.214

❿ **Ravello** Staying here overnight is something special, and feels quite separate from the scrum of the rest of the coast. See p.220

⓫ **Paestum** The three grand temples of Paestum form one of the greatest Hellenistic sites in Italy, an evocative sight at any time, but wonderful in the early morning or late evening when there's no one around. See p.230

OUTDOORS IN CAMPANIA

Allow a week to ten days for the following itinerary, which combines the best of the region's landscapes and activities, taking in mountains and seas, walking and watersports.

❶ **Cratere degli Astroni** This WWF nature reserve occupies the crater of a formerly active volcano, and is a paradise for birdwatchers and walkers. See p.109

❷ **Vesuvius** Why visit Naples and not take the chance to hike up to the top of mainland Europe's only active volcano? See p.118

❸ **Punta Campanella** The region's only marine nature reserve, well worth visiting if you can get permission. See p.143

❹ **Positano** Most people come for the town and its beach and chi-chi shops and restaurants, but Positano is also beautifully placed for hikes up into the mountains. See p.208

❺ **Amalfi** There are lots of paths that converge on Amalfi and Ravello, from where you can escape the crowds and explore the wilds of the coastal mountains. See p.214

❻ **Benevento** The wooded and hilly countryside around the inland town of Benevento begs to be explored on foot – and the beauty is you won't find many others doing the same. See p.199

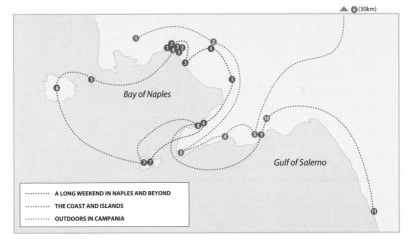

Bay of Naples

Gulf of Salerno

········· A LONG WEEKEND IN NAPLES AND BEYOND
········· THE COAST AND ISLANDS
········· OUTDOORS IN CAMPANIA

SCOOTER IN THE CENTRO STORICO, NAPLES

Basics

Getting there

The easiest way to get to Naples from the UK and Ireland is to fly, and the city is now on the radar of some of the low-cost operators. From the US and Canada there are no direct flights, and most people fly via London or another European gateway and pick up a cheap flight on from there, or fly direct to Rome and take an onward flight or (better) a train – a journey of just over an hour by the fastest rail connection. There are no direct flights to Italy from Australia, New Zealand or South Africa, but plenty of airlines fly to Rome via Asian or European hubs.

Airfares depend on the **season**, with the highest being around Easter, from June to August and from Christmas to New Year. Fares drop during the "shoulder" seasons – September to October and April to May – and you'll get the best prices during the November-to-March low season (excluding Christmas and New Year). Prices also tend to be cheaper if you travel on weekdays.

Flights from the UK and Ireland

Naples isn't a major tourist destination, and although there are scheduled flights it's not nearly as well served as Milan, Rome or other large Italian cities. Because Sorrento and the Amalfi Coast are popular holiday destinations, some carriers only operate services during the summer, which means that you can pay almost as much for flights out of season as you will at peak periods. Direct flight times are 2 hours and 40 minutes, and of the **full-service airlines**, British Airways and Alitalia fly daily from London Gatwick to Naples. Among the **low-cost carriers**, easyJet flies daily from both London Gatwick and London Stansted, and Meridiana from London Gatwick. During high season there are also regular flights operated by Thomsonfly from London Gatwick, London Luton, Birmingham, East Midlands, Manchester, Newcastle, Glasgow and Bristol. From **Ireland**, Aer Lingus flies direct from Dublin to Naples three times a week between April and October. Bear in mind also that flying to Rome and taking the train is always an option, if you can find a cheap fare.

Fares depend, as ever, on how far in advance you book and the time of year, and the cheapest tickets come with restrictions: any changes incur additional fees, and tickets are rarely valid for longer than a month. In general, between April and October you can expect to pay around £200–250 return. Book far enough in advance with one of the low-cost airlines and you might be able to pick up a ticket for £150 return including taxes, even in summer; book anything less than three weeks in advance and this can easily double. Low season fares can be as cheap as £100 return, even with scheduled carriers.

Flights from the US and Canada

There are no direct options to Naples from **North America**, and you'll get the widest choice of flights by flying to Rome and then taking either a connecting flight or a train. The Italian flag-carrier, Alitalia, has the most direct routes between the US and Rome, with daily flights from New York, Boston, Miami and Toronto. Among the national carriers, United flies from Newark, and US Airways from Philadelphia, while many European carriers fly to Italy (via their main hubs) from major US and Canadian cities – for example BA (via London), Lufthansa (via Frankfurt) and KLM (via Amsterdam).

The **fares** charged by each airline don't vary as much as you might think, and you'll often be basing your choice around flight timings, routes and gateway cities, ticket restrictions, and even the airline's reputation for comfort and service. It's quite a long flight – eight or nine hours from New York, Boston, Miami and the eastern Canadian cities – so it's as well to ensure that you're comfortable and arrive at a reasonably sociable hour. The cheapest return fares to Rome or Naples start at $800–1000, rising to around double that during high season.

Flights from Australia, New Zealand and South Africa

There are **no direct flights** to anywhere in Italy from Australia, New Zealand or South Africa, although plenty of airlines fly to Rome and Milan from Asian hubs. Return **fares** to Naples from the main cities in Australia go for around Aus$1500 in low and shoulder seasons, rising to Aus$2500 in high season, and from New Zealand from around NZ$2000 during low season to around NZ$3000 in high season. From South Africa, reckon on paying at least ZAR7000 return from Johannesburg or Cape Town.

A BETTER KIND OF TRAVEL

At Rough Guides we are passionately committed to travel. We believe it helps us understand the world we live in and the people we share it with – and of course tourism is vital to many developing economies. But the scale of modern tourism has also damaged some places irreparably, and climate change is accelerated by most forms of transport, especially flying. All Rough Guides' flights are carbon-offset, and every year we donate money to a variety of environmental charities.

Trains

Travelling **by train** to Italy isn't a particularly economical option, but you can at least break up your journey en route. The most direct route is to take the Eurostar from London to Paris, then the "Thello" overnight sleeper from Paris to Milan, changing there to a fast train to Naples (in summer Thello sleepers run as far as Rome). Total journey time is around 24 hours, and if you book far enough in advance you can get a one-way ticket for a little over £100 in low season, though peak prices can be upwards of £300. Discounts for under-26s are sometimes available and advance booking is essential. If Italy is just one stop on a longer European trip you could invest in a **rail pass** – the Rail Europe website is a useful source of information.

AIRLINES

Aer Lingus W aerlingus.com.
Alitalia W alitalia.com.
British Airways W ba.com.
easyJet W easyjet.com.
KLM (Royal Dutch Airlines) W klm.com.
Lufthansa W lufthansa.com.
Meridiana W meridiana.it
Thomsonfly W thomson.co.uk.
United Airlines W united.com.
US Airways W usair.com.

DISCOUNT FLIGHT AGENTS

Flight Centre UK W flightcentre.co.uk, US W flightcenter.com, Australia W flightcentre.com.au, NZ W flightcentre.co.nz. Specializes in budget flights and holiday packages.
North South Travel UK W northsouthtravel.co.uk. Friendly, competitive travel agency, offering discounted fares worldwide. Profits are used to support projects in the developing world, especially the promotion of sustainable tourism.
STA Travel W statravel.com. Worldwide specialists in independent travel; also student ID, travel insurance, car rental, rail passes and more. Good discounts for students and under-26s.
Trailfinders W trailfinders.com. One of the best-informed and most efficient agents for independent travellers.

RAIL CONTACTS

European Rail UK T 020 7619 1083, W europeanrail.com.
Eurostar UK T 03448 242 524 W eurostar.com.
Rail Europe/Voyages SNCF Australia T 03 9642 8644, W raileurope-world.com; Canada T 1 800 361 7245, W raileurope.ca; South Africa T 11 628 2319, W raileurope-world.com; UK T 0844 248 2483, W raileurope.com; USA T 1 800 622 8600, W raileurope.com.
The Man in Seat 61 W seat61.com.
Trainseurope T 0871 700 7722, W trainseurope.co.uk.
The Train Line W thetrainline-europe.com.

TOUR OPERATORS

UK

Alternative Travel Group W atg-oxford.co.uk. Inclusive 5-to 8-day walking holidays on the Amalfi Coast.
Citalia W citalia.com. Long-established company offering packages in Sorrento, the Amalfi Coast, Capri and Ischia.
GoLearnTo W golearnto.com. Excellent learning holidays specialist offers a range of cookery courses in Sorrento.
Italiatours W italiatours.co.uk. Package deals, city breaks and specialist Italian-cuisine tours. Also offers tailor-made itineraries and can book local events and tours.
Long Travel W long-travel.co.uk. Specialists in southern Italian holidays, with plenty of boutique hotels and villas in Naples, Sorrento, the Amalfi Coast and Ischia.
Martin Randall Travel W martinrandall.com. Inclusive, small-group cultural packages, including a Pompeii and Herculaneum tour.
Ramblers Worldwide Holidays W ramblersholidays.co.uk. One- and two-week walking holidays on the Sorrento peninsula.
Sunvil Holidays W sunvil.co.uk. Package holidays and tailor-made tours based at well-chosen hotels in Amalfi, Ravello, Positano and Sorrento.

US AND CANADA

Adventure Center W adventurecenter.com. Week-long tours of the Amalfi Coast, the Bay of Naples and the islands.
The International Kitchen W theinternationalkitchen.com. Cooking holidays in Ravello, Sorrento and elsewhere, including the Don Alfonso in Sant'Agata, and the Relais Blu in Termini.
Italian Connection W italian-connection.com. Walking tours and cooking tours on the Amalfi Coast and Capri.

Arrival

Arriving in Naples is more painless than you might think – the train station is central and the airport not far out of town. But it's worth knowing that the airport is something of a hub for the region, and is almost as well connected to Sorrento, Salerno and the Amalfi Coast as it is to Naples' city centre. The city's main train station is also very well integrated with the public transport system, not only across the city but also around the Bay of Naples and beyond.

By plane

Naples' Capodichino **airport** (☎081 789 6111, ⓦgesac.it) is a little way north of the city centre, connected with Naples' Piazza Garibaldi by **bus** #C68 every half an hour; the journey takes 20 to 30 minutes. Buy tickets (€1.30) from the *tabacchi* in the departures hall. When going to the airport, catch the bus at the stop in front of the station near the McDonald's. There is also an official airport bus, Alibus, operated by ANM (☎081 763 2177), which runs to Piazza Garibaldi every 20 minutes between 6.30am and midnight; it isn't very much quicker and is a bit more expensive (€3 in advance, €4 on the bus), but it does continue to the Molo Beverello, which is handy for the islands. It leaves from outside McDonald's across the road from the Departures building and takes around 15 minutes to reach the station, 25 minutes to the Molo Beverello. **Taxis** tend to take almost as long as buses to reach the city centre, and cost a flat fare of €16 to the station; up to €23 if you're going further – for example to Vomero or Chiaia. Curreri Viaggi (ⓦcurreriviaggi .it) runs around six buses a day – more in high season – to **Sorrento**; they take an hour and a quarter and cost €10 one way. A couple of bus companies run to **Salerno** (about €4), which is just over an hour from the airport: SITA (ⓦsitasudtrasporti .it), with two buses Monday to Friday except in August; and Buonobus (ⓦbuonobus.it), with two buses Monday to Saturday.

By train

By train, you're most likely to arrive at **Napoli Centrale**, situated on the edge of the city centre at one end of Piazza Garibaldi, at the main hub of city and suburban transport services; there's a **left luggage** office here (open 24hr). Some trains also pull into Stazione Mergellina, on the opposite side of the city centre, which is connected with Piazza Garibaldi by the underground Metropolitana. For train enquiries phone ☎848 888 088, check ⓦtrenitalia.com or go to the information booths at Napoli Centrale (daily 7am–9pm) and be prepared to queue.

By bus

City, suburban and inter-city **buses** also stop on Piazza Garibaldi, and the main companies operate from here. CTP (☎081 700 1111, ⓦctpn.it) run services to Caserta, and SITA (☎081 552 2176, ⓦsitabus.it) go to Pompeii, Sorrento, Positano, Amalfi and Salerno. You'll need to check the stops carefully as they are not well signed and subject to change.

Getting around

The only way to get around central Naples and stay sane is to walk. Driving can be a nightmare, and negotiating the narrow streets, hectic squares and racetrack boulevards on a scooter takes years of training. In any case, you'd miss a lot by not getting around on foot – Naples is the kind of place best appreciated from street level. For longer journeys – and Naples is a big, spread-out city – there are a number of alternatives, both for the city itself and the bay as a whole; for travel beyond Naples, see p.148 and p.206.

Naples transport

The city transport system is run by ANM. Buses will get you pretty much everywhere, and although they are crowded and slow, they remain much the best way of making short hops across the city centre. The bus system is supplemented by the **Metropolitana**, a small-scale underground network that crosses the city centre. Line 1 is in the process of being extended beneath the heart of the centre so that you will be able to travel direct from Napoli Centrale to Piazza Dante, with new stations at Duomo, Università, Municipio and Toledo, but at the time of writing only the first two of these were open. Line 2 runs from Gianturco to the east of the central train station and has five city centre stops – at Garibaldi, Piazza Cavour, Montesanto, Amedeo and Mergellina

TRANSPORT IN NAPLES AND AROUND THE BAY

Pomigliano, Acerra, Baiano

Ottaviano, Poggiomarino & Sarno

Pompei Santuario & Poggiomarino

Metropolitana line 1 (under construction)
Metropolitana line 2
Metropolitana line 6 (under construction)
Circumvesuviana
Cumana
Circumflegrea

Montesanto Funicular: Montesanto–Morghen
Central Funicular: Augusteo–Piazza Fuga
Chiaia Funicular: Piazza Amedeo–Cimarosa
Mergellina Funicular: Mergellina–Manzoni

TICKETS

Uniconapoli **tickets** for all forms of city transport cost a flat €1.30 for all journeys and forms of transport (valid 90min) within the city and must be bought in advance from *tabacchi*, newsstands and stations. An all-day ticket costs €3.70 (weekends €3.10), or you can buy a three-day tourist ticket for €20, which also covers the Alibus to the airport, buses to Vesuvius and public transport on the Amalfi Coast and the islands. The Campania Artecard, which combines unlimited transport with free entry to various sights and museums is also worth investing in (see p.34). Full information (in English as well) is available at ⊕unicocampania.it.

– running out to Pozzuoli in about half an hour. Line 6 is also in the process of being extended and will eventually run from the new station being built at Municipio to Mostra on the western edge of the city, with stops in Chiaia and Mergellina.

In addition, three **funiculars** scale the hill of the Vomero: the Funicolare di Chiaia, which runs from just above Piazza Amedeo to Cimarosa, just below Piazza Vanvitelli; the Funicolare Centrale, which runs from near the Augusteo station, just off the bottom end of Via Toledo, to Piazza Fuga, also a short walk from Vanvitelli; and a third, the Funicolare di Montesanto, running from the station on Piazza Montesanto to Morghen, which is handier for Vomero's main museums. There is a fourth funicular, from Mergellina to Manzoni, but it's much less useful, particularly for tourists. The funiculars are either *misto* – stopping at all stations – or *diretto* – non-stop to the top.

Taxis

There are fixed taxi fares to some key destinations, for example the station to the Molo Beverello costs €11, the station to the airport €16. If you're not taking one of these routes, make sure the driver switches on the meter when you start (they sometimes don't). It is also quite common for the driver to write down the agreed fare before leaving. Fares start at €3.50 for the initial journey, €6 after 10pm and on Sundays; the minimum fare is €4.50. There are taxi ranks at the train station, on Piazza Dante, Piazza del Gesù and Piazza Trieste e Trento, among other places.

CITY TRANSPORT ROUTES

Buses ⊕ 800 639 525, ⊕ anm.it
#R2 Piazza Garibaldi–Corso Umberto I–Piazza Bovio–Via Depretis–Piazza Municipio–Via San Carlo–Piazza Trieste e Trento–Piazza Municipio–Via Medina–Via Sanfelice–Corso Umberto I–Piazza Garibaldi.
#R3 Piazza Sannazzaro–Via Mergellina–Via Riviera di Chiaia–Piazza Municipio–Via Medina–Via Toledo–Piazza Municipio–Via San Carlo–Piazza Trieste e Trento–Piazza Municipio–Via Riviera di Chiaia– Piazza Sannazzaro.

#R4 Via Cardarelli–Via Capodimonte–Piazza Dante–Via Depretis– Piazza Dante–Via Capodimonte–Via Cardarelli.
#E1 Piazza del Gesù–Via Mezzocannone–Via Santa Chiara–Via Duomo–Via dei Tribunali–Via Duomo–Corso Umberto I–Via Monteoliveto–Piazza del Gesù.
#140, Capo Posillipo–Via Mergellina–Piazza Vittoria–Via Riviera di Chiaia–Via Santa Lucia–Via Riviera di Chiaia–Via Mergellina–Capo Posillipo.
#201 Piazza Garibaldi–Via Foria–Piazza Cavour–Piazza Dante– Piazza Municipio.
#401 (night bus) Piazza Garibaldi–Via Depretis–Piazza Municipio–Riviera di Chiaia–Viale Augusto–Via Diocleziano– Pozzuoli.
Metropolitana ⊕ 800 639 525, ⊕ anm.it. City-centre stops include Piazza Garibaldi, Piazza Cavour, Montesanto, Piazza Amedeo, Vanvitelli, Mergellina, Museo, Dante, Università and Duomo – with stops at Municipio and Toledo, among others, to come. Trains every 8min.
Funiculars ⊕ 800 639 525, ⊕ anm.it. Funicolare Centrale, Piazza Augusteo–Piazza Fuga (daily 6.30am–10pm; every 10min). Funicolare di Montesanto, Montesanto FS–Via Morghen (daily 7am–1pm; every 10min). Funicolare di Chiaia, Parco Margherita–Via Cimarosa (daily 6.30am–10pm; every 12min). Funicolare di Mergellina, Mergellina–Manzoni (daily 7am–10pm; every 10min).

Around the Bay of Naples

For **trips around the bay** in either direction – or indeed to get from one side of the centre to another, there are three more rail systems. The **Circumvesuviana** runs from its own station on Corso Garibaldi, near to Napoli Centrale where it also stops, right round the Bay of Naples about every thirty minutes, stopping everywhere as far south as Sorrento, which it reaches in about an hour. In the opposite direction, the **Ferrovia Cumana** operates every 10 minutes from its terminus in Piazza Montesanto west to Pozzuoli and Baia, as does the **Circumflegrea**, which takes a different route to the same terminus at **Torregevata**. Uniconapoli **tickets** are valid for all these suburban lines, though you will need to buy one that covers more zones than the basic ticket.

BAY TRANSPORT ROUTES

Unicocampania Ⓦ unicocampania.it. Campania's many and varied public transport options are excellently managed as an integrated network by this organization, and their website is a good place to find information on all the options around the city, bay and beyond.

Circumvesuviana ☎ 081 772 2444, Ⓦ eavcampania.it. A rail line running between Naples and Sorrento, with many stops around the southern part of the bay, including Ercolano and Pompeii, every 30min, from 5.09am to 10.42pm.

Circumflegrea and Ferrovia Cumana ☎ 800 001 616, Ⓦ eavcampania.it. These two lines connect Naples Montesanto to Fuorigrotta, Agnano, Bagnoli, Pozzuoli, Fusaro, Cumae and Torregaveta. Departures every 20min.

By ferry and hydrofoil

If you're doing any travelling at all around the Bay of Naples, sooner or later you're going to have to take a **ferry**, **hydrofoil** or **catamaran**, and the good news is that the entire region is extremely accessible by sea, with plentiful connections both to the islands and all around the bay and along the Amalfi Coast. Ferries are cheaper, slower and carry vehicles; as a foot passenger, catamarans and hydrofoils are often the better option but tickets are more expensive. The main operators to the islands are Alicost, Alilauro, Caremar, Medmar, SNAV, Travelmar and Coop Sant'Andrea. We've included more details of ferry services in the relevant chapters, on p.148 and p.207, while the Naples daily newspaper, *Il Mattino*, carries timetables for most services.

By car, motorbike and scooter

Travelling **by car** in Naples is fairly challenging: the city centre is crazy and congested and the ring roads that surround it almost impenetrable. Bear in mind too that the **traffic** can be heavy on the main roads down towards Sorrento and along the Amalfi Coast, particularly during the holiday season.

Having said that, there's nothing like driving the Amalfi Coast road for a thrill, and renting a scooter or car either to get around Naples itself or some of the towns around can be a fun thing to do – though it's no place for a beginner. Reckon on paying around €300 per week in high season for a small hatchback, with unlimited mileage, if booked in advance. The major chains have offices in all the larger cities and at airports, train stations, and so on. You need to be over 21 to rent a car in Italy and will need a credit card to act as a deposit when picking up your vehicle.

Rules of the road are straightforward: drive on the right; at junctions, where there's any ambiguity, give precedence to vehicles coming from the right; observe the speed limits – 50kph in built-up areas, 110kph on dual carriageways and 130kph on *autostrada* (for camper vans, these limits are 50kph, 80kph and 100kph respectively); and don't drink and drive. Drivers need to have their dipped headlights on while using any road outside a built-up area.

Parking can be a problem pretty much everywhere, and attendants are especially active in tourist areas. Look for the **blue-zone** parking spaces which usually have a maximum stay of one or two hours; they cost around €1–1.50 per hour (pay at meters or buy scratch-cards from local tobacconists) but are sometimes free after 8pm and on Sundays. Much coveted **white-zone** spaces (white lines) are free; **yellow-zone** areas (yellow lines) are reserved for residents. On the Amalfi Coast you may want to check whether your hotel has parking, and what it charges; they usually use small enclosed garages, but these can cost up to €20 a day in the main resorts.

Although Italians are by no means the world's worst drivers, they don't win any safety prizes either. The secret is to make it very clear what you're going to do – and then do it. A particular danger for unaccustomed drivers is the large number of scooters that can appear suddenly from the blind spot or dash across junctions and red lights with alarming recklessness. Never leave anything visible in the car when you're not using it, including the radio. In Naples some rental agencies won't insure a car left anywhere except in a locked garage.

CAR-RENTAL AGENCIES IN NAPLES

Avis ☎ 081 780 5790, Ⓦ avis.com.
Europcar ☎ 081 780 5643, Ⓦ europcar.com.
Hertz ☎ 081 231 1200, Ⓦ hertz.com.
Maggiore ☎ 081 780 3011, Ⓦ maggiore.it.
Sixt ☎ 081 751 2055, Ⓦ sixt.com.

Accommodation

Accommodation can be a major cost in certain parts of the region, such as the glitzy Amalfi Coast, where hotel prices can be off the scale. Naples itself has its fair share of pricey hotels but as it's not a tourist centre it tends to be cheaper than many other Italian cities, and it's not hard to find decent mid-range options as well as really personable B&Bs and hostels, and there are often real bargains to be had at weekends.

AGRITURISMO

An increasingly popular accommodation option is **agriturismo**, a scheme whereby farmers rent out converted barns and farm buildings. Usually these comprise a self-contained flat or building, though a few places just rent rooms on a bed-and-breakfast basis. This market has boomed in recent years, and while some rooms are still annexed to working farms or vineyards, many are simply smart, self-contained rural vacation properties. Attractions may include home-grown food, swimming pools and a range of activities from walking and riding to archery and mountain biking. Bear in mind though that many agriturismo properties have a **minimum-stay requirement** of one week in busy periods. Tourist offices keep lists of local properties, or you can search one of the growing number of agriturismo websites – there are hundreds of properties at ⓦagriturismo.com, ⓦagriturismo.net and ⓦagriturist.it.

In high season it is always a good idea to **book rooms in advance**, especially in the major resorts. The same applies during religious holidays (notably Easter), and anywhere where a festival is taking place. Most tourist offices carry full **lists of hotels** and other accommodation such as B&B and agriturismo options. They may be able to help you find a room at short notice, but few have dedicated accommodation services, and you're usually better off booking direct or through a hotel booking site like ⓦvenere .com. Always establish the full price of your room – including breakfast and other extras (tax and service charges are usually included) – before you accept it. It's often a good idea to call or email a day or so before arrival to **confirm your booking**. If you're going to arrive late in the evening, it's even worth another call that morning to reconfirm.

Hotels

Hotels – or *alberghi* – in Italy are **star-rated** from one to five. As with most European countries these days, prices fluctuate with demand, but as a general rule one- and two-star hotels go for about €80–100 for a double room; three- and four-star places go for €120–180, while you'll pay anything from €200 to €500 at the best hotels. In Naples prices are at the low end of the range and deals abound, especially at weekends, while in Capri and on the Amalfi Coast, you'll be looking at the higher prices and deals are harder to come by, especially during summer.

In the more popular centres, along the Amalfi Coast and on the islands, it's not unusual for hotels to impose a **minimum stay** of two or sometimes three nights in summer – usually July and August – or insist on you taking halfboard (breakfast and dinner) where they have a restaurant. Note also that single rooms nearly always cost far more than half the price of a double, although kindlier hoteliers – if

they have no singles available – may offer you a double room at the single rate, which is, again, more likely outside high season. In Naples, you will find hotels are cheaper at weekends so, if you look hard enough, you could pick up a real bargain at one of the swankier places.

Bed and breakfast

There's been a huge growth in **B&Bs** in Campania since deregulation at the end of the 1990s. Prices at the lower end of the scale are comparable to one- and two-star hotels – €80–100 a night – but you'll also find a number of upscale B&Bs, situated in noble *palazzi* and large private homes, where you'll pay €150 a night and up. Tourist offices and local websites often carry lists of B&Bs, and ⓦbed-and -breakfast.it is another useful resource. In addition to registered B&Bs you'll also find **rooms for rent** (*affitacamere*) advertised in some towns. These differ from B&Bs in that breakfast is not always offered, and they are not subject to the same regulations as official B&Bs; nearly all *affitacamere* are in the one-star price range.

Hostels and student accommodation

There are several excellent non-official **hostels** in Naples and some of the major resorts, and many hostels belonging to the **Hostelling International (HI)** network, ⓦhihostels.com. At the latter you strictly speaking need to be an HI member to stay at them, but many allow you to join on the spot, or simply charge a small supplement. Whether or not you're an HI member, you'll need to **book ahead** in the summer months.

Camping

There are plenty of **campsites** to choose from in the Campi Flegrei area, in inland Campania and of course along the Amalfi Coast and on the islands. Prices in high season tend to start at around €10 per person, plus around €10 per pitch. We've listed a few sites in the guide, and you can even camp and visit Naples if you want, but if you're camping extensively it's worth checking Italy's informative camping website, ⓦcamping.it, for details of sites and booking facilities.

Food and drink

You could be forgiven for coming to Naples solely to eat. Even in a country famous for its food, Naples is something special, and the staples of its cuisine – most notably its world-famous pizza – contribute hugely to the reputation of Italian cuisine worldwide.

Eating out

Restaurant meals are served in either a trattoria or a *ristorante*. Traditionally, a trattoria is a cheaper and more basic purveyor of home-style cooking, while a ristorante is more upmarket, although the lines are pretty blurred these days. Pizzerie obviously serve pizza but usually also include a handful of basic

---

ICE CREAM

Italian **ice cream** (*gelato*) is deservedly famous, and a cone (*cono*) or "cup" (*coppa*) is an indispensable accessory to the evening *passeggiata*. Most bars have a fairly good selection, but for real choice go to a **gelateria** (we've listed our favourite places in the Guide), where the range is a tribute to Neapolitan imagination and flair for display. There's usually a veritable cornucopia of flavours (*gusti*) ranging from those regarded as the classics – like lemon (*limone*) and pistacchio – through staples including *stracciatella* (vanilla with chocolate chips), strawberry (*fragola*) and *fiordilatte* (similar to vanilla), to house specialities that might include cinnamon (*cannella*), chocolate with chilli pepper (*cioccolato con peperoncino*) or even pumpkin (*zucca*).

---

pasta dishes on the menu, as well as delicious *fritti* – fried, savoury snacks that are as Neapolitan as pizza, and consist of such delights as *arancini* (deep-fried rice balls), potato *crochette*, even *pizzette fritte*. *Osterie* – basically old-fashioned trattorias or pub-like places – specialize in home cooking, though some upmarket places with pretensions to established antiquity borrow the name. It's hard to generalize with regard to **costs**, but in most mid-range places you'll pay €8–12 for a starter or pasta dish, while the main fish or meat courses will normally set you back between €10 and €15.

The menu and the bill

Traditionally, lunch (*pranzo*) and dinner (*cena*) start with the **antipasto** (literally "before the meal"), a course consisting of various cold cuts of meat, seafood and cold vegetable dishes. Some places offer self-service antipasto buffets. The next course, the **primo**, consists of a soup, risotto or pasta dish, and is followed by the **secondo** – the meat or fish course, usually served alone, except for perhaps a wedge of lemon or a garnish. Watch out when ordering fish, which will either be served whole or by weight – 250g is usually plenty for one person – or ask to have a look at the fish before it's cooked. Note that by law, any ingredients that have been frozen need to be marked (usually with an asterisk) on the menu. Vegetables or salads – **contorni** – are ordered and served separately, and there often won't be much choice:

BREAKFAST

Most Neapolitans start their day in a bar, their **breakfast** (*colazione*) consisting of a coffee and a *cornetto* – a sweet croissant often filled with jam, custard or chocolate, which you usually help yourself to from the counter and eat standing at the bar. It will cost between €1 and €1.50. Breakfast in cheaper hotels is all too often a limp affair of watery coffee, bread and processed meats, and sometimes you're better off just going to a bar.

WINE

The volcanic slopes of Mount Vesuvius are among the most ancient wine-producing areas in Italy, but in spite of this the region doesn't have a great reputation for **wine**. The best choices among the Campanian whites are **Greco di Tufo**, **Fiano di Avellino** and **Falanghina** – all fruity yet dry alternatives. Ischia nowadays produces good white wine, notably **Biancolella**, while **Lacryma Christi**, from the slopes of Vesuvius, is available in red and white varieties and is enjoying a new-found popularity after years of being considered cheap plonk. Among the pure reds, there's the unusual but delicious **Gragnano**, a sparkling wine that's best served slightly chilled, and **Taurasi** – like the best wines of the region made from the local *aglianico* grape, which produces rich, elegant wines that can command high prices.

potatoes will usually come as fries (*patate fritte*), while salads are either green (*verde*) or mixed (*mista*); vegetables (*verdure*) generally come very well boiled. Afterwards, you nearly always get a choice of fresh local fruit (*frutta*), ice cream (*gelato*) and a selection of **desserts** (*dolci*).

The great thing about an Italian menu is that you can dive in and out just as much or as little as you want. You will need quite an appetite to tackle four courses (antipasto, *primo*, *secondo*, *dolce*), but if your stomach – or wallet – isn't up to it, it's perfectly acceptable to have less. If you're not sure of the size of the portions, start with a pasta dish and ask to order the *secondo* afterwards. And don't feel shy about having just an antipasto and a *primo*; they're probably the best way of trying local specialities anyway. If there's no menu, the verbal list of what's available can be bewildering; if you don't understand, just ask for what you want – if it's something simple they can usually rustle it up. Pretty much everywhere will have pasta with tomato sauce (*pomodoro*) – always a good standby for kids.

At the end of the meal ask for the **bill** (*il conto*), and bear in mind that almost everywhere you'll pay a **cover charge** (*coperto*) of €1–3 a head. In many trattorias the bill amounts to little more than an illegible scrap of paper; if you want to check it, ask for a **receipt** (*ricevuta*). In more expensive places, service (*servizio*) will often be added on top of the cover charge, generally about ten percent. If service isn't included then it's fine just to leave a few coins as a **tip** unless you're particularly pleased (or displeased) with the service.

Drinking

Most **bars** in Naples are functional places to come for a coffee in the morning or a quick snack during the day. It's cheapest to drink standing at the counter, in which case you pay first at the cash desk (*la cassa*), present your receipt (*scontrino*) and give your order. There's always a list of prices (*listino prezzi*) behind the bar and it's customary to leave a small coin on the counter as a tip for the barperson, although no one will object if you don't. If there's waiter service, just sit where you like, though bear in mind that to do this can cost up to twice as much as drinking at the bar, especially if you sit outside (*fuori*) – the difference is shown on the price list as *tavola* (table) or *terrazzo* (any outside seating area).

An **osteria** can be a more congenial setting, often a traditional place where you can usually try local specialities with a glass of wine. Real enthusiasts of the grape should head for an **enoteca**, though many of these are more oriented towards selling wine by the case than by the glass. Naples has a lively after-dark scene, and many of its bars have live music or DJs. Some of these have taken to calling themselves **pubs**, with beer, particularly in its draught form – *alla spina* – an increasingly popular drink.

Coffee and tea

If pizza is Naples' most sacred food, then coffee is its liquid counterpart. It is consumed early and often and is almost always *espresso* or just *caffè*. An *espresso* will cost you €0.80–€1, a *cappuccino* about €1.30. Neapolitans are fiercely devoted to their favourite bar, even *barista*, and are chronically dissatisfied by coffee they consume outside the city limits. Often just like anywhere else you put in your own sugar, but in Naples sometimes the barista will do it for you, so you need to tell them how you want it: *amaro* (without sugar) or *zuccherato* (with sugar). Coffee can also be ordered *stretto* (extra short) or *lungo* (long). *Baristi* will begrudgingly make extra-long *café americano* when asked, but have been known to refuse making a *cappuccino* after noon. In the summer, look for *caffè freddo* and *cappuccino freddo*, cold versions of old favourites. An *espresso* with a drop of hot milk is *caffè macchiato*; very milky coffee is *caffè latte* (ordering just a "*latte*" will get you a glass of milk); coffee with

CUCINA NAPOLETANA

The most famous elements of the Italian diet – pasta, pizza and pastries – are the staples of Neapolitan cuisine. But it's not all home-grown: restaurant menus here read like a veritable history of foreign occupation. The Greeks brought olive trees and grapevines; the Romans imported grains used to make bread; and Arab traders promoted citrus and aubergine cultivation and introduced durum wheat. And the locals have the Spanish to thank for another staple of *cucina napoletana*: the humble tomato, a key ingredient in the venerable *pizza marinara*.

VEGETABLES AND CHEESE

This traditionally poor cuisine based on fresh produce featured little meat until the mid-twentieth century. Typical *contorni* (vegetable dishes) include bitter, leafy **greens** like *scarola* and *friarielli*, served sautéed in oil and garlic; *zucchine alla scapece* (sweet-and-sour courgettes); and *caponata* (a cooked vegetable salad made with aubergine, tomato and capers). Local **cheeses** such as cow's-milk *scamorza* and the softer mozzarella *di bufala*, made with buffalo milk, are widely available (the regions to the north and east of Naples are important mozzarella-producing areas).

PASTA AND MAIN COURSES

Pasta is often served with just a simple sauce of fresh tomatoes and basil laced with garlic; in Neapolitan sauces, garlic, onion and parmesan are rarely combined. Aubergines and courgettes turn up endlessly in sauces, as does the tomato-and-mozzarella pairing – particularly good as *gnocchi alla sorrentina*. You should also try the classic *pasta alla genovese* (with slow-cooked meat and onions). Of the seafood pastas, clams combine with garlic and oil for superb *spaghetti alle vongole*; mussels are often prepared as *zuppa di cozze* (with abundant chilli and croutons); and fresh squid and octopus are ubiquitous. The baked dishes *sartù di riso* (rice timbale) and *gattò di patate* (mashed-potato cake with diced ham and cheese) are common *trattoria* lunch options. **Meat** specialities include *braciole* (meat rolls stuffed with breadcrumbs, pine nuts and raisins) and *polpette* (meatballs) cooked in a rich tomato sauce; among the **fish** mains are *polipetti affogati* (literally, "drowned octopus"), sautéed in white wine, and *fritto misto* – small fish from the bay served deep-fried, bones and all.

a shot of alcohol – and you can ask for just about anything – is *caffè corretto*.

Hot tea (*tè caldo*) comes with lemon (*con limone*) unless you ask for milk (*con latte*). Milk itself is drunk hot as often as cold, or you can ask for it with a dash of coffee (*latte macchiato*) and sometimes as a milkshake – *frappè* or *frullato*.

Soft drinks and water

Among the **soft drinks** (*analcolici*), there are a number of slightly fizzy, bitter home-grown drinks like Sanbittèr or Crodino, or the cola-like Chinotto, or try a **spremuta** or fresh fruit juice, squeezed at the bar. A crushed-ice **granita** is a great summer cooler, plus there's the usual range of fizzy drinks and concentrated juices. **Tap water** (*acqua dal rubinetto*) is quite drinkable, and you won't pay for a glass in a bar (often you'll be given one with your coffee), though Italians prefer **mineral water** (*acqua minerale*) and drink more of it than any other country in Europe. It comes either still (*senza gas, liscia* or *naturale*)

or sparkling (*con gas* or *frizzante*). The local brands are the naturally sparkling Ferrarelle and Lete – the latter long-time shirt sponsors of the Napoli football team.

Beer and spirits

Beer (*birra*) is usually a lager-type brew (*birra chiara*), which comes in one-third or two-third litre bottles, or on tap (*alla spina*) – measure for measure more expensive than the bottled variety. A small beer is a *piccola* (20cl or 25cl), a larger one (usually 40cl) a *media*. The cheapest and most common Italian brands are Peroni, Moretti and Dreher, all of which are very drinkable, although craft beers are becoming popular in Italy and new artisanal breweries, producing tastier, more exotic ales, are springing up all the time. If you want Italian beer, either state the brand name or ask for *birra nazionale* – otherwise you could end up with a more expensive imported beer.

All the usual **spirits** are on sale and known mostly by their generic names. There are also Italian brands

PIZZA

Naples' most affordable food is also its most sacred; a local saying goes "you can insult my mother but never my pizzamaker". Crusty **pizza** baked rapidly in a searingly hot wood-fired oven and doused in olive oil is a speciality of the city-centre pizzerias (see p.85), though great pizza is readily available all over the region. The archetypal Neapolitan pizza is the *marinara* – not, as you might think, anything to do with seafood, but topped with just tomato, garlic and basil, no cheese. The simplest toppings tend to be the best – *margherita* (with tomatoes and cheese), or perhaps *salsiccia e friarelli* (sausage and local bitter greens).

PASTRIES AND DESSERTS

Neapolitans take their **desserts** very seriously, and the pastries and *gelato* served here are often *artigianale* or *di produzione propria* (home-made). Queues are commonplace at the top *pasticcerie*, particularly on Sundays, when locals take home fancy parcels of cakes to round off their slap-up lunch. Perhaps the best known of the region's celebrated pastries are **sfogliatelle**, ricotta-filled sweets made in two forms – "*riccia*" (shell-shaped with a crunchy, flaky crust) and "*frolla*" (flat and round with a shortbread crust). Another civic symbol is *babà*, a brioche soaked in a sugary rum syrup, sometimes split open and stuffed with cream. *Torta caprese*, a chocolate and hazelnut cake dusted with powdered sugar, makes a delicious accompaniment to Naples' world-class coffee. If you happen to be in the area during March, look out for *zeppole di San Giuseppe*, deep-fried doughnuts stuffed with custard, made in the weeks preceding and following the saint's day on March 19.

STREET FOOD

A plethora of food stalls or *friggitorie* sell delectable fried snacks; the Neapolitan classics below are perfect for lunch on the run (see p.90).

arancini large, breaded rice balls filled with meat or mozzarella
crocchè potato croquettes
fiorilli courgette flowers in batter
pizzette bite-sized pizzas
panzarotti ravioli parcels

panini napoletani pizza dough stuffed with ham, cheese and mortadella, folded into quarters and wrapped in paper to take away
scagliuozze fried polenta
sciurilli fried courgette flowers

of the main varieties: the best Italian brandies are Stock and Vecchia Romagna. A generous shot of these costs about €1.50, imported stuff much more. You'll also find **fortified wines** like Martini, Cinzano and Campari; ask for a Campari-soda and you'll get a ready-mixed version from a little bottle; lemon is *limone*, ice is *ghiaccio*. Aperol is a popular aperitif, a herby concoction not unlike Campari and often consumed with Prosecco or soda water – the perfect start to a summer evening. You might also try Cynar – believe it or not, an artichoke-based sherry also drunk as an aperitif with sparkling water.

There's also a daunting selection of **liqueurs**. Amaro is a bitter after-dinner drink or *digestivo*, the best-known version of which is Fernet-Branca; Amaretto is much sweeter, with a strong taste of almond; Sambuca a sticky-sweet aniseed concoction, traditionally served with a coffee bean in it and set on fire (though, increasingly, this is something put on to impress tourists). Another sweet alternative is *limoncello* or *limoncino* from Sorrento, a lemon-based liqueur traditionally drunk in a frozen

vase-shaped glass. Strega is another drink you'll see behind every bar, yellow, herb-and-saffron-based stuff in tall, elongated bottles: about as sweet as it looks but not unpleasant.

The media

Italy's decentralized press serves to emphasize the strength of regionalism in the country, and Naples is no exception, with strong local papers and supplements, although you may find yourself turning to foreign TV channels or papers if you want an international outlook on events.

Newspapers

Naples' daily **newspaper** is *Il Mattino* – like most Italian papers, not particularly comprehensible even if you speak Italian, but useful for local museum opening hours, ferry and train timetables and the like. Of the nationals, the posh paper is the right-of-centre *Corriere della Sera*, to which *La Repubblica* is the left-of-centre alternative, and both have Naples sections that are useful for listings whether or not you speak Italian. The tourist office publication, *Qui Napoli*, is also good for events information. The sports coverage in all these papers is relatively thin; if you want in-depth football reporting you need to try one of three national sports dailies – either the pink *Gazzetto dello Sport*, the Rome-based *Corriere dello Sport*, or *Tuttosport*. Finally, **English-language newspapers** are available on the day after publication at newsstands all over the region. *The International New York Times*, available at most newsstands on the day of publication, is printed in Italy and includes an Italian news supplement.

TV and radio

Italian **TV** has a justified reputation for ghastly quiz shows, mindless variety programmes and chat shows squeezed in between countless advertisements. There are three state-owned channels – Rai 1, 2 and 3 – along with the channels of Berlusconi's Mediaset empire – Italia 1, Rete 4, Canale 5 – and a seventh channel, Canale 7. Satellite television is fairly widely available, and some hotels will offer a mix of BBC World, CNN and French-, German- and Spanish-language news channels, as well as MTV and Eurosport.

Rai dominates Italian **radio** too, with three main stations. There are one or two decent local stations – Amore (105.8), Kiss Kiss Napoli (103), Radio Club 91 (91.0) – but on the whole the output is virtually undiluted Europop.

Check the following websites for details of the global frequencies of **world service** stations: BBC ⓦbbc.co.uk/worldservice; Radio Canada ⓦrcinet .ca; Voice of America ⓦvoa.gov.

Festivals

Naples is a city that likes to enjoy itself, and the lively festivals and events that punctuate the year, both in the city and the surrounding area, can be worth organizing a visit around.

In Naples itself the biggest event is undoubtedly the festival of the city's patron saint **San Gennaro**, which takes place three times a year, but the more explosive **Santa Maria del Carmine** festival in July and the **Festa di Piedigrotta** in September also draw the crowds.

There's no shortage of music, theatre or **cultural events** either, whether it's the Maggio dei Monumenti in May, the Napoli Teatro Festival in June or one of several film festivals that are held in Naples throughout the year, which offer pretty much the city's only opportunity to view English-language cinema. Outside Naples, **Ravello's arts festival** is gaining in stature as an annual event, and offers the chance to attend concerts in some unique settings, as does June's **Vesuvian Villas festival**, while inland Campania sees some fantastic *sagre* (food-based festivals) from September through to November (see box, p.193). Festivals are detailed in the relevant chapters of the Guide, along with other, smaller events, some of which you may just be lucky to stumble across on your trip.

Festival calendar

JANUARY

La Befana (Jan 6) Naples. The feast of Epiphany is celebrated in Naples with gifts for good children, coal for naughty ones, and there's a market in Piazza del Plebiscito.

FEBRUARY

Carnevale Naples. Celebrated every year in Naples and some of the towns around. There's no real parade, but everyone takes to the streets in costume, and at home people traditionally eat lasagne to mark the last meal before Lent.

Sant'Antonino (Feb 14) Sorrento. A big parade and lots of fireworks to celebrate Sorrento's saint's day.

MARCH–APRIL

Easter Naples, Procida & Sorrento. During the Settimana Santa, solemn processions mark the lead-up to Easter, and are particularly resonant in some of the towns around the bay.

Naples Marathon (Sun in mid-April) ⓦ napolimarathon.it. A full marathon, half-marathon or a 4km fun run, held annually in April.

MAY

Festa di San Gennaro (first Sat in May) Naples. Festival for the city's patron saint, with crowds gathering in the cathedral to witness the liquefaction of San Gennaro's blood (see p.43).

Maggio dei Monumenti (weekends in May) Naples. Buildings and monuments that are usually kept closed open their doors, for exhibitions, concerts and readings, or just for visits.

JUNE

Regata delle Quattro Antiche Repubbliche Marinare (first Sun in June, every four years) Amalfi. An ancient boat race between the cities of Venice, Genoa, Pisa and Amalfi (see p.214). Next one 2016.

Napoli Teatro Festival (three weeks in June)
Ⓦ napoliteatrofestival.it. A festival, showcasing Italian and foreign-language drama, song and dance in some fantastic venues around town.

Napoli Film Festival (ten days in June), Ⓦ napolifilmfestival.com. Featuring shorts, feature-length films and documentaries in their original language.

Independent Film Show (three days late June) Naples
Ⓦ em-arts.org. Festival of experimental film, with screenings in the original language.

Ravello Festival (end June–Sept), Ⓦ ravellofestival.com. A festival of music, dance, literature and the visual arts, with big names coming to perform in great indoor and outdoor venues around the hill-town (see p.223). Whatever you see, the settings are magical, and the auditorium spectacular.

Estate a Napoli (June–Sept). Free outdoor concerts and events in atmospheric venues across the city.

JULY

Festa della Madonna del Carmine (July 16) Naples. The fireworks at this festival are among the city's best.

Neapolis Festival (three days mid-July) Naples Ⓦ neapolis.it. This three-day rock event held in the Arena Flegrea in Fuorigrotta is Southern Italy's biggest, with an array of international as well as Italian names.

Festa di Sant'Anna (July 26) Ischia. The island celebrates its saint's day with a parade of fishing boats and fireworks around the Castello Aragonese.

Amalfi Coast Music and Arts Festival Vietri sul Mare
Ⓦ amalfi-festival.org. Chamber music and piano and vocal recitals in Vietri and other Amalfi Coast towns throughout July.

Festa delle Ville Vesuviane (end July) Ercolano, Portici
Ⓦ festivalvillevesuviane.it. A long-running festival of classical music concerts hosted in the best of the Bourbon villas in the towns immediately south of Naples.

AUGUST

Ferragosto (Aug 15) Pozzuoli. August 15 is a national holiday in Italy, and celebrations are particularly serious in Pozzuoli where locals compete to climb a greased pole and there's a spectacular fireworks display (see box, p.103).

SEPTEMBER

Festa di Piedigrotta (early to mid-Sept) Naples
Ⓦ festadipiedigrotta.it. One of the biggest events of the year, with a massive procession through the city centre from Mergellina, and ten days of special events.

Festa di San Gennaro (Sept 19) Naples. The second chance to witness the liquefaction of the blood of the city's patron saint (see box, p.43).

Pizzafest (two weeks mid-Sept) Naples Ⓦ pizzafest.info. Held for over ten years in the Mostra d'Oltremare showground in Fuorigrotta, this ten-day event is a celebration of Naples' most famous gift to the world, with food stalls, demonstrations and plenty of cheesy entertainment.

OCTOBER

Artecinema (three days mid-Oct) Naples Ⓦ artecinema.com. A documentary film festival, with films in their original language.

DECEMBER

Festa di San Gennaro (Dec 16) Naples. The third and last San Gennaro event of the year.

Natale Naples. Nowhere does Christmas cribs or *presepi* like the Neapolitans, and the city is appropriately festive during the month of December, but otherwise Christmas is a family affair, with a big – and traditionally meat-free – feast on Christmas Eve.

Capodanno (Dec 31) Naples. New Year is celebrated in style, with the festival of San Silvestro, which not only entails the throwing of old furniture out of windows but also traditional Italian food – *cotechino* sausage and lentils. Naples also hosts one of the country's best New Year's Eve firework displays, over the Castel dell'Ovo.

Travel essentials

Costs

Prices have risen considerably in Italy over the past decade, in particular accommodation costs, and although Naples is still cheaper than the cities of the north, the Amalfi Coast is one of the most expensive areas in the country when it comes to food and accommodation. You'll pay more every-where during the height of summer, although again in Naples itself prices are fairly competitive even then.

Crime and safety

Naples is a big city with an even bigger reputa-tion for petty **crime** – one that's not entirely without foundation but which also tends to be overplayed. With a bit of common sense, the city is for the most part no more dangerous than any other large city of a million or so inhabitants.

EMERGENCY NUMBERS

Police or any emergency service, including ambulance (Soccorso Pubblico di Emergenza) ☏ 113.
Carabinieri ☏ 112.
Ambulance (Ambulanza) ☏ 118.
Fire brigade (Vigili del Fuoco) ☏ 115.
Road assistance (Soccorso Stradale) ☏ 116.

There are some districts where it's wise to be cautious, or to avoid entirely late at night – areas around Piazza Garibaldi and Forcella, the Quartieri Spagnoli and La Sanità among them. Wherever you are, you should take the usual big-city **precautions**: walk with a purpose; try to avoid looking too much like a tourist; and plan your route in advance, so that you don't constantly have to resort to a map. If you own expensive jewellery or a flashy watch, think about leaving them in your hotel room; don't brandish expensive cameras, mobile phones or other desirable gadgetry in too ostentatious a way; and keep your bag close to your body with the strap in your hand in case of drive-by bag-snatchers (*scippatori*). Finally, don't let all this advice worry you unduly or stop you from enjoying Naples.

To **report a crime**, you will need to make a *denuncia* (statement) at the police station. In Italy the **police** come in many forms, but the two most visible branches are the Carabinieri, with their military-style uniforms and white shoulder belts, who deal with general crime, public order and drug control, and the Polizia Statale, the other general crime-fighting force, who enjoy a fierce rivalry with the Carabinieri and are the ones who deal with thefts. Other branches of law enforcement are the Guardia di Finanza, responsible for investigating smuggling, tax evasion and other finance-related felonies; the Vigili Urbani, mainly concerned with directing traffic and issuing parking fines; and the Polizia Stradale, who patrol the *autostrada*.

Electricity

The supply is 220V, though anything requiring 240V will work. Most plugs are two round pins: UK equipment will need an adaptor, US equipment a 220-to-110 transformer as well.

Entry requirements

All EU citizens can enter Italy and stay as long as they like on production of a valid **passport**. Citizens of the United States, Canada, Australia and New Zealand also need a valid passport, but are limited to stays of three months. All other nationals should consult the relevant embassy about **visa requirements**. Legally, you're required to register with the police within three days of entering Italy, though if you're staying at a hotel this will be done for you.

ITALIAN EMBASSIES AND CONSULATES ABROAD

Australia Embassy: 12 Grey St, Deakin, Canberra, ACT 2600 ☎ 02 6273 3333, ⓦ ambcanberra.esteri.it. Consulates in Melbourne ☎ 03 9867 5744; Sydney ☎ 02 9392 7900; Adelaide ☎ 08 8337 0777; Brisbane ☎ 07 3299 8944; Perth ☎ 08 9322 4500.

Canada Embassy: 275 Slater St, Ottawa, ON, K1P 5H9 ☎ 613 232 2401, ⓦ ambottawa.esteri.it. Consulates in Montréal ☎ 514 849 8351; Toronto ☎ 647 722 0450; Vancouver ☎ 604 684 7288; Edmonton ☎ 780 423 5153.

Ireland Embassy: 63–65 Northumberland Rd, Dublin 4 ☎ 01 660 1744, ⓦ ambdublino.esteri.it.

New Zealand Embassy: 34–38 Grant Rd, PO Box 463, Thorndon, Wellington ☎ 04 473 5339, ⓦ ambwellington.esteri.it.

South Africa Embassy: 796 George Ave, Arcadia 0083, Pretoria ☎ 012 423 0000, ⓦ ambpretoria.esteri.it. Consulates in Johannesburg ☎ 011 728 1392; Cape Town ☎ 021 487 3900.

UK Embassy: 14 Three Kings Yard, London W12K 4EH ☎ 020 7312 2200, ⓦ amblondra.esteri.it. Consulates in Manchester ☎ 0161 236 9024; Liverpool ☎ 0151 666 2866; Edinburgh ☎ 0131 226 3631.

US Embassy: 3000 Whitehaven St NW, Washington DC 20008 ☎ 202 612 4400, ⓦ ambwashingtondc.esteri.it. Consulates in cities nationwide, including Boston ☎ 617 722 9201; Chicago ☎ 312 467 1550; Detroit ☎ 313 963 8560; Los Angeles ☎ 310 820 0622; New York ☎ 212 737 9100; Philadelphia ☎ 215 592 7329; San Francisco ☎ 415 292 9200.

FOREIGN CONSULATES AND EMBASSIES ITALY

Australia Via Bosio 5, Rome ☎ 06 852 721, ⓦ italy.embassy.gov .au/rome/home.html.

Canada Via Carducci 29, Naples ☎ 081 401 338, ⓦ canadainternational.gc.ca/italy-italie.

Ireland Via Giacomo Medici 1, Rome ☎ 06 585 2381, ⓦ embassyofireland.it.

New Zealand Via Clitunno 44, Rome ☎ 06 853 7501, ⓦ nzembassy.com/italy.

South Africa Via Tanaro 14, Naples ☎ 081 852 541, ⓦ sudafrica.it

UK Via XX Settembre 80/a, Rome ☎ 06 4220 2431, ⓦ gov.uk /government/world/organisations/british-embassy-rome

USA Piazza della Repubblica, Naples ☎ 081 583 8111, ⓦ naples .usconsulate.gov.

Gay and lesbian travellers

Attitudes to gays and lesbians are fairly tolerant in Naples and the main resorts especially, although it's as well to be discreet in the smaller provincial towns and the old centre of Naples itself. The national gay organization Arcigay has a branch in Naples (Vico San Geronimo 19, ☎ 081 552 8815), which can provide information on local events, while the website ⓦgay.it has a wealth of information on the scene in Italy. The age of consent in Italy is 18.

Health

As a member of the European Union, Italy has free reciprocal health agreements with other member states. **EU citizens** are entitled to free treatment within Italy's public health-care system on production of a European Health Insurance Card (EHIC). However, you do need to make sure you use a Servizio Sanitario Nazionale (SSN)-approved doctor or hospital when seeking treatment. You can obtain an EHIC by picking up a form at the post office or applying online at ⓦnhs.uk /NHSEngland/Healthcareabroad/EHIC. Allow up to 21 days for delivery. The EHIC is free of charge, valid for at least five years, and basically entitles you to the same treatment as an insured person in Italy. The Australian Medicare system also has a reciprocal health-care arrangement with Italy. Note, however, that this and the EHIC won't cover the full cost of major treatment (or dental treatment), and the high medical charges make travel insurance essential. You normally have to pay the full cost of emergency treatment upfront, and claim it back when you get home (minus a small excess); make sure you hang onto full doctors' reports, signed prescription details and all receipts to back up your claim.

In an **emergency**, go straight to the **Pronto Soccorso** (A&E) of the nearest hospital, or phone ❶ 118 and ask for *ospedale* or *ambulanza*.

A **pharmacist** (*farmacia*) is well qualified to give you advice on minor ailments and to dispense prescriptions; in Naples there are a number that are open outside normal hours (see p.95). If you need a **doctor** (*medico*) or a **dentist** (*dentista*), ask at your hotel or the local tourist office. Again, keep all receipts for insurance claims.

Insurance

Even though EU health-care privileges apply in Italy, you'd do well to take out an **insurance policy** before travelling to cover against theft, loss, illness or injury. A typical policy usually provides cover for the loss of baggage, tickets and – up to a certain limit – cash or cheques, as well as cancellation or curtailment of your journey. Many policies can be chopped and changed to exclude coverage you don't need – for example, sickness and accident benefits can often be excluded or included at will. If you do take out medical coverage, ascertain whether benefits will be paid as treatment proceeds or only after your return home, and whether there is a 24-hour medical emergency number. When securing baggage cover, make sure that the per-article limit – typically under £500 – will cover your most valuable possession. If you need to make a **claim**, you should keep receipts for medicines and medical treatment, and in the event you have anything stolen, you must obtain an official statement (*denuncia*) from the police.

Internet

Most hotels, hostels and B&Bs offer wi-fi access these days, although a few still have the nerve to charge for it. Many cafés and bars have free wi-fi, and some places will also have a terminal you can use for a modest charge.

Mail

Post office **opening hours** are usually Monday to Friday 8.30am until 7.30pm, and on Saturday until 1pm. **Stamps** (*francobolli*) are sold in *tabacchi* and some gift shops, as well as post offices. The Italian postal system is one of the slowest in Europe, so if your letter is urgent make sure you send it *posta prioritaria*, which has varying rates according to

---

ROUGH GUIDES TRAVEL INSURANCE

Rough Guides has teamed up with WorldNomads.com to offer great **travel insurance** deals. Policies are available to residents of over 150 countries, with cover for a wide range of adventure sports, 24hr emergency assistance, high levels of medical and evacuation cover and a stream of travel safety information. Roughguides.com users can take advantage of their policies online 24/7, from anywhere in the world – even if you're already travelling. And since plans often change when you're on the road, you can extend your policy and even claim online. Roughguides.com users who buy travel insurance with WorldNomads.com can also leave a positive footprint and donate to a community development project. For more information go to ⓦroughguides.com/shop.

DISCOUNT CARDS

You can cut the price of sightseeing by investing in the **Campania Artecard**, which gives free travel in Naples, on buses to Pozzuoli and Caserta, and on the Circumvesuviana, Circumflegrea and Cumana lines, plus free entry to several key sights, as well as large discounts on others. There is a range of options, all a little cheaper if you're under 26: a standard, three-day option that includes key city-centre sights and transport (€21); another that also covers sights in the Campi Flegrei and the rest of the region and is valid for either three days (€32) or seven days (€34), though the latter doesn't cover transport; and a third valid for a year and covering the main sights of the region but no transport (€43). More information is available on ☎ 800 600 601 or ⓦ campaniaartecard.it.

Many state museums and archeological sites offer cut-price admission to **EU citizens**, with entrance often free to those under 18 and over 65, and a 50 percent discount to those aged between 18 and 25. ISIC cards are not accepted at many sights because entry prices are based on age, rather than student status, so official ID such as a passport or driver's licence is best.

If you're planning to visit Herculaneum as well as Pompeii, and have your own transport, it's worth knowing that there's a joint ticket that covers entry to both sights, plus nearby Villa Oplontis, Stabiae and Boscoreale, for €20 (valid for 3 days).

weight and destination. Letters can be sent **poste restante** (general delivery) to any Italian post office by addressing them "*Fermo Posta*" followed by the name of the town.

Maps

The **maps** in this Guide should be fine for most purposes, and the tourist offices hand out free maps. The Campania tourist office produces an excellent series of maps to the whole region, including plans of all the major towns, cities and islands. Among commercial maps, the *Touring Club Italiano* map is probably the best stand-alone city plan of Naples, and they do a decent map of the Bay of Naples too, while the Kompass map of the *Sorrentine Peninsula and Amalfi Coast* should be more than detailed enough for any trip.

Money

Italy's currency is the **euro** (€), which is split into 100 cents. There are seven euro notes – in denominations of 500, 200, 100, 50, 20, 10 and 5 euros, each a different colour and size – and eight different coin denominations, with 2 and 1 euros, then 50, 20, 10, 5, 2 and 1 cents. For the latest rates check ⓦ xe.com.

Banks usually offer the best rate of exchange and you can get cash out of ATMs (*bancomat*) everywhere; there's usually a charge, but you won't spend more getting money this way than any other. If you need to go to a bank,

hours are normally Monday to Friday from 8.30am until 1.30pm, and from 2.30pm until 4pm. There are plenty of exchange bureaux and post offices will exchange American Express travellers' cheques and cash commission-free, plus they also have their own cash machines. You can also use a credit card to get cash but remember that all cash advances are treated as loans, with interest accruing daily from the date of withdrawal, plus there is often a transaction fee on top.

Opening hours and public holidays

Naples has plenty to see but there was a time when many sights were closed to the public. Things have improved dramatically since then, but as the city's economy has struggled sights have been closing more frequently for no obvious reason. Exhibits are moved around or sections of museums are closed

VISITING CHURCHES AND RELIGIOUS SITES

The rules for visiting churches, cathedrals and religious buildings are much the same as they are all over the Mediterranean and are strictly enforced everywhere: **dress modestly**, which means no shorts (not even Bermuda-length ones), and covered shoulders for women, and try to avoid wandering around during a service.

due to budget cuts, lack of staff or who knows what, making it hard to say with precision what you'll see at any given attraction. Some places may be closed altogether, but that's Naples – best to go with the flow.

Opening hours have become a bit more flexible in general, but the city and most of the region still follow a traditional Italian routine, with most **shops and businesses** open Monday to Saturday from around 8am until 1pm, and then again from about 4pm until 7pm or 8pm, although many shops also close on Saturday afternoons and Monday mornings. Traditionally, everything except bars and restaurants closes on Sunday, though there's usually a *pasticceria* (pastry shop) open in the mornings, and in general Sunday opening is becoming more common.

Most Naples **churches** open in the early morning, around 8am, and close around noon or 1pm, opening up again at 3pm or 4pm and closing at around 7pm, but there are subtle variations and we've tried to give the most up-to-date times in the text. Sometimes a church or sight will be kept locked and if you're determined to take a look you have to ask for the key; we've given the details of custodians where they exist.

The majority of **museums** are closed on Mondays, and you'll find that a number choose another day of the week to close. The opening times of **archeological sites** around the bay are more flexible: most are open every day, Sunday included, from 9am until one hour before sunset. In winter, times are drastically cut because of the darker evenings; 4pm is a common closing time.

In **August** most of Naples gets out of town, and many shops, bars and restaurants close, leaving the city to the tourists. On official **national holidays** everything closes down except bars and restaurants.

NATIONAL HOLIDAYS

January 1
January 6 (Epiphany)
Easter Monday (Pasquetta)
April 25 (Liberation Day)
May 1 (Labour Day)
June 2 (Day of the Republic)
August 15 (Ferragosto; Assumption)
November 1 (Ognissanti; All Saints' Day)
December 8 (Immacolata; Immaculate Conception of the Blessed Virgin Mary)
December 25
December 26

CALLING HOME FROM ABROAD

To make an international call, dial the international access code (in Italy it's 00), then the destination's country code, before the rest of the number. Note that the initial zero is omitted from the area code when dialling the UK, Ireland, Australia and New Zealand from abroad.
Australia + 61.
New Zealand + 64.
UK + 44.
US and Canada + 1.
Republic of Ireland + 353.
South Africa + 27.

Phones

You will hardly see an Italian without a **mobile phone** – or *telefonino* – clasped to their ear. Most European travellers can use their phones as normal, but far fewer American or Canadian phones work in Italy – check with your provider before travelling. If you are using your regular phone and SIM you are likely to be charged extra for incoming calls, and calls and texts to other foreign mobiles, even your travelling companions in Italy, will be charged at international rates. It may be worth then investing in an Italian SIM card, which can be bought for about €10 from Italian providers TIM, Wind or Vodafone; ask for a "SIM *prepagato*". However, be aware that you will have to contact your regular provider so they can unlock your phone. For further information about using your phone abroad contact your network or check out ⓦ which.co.uk /technology/phones/guides/using-mobile-phones-abroad/using-international-sim-cards. Locally, any numbers that start with a 3 are mobile numbers and consequently more expensive to call.

Public telephones, run by Telecom Italia, come in various forms, but they usually have clear instructions in English. Coin-operated machines are increasingly hard to find and you will probably have to buy a **telephone card** (*carta* or *scheda telefonica*), available from *tabacchi* and newsstands in denominations of €5 and €10. You always need to dial the local code, regardless of where you are; all **telephone numbers** listed in this guide include the local codes – 081 for Naples and around, 089 for the Amalfi Coast. Numbers beginning ☏800 are free, ☏170 will get you through to an English-speaking operator, ☏176 to international directory enquiries.

USEFUL WEBSITES

Naples and the area around are not particularly well-served by websites and online information that's up-to-date, but the following sites are often good sources of recommendations, features and the latest on the city's transport situation.

ⓦ **baiadinapoli.it** General Bay of Naples site that may have what you're looking for, or at least a link to it.

ⓦ **comune.napoli.it** Main city council website, with lots of info in English about the city.

ⓦ **incampania.com** Official site of the Campania regional tourist organization and as such a lead-in to lots of interesting stuff on Naples and around.

ⓦ **capri.net** All-round source of practical travel listings and what's-on information for the fabled island.

ⓦ **ischiaonline.it** General information source and home to webcams trained on points all over the island.

ⓦ **inaples.it** The official tourist board site is a comprehensive source of information on Naples. You can also download the *Qui Napoli* booklet from here, which is handy for all sorts of information, from ferry schedules to events listings.

ⓦ **napoli.com** Articles about the city, as well as cultural itineraries and listings, with English translation.

ⓦ **napoliunplugged.com** A cyber-homage to the city in the form of personal and contemporary articles and blogs, what's on information, etc. A bit hit and miss, but worth a browse.

ⓦ **sorrentoinfo.com** A wealth of practical details on the town, including listings of hotels, restaurants and shops.

Italian **phone tariffs** are expensive, especially if you're calling long-distance or internationally, and many people use phone calling cards for **long-distance calls**, which you can buy from *tabacchi* for upwards of €5. To use one of these cards, you dial a central number and then enter a PIN code given on the reverse of the card, before dialling the number you want to reach. Finally, you can make international reversed-charge or collect calls (*chiamata con addebito destinatario*) by dialling ☎ 170 and following the recorded instructions.

Time

Italy is on Central European Time – one hour ahead of Britain, six hours ahead of EST and nine hours ahead of PST in North America. It's also nine hours behind Perth, eleven hours behind Sydney, and one hour behind Cape Town and Johannesburg.

Tourist information

The **Italian State Tourist Board** (ENIT; ⓦ enit.it) can be useful for maps and accommodation listings before you go – though you can usually pick up fuller information from tourist offices in Italy. Details of every town's tourist offices are given in the Guide.

ITALIAN STATE TOURIST OFFICES ABROAD

Australia Level 4, 46 Market St, Sydney, NSW 2000 ☎ 02 9262 1666.

Canada 110 Yonge St, Suite 503, Toronto, ON M5C 1T4 ☎ 416 925 4882.

UK 1 Princes St, London W1B 2AY ☎ 020 7408 1254.

USA 630 Fifth Avenue, Suite 1965, New York, NY 10111 ☎ 212 245 5618; 500 North Michigan Ave, Suite 506, Chicago, IL 60611 ☎ 312 644 0996; 10850 Wilshire Boulevard, Suite 575, Los Angeles, CA 90024 ☎ 310 820 1898.

Travellers with disabilities

Facilities in Naples aren't geared towards travellers with disabilities, though progress is slowly being made to make hotels, transport and public buildings more accessible. In Naples, cobbled streets, high kerbs, ad hoc parking and building works can make life difficult for those in wheelchairs and the partially sighted, while the steep hillsides of the Amalfi Coast in particular can present their own problems. On car-free Capri, the lack of stairs makes getting around somewhat easier, though the slopes are very steep and the buses aren't wheelchair accessible. **Public transport** in general can be challenging, although some trains have disabled facilities; call ☎ 081 567 2991 in advance for assistance. You can ask at the local tourist office to give you a hand with finding adapted **accommodation**. The website ⓦ turismoaccessibile.org is an excellent resource, with a wealth of useful information on everything from accessible hotels to wheelchair-friendly monuments and churches in Naples and the surrounding area.

Travelling with children

Children are adored in Italy and will be made a fuss of in the street, and welcomed and catered for in bars and restaurants. Hotels normally charge around thirty percent extra to put a bed or cot in your room, though kids pay less on trains and can generally expect discounts for museum entry; prices vary, but 11–18-year-olds are usually admitted at half price on production of some form of ID (although sometimes this applies only to EU citizens). Under-11s – or sometimes only under-6s – have free entry.

Supplies for **babies** and small children are pricey: nappies and milk formula can cost up to three times as much as in other parts of Europe.

Discreet breastfeeding is widely accepted – even smiled on – but nappy-changing facilities are few and far between. Branches of the children's clothes and accessories chain, Prenatal, have changing facilities and a feeding area, but otherwise you may find you have to be creative. Highchairs are rare too, although establishments in areas that see a high volume of foreign visitors tend to be better equipped.

Naples

PROCESSION, FESTA DI SAN GENNARO

Naples

The de-facto capital of the Italian south, Naples is a hard city to like, at least at first. But spend any time here and you will be smitten. Some of the myths are of course true. It's a huge, filthy, crime-ridden place and in parts falling apart; it's edgy and atmospheric, with a faint air of menace; and it is definitely like nowhere else in Italy. Yet Naples has bags of charm, making the noise and disorder easily endurable, even enjoyable, for most first-timers. Compared to the cities of the north, it doesn't attract many visitors, and is refreshingly lacking in tourist gloss. However it's also a grand and beautiful place, with monumental squares, world-class museums, down-at-heel churches crammed with Baroque masterpieces and all manner of historic nooks and crannies – plus innumerable places to enjoy what is arguably Italy's best and most delicious regional cuisine.

Given its great location and the host of things to see in its environs, Naples could reach far greater heights and properly join the European tourist mainstream. But the city is almost too complex for that; indeed its problems – of organized crime, infrastructure and poverty – are the very things that help to keep it unique. It's possible that neither the locals, nor its increasing numbers of admiring visitors, would have it any other way; you can spend a couple of days here and end up as staunch a defender of the place as its most devoted inhabitants.

The **Centro Storico** is the heart of the city, a crowded, buzzing quarter, where Renaissance *palazzi* rise up above streets that hardly see any light, and shrines to the Virgin and San Gennaro – the city's patron saint – hide in dark corners (Naples is a very Catholic place). It's this part of town that rightly gets the most attention, with a dense concentration of sights, the legacy of the city's chequered history. Naples is far less homogenized than most other large European cities, with a layout that follows the grid of the ancient Greek and Roman city underneath, with the palaces and churches of the French and Spanish eras grafted on top. There's always something to see in this part of town, and you could spend a couple of days happily wandering the streets here. But give time too to the modern neighbourhoods beyond: stretching up the city's hills and around the bay, these areas have an altogether different appeal, not to mention a handful of outstanding museums, and some amazing views from the most elevated points.

Orientation

Naples is large and sprawling, and although its centre, focusing on the Centro Storico and the shopping artery of Via Toledo, is clear enough, there are a

Highlights

❶ Centro Storico The best thing to do when you arrive in Naples is to wander the streets of its unique and vibrant old city – still laid out along the lines of the original Greek settlement. **See p.43**

❷ The Duomo The heart and soul of the city, home to the blood of San Gennaro and a host of other features besides. **See p.43**

❸ Napoli Sotterranea There's virtually another city under the paving stones and cobbles of Naples' ancient centre. This intriguing tour takes in some of the best bits. **See p.50**

❹ Cappella Sansevero Perhaps the most macabre attraction in a city full of grotesque treasures. **See p.54**

❺ Museo Archeologico Nazionale One of the world's greatest archeological collections, home to the cream of the treasures from Pompeii and Herculaneum. **See p.67**

❻ Museo Nazionale di Capodimonte The eighteenth-century palace of the Bourbon monarchs overlooks the city from on high and houses a great collection of art. **See p.71**

❼ Football Napoli are the pride of the city, and a visit to the Stadio San Paolo is one of the best Naples experiences. **See p.79**

HIGHLIGHTS ARE MARKED ON THE MAP ON P.42

1

number of different and distinct neighbourhoods. For simplicity, we've divided the metropolis into seven main areas. You may arrive in the area around **Piazza Garibaldi**, one of the city's main transport hubs and location of the train terminus, Stazione Centrale. It's a scruffy, unenticing introduction to the city; you'll find more of interest in the areas beyond the square – up towards the edge of the old city, in **Forcella**, and down towards the port. West of here lies the ancient heart of the city, the **Centro Storico**, roughly corresponding to Roman Neapolis and with the main streets still following the path of the old Roman roads. This is much the liveliest part of town, an open-air kasbah of hawking, yelling humanity that makes up in energy what it lacks in grace. Buildings rise high on either side of the narrow, crowded streets, cobwebbed with washing; there's little light, and not even much sense of the rest of the city outside – certainly not of the proximity of the sea. Beyond here, Naples' commercial and modern centre has **Via Toledo** as its spine, from Piazza Trieste e Trento and the Palazzo Reale at its southern end to the Museo Nazionale Archeologico at the top. North of here, the districts of **Montesanto**, **La Sanità** and **Capodimonte** represent Naples at both its poorest and most grand, while in the opposite direction the neighbourhoods stretching around the bay towards Posillipo are the city's most salubrious; indeed anyone strolling from the station might think they'd reached a different city by the time they came across the elegant storefronts of **Chiaia**. There's an upscale feel, too, on the nearby waterfront, around the statuesque hotels of **Santa Lucia** and along the wide boulevards that connect this part of town to the port at **Mergellina** and to **Posillipo** just beyond, in parts of which you might almost fancy you had reached the Amalfi Coast itself. High above the city and reachable by funicular, **Vomero** has a similarly prosperous atmosphere, and is home to some of the city's most classic views of the bay and beyond.

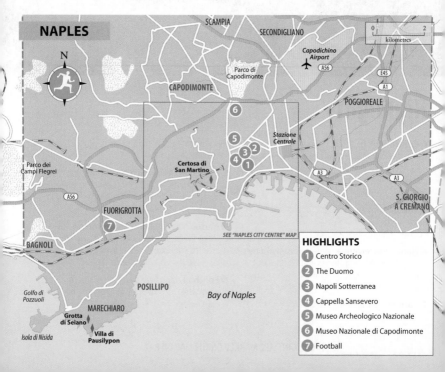

HIGHLIGHTS

1 Centro Storico
2 The Duomo
3 Napoli Sotterranea
4 Cappella Sansevero
5 Museo Archeologico Nazionale
6 Museo Nazionale di Capodimonte
7 Football

The Centro Storico

The UNESCO-protected **CENTRO STORICO** covers the area of the old Roman Neapolis, much of which is still unexcavated below the ground. Its two main streets are **Via dei Tribunali** and **Via San Biagio dei Librai** (the latter also known as Spaccanapoli for the way it splits old Naples): narrow thoroughfares, lined with old arcaded buildings, which lead due west on the path of the *decumanus maior* and *decumanus inferior* respectively of Roman times. Both streets are charged with atmosphere throughout the day, a maelstrom of hurrying pedestrians, revving cars and buzzing, dodging scooters. A third street, known as the **Anticaglia**, follows the *decumanus superior* across the top end of the ancient centre; it's quieter and has fewer sights as such, but still repays a wander.

The Duomo

Via Duomo 147 • Mon–Sat 8am–1.30pm & 2.30–8pm, Sun 8am–1.30pm & 4.30–7.30pm • Free • ☎ 081 449 097

Tucked away unassumingly off Via Duomo, Naples' **Duomo** is a Gothic building from the early thirteenth century (though with a late nineteenth-century neo-Gothic facade), dedicated to the patron saint of the city, **San Gennaro**. Both church and saint are key reference points for Neapolitans: San Gennaro was martyred at Pozzuoli, just outside Naples, in 305 AD under the purges of Diocletian. Tradition has it that when his body was transferred here, two phials of his dried blood liquefied in the bishop's hands. Since then, the "miracle" has continued to repeat itself no fewer than three times a year: on the first Saturday in May (when a procession leads from the church of Santa Chiara to the cathedral) and on September 19 and December 16. There is still a great deal of superstition surrounding this event: San Gennaro is seen as the saviour and protector of Naples, and if the blood refuses to liquefy – which luckily is rare – disaster is supposed to befall the city, and many still wait with bated breath to see if the miracle has occurred. Interestingly, one of the few occasions in recent times that Gennaro's blood hasn't turned was in 1944, an event followed by Vesuvius's last eruption. The most recent times were in 1980, the year of the earthquake, and in 1988, the day after which Naples lost an important football match to their rivals, Milan. The miraculous liquefaction takes place during a special Mass in full view of the congregation (see box below), though the church authorities have yet to allow any close scientific examination of the blood. Whatever the truth, there's no question it's still a significant event in the Neapolitan calendar, and one of the more bizarre of the city's institutions.

THE MIRACLE OF SAN GENNARO

If you're in Naples at the right time (see pp.30–31) it's possible to attend the service to witness the **liquefaction of San Gennaro's blood**, but you must be sure to arrive at the Duomo early. The Mass starts at 9am, but queues begin to form two hours before that; arrive much after 7am and there's a chance you won't get in. Once the line of Carabinieri has opened up the church everyone will make a dash for the front; for a good view of the proceedings you'll have to join them. Pushing and shoving is very much part of the procedure, and throughout the service the atmosphere in the church is boisterous. The preliminary Mass goes on for some time, the chancel of the church ringed by armed policemen and flanked by a determined press corps, until a procession leads out of the saint's chapel holding the (still solid) phial of blood aloft, to much applause and neck-craning, and cries of "*Viva San Gennaro!*" After ten minutes or so of emotional imprecations the reliquary is taken down from its holder and inspected – at which point, hopefully, it is declared to tumultuous applause and cheering that the saint's blood is indeed now liquid, and the phial is shaken to prove the point. Afterwards the atmosphere is festive, stallholders setting up outside the church and the devout queuing up to kiss the phial containing the liquefied blood – a process that goes on for a week.

1

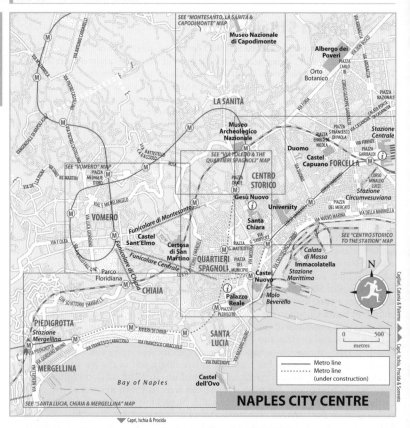

Capri, Ischia & Procida

Inside, the third chapel on the right is dedicated to **San Gennaro**. It's an eye-bogglingly ornate affair, practically a church in its own right, containing the precious phials of the saint's blood and his skull in a silver bust-reliquary from 1305 (stored behind the altar except for ceremonies). Further down the nave, there are paintings by seventeenth-century Neapolitan artists Luca Giordano and Francesco Solimena in the transepts, and some scraps of ancient fresco in the Minutolo chapel in the right transept, together with a large and gaudy Gothic funerary monument, next to which is a painting of *Our Lady of the Assumption* by Perugino. Down below, the **crypt** of San Gennaro holds an altar dedicated to the saint – complete with bones – and a statue of a kneeling Cardinal Carafa, the crypt's founder.

The basilica of Santa Restituta, baptistry and excavations

Off the left-hand side of the nave, the basilica of **Santa Restituta** is actually a separate church, officially the oldest structure in Naples, erected by Constantine in 324 and supported by columns that were taken from a temple to Apollo on this site. To the right of the main altar, the **baptistry** (Mon–Sat 8.30am–12.30pm & 4–6.30pm, Sun 8.30am–1pm; €1.50) contains Christian mosaics dating back to the late fifth century, and a sunken font believed to have been taken from a temple to Dionysus. Beyond the baptistry there are the remains of another ancient church, along with relics from the Roman and even the Greek ancient cities, covering a vast area and well laid out with raised walkways taking you past remnants of Greek-era wall and road, Roman gutters

ART AND ARCHITECTURE: NAPLES' GOLDEN AGE

The greatest age of Neapolitan art and architecture was during the **seventeenth and eighteenth centuries**, when the Counter-Reformation under the pious Spanish viceroys really took hold in the city, and as in Rome was expressed in a fervent flowering of the Baroque style. It was Naples' defining era, when it basked in its status as one of Europe's largest, most elegant and most prosperous cities.

ART

The most famous artist to work in Naples, **Caravaggio** (1571–1610), fled here from Rome in 1606 and quickly became the city's most celebrated painter and a major influence on a generation of Neapolitan artists. One of these was **Giuseppe Ribera** (1591–1652), actually a Spaniard from Valencia (he was known as *Lo Spagnoletto* or "Little Spaniard"), and perhaps the best-known artist from the early part of the Neapolitan Baroque period. Not surprisingly, he was popular with the Spanish in the city, who made sure he landed the plum commissions, and his style is typical of the period, heavily influenced by Caravaggio in its use of *chiaroscuro*, and tending to dramatic themes rendered in a deliberately theatrical style. Ribera was said to be the head of a group of painters who sometimes used violent means to eliminate their competitors, although this didn't do him much good as he died in poverty, despite the fact that his daughter married a prominent Spanish nobleman. A member of the same group, Giovanni Battista or **Battistello Caracciolo** (1578–1637) was, unlike Ribera, a native of Naples, but he was also heavily influenced by Caravaggio and painted in a dark and histrionic style that was the epitome of Neapolitan Baroque. His pupil, **Mattia Preti** (1613–99), also worked in Naples for a period, and a number of his works remain.

The most prolific painter of the era, however, was unquestionably **Luca Giordano** (1632–1705), known as *Luca fa presto*, or "Luca does it quickly" for the speed with which he could churn out works – a skill which was useful for the number of commissions it attracted, but which also meant he was not always taken seriously by his patrons. In fact, he was a great artist, and his paintings are dotted all over Naples, although arguably his greatest works were done elsewhere (in the Escorial in Spain, for example).

Among other Baroque artists who left their mark all over the city was **Massimo Stanzione** (1585–1656), another follower of Caravaggio, though with a style that was a little more refined than that of Giordano and Ribera, earning him the tag of the Neapolitan Guido Reni (1575–1642), whose smooth and elegant paintings are similar. The works of **Giovanni Lanfranco** (1582–1647), a native of Parma, can be seen in the Duomo and the church of Santi Apostoli, which he decorated in a dramatic, Mannerist style that influenced the local painters almost as much as Caravaggio. One of Stanzione's pupils was **Bernardo Cavallino** (1616–56), who died during the Neapolitan plague and left behind precious little work, but was arguably the better painter, as can be seen by a couple of works in the Capodimonte, museum. His contemporary, **Andrea Vaccaro** (1600–70), the son of a family of painters, lived longer and left a lot more behind, most notably in the Certosa di San Martino, Capodimonte, and in a number of churches, again mostly in Caravaggesque style.

The painter who really closes the Neapolitan Baroque era is **Francesco Solimena** (1657–1747) – immensely prolific, and extremely successful too, much in demand in the court of Naples. He had a large studio, and many pupils, among them **Francesco de Mura** (1696–1784), who painted a series of frescoes in the Nunziatella, **Giuseppe Bonito** (1707–89) and **Sebastiano Conca** (1680–1764), who were the two main artists of the Neapolitan Rococo period; perhaps the best-known artist of this period, however, was the landscapist **Gaspar van Wittel** (1653–1736), a Dutchman who spent his last years in Naples, where his son, the future architect Luigi Vanvitelli, was born.

and drainage systems, and mosaic floors from the fifth-century basilica. The excavations are often closed to the public.

Museo del Tesoro di San Gennaro

Via Duomo 149 • Mon, Tues, Thurs–Sun 9am–5pm • €5, also includes entry to Complesso Monumentale dei Girolamini (see p.46) • ☏ 081 294 980, ⓦ museosangennaro.it

Next door to the cathedral, the **Museo del Tesoro di San Gennaro** contains an array of reliquaries, statuary and suchlike, among them a series of bejewelled early

1

nineteenth-century monstrances, lots more silver busts and the eighteenth-century sedan chair used for carrying San Gennaro's relics and a large solid silver throne from the same era. There are older exhibits too, including a painting of the saint by Francesco Solimena, dating from 1701. The chapel and sacristy that house part of the museum are also worth seeing, elaborately decorated in the mid-seventeenth century by Luca Giordano, among others.

Complesso Monumentale dei Girolamini

Via Duomo 142 • Mon, Tues, Thurs & Fri 9am–5pm, Sat & Sun 9.30am–2pm • €5, also includes Museo del Tesoro di San Gennaro (see p.45)

Just across the road from Naples' cathedral is the entrance to the late sixteenth century **Complesso Monumentale dei Girolamini**, the former home of the Order of Oratorians founded by St Philip Neri in 1561. Its enormous church has striped marble pillars and a large fresco by Luca Giordano above the west door depicting Christ casting the Merchants from the Temple. The complex also houses a small picture gallery, on the other side of the cloisters, whose half a dozen rooms mostly contain paintings of the Neapolitan school – dark, brooding works, the best of which are Giuseppe Ribera's depictions of St Andrew and St Peter and a handful of paintings by Luca Giordano and Battistello Caracciolo. There's also a magnificent ancient library, though this is rarely open to the public.

Via del Duomo

Via del Duomo borders the Centro Storico to the east, a dead straight thoroughfare laid out after the 1880s cholera epidemic decimated this part of the city, leading in one direction up to Via Foria and in the other across Corso Umberto and down to the port. A little way down, the right aisle of the large church of **San Giorgio Maggiore** at Via Duomo 237 (Mon–Sat 8am–1pm & 4–7pm, Sun 8am–1pm) was demolished to make way for the street, which explains its somewhat lopsided appearance. It doesn't look it, but it is one of Naples' oldest churches, as you'll see from the semicircular entrance, which was formerly the apse of an early Christian basilica and is the only part to have survived a mid-seventeenth-century earthquake – which probably qualifies San Giorgio as the city's most messed-about church. Further down on the Centro Storico side, the street widens out into a small square at the rusticated rectangular block of the **Palazzo Cuomo**. The square is named after the Filangieri museum of paintings and applied arts that was housed in the building for many years, but has been closed for some time and shows no sign of reopening.

Via dei Tribunali

About halfway up, Via del Duomo is crossed by **Via dei Tribunali**, one of the two main streets of old Naples, which leads straight through the heart of the old city to link to the modern centre around Via Toledo. It's richer in interest and sights than almost any other street in Naples, and you can spend many happy hours picking your way through its churches, palaces and underground caverns, stopping off for pizza at one of its numerous pizzerias before emerging at Piazza Bellini and strolling up to the archeological museum (see p.67).

Pio Monte della Misericordia

Via dei Tribunali 253 • Mon, Tues, Thurs–Sun 9am–2pm • €7 • ☎ 081 446 944, ⓦ piomontedellamisericordia.it

On the Forcella side of Via dei Tribunali you'll find the headquarters of **Pio Monte della Misericordia**, a still-functioning charity that was set up in the early seventeenth century to alleviate the plight of the poor. It's one of the artistic treasure houses of Naples, and most people come to see the charity's **chapel**. This beautiful octagonal structure is best known for Caravaggio's moving *Seven Acts of Mercy* in pride of place over its high altar, but it also has a beautiful and emotional *Deposition* by the late seventeenth-century Neapolitan artist Luca Giordano – easy to miss as you come in – and Battistello Caracciolo's *The Freeing of St Peter* in the chapel next to it. You can also visit the rooms of the organization's **picture gallery** upstairs, some of which are functioning offices and meeting rooms. The trustees of the charity still meet in the Sala del Governo at the far end, overlooked by four powerful paintings of Christ by Mattia Preti, and next door a little balcony looks down onto the church, and has several Caravaggio-like paintings from the same era, notably the *Incredulity of St Thomas* by the Dutch painter Dirk van Baburen. The highlight of the other rooms is a rare self-portrait by Luca Giordano, showing the face of an arrogant and ill-tempered intellectual, glasses perched on his nose.

Piazza Girolamini

Via dei Tribunali continues past **Piazza Girolamini**, on which a plaque marks the house where, in 1668, Giambattista Vico was born. Vico was a late Renaissance Neapolitan philosopher who advanced theories of cyclical history that were far ahead of their time and still echo through modern-day thinking: James Joyce's *Finnegan's Wake* was based on his writings. Vico lived all his life in this district and is buried in **Complesso Monumentale dei Girolamini** (see p.46).

San Paolo Maggiore

Piazza San Gaetano 76 • Mon–Sat 9am–6pm, Sun 10am–12.30pm • Free • ☎ 081 454 048, ⓦ sanpaolomaggiore.it

Via dei Tribunali opens out at **Piazza San Gaetano**, on the site of the agora or **forum** of the ancient Greek and Roman cities, and marked by the statue of the saint. On the right, the basilica of **San Paolo Maggiore** stands on the site of a Roman temple that was rebuilt as a Christian basilica, its ancient roots manifest in a couple of Roman columns which help support the facade with its double staircase. The current church, dating from the seventeenth century, is a huge marbled structure with a wide central nave, decorated with some (sadly damaged) frescoes by Massimo Stanzione. There's little else of interest, apart from the sacristy to the right of the main altar, which is a confection of late seventeenth-century frescoes by Francesco Solimena, with the *Conversion of St Paul* depicted in typically melodramatic style.

San Lorenzo Maggiore

Via dei Tribunali 316 • Daily 7.30am–7pm • Free • ☎ 081 211 0860, ⓦ sanlorenzomaggiorenapoli.it

Almost opposite San Paolo Maggiore, at the top end of Via San Gregorio Armeno, the church of **San Lorenzo Maggiore** is a light, spacious Gothic structure, unspoiled by postwar additions and with a soaring Gothic ambulatory in its apse – unusual in Italy, even more so in Naples. It's a mainly thirteenth- and fourteenth-century building, though with a much later facade, built during the reign of the Angevin king Robert the Wise on the site of the Roman forum – the remains of which are in the cloisters, and the shape of which is marked out on the floor of the nave, along with the fragments of mosaic floor under glass. Scraps of medieval fresco, believed to have been painted by a pupil of Giotto, and several Renaissance funerary monuments point to its later history. The church was at the centre of the golden age that Naples enjoyed under Robert, and the focus of its cultural activity. Petrarch stayed in the adjacent convent, and Boccaccio is said to have met the model for his Fiammetta – believed to be Robert's daughter – during Mass here in 1334.

Museum and excavations

Mon–Sat 9.30am–5.30pm, Sun 9.30am–1.30pm • €9

The real draw of the complex is the excavations, although you can also visit various bits of the **convent** and there's a small **museum**, on several floors, which has frescoes and

1

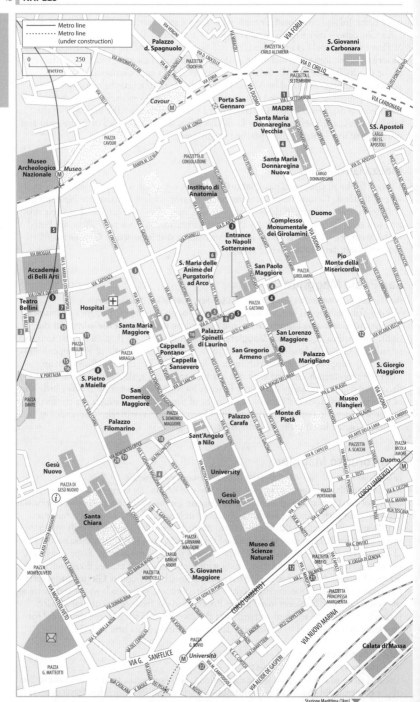

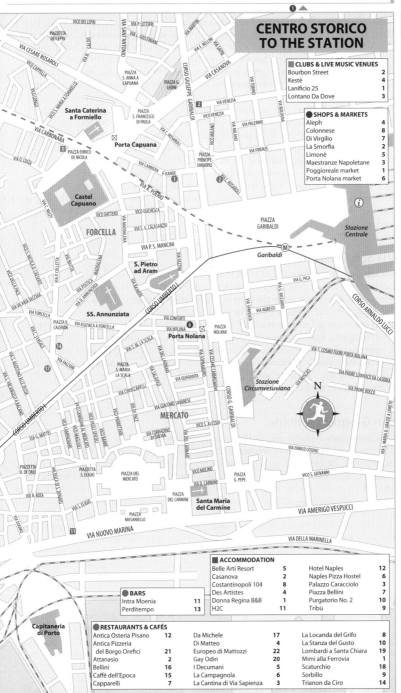

CENTRO STORICO TO THE STATION

CLUBS & LIVE MUSIC VENUES

Bourbon Street	2
Kestè	4
Lanificio 25	1
Lontano Da Dove	3

SHOPS & MARKETS

Aleph	4
Colonnese	8
Di Virgilio	7
La Smorfia	2
Limonè	5
Maestranze Napoletane	3
Poggioreale market	1
Porta Nolana market	6

ACCOMMODATION

Belle Arti Resort	5	Hotel Naples	12
Casanova	2	Naples Pizza Hostel	6
Costantinopoli 104	8	Palazzo Caracciolo	3
Des Artistes	4	Piazza Bellini	7
Donna Regina B&B	1	Purgatorio No. 2	10
H2C	11	Tribù	9

BARS

Intra Moenia	11
Perditempo	13

RESTAURANTS & CAFÉS

Antica Osteria Pisano	12	Da Michele	17	La Locanda del Grifo	8
Antica Pizzeria del Borgo Orefici	21	Di Matteo	4	La Stanza del Gusto	10
Attanasio	2	Europeo di Mattozzi	22	Lombardi a Santa Chiara	19
Bellini	16	Gay Odin	20	Mimi alla Ferrovia	1
Caffè dell'Epoca	15	I Decumani	5	Scaturchio	18
Capparelli	7	La Campagnola	6	Sorbillo	9
		La Cantina di Via Sapienza	3	Trianon da Ciro	14

statues from the church, arrayed around a lovely painted small atrium, and, on the top floor, a series of painted wooden figures from large-scale eighteenth-century *presepi*. Off the courtyard of the convent are a few rooms from the old Angevin-era building, including the long, frescoed Sisto V room and the adjoining chapterhouse, its walls decorated with portraits of members of the religious orders based here in the late sixteenth century. As for the **excavations**, you can explore the remains of the Roman forum as you walk along the old Roman pavement, passing a barrel-vaulted bakery, a laundry and an area of sloping stone banquettes, where it is thought that Romans reclined and debated the great issues of the day, kept warm by a fire beneath the stone.

What was likely to have been the town's treasury shows a remarkable resemblance to a contemporary bank, with visitors having to negotiate a security-conscious double doorway before reaching the main area for business. The great tufa foundations of the Roman forum were built over the earlier Greek agora; a scale model shows how the latter was laid out, with the circular *tholos*, where some goods were sold, at its centre. It's a rare chance to see exactly how the layers of the city were built up over the centuries, and to get some idea of how Naples must have looked back in the fifth century BC.

Via San Gregorio Armeno

Via San Gregorio Armeno leads from Piazza San Gaetano to the other main axis of the old centre, Via San Biagio dei Librai, and is one of the old city's most picturesque streets, lined with places specializing in the making of **presepi** (Christmas cribs), a Neapolitan tradition that endures to this day, although the workshops along here turn them out more or less year-round. The often inventive creations now incorporate modern figures into the huge crib scenes, which can also contain water features, illuminated pizza ovens and tons of moss and bark. "Goodies" such as ex-mayor Antonio Bassolino are distinguished from such "baddies" as Silvio Berlusconi by their haloes, while dear, departed saintly figures like Mother Teresa, Princess Diana and Gianni Versace are also commemorated.

San Gregorio Armeno

Via San Gregorio Armeno 1 • Daily 9am–noon, Tues till 1pm; cloister daily 9.30am–noon, Sun 9.30am–1pm • Free

The church of **San Gregorio Armeno** is a sumptuous Baroque edifice with frescoes above the entrance by Luca Giordano, not to mention two stupendously ornate gilded organs, one on each side of the nave. It's also home to the relics of Santa Patrizia, another Neapolitan saint whose blood – like that of San Gennaro (see p.43) – liquefies on her saint's day (Aug 25), as well as every Tuesday morning. The saint's remains lie in a chapel on the right, while up above the south aisle you'll notice a series of grilles, through which the Benedictine nuns would view the services from the **Chiostro di San Gregorio Armeno** next door. You can sit in the cloister yourself by walking up the street to the convent entrance on the left. It's a wonderfully peaceful haven from the noise outside, planted with limes and busy with nuns quietly going about their duties.

Napoli Sotterranea

Piazza San Gaetano 68 • Daily tours hourly 10am–6pm, Thurs until 9pm • €10 • ☎ 081 296 944, ⓦ napolisotterranea.org

Next door to the church of San Paolo in Piazza San Gaetano is the entrance to **Napoli Sotterranea**, whose ninety-minute underground **tours** explore what's left of the Greek city of Neapolis. The visit starts by exploring remnants of a Roman theatre – which is actually not far underground at all, and is accessed by way of an old one-room Neapolitan apartment or *basso* – artfully furnished as it would have been when they made the discovery forty years ago. You can see a couple of aisles of the theatre – though it's hard to

SUPERSTITIOUS NAPLES

Naples must be one of the most **superstitious** places on earth – and, in some ways, the most cultish, at least by European standards. For a start, there's the enduring belief that the liquefaction of the blood of a **saint** who died two thousand years ago will keep the city from harm (see box, p.43). But it doesn't stop there. There are other local saints that are believed to bring luck and succour to the afflicted – San Vicenzo in La Sanità, the Madonnas of the Piedigrotta and Carmine churches, and modern-day saints like San Giuseppe Moscati who is remembered by a shrine in the Gesù Nuovo.

There's also an unhealthy fascination with **death**. Perhaps it's the presence of Vesuvius glowering on the horizon at every turn, but the notion of the end being just around the next corner is strong in Naples, and is manifest in the city's various death cults: shrines in the streets are regularly stocked with fresh flowers and votive offerings; people until recently used to "adopt" a skull in the city's underground cemeteries to cure illnesses; and in the church of **Santa Maria delle Anime del Purgatorio ad Arco** in the Centro Storico, Neapolitans still secretly make offerings to the dead, although the practice was banned by the Church years ago.

Then there's the **lottery**, just a game of luck and numbers to some, but taken much more seriously in Naples, where an inbred belief in signs and omens, fortune and chance is so strong – and where there are also so many people looking for a stroke of good fortune to pull them out of the gutter. The rules are different here, too, because the numbers have meanings, as determined by **La Smorfia**. This ancient Neapolitan book of dreams and their interpretations ascribes a number to just about anything you might dream about – for example, a pig would always be number 4, a nude woman 21, a hunchback 57, a bride 63, and so on; people who can interpret dreams and the Smorfia are in high demand.

Among countless Neapolitan legends is the **munaciello**, literally "little monk", a sprite who hovers around houses playing pranks on the inhabitants, leaving notes or moving things, breaking furniture or whispering in the ears of people while they're asleep. These figures were originally associated with the tunnels and cisterns underneath Naples, from where they could gain access to people's houses and play tricks – any kind of disorder could be down to the *munaciello*. However, although you may notice their presence in your house, it's considered extremely bad luck to tell anyone about it.

As in many places in Southern Europe, Neapolitans also traditionally fear people with the *malocchio* or **evil eye** – folk who are perceived to have evil powers. Again, it's rooted in the city's obsession with fate and fortune, and naturally there are all sorts of ways of combating the bad luck or *jettatura* that the evil eye can cause. The leaves of various plants are said to be effective, and garlic of course; and historically men touching their genitals was supposed to avert misfortune. But the commonest and most effective way of dealing with the evil eye is to make the sign of horns by holding up your index and little finger and pointing at the ground, or to carry an amulet with the sign of horns – effective as long as they are red, pointed, twisted and given as a present: not hard to do given that they are sold as trinkets all over the city centre.

get a sense of the whole – and it's incredibly well integrated with the buildings above. This is even more evident on Via Anticaglia itself, where two arches over the street are formed by the highest tier of the theatre, and the street curves slightly to follow its shape.

The other part of the tour takes in the **aqueducts** and cisterns that honeycomb the ground beneath the city, used from ancient times until the late nineteenth-century cholera outbreak, and then again as bomb shelters during World War II. The best bit is a candlelit squeeze through some narrow passageways to a couple of cisterns that have been refilled with water. For more opportunities to get beneath the streets, check out the Acquedotto Carmignano (see box, p.65) and the Galleria Borbonica (see p.75).

Santa Maria delle Anime del Purgatorio ad Arco

Via dei Tribunali 39 • Mon–Fri 9.30am–1pm, Sat 10am–5pm • €3 • ☎ 333 383 2561, ⓦ purgatorioadarco.com

Down the street from Piazza San Gaetano, the skulls on the posts outside the church of **Santa Maria delle Anime del Purgatorio ad Arco** give you a clue that this is one of

1

Naples' more morbid attractions: the site of a death cult that was outlawed in the 1960s by the Catholic authorities but still lives on in a semi-secret fashion in its downstairs **hypogeum**. In the church upstairs skulls flank a painting by Stanzione in the apse, showing souls rising to heaven, and the dusty chapels down below hold tiled shrines to the anonymous dead who were worshipped here, revered as intermediaries between the earthly and divine, and given names that endeared the keepers of their graves to them. Some – to "Lucia" for example – are full of flowers and bones, and strewn with notes from well-wishers, though no one knows who she was, or even whether that was really her name. It's a peculiar place: neglected, yet still very much in use.

Palazzo Spinelli di Laurino

Via dei Tribunali 362 • Free

Just beyond the church of Santa Maria, the eighteenth-century **Palazzo Spinelli di Laurino** is worth a peek. The walls are studded with medallions depicting classical themes, and the oval courtyard and monumental staircase tucked into the far corner are great examples of how rooted these grand old *palazzi* are in modern Neapolitan life: festooned with plants and satellite dishes, but with a real elegance beyond the chipped plaster and peeling paint. If you want to experience the place from the inside you can stay at Nathalie de St-Phalle's unique gallery and B&B, *Purgatorio No. 2*, on the first floor (see p.82).

Santa Maria Maggiore alla Pietrasanta and the Capella Pontano

Just past Palazzo Spinelli, the brick campanile of the church of **Santa Maria Maggiore alla Pietrasanta** stands out like a sore thumb. Naples' only surviving large-scale medieval monument, it dates from the eleventh century, and is actually a lot more interesting than the church itself just behind: little more than a large, domed shed put up in Cosimo Fanzago in 1653. There's another interesting feature just outside, the **Cappella Pontano** (Mon–Sat 9am–6pm), a late fifteenth-century structure that looks like a Roman temple, commissioned by one Giovanni Pontano in 1492 as a funerary monument to his wife. Pontano was principal secretary to the Aragonese rulers of Naples, in particular Ferdinand I, and one of the most refined and accomplished men in Europe at the time. Renowned as a poet and humanist, he penned the Latin inscriptions that cover the walls, and the floor of the building is paved with fifteenth-century majolica tiles, each with a subtly different design, interspersed fish, animals and the odd human profile.

San Pietro a Maiella

Via San Pietro a Maiella 35 • Daily 9am–2pm • Free

The fourteenth-century church of **San Pietro a Maiella**, which anchors the end of Via dei Tribunali at Piazza Miraglia, seems oddly out of place, with a stone tower that has the feel of a French provincial church. Built as an Angevin church in the fourteenth century, it's a theme that's continued in the interior, which has been restored to its full Gothic splendour. High, bare stone arches give way to the building's main decorative feature: a magnificent painted wooden ceiling by Matteo Preti dated 1657. Look too at the chapel to the left of the apse, which is covered with fragments of delicate frescoes done by the same Giotto follower who worked in San Lorenzo Maggiore (see p.47). Attached to the church is a convent that houses the **Naples Conservatory of Music**, home to a fabled library of books and music, and whose cloister regularly resounds to the sound of piano music and shrill operatic voices (Via San Sebastiano, around the corner, is lined with music stores).

Piazza Bellini

Just past the church of San Pietro a Maiella, **Piazza Bellini** is a rectangular open space which marks the end of the old city, and indeed always has: the ruins of the old Greco-Roman walls can still be seen at the bottom end of the square. It's a rare pocket of tranquillity in central Naples, at least during the day, a pleasant, leafy square lined with terraced cafés, a good spot for a coffee and a break from sightseeing. At night it's a major hub, with the cafés packed and the square full of cool folk hanging out and shooting the breeze.

Spaccanapoli

Running parallel to Via dei Tribunali, **Spaccanapoli** (literally, "Splitting Naples") cuts cleanly through the old city. It's a long street, and changes name several times: at the Via del Duomo end, it's **Via San Biagio dei Librai**, becoming **Via Benedetto Croce** at its western end, where it opens out at the large square of the Gesù Nuovo and the edge of old Naples.

Via San Biagio dei Librai

West from Via del Duomo, **Via San Biagio dei Librai** leads past some impressive palaces. Renaissance **Palazzo Marigliano**, at no. 39, is one of the city's most beautiful, built in 1513, although it's hard to stand back far enough to appreciate its elegant facade; peek if you can into its courtyard, with its double staircase. It is rather run-down, like most buildings of this kind in the centre, but at least looks better than it did in the 1980s, when it was one of the city centre's most famous radical squats. The rather grander **Palazzo Monte di Pietà** at no. 114, now owned by the Banco di Napoli, has a chapel with seventeenth-century frescoes by Corenzio. Off to the left, the sacristy has more frescoes, best of which are those by Bonito, painted a century later, representing the good deeds of the charity. Outside, the figures in the niches are by Pietro Bernini, father of the more famous Gianlorenzo, who sculpted half of Rome but never made it to Naples, and there's a small display of paintings and sculpture in the rooms off the courtyard.

Further on, the **Palazzo Carafa**, at no. 121, boasts its Florentine original gates, dating from its construction in 1444, and has a terracotta horse's head in the courtyard, a gift from Lorenzo de' Medici. Just beyond, on the opposite side of the street, **Largo del Corpo di Nilo** is home to a famous Roman statue of a reclining old man, thought to have been sculpted in Nero's time – a representation of the Nile that has a habit, it's claimed, of whispering to women as they walk by. Opposite, there's a monument of a different kind, where the **Bar Nilo** has a much-photographed – and venerated – shrine to Diego Maradona, the Argentine football genius who led Napoli to their last *scudetto* in 1990. The shrine used to be inside the bar but was recently moved outside by the exasperated owners, fed up with fans and tourists dropping by for a peek but not ordering a coffee.

Sant'Angelo a Nilo

Piazzetta Nilo 23 • Mon–Sat 9am–1pm & 4.30–7pm, Sun 9.30am–1pm • Free

The little church of **Sant'Angelo a Nilo** is home to the city's earliest piece of Renaissance art: the funerary monument to Cardinal Rinaldo Brancaccio, who built the church adjacent to his palace, which was – and still is – home to Naples' first public library. It was commissioned by his executor Cosimo de' Medici, and made in Pisa in 1426 by Michelozzo and Donatello, and is a tall, columned affair, with an evocative, apparently very true-to-life figure of the cardinal supported by three caryatids and a delicate relief of the *Assumption* on the front by Donatello. Also worth a look is the *St Michael* on the high altar, a late sixteenth-century painting by another Tuscan artist, in this case Marco Pino, and a colourful and expressive piece of work.

1

The University and its museums

Centro Musei delle Scienze Naturali: Via Mezzocannone 8 • Tues, Wed & Fri 9am–1.30pm, Mon & Thurs 9am–1.30pm & 3–5pm, Sat & Sun 9am–1pm • €2.50, €4.50 for all four museums • ⓦ musei.unina.it

Down Via San Biagio is Naples' main **University** building, set between Via Paladino and Via Mezzocannone. The streets around here teem with students, and there's a lively buzz to the area. **Largo San Giovanni**, to the west of Via Mezzocannone, is a pleasant open space by Naples' standards – and you can wander through the university's courtyards from Via Paladino to Via Mezzocannone. You may want to visit in order to see the four small collections that make up Naples' natural history museum – the **Centro Musei delle Scienze Naturali**. These are of limited appeal, but you could stop off at the small zoological museum on the second floor, which has two large rooms of glass cases full of stuffed mammals, as well as various birds and molluscs. The small anthropological collection upstairs focuses on reconstructions of human features, based on African models, as well as the inhabitants of ancient Herculaneum. Next door, there's a museum of mineralogy and paleontology, with a skeleton of a large allosaurus.

Piazza San Domenico Maggiore

Further along Via San Biagio from Piazzetta Nilo, **Piazza San Domenico Maggiore** is marked by the **Guglia di San Domenico**, one of the many whimsical Baroque obelisks that were originally put up in the city after times of plague or disease. This was built in the 1650s to give thanks for the deliverance of the city from plague a couple of decades earlier, although it's hard to say whether thanks were really due as two-thirds of the population had been wiped out. The top corner is anchored by the bulky, seventeenth-century **Palazzo di Sangro**, on the corner of Vico San Domenico Maggiore, home of the notorious alchemist Prince Raimondo di Sangro, whose remarkable chapel, just around the next corner, is one of the city's most compelling sights (see below).

San Domenico Maggiore

Piazza San Domenico Maggiore 8 • Mon–Sat 8.30am–noon & 4–7pm, Sun 9am–1pm & 4.30–7.15pm; Treasury Sat 9.30am–noon & 4–7pm, Sun 9.30am–noon ; Cloister Mon–Sat 10am–5pm • Free

The partially fortified church of **San Domenico Maggiore** flanks the northern side of the square, a long, high, originally Gothic building from 1289, though much reconstructed over the years, and with a large convent complex behind, where a small **cloister** is devoted to temporary exhibitions. The frescoes in the Brancaccio chapel – second on the right – are its oldest feature, the work of Pietro Cavallini and dating back to the early fourteenth century. Their clear, bright colours depict the *Martyrdom of St John the Baptist* and a crucifixion scene with Dominican saints. Another chapel, further down on the same side, holds a miraculous painting of the Crucifixion which is said to have spoken to St Thomas Aquinas during his time at the adjacent monastery, while in the sacristy, off the right aisle, there are much later frescoes by Francesco Solimena, representing the *Triumph of the Dominicans*, and a small **treasury**. However, the sacristy's real feature is the velvet-clad coffins of the Aragonese rulers of Naples stacked up on the balcony that runs all the way round – an odd sight, but an apt one, for it was the Spanish kings who made the San Domenico square and church the centre of their court in Naples.

Cappella Sansevero

Via Francesco di Sanctis 19/21 • Mon & Wed–Sat 9.30am–6.30pm, Sun 9.30am–2pm • €7 • ☎ 081 551 8470, ⓦ museosansevero.it

Branching off the top end of Piazza San Domenico, Via de Sanctis leads off right to one of the city's odder monuments, the **Cappella Sansevero**, tomb-chapel of the Di Sangro family, sculpted by Giuseppe Sammartino in the mid-eighteenth century. The decoration is extraordinary: the centrepiece a carving of a dead Christ, laid out flat and covered with a veil of stark realism, ingeniously, and remarkably, carved out of a single piece of marble.

Even more accomplished, though by different sculptors, is the veiled figure of *Modesty* on the left, and, on the right, *Disillusionment*, in the form of a woeful figure struggling with the marble netting of his own disenchantment. Look, too, at the effusive *Deposition* on the high altar and the memorial above the doorway, which shows one Cecco di Sangro climbing out of his tomb, sword in hand, both by Francesco Celebrano. The man responsible for the chapel, Prince Raimondo, was a well-known eighteenth-century alchemist (whose palace still stands on Piazza San Domenico Maggiore, see p.54), and **downstairs** are the results of some of his experiments: bodies of an upright man and woman, behind glass, their capillaries and most of their organs preserved by a mysterious liquid developed by the prince – who, incidentally, was excommunicated by the pope for such practices. Even now, the black entanglements make for a gruesome sight.

Via Benedetto Croce

The last stretch of Spaccanapoli is known as **Via Benedetto Croce**. The twentieth-century philosopher, after whom the street is named spent much of his life in this neighbourhood, and used to live in the **Palazzo Filomarino**, across from the campanile of the church of Santa Chiara. Croce died here in 1952, and the building is now given over to the library of the Italian historical institute, which he founded (closed to the public).

Santa Chiara

Via Santa Chiara 49 • Daily 7.30am–1pm & 4.30–8pm • Free • ⓦ monasterodisantachiara.eu

Effectively marking the boundary of the Renaissance city, the church of **Santa Chiara** is quite different from any other building in Naples – a Provençal-Gothic structure built in 1328. It was completely destroyed by Allied bombs during World War II, and on rebuilding was restored to its original bare Gothic austerity: quite refreshing after the excesses of most Neapolitan churches. There's not much to see **inside**, but the eighteenth-century majolica floor survived the bombing, as did the fine medieval tombs of the Angevin monarchs at the far end, which include that of Robert of Anjou, sculpted in Florence in 1345. It has two images of the king – as a powerful figure in full regalia above, and lying on his deathbed in a monk's habit below. There are equally grand and finely sculpted monuments to Robert's son, Charles of Calabria, and Mary Valois, Charles's second wife, while the so-called Clares' Choir behind has traces of frescoes once thought to have been by Giotto; the choir, however, is rarely open to non-worshipping tourists.

Cloister

Mon–Sat 9.30am–5.30pm, Sun 10am–2.30pm • €6

That's not it for Santa Chiara. The convent to the left of the church, established by Robert's second wife, Sancia, has a **cloister** that is one of the gems of the city. A shady haven planted with neatly clipped box hedges, it is furnished with benches and low walls covered with colourful majolica tiles depicting bucolic scenes of life outside the convent walls – the work of Domenico Antonio Vaccaro. There's also a giant **presepe** or Christmas crib, to the right as you enter, and in the far corner a very well-organized **museum**, with a collection of pieces from the church before the bombing. The partially reconstructed frieze showing the Angevin kings is by Tino di Camaino, who sculpted many of the royal tombs, and the bits of stonework and statuary, and photos of the complex before and after the bombing, are all beautifully displayed. Outside, the excavated remains of a Roman bath complex – viewed by way of a series of raised walkways – provide yet more evidence of the ancient foundations upon which Naples stands. Finally there's a little café just outside the cloister if you want a rest and a drink.

Gesù Nuovo

Piazza Gesù Nuovo • Daily 7am–12.30pm & 4–7pm • Free • ⓦ gesunuovo.it

Just past Santa Chiara the street broadens out at **Piazza del Gesù Nuovo**, centring on the ornate **Guglia dell'Immacolata**, much larger than the San Domenico obelisk, and

1

commissioned in 1743 by the Jesuits. The **Gesù Nuovo** church is distinctive for its lava-stone facade, originally part of a fifteenth-century palace, prickled with pyramids that give it an impregnable, prison-like air. The building was taken over by the Jesuit order in the 1580s and consecrated as a church at the turn of the seventeenth century.

The **interior** is as over-sized and over-decorated as most Jesuit churches, although its most interesting feature is perhaps the simple chapel and set of rooms on the far right, dedicated to San Giuseppe Moscati, a local doctor who died in 1927 and was reputed to perform medical miracles – as you can see from the votive plaques, poems and scribbled thanks that cover the walls. There's also a re-creation of his consulting rooms and bedroom, arranged as they were on the day he died, complete with desk, couch and the doctor's bed, and a display on his short life; he died in his late forties. Back in the main church there's a statue of Moscati, its hands worn lighter by the touch of regular supplicants, in the Chapel of the Visitation, where his body lies in a sarcophagus under the altar.

The rest of the church is rich in ornament and **paintings**, the most prominent being the large *Expulsion of Eliodoro from the Temple* (1725) by Francesco Solimena above the entrance. The frescoes of the apostles in the pendentives of the cupola are by Lanfranco, echoing his work in the Santi Apostoli church nearby (see p.57); the same artist decorated the rest of the dome but this collapsed in the 1688 earthquake. The altar in the left transept – dedicated to St Ignatius, founder of the Jesuit order – sports paintings and sculpture by the great Neapolitan Baroque artist Cosimo Fanzago, the statues either side decorated with his trademark garlands of fruit. To the left of the main altar, the Cappella Ravaschiera holds around sixty wooden head reliquaries of Jesuit saints, all lined up as if for a performance – which seems appropriate, in this most theatrical of Neapolitan churches.

The Anticaglia

The third of the Centro Storico's Greco-Roman streets is the **decumanus superior**, which runs parallel to Via dei Tribunali a block further up Via del Duomo. Formed of four streets – Via della Sapienza, Via Pisanelli, Via del Anticaglia and Via dei Santi Apostoli – and known as the **Anticaglia**, it's the least busy and least visited of the old city's three main thoroughfares, but it does have a few low-key attractions. It feels much more off the beaten track than the other two streets, and less straight too, swerving in two semicircles around the foundations of a Greek theatre, whose arches still straddle the street and are incorporated into the buildings on both sides.

Santa Maria Donnaregina Nuova: the Museo Diocesano

Largo Donnaregina • Mon & Wed–Sat 9.30am–4.30pm, Sun 9.30am–2pm • €6 • ☎ 081 557 1365, ⓦ museodiocesanonapoli.com

Situated on its own peaceful square just off of Via del Duomo, the seventeenth-century church of **Santa Maria Donnaregina Nuova** has been splendidly restored and converted to house the city's **Museo Diocesano**. Two vast paintings of the *Miracles of Christ* by Luca Giordano face each other across the high altar, while the museum ranges around the sacristy and other rooms on the ground floor, as well as the upper galleries on either side. It's chock-full of dead Christs, martyred saints and all manner of gloom and gore by many of the better-known Neapolitan painters (Solimena, Vaccaro and Paolo de' Matteis, among others), but the exhibits are well displayed and the views of the church from the upper levels spectacular.

Santa Maria Donnaregina Vecchia

Vico Donnaregina 25 • Times vary • Free

Take the alley that runs up the side of Santa Maria Donnaregina Nuova to reach its fourteenth-century counterpart, **Santa Maria Donnaregina Vecchia**. The church was abandoned for the best part of two hundred years and has now been deconsecrated, a bare Gothic building that is officially part of the Naples modern art museum, MADRE, and given over to exhibitions. Whether or not there's anything interesting on, you may want to take a look, not only for the building itself but also to see the fourteenth-century marble tomb of Queen Mary of Hungary in the nave, supported by angels and studded with colourful mosaics, the work of the sculptor Tino di Camaino. Beautiful frescoes decorate a downstairs chapel, including a Baptism of Christ, and now you can also climb the stairs to see the upstairs nuns' gallery, which is almost a separate church and has a fantastic albeit faded series of frescoes by Pietro Cavallini.

MADRE

Via Settembrini 79 • Mon & Wed–Sat 10am–7.30pm, Sun 10am–8pm • €7, Mon free • ☎ 081 1931 3016, ⓦ museomadre.it

Just steps away from Donnaregina Nuova, the Museo d'Art Contemporanea Donnaregina – or **MADRE** for short – is emblematic of Naples' struggles to reinvent itself over recent years. Created in Palazzo Donnaregina in 2005, it hosts temporary exhibitions on the ground and top floors and has a small permanent collection on its first and second floors, including a series of conceptual works that were created by some big-name contemporary artists specifically for the museum. The most prominent of these is the **mural** by Francesco Clemente, a New York-based Neapolitan artist who created the large fresco of Naples across the two floors on his return to the city for his first retrospective – a colourful work full of giant figures and riotous figurative detail. But there are also **first floor** works by Jeff Koons, Anish Kapoor and Richard Serra, the Italian Mimmo Paladino, as well as a massive anchor – embodying the city's maritime roots – by Jannis Kounellis. The **second floor** gives a quick chronological, revolving rundown of some of the work of major figures of contemporary art, from Sixties artists Robert Rauschenberg, Claus Oldenberg, Roy Lichtenstein and Carl Andre, right up to more contemporary work by artists like Georges Baselitz, Damien Hirst, Gilbert and George and Anselm Kiefer. All in all, it's a nicely assembled collection, and there's a good café and bookshop too. Afterwards you can ascend to the roof terrace for a view over the surrounding buildings, including the next-door church of Santa Maria Donnaregina Vecchia (see p.56).

Santi Apostoli

Largo Santi Apostoli • Daily 9am–7.30pm • Free

At the far end of the *decumanus superior*, the mid-fifteenth-century church of **Santi Apostoli**, on its own small square, is yet another Tardis-like Naples structure that feels vast when you step inside. It's also a real treasure trove, principally for its mid-seventeenth-century frescoes by Giovanni Lanfranco, which fill the panels and pendentives of the ceiling with scenes of the martyrdom of the apostles: realistic, action-packed pieces with plenty to draw the eye. There's a great deal of neck-craning involved, however, and sadly the paintings are partially damaged and in need of restoration. Some of the other paintings in the church are in a similar state, though Lanfranco's depiction of the healing Pool of Probatica above the entrance is beautifully clear and bright.

Piazza Garibaldi, Forcella and the Port

Marking the far eastern edge of the city centre, **PIAZZA GARIBALDI** is the city's main transport hub, a long, wide square crisscrossed by traffic lanes that cuts into the city centre from the modern train station. Most buses leave from here, as do the Metropolitana and Circumvesuviana lines, and it's one of Naples' most hectic junctions – indeed it's Piazza Garibaldi, perhaps more than any other part of the city, that puts people off Naples, especially at the moment: the entire piazza is currently a vast construction site due to work on the new metro, and pedestrians are blocked by steel walls and challenged by traffic at every turn. Of late, the area has also become a centre for the city's growing immigrant community, with a number of African restaurants and Moroccan grocery stores, and don't be surprised to hear Slavic accents too – many Ukrainians find their way here to work as housekeepers in the city.

1

Porta Capuana and the Castel Capuano

Off the northwestern corner of Piazza Garibaldi, the **Porta Capuana** is one of several relics from the Aragonese city walls, a sturdy defensive gate dating from 1490, delicately decorated on one side in Florentine Renaissance style – one tower is said to represent Honour, the other Virtue. Across the road the much renovated **Castel Capuano**, with its decorative white plaster facade, was the residence of the Norman king William I, and later, under the Spanish, became a courthouse – which it still is, although parts are also sporadically open to the public.

Santa Caterina a Formiello

Piazza Enrico de Nicola 49 • Daily 9am–noon & 4–7pm • Free

Next door to the Porta Capuana, and worth a look if you're passing, is the large, early fifteenth-century domed church of **Santa Caterina a Formiello**, one of the city's most highly decorated Renaissance churches, with every surface covered with paintings, sculptures or some sort of embellishment. Originally part of a convent (the buildings of which became a wool factory and still stand nearby), its dome was one of the first in the city, and is decorated with paintings by the Neapolitan artist Paolo de' Matteis.

San Giovanni a Carbonara

Via Carbonara 5 • Mon–Sat 9am–6pm • Free

The church of **San Giovanni a Carbonara**, which lies across Via Carbonara, marks the end of the *decumanus superior* and is something of a find in what is by any standards not Naples' most attractive quarter. Fronted by an elegant curving double staircase, the interior is notable for its Renaissance funerary monuments, none more monumental than the massive fourteenth-century memorial to Ladislas of Durazzo, son of the fourteenth-century king of Naples, Charles III, and his sister Joan II, which dominates the nave. It only just outdoes the monument in the round chapel behind, decorated with frescoes and majolica floor tiles from the 1440s, where Joan's lover Sergianni Caracciolo is remembered; the marbled magnificence of the Caracciolo di Vico chapel, off to the left, commemorates other members of the influential family.

The Albergo dei Poveri and Orto Botanico

Ten minutes' walk north of Piazza Garibaldi, on the large Piazza Carlo III, is the enormous facade – actually only one-fifth of the size originally planned – of the **Albergo dei Poveri**, a workhouse built in 1751. Believe it or not, it's looking better than it has done for some time, with a fresh coat of paint that's part of an ongoing restoration that will probably never be completed. Small wonder, given the building is so large. Next to it, the high walls don't enclose a prison but the **Orto Botanico** or Botanic Gardens, founded in 1777 by Ferdinand IV, a small oasis of lush vegetation that feels quite at odds with the location (Mon–Fri 9am–2pm, by appointment only; ☎081 253 3937, ⊕ortobotanico.unina.it).

Forcella

City-centre stronghold of the Camorra, and one of Naples' poorest areas, the **Forcella** quarter forms the most easterly part of old Naples, spreading down from the Castel Capuano to Corso Umberto I. It's always been poor, but it's also something of a vibrant open-air market, where sellers of knock-off CDs and sunglasses hawk their wares alongside a vast quantity of food stalls – not to mention a couple of the city's most authentic pizzerias (see pp.86–87).

THE PORT OF NAPLES

1

Naples' **port** is the engine of the city, squalid and edgy, its quaysides and piers, yards and warehouses occupying nearly 11km of the waterfront. A mass of flyovers, decaying warehouses and factories stretches from the **Molo Beverello** passenger terminal to the merchant shipping docks further south, all the way down to the suburb of San Giovanni a Teduccio and beyond, littered with piles and piles of containers, mostly from China. Naples handles a huge percentage of the EU's trade with China – which in itself is a large percentage of the EU's trade overall – so the amount of business passing through is immense. The port looks like a secure area, but it's not: according to the anti-Camorra author Roberto Saviano, well over half of all goods arriving in Naples are not inspected by customs, and most are prey to a series of mafia-sponsored scams that used to involve mainly cigarettes but now consist of more or less anything that will make money.

Most of the port was redeveloped in the late nineteenth century, when the main Via Cristoforo Colombo that leads alongside the waterfront was built. From a tourist's point of view there's nothing to see, and you wouldn't want to spend any of your time in Naples anywhere near here. But you may notice one building from an earlier time: the **Immacolatella**, on its own jetty about 200m past Molo Beverello, a former quarantine station which dates from 1740 and was the work of the painter and architect Domenico Vaccaro, who was also responsible for the much more visible cloister of Santa Chiara, and much else in Naples besides. The arch and fountain that used to stand alongside have been relocated to the waterfront near the Castel dell'Ovo (see p.73).

Santissima Annunziata

Via dell'Annunziata 34 • Mon–Sat 9am–6pm • Free

Perhaps the most tangible manifestation of the Forcella district's ingrained poverty is the church of **Santissima Annunziata**, which lies on Via dell'Annunziata, one of the neighbourhood's busiest streets. The church was remodelled by Vanvitelli in the eighteenth century, and has a big, white wedding cake of an interior. The real interest is next door, in a building that was once an orphanage, now a hospital. Through a little portico on the left, you can get a close look at the restored *ruota*, or wheel, in which unwanted babies used to be left for the church to look after. The space in the wheel is chillingly baby-sized, while a few displays in the next room summarize the work of the institution and include lists from the seventeenth century of babies who were left here – all named – in case you're in any doubt as to how much it was used in its heyday. Outside, you can see the window through which the babies would have been placed in the wheel, now bricked up and marked with the date – June 27, 1875 – when they stopped taking them in.

Santa Maria del Carmine

Piazza del Carmine 5 • Mon, Tues & Thurs–Sat 6.30am–12.30pm, Wed 6.30am–1.30pm, Sun 6.30am–2pm • Free

Towards the end of Corso Garibaldi, past the main Circumvesuviana rail terminal and off to the right, is the thirteenth-century church of **Santa Maria del Carmine**. Landmarked by its distinctive curvaceous campanile, it is traditionally the church of the poor in Naples, particularly fishermen and mariners. Axel Munthe, the Swedish writer and resident of Capri, used to sleep here after tending to victims of the 1884 cholera outbreak. It's a heavily decorated church, quite a contrast to the shabby square outside, and is known for the miraculous properties of a couple of objects inside: a wooden crucifix, hidden away in a wooden tabernacle below the arch of the transept, which dodged a cannonball during a siege in 1439 and has been revered ever since; and the Byzantine icon of the so-called *Madonna Bruna* or "Dark Madonna" behind the high altar, which is supposed to have saved the bell tower from a fire and is now celebrated every July 16 with a massive display of fireworks; go through the sacristy for a close-up look. Incidentally, the church's cloister, off to the right, is lovely, shaded by overhanging lemons and limes.

1

Corso Umberto I

Leading from Piazza Garibaldi to the city centre, dead-straight **Corso Umberto I**, also known as the *Rettifilo*, was built in the 1880s not only as a traffic artery but also to separate the heart of the old city from the port during the cholera outbreak. The street spears through the old part of the city, from the seedy gatherings of prostitutes and kerb-crawlers at its Piazza Garibaldi end, past mainstream shops, to Piazza Nicola Amore, where Via del Duomo heads up the hill, dividing Forcella from the Centro Storico. From Piazza Nicola Amore it continues past the **University** (see p.54), from where you can either cut through into the heart of the Centro Storico, or continue on to symmetrical **Piazza Bovio** and its elegant seventeenth-century Fontana di Nettuno. Off to the left, between the Corso and the waterfront boulevard, is the **Borgo Orefici** or "Gold Quarter", a secretive and ancient haven of jewellers and gold and silver outlets that merits a brief detour before heading on towards Castel Nuovo and Piazza Municipio, the city's modern centre.

Via Toledo and around

If you asked most people what they thought of as the centre of Naples, they'd say **VIA TOLEDO**, sometimes known as Via Roma: the shop-lined modern thoroughfare that provides the modern city's spine. Its southern end is anchored by Piazza Trieste e Trento, which in turn is edged by some of the centre's most monumental buildings: the Palazzo Reale, Galleria Umberto I and the Castel Nuovo. From here, Via Toledo leads north in a dead-straight line, climbing the hill towards the **Museo Archeologico Nazionale** and separating the city into two very distinct parts. To its right, as far as Piazza del Gesù Nuovo, the streets and buildings are modern and spacious, centring on the unmistakable mass of the Fascist-era central **Post Office**, while to the left are two of the city's most densely populated and poorest neighbourhoods, the **Quartieri Spagnoli** and **Montesanto** (see p.66).

Piazza del Municipio

Piazza del Municipio sits between the old city and the sea, a busy traffic junction that stretches from the ferry terminal up to the Palazzo Municipale, or city hall. It's a pleasant enough open space, but a mess at present, dominated as it is by the works to extend the city's metro. These in turn have been delayed due to the extent of archeological finds, including Roman ships (this used to be the port of the ancient city). You can look down into the excavations from the walkways built to get pedestrians from one side to the other.

The Castel Nuovo and Museo Civico

Piazza Municipio • Mon–Sat 9am–7pm • €6

Across the piazza is the brooding hulk of the **Castel Nuovo** or the "Maschio Angioino" (Angevin fortress), whose squat, crenellated turrets are the first view of the city for the thousands of visitors who arrive in Naples by cruise ship. It's as impressive a monument on dry land as it is from the water, erected in 1282 by the Angevins and later converted as the royal residence of the Aragon monarchs. The entrance incorporates a carved marble triumphal arch from 1454, the work of Pietro di Milano and Francesco Laurana, which commemorates the taking of the city by Alfonso I, the first Aragon ruler, and shows details of his triumph topped by a rousing statue of St Michael.

Nowadays the Castel Nuovo is home to the city's Museo Civico, but first visit the imposing courtyard, and the Sala dei Baroni on the far left, a huge Gothic hall, 28m high in the middle, whose magnificent umbrella-ribbed vaults were once covered in frescoes by Giotto – sadly long faded. It's still used as the debating chamber of the city council. Also accessible from the courtyard is the ground-floor Cappella Palatina, a high, bare,

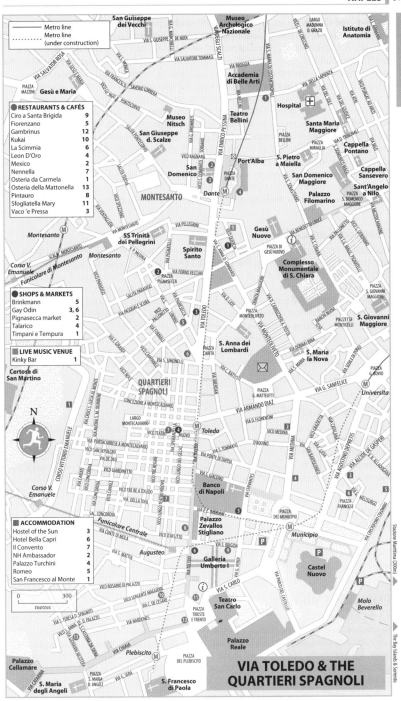

RESTAURANTS & CAFÉS
Ciro a Santa Brigida	9
Fiorenzano	5
Gambrinus	12
Kukai	10
La Scimmia	6
Leon D'Oro	4
Mexico	2
Nennella	7
Osteria da Carmela	1
Osteria della Mattonella	13
Pintauro	8
Sfogliatella Mary	11
Vaco 'e Pressa	3

SHOPS & MARKETS
Brinkmann	5
Gay Odin	3, 6
Pignasecca market	2
Talarico	4
Timpani e Tempura	1

LIVE MUSIC VENUE
Kinky Bar	1

ACCOMMODATION
Hostel of the Sun	3
Hotel Bella Capri	6
Il Convento	7
NH Ambassador	2
Palazzo Turchini	4
Romeo	5
San Francesco al Monte	1

VIA TOLEDO & THE QUARTIERI SPAGNOLI

1

single-naved church with a fifteenth-century marble portal and rose window and a handful of artistic objects, including fourteenth- to sixteenth-century frescoes from Caserta. A number of sculptural depictions of the Madonna and Child decorate the far end of the church and also the sacristy, one of them rescued from a piazza in the Materdei quarter of the city and others by the same sculptors as the triumphal arch outside.

Upstairs from here, the first-floor galleries of the **Museo Civico** host undistinguished canvases by the leading lights of the Neapolitan artistic canon – Luca Giordano and Francesco Solimena, among others – and the castle's original bronze doors from 1468, which show scenes from Ferdinand of Aragon's struggle against the local barons. The cannonball wedged in the lower left-hand panel dates from a naval battle in 1495 between the French and the Genoese that took place while the former were pillaging the castle's doors – the doors on the front of the castle have a similar rip. On the second floor there are later, mainly nineteenth-century works depicting Naples at the time, and sculptures by the prolific local artist Vincenzo Gemito. But ultimately it's the views from the top terrace that steal the show – over the harbour, the cruise ships and the bay beyond.

Teatro di San Carlo

Via San Carlo 98 • Tours every hour Mon–Sat 10.30am–4.30pm, Sun 10.30am–12.30pm • €6 • ☎ 081 797 2468, ☯ teatrosancarlo.it

Just beyond the Castel Nuovo, the **Teatro di San Carlo** is an oddly unimpressive building from the outside, but it was the envy of Europe when it opened in 1737, in time for the birthday of Charles of Bourbon, for whom it was built (it's conveniently connected to the royal palace behind). Destroyed by fire in 1816 and rebuilt, it's still the largest – and oldest – opera house in Italy, and one of the most distinguished in the world. There's a statue of the Naples-born tenor Caruso in the foyer, although oddly the singer was badly received on his debut in 1900 and never again sang in the city. There are regular guided tours, although to properly appreciate the interior you should come to a performance (see p.92). There's also an exhibition on the opera house in part of the Palazzo Reale immediately behind (see p.65).

Galleria Umberto I

Opposite the Teatro di San Carlo, the **Galleria Umberto I** is an impressive monument. Neglected over the years, its high arcades, erected in 1887, are only now beginning to recover some of their original elegance with a much-needed restoration. Some of the commercial life from Via Toledo is seeping back into the massive structure, although it still has some way to go before it attains the elegance of its counterparts in Rome or Milan.

Piazza Trieste e Trento

Piazza Trieste e Trento – sometimes known as Piazza San Ferdinando after the church on its corner – is probably as close to central Naples as you can get. Although more of a roundabout than a piazza, it's nevertheless a good place to watch the world go by while sipping a pricey drink on the terrace of the historic *Caffè Gambrinus* (see p.87).

Piazza del Plebiscito

To the left of the *Caffè Gambrinus*, the expanse of **Piazza del Plebiscito** is a decent attempt to create a bit of civic grandeur, laid out in the early nineteenth century with a curve of columns modelled on Bernini's Piazza San Pietro in Rome, and spruced up over recent years. It's a favourite place to stroll in the evening, and hosts occasional summertime installations by renowned contemporary artists, despite the fact that its colonnades are rather graffitied and run-down in places, and the whole square has a rather forlorn air.

CLOCKWISE FROM TOP LEFT PIZZA (P.29); GALLERIA UMBERTO I (P.62); PIAZZA TRIESTE E TRENTO (P.62) >

1

San Francesco di Paola

Piazza del Plebiscito 10 • Mon–Sat 8.30am–noon & 3.30–7pm • Free

Flanked by the buildings of the Naples prefecture on each side, and with the Palazzo Reale on the left, is the church of **San Francesco di Paola**, a monumental building from 1836 that was modelled on the Pantheon. Inside, it's a rather chilling structure, with an enormous dome that dwarfs even the Neoclassical features of its interior, let alone its hapless congregation.

Palazzo Reale

Piazza del Plebiscito • Mon, Tues, Thurs–Sun 9am–7pm; Memus Mon–Sat 9am–5pm, Sun 9am–2pm • €4, €6 including Memus • Ⓦ palazzorealenapoli.it, Ⓦ memus.org

The **Palazzo Reale** forms the fourth side of Piazza del Plebiscito, and is a vast and very grand affair, hogging all the best views of the sea from this part of town. That said, it's a bland, derivative building for the most part, and even a bit of a fake: it was thrown up hurriedly in 1602 by Domenico Fontana to accommodate Philip III on a visit here and was never actually occupied by a monarch long-term. Indeed, it's more of a monument to monarchies than monarchs, with the various dynasties that ruled Naples by proxy for so long represented in the niches of the facade, from Roger the Norman to Vittorio Emanuele II, taking in, among others, Alfonso I and a slightly comic Murat on the way.

You can wander into the gardens and back and forth through the building's many large courtyards, but the main things to see are the palace's **first-floor rooms**, decorated with Baroque excess: gilded furniture, trompe-l'oeil ceilings, overbearing tapestries, impressive French Empire pieces and scores of seventeenth- and eighteenth-century paintings, including works by Guercino, Carracci and Titian, as well as Flemish old masters.

The staircase and theatre

The grand, white marble double staircase, which sweeps up one side of the palace's central courtyard, is probably the finest in a city not short of sweeping staircases, and at the top on the right is one of the gems of the palace – the private **theatre**. Built in 1768 by Ferdinando Fuga to celebrate the marriage of Maria Carolina of Austria and Ferdinand IV, the lavish theatre is decorated with large papier-mâché statues and an equally fake royal box.

The throne room to the Flemish Room

Numerous rooms and antechambers follow: the throne room has a ceiling studded with gilded figures representing different parts of the Kingdom of Two Sicilies in 1818, as well as a rather shabby gilded throne; the Great Captain's Room looks out onto the terrace's "hanging gardens" and has ceiling frescoes by the Neapolitan master Battistello Caracciolo, depicting the conquest of the kingdom of Naples in 1502 by the Spanish; and the Flemish Room, so named for its collection of Dutch art, includes a painting by one of Rembrandt's most gifted pupils, Nicolas Maes, and the brilliant *Tax Collectors* (1465) by Marinus van Roymerswaele.

The Hercules Room and chapel

Rooms 14–19 hold the cream of the palace's art collection, including large-scale works by Luca Giordano, Andrea Vaccaro and various followers of Caravaggio, Mattia de' Preti and the Dutch painter Gerrit van Honthorst among them. The **Hercules Room** or Ballroom, at the end, is suitably vast, although its name comes from the fact that the archeological museum's *Farnese Hercules* used to reside here. Next door but one is the **chapel**, whose sixteenth-century doors come from Toledo's old royal palace and whose *presepe* (Christmas crib) is one of the city's largest, filled with mainly eighteenth-century figures – 210 in all.

THE ACQUEDOTTO CARMIGNANO

The city's most elegant café, the *Gambrinus*, Via Chiaia 1, may seem an unlikely point of departure for a journey to underground Naples, but this is the place if you want to explore the **Acquedotto Carmignano**, a vast network of gullies and water cisterns, in use right up to the cholera epidemic of the 1880s. Hour-long **tours** leave from the café (Thurs 9pm, Sat 10am, noon & 6pm, Sun 10am, 11am, noon & 6pm; €10), but the visit actually begins at Vico Sant'Anna di Palazzo 40, in the Quartieri Spagnoli, where you descend 40m underground. Tours are mostly in Italian, but there's plenty to appreciate even if you can't follow the guide's narrative, such as graffiti from World War II, when the tunnels were used as bomb shelters, and any number of spooky caverns and passages. It's fun, too, to squeeze through some of the gaps in the rock, but be warned that some of the spaces you need to get through are very narrow indeed, and not for the claustrophobic. Details on ☎ 081 400 256 or at ⓦ lanapolisotterranea.it.

Memus

Finally there's **Memus** (or Museo e Archivio Storico del Teatro di San Carlo), which you reach from the bottom of the main staircase, and consists of a couple of floors of photos, costumes, set designs and programmes from the Teatro San Carlo, the venerable old opera house that is actually attached to the Palazzo Reale. The museum hosts a film chronicling its history, but there's not much for someone who isn't a real opera devotee and doesn't speak at least a bit of Italian – although the faintly psychedelic 3D theatre, playing various opera standards, is fun.

Palazzo Zevallos Stigliano

Via Toledo 185 • Tues–Sun 10am–6pm, Sat open until 8pm • €4 • ☎ 0800 1605 2007, ⓦ palazzozevallos.com

A little way up Via Toledo from Piazza Trieste e Trento, the **Palazzo Zevallos Stigliano** was the work of Cosimo Fanzago. Now home to the Intesa San Paolo bank, you can wander in to inspect its (now disused) old-style banking hall, although most people come to see one of the very last works by Caravaggio in Naples on the first floor, the *Martyrdom of St Ursula*. A typically shadowy and very theatrical painting showing the piercing of the saint's breast by an arrow fired from the bow of Attila the Hun, it is reverentially displayed in a room on its own, with lots of background info and a short film (all in English). There's also a fantastic sketch map of the city in 1629 and a handful of eighteenth-century cityscapes by Dutch painters, although the entry fee seems like a lot to view what amounts to little more than one painting.

Banco di Napoli

Via Toledo 177 • Free

Next to the Palazzo Zevallos Stigliano in what is effectively a parade of monumental buildings on Via Toledo, the **Banco di Napoli** is of a different vintage altogether from its neighbour. The bank's headquarters was completed on the eve of World War II by Mussolini's favourite architect, Marcello Piacentini, and is as deliberately awe-inspiring as you might expect, with a large and very grand main banking hall that's worth a quick peek even if you're not a devoted student of modern architecture.

The Quartieri Spagnoli

Scaling the slopes of Vomero to the west of Via Toledo are some of the city's narrowest and most crowded streets. The grid of alleys was laid out to house Spanish troops during the seventeenth century, hence the name: the **Quartieri Spagnoli**. In some ways it's an enticing area, in that it's what you expect of Naples, with the buildings so close

1

together as to barely admit any sunlight. But it's a poor, densely populated part of town too, home to the notorious Neapolitan *bassi* – one-room windowless dwellings that open directly onto the street – and one you'd be wise to avoid wandering too deeply into at night.

Piazza Matteotti

On the other side of Via Toledo from the Quartieri Spagnoli, immediately east of **Piazza Carità**, the streets are modern and less obviously appealing. The main focus is the busy junction of **Piazza Matteotti**, which is surrounded by some brutalist yet elegant modern architecture, and anchored by the broad sweep of the **Post Office** building – a huge and stylish homage to the art of delivering the post on time (ironic in any part of Italy, where the postal system is considered a joke). Built in the 1930s, up close it's a bit worse for wear, but it is at least elegantly echoed by the resoundingly Modernist police headquarters across the square.

Santa Maria la Nova

Piazza Santa Maria la Nova 44 • Daily 9am–6pm • Free • ⓦ santamarialanova.info

Just across the road from the post office, the church of **Santa Maria la Nova** was built during the thirteenth century to replace a church that was knocked down when the Castel Nuovo went up. It contains a series of frescoed ceiling panels that were the work of a number of Neapolitan artists, including Luca Giordano, while next door are two cloisters – one a pleasant garden, the other decorated with fifteenth-century frescoes and now home of **ARCA**, Naples' museum of contemporary religious art.

Sant'Anna dei Lombardi

Piazza Monteoliveto 44 • Mon–Thurs 10am–1.30pm & 2–4pm, Fri & Sat 10am–1.30pm & 2–6pm, Sun 9am–1pm • Free

Behind the post office, on the edge of the old part of the city, the little square of Piazza Monteoliveto is home both to the Carabinieri and the church of **Sant'Anna dei Lombardi** – rebuilt after wartime bombing and holding some of the city's finest Renaissance art. The best-known of these is a fabulous sacristy painted in 1544–45 by Giorgio Vasari with allegorical frescoes showing *Religion*, *Faith* and *Eternity* on the three Gothic vaults of the long room, which is in turn lined with late fifteenth-century intarsia panels. Next door is a rather startling group of eight almost life-sized figures mourning the dead Christ by Guido Mazzoni (the faces are said to be portraits), from 1492. Don't miss the two works by the fifteenth-century sculptor Antonio Rossellino in the chapel to the left of the entrance: a nativity scene from 1475 and the tomb of Mary of Aragon, daughter of Ferdinand I. A beautiful *Annunciation* by Benedetto di Maiano lies in the chapel on the right.

Montesanto, La Sanità and Capodimonte

Off Via Toledo to the west, just beyond Piazza Carità, is the atmospheric district of **MONTESANTO**, with its appealing main drag, Via Pignasecca, leading to lively **Piazza Pignasecca** and the Montesanto funicular station. It's as vibrant a part of Naples as you'll find, with any number of food stalls, tripe joints and grocery stores, particularly around Piazza Pignasecca. A little further north, beyond the archeological museum, you can delve into the old quarter of **LA SANITÀ**, whose name literally means "health" due to its position outside the walls of the old city. Though one of the city's poorer neighbourhoods, it's also full of Neapolitan folklore, and is the birthplace of the revered Italian comic actor Totò. It's well worth a wander for its street-level commerce, sometimes more reminiscent of downtown Mumbai than Italy. However, the real interest lies in between the two neighbourhoods, at the city's fantastic archeological museum, situated at one end of the busy nineteenth-century triangle of **Piazza Cavour**. If you see only one major Naples sight, make it this one.

Museo Nitsch

Vico Lungo Pontecorvo 29/d • Mon–Fri 10am–7pm, Sat 10am–2pm • €10 • ☎ 081 564 1655, ⓦ museonitsch.org

The Montesanto area harbours just one real sight, the **Museo Nitsch**, which occupies a fantastic position in a former electricity substation, tucked away in the heights of the neighbourhood, with a terrace overlooking densely packed rooftops and offering perfect views of a glowering Vesuvius. Part of local art impresario Giuseppe Morra's Fondazione Morra, the museum itself is a somewhat bizarre collection of the works of the Austrian performance artist Hermann Nitsch, who specializes in large-scale events in which naked men and women are "crucified" with dead sheep parts and entrails draped around their bodies, usually witnessed by crowds of devotees. There are photos and videos – complete with soundtrack – along with exhibits of the tools of his trade: bloodstained cloths, surgical instruments and liturgical garments. Though the display makes disquieting viewing, and certainly won't be to everyone's taste, it's somehow thoroughly Neapolitan in its theatrical shockability, and strangely doesn't seem out of place here at all.

Piazza Dante

Piazza Dante, designed by Luigi Vanvitelli during the eighteenth century, cuts an elegant semicircle around a graffiti-covered statue of the poet. Cross the square and cut through the seventeenth-century **Port'Alba** for the very appealing **Piazza Bellini** (see p.53) and the old city, or push straight on up the street to the archeological museum, housed in a grandiose, late sixteenth-century army barracks on the corner of Piazza Cavour.

Accademia di Belle Arti

Via Costantinopoli 107 • Tues–Sat 10am–2pm • Free • ☎ 081 444 245, ⓦ accademiadinapoli.it

The **Accademia di Belle Arti** is the city's art school, and a very grand one too, with a small gallery of paintings and sculptures on its second floor. There are a few pre-nineteenth-century paintings, among them a *St Catherine* by Mattia de' Preti, but otherwise it's mainly work from the nineteenth century and beyond: busts by local sculptor Vincenzo Gemito, paintings by the important nineteenth-century Neapolitan artist Domenico Morelli, who was president of the academy for the last two years of his life, and work by his more impressionistic student Antonio Mancini. There's also a section representing the 1960s right up to the present day.

Museo Archeologico Nazionale

Mon, Wed–Sun 9am–7.30pm • €8 • ☎ 081 442 2149, ⓦ cir.campania.beniculturali.it/museoarcheologiconazionale

Naples isn't really a city of museums – there's more than enough to observe on the streets – and most displays of interest are kept in the city's churches and palaces. The **Museo Archeologico Nazionale** is an exception, home to the Farnese collection of antiquities from Lazio and Campania and the best of the finds from the nearby Roman sites of Pompeii and Herculaneum. Despite the pedigree of the exhibits, however, the museum is at best tatty and at worst in a state of complete disarray, with endless reorganizations. Because of this, locations of exhibits are liable to change, and departments may close at short notice. The core collection of paintings and mosaics is generally on display, however, and they are one of the city's true highlights.

1

MONTESANTO, LA SANITÀ AND CAPODIMONTE

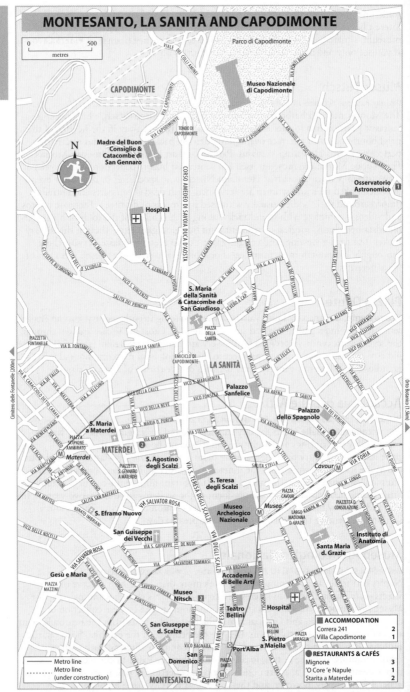

Parco di Capodimonte

0 — 500 metres

VIALE DEI COLLI AMINEI

CAPODIMONTE

Museo Nazionale di Capodimonte

VIA CAPODIMONTE

TONDO DI CAPODIMONTE

Madre del Buon Consiglio & Catacombe di San Gennaro

N

VIA CAPODIMONTE

VIA S. ANTONIO A CAPODIMONTE

SALITA MOIARIELLO

Osservatorio Astronomico

Hospital

CORSO AMEDEO DI SAVOIA DUCA D'AOSTA

SALITA DELLA BUCCA

SALITA MIRADOIS

VIA DI MIANO

SALITA DELL' O. SCUDILLO

VIA S. GENNARO DEI POVERI

VIA GIUSEPPE DU ONUOMO

VICO S. VINCENZO

VICO TAVERNOLA

VICO TESSITORI

VICO DEI MIRACOLI

SALITA DEI PRINCIPI

S. Maria della Sanità & Catacombe di San Gaudioso

PIAZZA DELLA SANITÀ

PIAZZETTA FONTANELLE

VIA D. FONTANELLE

EMICICLO DI CAPODIMONTE

LA SANITÀ

VIA DELLA SANITÀ

Palazzo Sanfelice

Palazzo dello Spagnolo

S. Maria a Materdei

VICO DELLA CALCE

VICO DELLA NEVE

VIA ARENA

D. SANITÀ

VIA DEI VERGINI

Materdei (M)

MATERDEI

S. Agostino degli Scalzi

S. Teresa degli Scalzi

Cavour (M)

VIA FORIA

S. Eframo Nuovo

SALVATOR ROSA

Museo Archeologico Nazionale

Museo (M)

PIAZZA CAVOUR

Santa Maria d. Grazie

Instituto di Anatomia

San Giuseppe dei Vecchi

Gesù e Maria

PIAZZA MAZZINI

Accademia di Belle Arti

Museo Nitsch

Teatro Bellini

Hospital

San Giuseppe d. Scalze

San Domenico

Port'Alba

S. Pietro a Maiella

PIAZZA DANTE

MONTESANTO

Dante (M)

ACCOMMODATION
Correra 241	2
Villa Capodimonte	1

RESTAURANTS & CAFÉS
Mignone	3
'O Core 'e Napule	1
Starita a Materdei	2

— Metro line
···· Metro line (under construction)

Cimitero delle Fontanelle (200m)

Orto Botanico (1.5km)

1

Ground floor

The **ground floor** of the museum concentrates on sculpture from the **Farnese collection**, from the Palatine Hill and the Baths of Caracalla in Rome, one of the greatest collections of imperial-era sculpture you'll see anywhere. Displayed together are the *Farnese Bull* and *Farnese Hercules*, the former a Hellenistic work that is the largest piece of classical sculpture ever found, the latter a colossal statue that's a third-century AD Roman replica of a Greek original. There are also portrait busts of various Roman emperors and VIPs – a statue of Hadrian's boyfriend Antinous, a reclining woman, perhaps Agrippina, a huge bust of Vespasian with the top sliced off, as well as busts of Caracalla, Domitian, Commodus and others. Don't miss Ephesian Artemis, an alabaster and bronze statue with rows of bulls' scrota embellishing the goddess's chest, and bees, mini-beasts and sphinxes adorning her lower half.

Mezzanine floor

Campanian mosaics

Halfway up the double staircase, the **mezzanine floor** holds the museum's collection of **mosaics** – remarkably preserved works, giving a superb insight into Roman customs, beliefs and humour. The fascinating collection includes images of fish, crustacea, a wonderful scene of wildlife on the banks of the Nile, a cheeky cat and quail with still life beneath, masks, skulls and simple abstract decoration – all from the House of the Faun in Pompeii (see p.123). Highlights include a realistic *Battle Scene* (no. 10020), which perhaps shows Alexander the Great, *Three Musicians with Dwarf* (no. 9985), an urbane *Meeting of the Platonic Academy* (no. 124545) and a marvellously captured scene from a comedy, *The Consultation of the Fattucchiera* (no. 9987), with a soothsayer giving a dour and doomy prediction. Also worth looking out for are the lovely *Head of a Woman* (no. 124666), and *Antifrite and Poseidon* (no. 10007), from the House of Neptune and Amphitrite in Herculaneum (see p.115).

Gabinetto Segreto

At the far end of the mosaic rooms is the intriguing **Gabinetto Segreto** (Secret Room), containing erotic material – paintings and sculpture mainly – taken from the brothels, baths, houses and taverns of Pompeii and Herculaneum. The objects in the collection weren't always segregated in this way; it was the shocked Duke of Calabria who, having taken his wife and daughter to view the museum, decided that the offending objects should be removed from the gaze of ladies. From then until the time of Garibaldi they were kept under lock and key, disappearing again from public view in the twentieth century for long periods. The artefacts, from languidly sensual wall paintings to preposterously phallic lamps, bear testimony to Roman licentiousness, although the phallus was often used as a kind of lucky charm rather than as a sexual symbol – cheerfully hung outside taverns and bakeries to ward off the evil eye. There's a group of paintings displaying a variety of sexual positions, and a lot of erotic mythological art, making this an admirably serious and smut-free collection, though it's hard to repress a giggle at the sculpture of a headless man whose toga is failing to mask an erection, or the graphic but elegantly executed marble of Pan "seducing" a goat.

Coins and commercial artefacts

On the other side of the mezzanine floor are displays of **money and commercial artefacts** – mainly Roman but going right up to the Bourbons. There are examples of very early Roman and Hellenistic currency, and later Roman coinage – a gold coin with an image of Augustus, several large hoards from Pompeii, including golden Republican and imperial coins from the Porta di Sarno, as well as an amazing studded chest, sets of scales from Minturno and even stamps for receipts.

1

First floor
Salone della Meridiana

Upstairs, the enormous **Salone della Meridiana** holds a sparse but fine assortment of Roman figures, notably a wonderfully strained Atlas – again a Roman copy of a Greek original.

Campanian wall paintings

The further rooms of the first floor show Campanian **wall paintings**, lifted from the villas of Pompeii and Herculaneum and other sites around the bay, and amazingly rich in colour and invention. It's worth devoting time to this section, which includes works from the Sacrarium – part of Pompeii's Egyptian temple of Isis, the most celebrated mystery cult of antiquity – the discovery of which gave a major boost to Egyptomania at the end of the eighteenth century. In the next series of rooms, some of the smallest and most easily missed works are among the most exquisite. Among those to look out for are a paternal *Achilles and Chirone* (no. 9109); the *Sacrifice of Iphiginia* (no. 9112), one of the best preserved of all the murals; and the dignified *Dido Abandoned by Aeneas and the Personification of Africa* (no. 8998). Look out too for the group of four small allegorical pictures, including a depiction of a woman gathering flowers entitled *Allegoria della Primavera* (no. 8834) – a fluid, impressionistic work capturing both the gentleness of spring and the graceful beauty of the woman; a snapshot-like portrait of a young man and woman, *The Baker Terentius and his Wife* (no. 9058); and a nearby *Perseus and Andromeda* (no. 8995).

Beyond the murals are the actual finds form the Campanian cities – everyday items like glass, silver, ceramics, charred pieces of rope, even foodstuffs (petrified cakes, figs, fruit and nuts), together with a model of Pompeii in cork.

Villa dei Papiri

On the other side of the first floor, there are finds from the **Villa dei Papiri** in Herculaneum (see p.117), containing mainly sculptures in bronze. In the centre of the second room, *Hermes at Rest* with the god overcome with exhaustion is perhaps the most arresting piece, but around are other adept statues – of dramatically poised athletes, suffused with movement; a languid *Sleeping Satyr*; the convincingly jolly *Drunken Silenus*; and a number of portrait busts of soldiers and various local bigwigs.

Via dei Vergini

Via dei Vergini leads through the heart of the Sanità district, passing the **Palazzo dello Spagnolo** at no. 13 (access to courtyard only), a gem of a building built in 1738 by the Neapolitan Baroque architect Ferdinando Sanfelice which has a fantastic series of staircases that double back on each other at the rear of the building's courtyard. Until recently, the building was the headquarters of the influential Morra foundation (see p.67), and is subsequently in a good state of repair – unlike the decrepit and slightly older **Palazzo Sanfelice** a little further up the street at Via Sanità 19, which ironically was the architect's own home.

Santa Maria della Sanità

Piazza Sanità 14 • Mon–Sat 10am–5pm guided tours every hour • €8 • ☎ 081 744 3714, ⓦ catacombedinapoli.it

At the far end of Via Sanità, the Dominican church of **Santa Maria della Sanità** stands on the piazza of the same name, a scrubby little square, right by the bridge that connects the city centre to Capodimonte. Built in the early seventeenth century, its design was based loosely on Bramante's for St Peter's in Rome, and it's certainly a grand building inside, although its most appealing features are on a smaller scale. Look out for a couple of paintings by the ubiquitous Luca Giordano: the *Virgin with Hyacinth and Rose* on the left as you go in, and a painting of San Vincenzo on the right.

The latter is a venerated piece; in fact the church is sometimes known as San Vincenzo for the esteem in which the saint is held.

Catacombe di San Gaudioso

Perhaps of most interest are the **Catacombe di San Gaudioso** beneath the church, an early Christian burial ground that like so much of Naples is an intriguing mix of different eras. The entrance is immediately beneath the high altar, where a Byzantine fresco of San Gaudioso, a bishop from Africa who came to Naples in the fifth century, gives way to frescoes and fragments of mosaics of the same period, along with shelves that were used to bury the dead, one of which was supposedly the last resting place of the saint himself. But this is not just an early Christian burial place; the Dominicans ended their days here too, in seated niches where they would desiccate and then be buried elsewhere. There's also a series of tombs for the great and the good of the Dominican order, and it was another tradition that their skulls be removed and set in the wall above a skeletal painting while their body rested behind. Oddly, you can find more fifth-century frescoes mixed up in all this, and tours end in a barrel-vaulted room that was a Roman cistern.

Cimitero delle Fontanelle

Piazza Fontanelle della Sanità 154 • Mon, Tues, Thurs–Sun 10am–5pm • Free

One of the most memorable sights in La Sanità, the **Cimitero delle Fontanelle** is an underground cemetery or ossuary hacked out of Naples' tufa foundations and is full of the bones of thousands who died in epidemics in the city during the seventeenth, eighteenth and nineteenth centuries. It's an eerie place and was closed for many years, partly because worship of the unknown dead had grown into a cult over time; local pressure has led to it being opened once again to public view. The vast hall of skulls is decorated with gifts from the living – trinkets and toys for deceased children, and for one skull, a Band-Aid – and is one of Naples' weirdest sights, but one perfectly in tune with the city's celebratory and strangely open relationship with death.

Catacombe di San Gennaro

Via Capodimonte 13 • Mon–Sat 10am–5pm guided tours every hour • €8 • ☎ 081 744 3714, ⓦ catacombedinapoli.it • Bus #R4 from Via Toledo, or #178 from the Archeological Museum

Right by the church of Santa Maria della Sanità, elevators link La Sanità with Corso Amedeo up above, the main road to **Capodimonte**, and from here it's about a ten-minute walk to another burial site, the **Catacombe di San Gennaro**, next door to the huge Madre del Buon Consiglio church, halfway up the hill to Capodimonte. Bigger and more open than the San Gaudioso catacombs, this site is best known for being the final resting place of San Gennaro, whose body was brought here in the fifth century. It's a Christian burial ground, where the wealthy were placed in chapels on shelves and the poor were dumped on the ground – a class system it's easy to discern even now. There are some early frescoes of San Gennaro and saints Peter and Paul in some of the niches, as well as earlier red Pompeiian-style ceiling frescoes next to a Byzantine Christ. Nearby, you can look down to the next level at Gennaro's supposed tomb, and a mosaic of the bishop that brought him here.

Museo Nazionale di Capodimonte

Via Miano 2 • Mon, Tues, Thurs–Sun 8.30am–7.30pm • €7.50, €6.50 after 2pm; audio guides €5 • ☎ 081 749 9111, ⓦ polomusealenapoli .beniculturali.it

At the top of the hill above central Naples the **Palazzo Reale di Capodimonte**, with its adjoining **park**, was the royal residence of the Bourbon King Charles III, built in 1738 and now housing the superb **Museo Nazionale di Capodimonte**, one of the best

1

collections of art in Italy. You could easily spend half a day here, taking in the many important works by Campanian and other, mainly Italian, artists as well as curious objets d'art and fine pieces of Capodimonte porcelain.

First floor

The three-storey museum is organized roughly chronologically, but also by its various collections, which were built up by the Borgia, Farnese and Bourbon rulers of the city. The museum starts on the first floor with the Farnese collection, and a grouping of portraits of the Farnese pope, Paul III, by Titian, alongside the same artist's portrayals of Charles V and Philip II, which face his portrait of Alessandro Farnese and Andre del Sarto's glowering depiction of Leo X. Subsequent rooms hold fragments of polyptychs by Massaccio and Masolino, the rest of which are to be found in various other major European galleries – the bottom half of Massaccio's 1426 Crucifixion is in London's National Gallery, as is the other major part of Masolino's beautiful polyptych next door, which was painted for the church of Santa Maria Maggiore in Rome.

Beyond are more works by Renaissance masters: Bellini's impressively coloured and composed *Transfiguration*; Lotto's odd *Madonna with St Peter*; Giulio Romano's dark and powerful *Madonna of the Cat*; Sebastiano del Piombo's haughty Clement VII; Marcello Venusti's small-scale 1549 copy of Michelangelo's *Last Judgement* – probably the only chance you'll get to see the painting this close up; and Titian's lascivious *Danaë*. There's not just Italian work here either: there's El Greco's flashy but atmospheric *Soflon*, a couple of Brueghels – *The Misanthrope* and *The Parable of the Blind* – two triptychs by Joos van Cleve and a whole room of giant food scenes by Brueckelaar. Beyond here are two rooms mainly devoted to the Carracci brothers, full of magnificent pieces like Annibale's *Mystical Marriage of St Catherine*.

Second floor

On the **second floor** are some outstanding Italian paintings from the fourteenth and fifteenth centuries, of which the most famous is the *St Ludovic of Toulose* by Simone Martini, a fascinating Gothic painting glowing with gold leaf. An overt work of propaganda, it depicts an enthroned Ludovic crowning his brother Robert of Anjou and thereby legitimizing his rule. Elsewhere there are paintings that used to hang in Naples' churches: Niccolò Colantonio's *St Jerome in his Study* was painted for the altar of San Lorenzo Maggiore, and the same artist's *Deposition* used to hang in San Domenico Maggiore. Further on, Vasari's dramatic, almost snapshot-like *Presentation in the Temple* was done for the city's Monteoliveto church, and there's a series of smaller works by the same painter for the sacristy of San Giovanni Carbonara, while Titian's *Annunciation*, further on, was done for the church of San Domenico Maggiore. The long series of rooms finishes off in fine style with one of Caravaggio's best-known works, his dark and brutal *Flagellation*, beyond which is the museum's collection of seventeenth-and eighteenth-century Neapolitan paintings, including a generally wonderful grouping of all the shining lights of the Neapolitan Baroque: *Christ Tied to a Column* and *Ecce Homo* by Caracciolo, Ribera's *St Jerome with an Angel*, and whole rooms of work by the prolific Luca Giordano, including his Apollo and Marsia, among other pale, tormented nudes depicting classical stories by the same artist, before giving way to the later work of Francesco de Mura and Solimena, including a rare and serious self-portrait by the latter. Finally, upstairs is a smattering of **twentieth-century works**, of which the most notable is a painting of an erupting Vesuvius by Andy Warhol.

Royal apartments

If you have time to spare, take a walk around the **royal apartments** on the first floor, smaller and more downbeat than those at Caserta (see p.191), but in many ways more enjoyable, not least because you can walk freely through the rooms. They're kept much as they would have been in the eighteenth century, and highlights include the airy,

1

mirrored ballroom, lined with portraits of various Bourbon monarchs and other European despots, and an entire room decked out with dripping, colourful porcelain, sprouting three-dimensional Chinese scenes, monkeys, fruit and flowers.

Santa Lucia and Pizzofalcone

Just south of Piazza del Plebiscito, the main road curves around towards the sea and the **Santa Lucia** district, whose main artery, **Via Santa Lucia**, leads off to the right from Via Cesario Console, beneath the hill of Monte Echia and the **Pizzofalcone** neighbourhood. A city block away, the seafront Via Partenope is home to several of the city's poshest hotels, which overlook the bulk of the Castel dell'Ovo and the marina and quayside restaurants that surround it. The sculptural **Fontana dell'Immacolatella** that anchors the nearby corner was the work of Pietro Bernini and used to stand outside the seventeenth-century Immacolatella quarantine building in the old container port (see p.59).

Castel dell'Ovo

Via Partenope • Mon–Sat 9am–6pm, Sun 9am–2pm • Free • ⓦ comune.napoli.it/casteldellovo

The grey mass of the **Castel dell'Ovo** or "egg-castle" takes its name from the whimsical legend that it was built over an egg placed here by Virgil in Roman times: it is believed that if the egg breaks, Naples will fall. Actually the islet on which it stands – Megaris – was developed in ancient times, then in the fifth century by a community of monks; the citadel itself was built by the Hohenstaufen king Frederick II and extended by the Angevins. It's had various functions over the years, and has been greatly modified. **Inside**, it's just a series of terraces and empty echoing halls, sometimes used for temporary exhibitions. But the **views** you get from its battlements are among the best in town: the 360-degree panorama over the entire bay and back over Naples itself is quite a sight. Come as late in the day as possible, clamber about on the cannons, take in the views as the sun sets over Posillipo, and then go for a drink or dinner at the quayside restaurants of the **Borgo Marinaro** below. Cheesy maybe, but the perfect end to a day in Naples.

Monte Echia and Pizzofalcone

The hill that rises up above the heart of the city at the bottom of Via Toledo, **Monte Echia**, was the birthplace of Naples, where Greek settlers founded a place they called Parthenope, after the siren whose body was said to have been laid to rest here. Later, when it outgrew its location, it became Paleopolis or "old city" – as opposed to Neapolis or "new city", which was built at the bottom of the hill and gave Naples its modern name, while the original settlement took on a more gentrified air over the years. In the seventeenth and eighteenth centuries it was considered to be one of the classier parts of town, and even today it retains a slightly separate feel, due partly to the fact that it's tucked out of the way on the hill. It also provides an interesting way of reaching the Castel dell'Ovo and Santa Lucia waterfront by taking the Galleria Borbonica (see p.75).

If you prefer to stay above ground, follow Via Serra to **Santa Maria degli Angeli** at the top, a large church with an enormous dome, and turn left down Via Monte di Dio, past the **Palazzo Serra di Cassano** on the left, and make a right to the military academy and its attached church, the **Nunziatella**. This Baroque jewellery-box of a church was built by Ferdinando Sanfelice in 1700 and is decorated with paintings by Francesco di Mura. Retrace your steps back across the main road to Via Egiziaca di Pizzofalcone, where there's another church, **Santa Maria Egiziaca di Pizzofalcone**, the creation of Cosimo Fanzago in 1651, whose lovely proportions and octagonal shape show the church of San Francesco immediately below just how it's done with domes; two works by Paolo de' Matteis face each other across the main altars. Follow the road around the

1

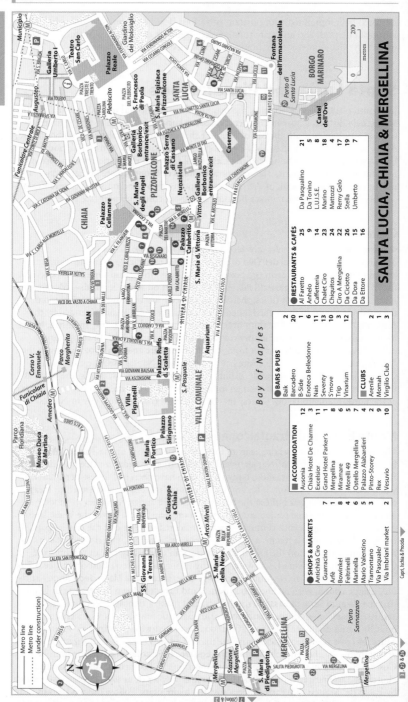

SANTA LUCIA, CHIAIA & MERGELLINA

● RESTAURANTS & CAFÉS

Al Faretto	25
Anhelo	9
Caffetteria	14
Chalet Ciro	23
Chiquitos	24
Ciro A Mergellina	22
Da Ciciotto	26
Da Dora	15
Da Ettore	16
Da Pasqualino	21
Da Tonino	5
L.U.I.S.E.	8
Marino	18
Mattozzi	4
Remy Gelo	17
Stella	19
Umberto	7

● BARS & PUBS

Baik	2
Barcadero	20
B-Side	1
Enoteca Belledonne	6
Nais	11
Seventy	13
S'move	10
Trip	3
Vinarium	12

■ CLUBS

Arenile	2
Momah	1
Virgilio Club	3

■ ACCOMMODATION

Ausonia	12
Chiaia Hotel De Charme	3
Excelsior	11
Grand Hotel Parker's	7
Mergellina	1
Miramare	8
Morelli 49	4
Ostello Mergellina	6
Palazzo Alabardieri	5
Pinto-Storey	3
Rex	9
Vesuvio	2

● SHOPS & MARKETS

Antichità Ciro	
Arfè	7
Bowinkel	8
Feltrinelli	4
Marinella	
Mario Valentino	
Tramontano	3
Via Pasquale/	
Via Imbriani market	
Guarracino	11

Metro line
Metro line (under construction)

Bay of Naples

0   200
metres

KIDS' NAPLES

Make no mistake – Naples is a great place to visit with kids. Its culture of extremes, the diversity of its attractions, not just in the city itself but in the surrounding area, and the sheer buzz of its streets are more than enough to keep children of all ages entertained. The following is a list of favourite children's attractions:

Catacombs The subterranean chambers of the dead hold an irresistible fascination. See p.71.

Castel dell'Ovo About as close to a classic castle experience as it's possible to get – with a great location and lots of passageways and levels to chase about on. See p.73.

Aquarium Fish and sea creatures never fail, and there's a petting pool for the really small. See p.76.

Herculaneum and Pompeii Where could be better for a fun-yet-educational day out than these fascinating ancient Roman sites? See p.112 & p.122.

Vesuvius The chance of scaling a real-life active volcano is not to be passed up. See p.118.

Via San Gregorio Armeno Children love the little figures and inventive crib scenes that are made and sold on this street. See p.50.

Napoli Sotterranea and the Acquedotto Carmignano It's grown-up sightseeing, but it also involves squeezing through narrow underground passages with a candle – great for imaginative kids. See p.50 & p.65.

Grotta di Seiano In a city of underground tunnels, this is one of the spookiest and best. See p.79.

edge of the military academy to a small **park**, where you can rest up and take in one of the best views of the city, before descending down a zigzagging road to the Santa Lucia quarter immediately below. Following this route without stopping would take 20–30 minutes, or a very pleasant hour or so if you take in the sights on the way.

Galleria Borbonica

Vico del Grottone 4 & Via Domnico Morelli 40 • Fri–Sun 1hr tours at 10am, noon, 3.30pm & 5.30pm • Free • ☎ 081 764 5808, Ⓦ galleriaborbonica.com

Accessed through an old vet's surgery down an alley off Via Serra (or through the Parcheggio Morelli on Via Domenico Morelli), the Galleria Borbonica is really three sights in one: a tunnel built by the nervous king Ferdinand II in the 1850s as a means of escape from the Palazzo Reale – it in fact runs from Piazza Carolina to Via Chiatamone, which was at the time on the Santa Lucia seafront; a series of cisterns that were used as the main water supply for this part of the city until the 1880s; and a series of bomb shelters from World War II which were fashioned out of the tunnel and a number of disused cisterns. Among many things to see is a host of abandoned cars mainly from the 1940s and 1950s (the oldest dates back to 1934), the cisterns themselves, including the steps hollowed out of the rock that the "*pozzari*" or water attendants would use to get in and out, and the bomb shelters, full of affecting graffiti done by the folk who once sheltered here – "*Noi Vivi*" one defiant scrawl proclaims, while another was written by a 10-year-old Neapolitan boy who famously returned as an old man in 2010 to view his handiwork.

Chiaia

The **Chiaia** neighbourhood displays a sense of order and classical elegance that is quite absent from the rest of the city, its buildings well preserved, its residents noticeably more affluent – although parts of the district, especially that which spreads up the hill towards Vomero, are as maze-like and atmospheric as anywhere in the city.

Via Chiaia to Piazza dei Martiri

Via Chiaia leads west from Piazza Trieste e Trento into a quite different Naples from the congested *vicoli* of the Centro Storico or Quartieri Spagnoli, at first a mainstream

1

pedestrianized shopping street but increasingly lined with fancy shops until it bends around to join with the elegant open space of **Piazza dei Martiri** – named after the nineteenth-century revolutionary martyrs commemorated by the column in its centre. It's fringed by a couple of pleasant cafés to take the weight off.

Palazzo delle Arti di Napoli

Via dei Mille 60 • Mon–Sat 9.30am–7.30pm • €8 (varies) • ☎ 081 795 8604, ⓦ palazzoartinapoli.net

You can get a taste of the neighbourhood by following the posh shopping street of Via G. Filangieri, which turns into Via dei Mille as far as **PAN**, or the Palazzo delle Arti di Napoli. Occupying the enormous Palazzo Rocella, this is an exhibition space for contemporary art, along with an art-house cinema and bookshop.

Santa Maria in Portico

Via Santa Maria in Portico 17 • Daily 8am–11.30am & 4–7pm • Free

Walk along Via Santa Teresa a Chiaia, which turns into Via Piscielli, and follow this as far as the church of **Santa Maria in Portico** – a stroll that gives a sense both of Chiaia's upscale commercialism and its authentic neighbourhood charm. The church of Santa Maria is in itself nothing special, but you may want to look in for the giant *presepe* (Christmas crib) in its sacristy, just to the left of the altar – an unsettling ensemble of almost life-sized figures in seventeenth-century costume.

Villa Comunale

Forming a strip along the waterfront from Santa Lucia to Mergellina, the **Villa Comunale** is Naples' most central city park, laid out by Vanvitelli in 1781 as a royal garden and richly adorned with classical sculpture – the *Farnese Bull* stood here until it moved to the city's archeological museum (see p.67) – and it offers the best position from which to appreciate the city as a port and seafront city, the views stretching right around the bay from the long lizard of its northern side to the distinctive silhouette of Vesuvius in the east, behind the cranes and far-off apartment blocks of the sprawling industrial suburbs. The main road that skirts the park, **Via Caracciolo**, is named after the Neapolitan sea captain, Francesco Caracciolo, who was executed by the British after defecting to the French cause in 1799, and it makes for a relaxed walk around the bay to Mergellina, particularly in the early evening when the lights of the city enhance the views. About two-thirds of the way to Mergellina, hot summer days see people swimming and sunbathing on two small patches of beach and artificial rocks.

The Aquarium

Villa Comunale • March–Oct Tues–Sun 9.30am–6.30pm; Nov–Feb Tues–Sun 9.30am–5pm • €1.50 • ⓦ szn.it

Right in the middle of the Villa Comunale, you might want to take in the Mediterranean marine life at the more than a century old but newly restored **Aquarium**. It comprises just one large room, lined with tanks filled with impressive giant turtles, eels and rays, as well as a couple of artificial rock pools.

Villa Pignatelli

Riviera Chiaia 200 • Mon, Wed–Sun 8.30am–2pm • €2 • ☎ 081 669 675, ⓦ polomusealenapoli.beniculturali.it

On the inland side of the Riviera di Chiaia, the gardens of the **Villa Pignatelli** are a peaceful alternative to the Villa Comunale, and the early nineteenth-century house itself, now a museum, is kept in much the same way as when it was the home of a

FROM TOP TEATRO SAN CARLO (P.62); QUARTIERI SPAGNOLI (P.65) >

1

prominent Naples family and a nineteenth-century meeting place for the city's elite. Built by the Anglo-Italian aristocrat Sir Ferdinand Acton in 1826, by the standards of some of Naples' palaces it's a rather modest affair: Palladian in style but with a grand Doric-columned portico, with half a dozen rooms on the ground floor, still decorated as they would have been in Acton's time. He only lived here until 1841, when the villa was bought by the Rothschilds and later the Pignatelli-Cortes family – descendants of the notorious Spanish conquistador, as evidenced by the bust of him in the ballroom, rescued from his pillaged funerary monument in Mexico City. The ballroom is a grand open space, divided between areas for the dancers and musicians; look in on the Pompeii-style ante-room at the end. The rest of the ground floor is equally sumptuous, from the central "red room", added by the Rothschilds, to the "green room" with its collection of Meissen and Capodimonte porcelain, and the dining room and library on either side. Upstairs, off the elegant circular vestibule, there's a small collection of artworks: pride of place goes to Guercino's arresting depiction of St George and a collection of sculptures of street urchins and old men by the nineteenth-century Neapolitan artist Vincenzo Gemito. There's also a room of local landscapes, notably a depiction of the "village" of Chiaia in 1700, by the Dutch painter Gaspar van Wittel.

Mergellina and Posillipo

Via Caracciolo stretches around the bay for just over 1km, at the far end of which lie the harbour and main square – **Piazza Sannazzaro** – of the **Mergellina** district, a pleasant seaside neighbourhood that's a departure point for hydrofoils to the bay's islands. There's not a lot to see here, but it's worth wandering down to the "*porticciolo*" for an ogle at the yachts and an ice cream or pastry at one of the chalets in the waterfront park; there's also a handful of fishing boats at the far end that sell their morning's catch from a couple of shacks on the beach. **Posillipo** – ancient Pausilypon, literally a "pause from care" – is an upmarket suburb of swanky villas and deep pockets but of not much appeal to tourists, though you may want to come out here to eat, either in Posillipo itself or in the seaside village of **Marechiaro**, reachable by taking bus #140 from Via Santa Lucia and then changing to bus #23. There's also the dense and lovely **Parco Virgiliano**, also reachable on bus #140, and, just beyond, another recently excavated Roman tunnel, the **Grotta di Seiano**, on Salita Coroglio.

Santa Maria in Piedigrotta

Piazza Piedigrotta 24 • Daily 9am–noon & 5–7pm • Free

The church butts up against the cliff and grotto, from which it – and the district – takes its name (literally "foot of the grotto"). Originally from the 1350s, and rebuilt in the sixteenth century, the church is mainly of interest for the Madonna that sits on the altar and is carried through the streets every September 8 in one of the city's most popular festivals.

Parco Virgiliano

Salita della Grotta 20 • Daily 9am–6.30pm • Free

Immediately behind the church, in the **Parco Virgiliano**, a path leads to a monument to Giacomo Leopardi, the doomed nineteenth-century Italian Romantic poet, who died in Naples of cholera at the ripe old age of 39, but is generally considered one of the lions of nineteenth-century Italian literature. From here, the path leads up to the entrance to a first-century BC tunnel that was built to connect Neapolis with Puteoli (modern-day Pozzuoli); it's said to be nearly 1km long but you can't go inside and instead have to make do with the medieval frescoes that decorate its entrance. The park takes its name from the fact that it was once thought that the poet Virgil was buried

FOOTBALL IN NAPLES

The district of **Fuorigrotta**, literally "beyond the grotto", the other side of the Mergellina hill, is not really of interest unless you're going to a football match, since it's home to SSC Napoli's **San Paolo** stadium. Football is something of a religion in Naples, and although support is not as fanatical as it used to be since the club's bankruptcy and subsequent relegation from the national *serie A*, they've recently been rescued by the movie mogul Aurelio De Laurentiis and have made it back to – and are thriving in – the top flight.

To get to a game, take the Cumana railway from Montesanto to Mostra and the stadium is right in front of you. Tickets are sometimes available from the offices facing you as you approach, or from the club's outlets in town, but you will need ID and even then it's not certain you'll be able to get hold of one. The other alternative is to buy online from sites like ⓦ 1st4footballtickets.com or ⓦ viagogo.co.uk. Prices range from €25 for seats in the end *curva* stands to €40 in the *distinti* or corner. For a seat in the side or *tribuna* stands, expect to pay over €60.

here, in the stone beehive to its side, and although there's no truth in this, the setting is lovely, and it's worth climbing up the steep steps to the right of the tunnel entrance for a closer look at Virgil's supposed last resting place.

Grotta di Seiano and the Villa di Pausilypon

Discesa Coroglio 36 • Grotta: Mon, Wed, Fri 9.30am–11.45am; Villa: Mon–Sat 9.30am–11.45am • Free • ☎ 081 230 1030 • Bus #140 from Piazza Vittoria to Mescita Osteria and then #C1

On the far side of the hill that lies beyond Mergellina and Posillipo is the **Grotta di Seiano**, a 770m-long tunnel that connects to the ruins of the Roman **Villa di Pausilypon** at the other end, once the home of one Vedius Pollio, a freed slave who built the villa and tunnel together for the convenient access it gave him to the city. The tunnel is high and slender, supported by round arches, and a fragment of an inscription at the entrance dates from its fourth-century AD restoration. As for the villa, it has been pillaged mercilessly over the years, and there's not much of it left, but you can still make out a small amphitheatre, the remains of a temple and a small shrine. The site itself, at the end of the promontory, is magnificent, while down below you can see the cove of **La Gaiola** with its small beach, reachable by a steep path.

Vomero

Like Chiaia below and Mergellina to the west, **Vomero** – the district topping the hill immediately above the old city – is one of Naples' relatively modern additions: a light, airy and peaceful quarter connected most directly with the teeming morass below by funicular railway. It's a large area but mostly residential, and you're unlikely to want to stray far beyond the streets that fan out from each of the three funicular stations, centring on the grand symmetry of **Piazza Vanvitelli**, fringed by cafés and the location of a vibrant summer-evening *passeggiata*.

Castel Sant'Elmo

Via Tito Angelini 22 • Mon, Tues, Thurs–Sun 8.30am–7pm • €5 • ☎ 081 229 4401, ⓦ polomusealenapoli.beniculturali.it

Five minutes' walk from the Morghen funicular station, the **Castel Sant'Elmo** occupies Naples' highest point and is an impressive fortification, a fourteenth-century structure once used for incarcerating political prisoners and now lording it grandly over the streets below. Its six-pointed star layout was cleverly designed to defend its position, requiring fewer men and arms than a conventional citadel, and it remained an important fortress right up to Bourbon times, when it was used to imprison dissidents

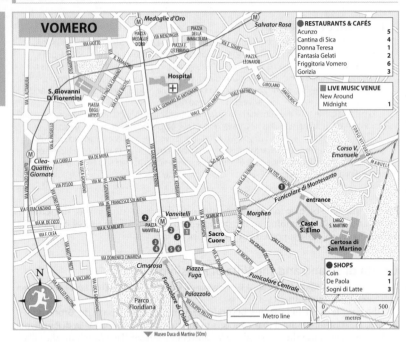

VOMERO

Medaglie d'Oro

PIAZZA MEDAGLIE D'ORO · VIA MENZINGER · PIAZZA DELLA IMMACOLATA · VIA E. SUAREZ

PIAZZA CELEBRANO · PIAZZA LEONARDO

Salvator Rosa

Hospital

S. Giovanni D. Fiorentini · PIAZZA DEGLI ARTISTI · VIA S. GENNARO AD ANTIGNANO · VIALE MICHELANGELO · VIALE RAFFAELLO · GIROLAMO SANTACROCE

Cilea-Quattro Giornate

Vanvitelli · Morghen · Castel S. Elmo · Funicolare di Montesanto · entrance · Corso V. Emanuele

Sacro Cuore · LARGO S. MARTINO · Certosa di San Martino

Cimarosa · Piazza Fuga · Funicolare Centrale

Parco Floridiana · Palazzolo · Funicolare di Chiaia

N · Metro line

● RESTAURANTS & CAFÉS	
Acunzo	5
Cantina di Sica	4
Donna Teresa	1
Fantasia Gelati	2
Friggitoria Vomero	6
Gorizia	3

■ LIVE MUSIC VENUE	
New Around Midnight	1

● SHOPS	
Coin	2
De Paola	1
Sogni di Latte	3

0 — 500 metres

▼ Museo Duca di Martina (50m)

against the regime, and then again as a military prison after Unification. Not surprisingly it has some of the best views in Naples and you can enjoy them from the top terrace of the castle before visiting the Napoli Novocento museum in the centre – a collection of paintings and sculpture by Neapolitan artists from the early twentieth century to the 1980s.

Certosa di San Martino

Largo San Martino 5 • Mon, Tues, Thurs–Sun 8.30am–7pm • €6 • ☎ 081 578 1769 • ⓦ cir.campania.beniculturali.it

The fourteenth-century monastic complex of the **Certosa e Museo di San Martino** is one of Naples' prime historical attractions, with a wealth of plunder from the city and beyond, though unfortunately with very little information in English. Founded by Charles of Calabria, the son of Robert of Anjou, in 1325, and renovated and restored over successive centuries, it's a sprawling complex, and one, along with the Castel Sant'Elmo, that you're somehow always aware of wherever you are in Naples. Indeed, the views from its cunningly constructed terraced gardens are worth the entrance fee alone – short of climbing Vesuvius, they're as good a vista of the Bay of Naples as you'll get – but there is much to see in the rest of the museum too.

The monastic **church** occupies the first courtyard, a highly decorated affair with a colourful pavement and works by some of the greats of Neapolitan painting. On the ceiling are frescoes by Giovanni Lanfranco depicting *Christ in Glory with Saints*; above the high altar, you can see an *Adoration of the Shepherds* by Guido Reni; and the chapels that fringe the small nave are decorated by Domenico Vaccaro, Massimo Stanzione, Battistelo Carraciolo and Francesco Solimena, among others. Have a look too in the rooms off the high altar, where there is a sacristy lined with sixteenth-century wood-inlay cupboards and, beyond, a series of frescoes recording the *Triumph of Judith* by Luca Giordano.

There are more paintings by the Neapolitan masters in the **museum** beyond, as well as two sculptures by Pietro Bernini – *San Martino on Horseback* and a *Virgin and Child* – and paintings by Stanzione in the former apartments of the prior. The library has frescoed walls and ceilings, and a meridian line and signs of the zodiac in majolica on the floor. It holds the museum's impressive collection of *presepi* or Christmas cribs, including one very large one with its own grotto dating from 1879, and some practically life-size polychromatic figures from the late-fifteenth century originally from the church of San Giovanni a Carbonara (see p.58). The large Baroque **cloister** – which you can sometimes also access through the back of the church – is lovely too, renovated by Cosimo Fanzago who added the monks' cemetery in the corner, identifiable by the skulls on the balustrade. It's surrounded by more rooms displaying paintings and sculpture of variable quality.

Museo Duca di Martina

Villa Floridiana, Via Cimarosa 77 • Mon, Wed–Sun 8.30am–2pm • Free • ☎ 081 578 8418, ⓦ polomusealenapoli.beniculturali.it

Vomero's third museum, close to the Chiaia funicular, five minutes' walk from Piazza Vanvitelli, is the **Museo Duca di Martina**, set in the Neoclassical **Villa Floridiana** which sits in its own park, a busy place – and a good place for a picnic – in the summer months, full of gangs of schoolchildren, canoodling couples and mums pushing buggies, and a large colony of cats. The villa itself, which was formerly the summer home of the wife of the Bourbon king Ferdinand, Lucia Migliaccio, was bought by the Italian state in 1927 and has been a museum of ceramics and porcelain ever since, though it's of fairly specialist interest and parts are only sporadically open. When it's fully open, you can see the main European porcelain collection, which varies from the beautifully simple to the outrageously kitsch, with examples of Capodimonte and Meissen work, as well as Venetian glass, eighteenth-century Limoges work and German and Viennese pieces. Also on the ground floor are ivory and enamel work as well as various devotional items, while the lower floors focus on Ming- and Qing-dynasty Chinese porcelain, Japanese pieces and some exquisite inlaid jade boxes and panels.

INFORMATION

Tourist offices Piazza del Gesù Mon–Sat 9am–5pm, Sun 9am–1pm ☎ 081 551 2701; Via San Carlo 9, Mon–Sat 9am–5pm, Sun 9am–1pm ☎ 081 402 394; Stazione Centrale daily 9am–6pm ☎ 081 268 779; ⓦ inaples.it. Each office gives out free city maps and the monthly *Qui* *Napoli*, a useful source of information on the city in general, with listings on sights, events and more. You can also download *Qui Napoli* at the Naples tourist office's website, which is in itself a good if sporadically updated source of information.

TOURS

CitySightseeing Napoli ☎ 081 551 7279, ⓦ napoli .city-sightseeing.it Operates a hop-on-hop-off service taking in the sights on several routes around town between May and October; tickets cost €22 for adults (children €11, families €66) and are valid for 24hr. Tours leave from just in front of the Castel Nuovo.

ACCOMMODATION

Perhaps the biggest change in Naples in recent years is its newly galvanized hotel industry. The palatial five-stars fronting the sea in Santa Lucia are still there, as are the faceless corporate options that dot much of the rest of the centre. But a number of places have been renovated, and **new hotels** and **B&Bs** have opened, giving the city a range of contemporary, boutique alternatives and lifting the general standard of accommodation to a new high. If you've travelled in the north of Italy, hotel **prices** may also come as a pleasant surprise, although it's actually hard to say what you'll pay as prices vary enormously. The city is not a massive tourist draw, and it is often possible to find bargains, particularly at weekends, when many places drop their prices.

CENTRO STORICO

Quite a few boutique hotels and small B&Bs have sprouted up in the Centro Storico in recent years, and in some respects, it is the most atmospheric part of Naples in which to stay. You don't get the views, but you are on hand for some of the city's best restaurants and pizzerias.

HOTELS

★ **Costantinopoli 104** Via S. Maria di Costantinopoli 104 ☎ 081 557 1035, ⓦ costantinopoli104.com; map pp.48–49. A contemporary boutique hotel with its own garden and small swimming pool in a secluded yet central location at the back of a Piazza Bellini *palazzo*. Some of the

1

rooms open onto the garden, others onto the upstairs terrace. Very peaceful, but also very convenient. **€200**

Des Artistes Via Duomo 61 ☎081 1925 5086, ⓦhoteldesartistesnaples.it; map pp.48–49. A comfortable place with simple rooms and young, friendly staff – plus free wi-fi. Just 200m from the Duomo and within easy striking distance of the archeological museum and the Centro Storico. **€70**

Piazza Bellini Via Santa Maria di Costantinopoli 101 ☎081 451 732, ⓦhotelpiazzabellini.com; map pp.48–49. Stylish yet unpretentious and friendly contemporary hotel within a light-flooded high-ceilinged Renaissance *palazzo*, right on the edge of the Centro Storico, off lively Piazza Bellini. There's a secluded courtyard, and 48 spacious rooms with unfussy custom-designed furniture – the best with huge terraces looking over the city to Vesuvius. Free wi-fi, plus a small bar and a book-sharing library for guests. **€150**

B&BS

Belle Arti Resort Via S. Maria di Costantinopoli 27 ☎081 557 1062, ⓦbelleartiresort.com; map pp.48–49. Contemporary design meets historic elegance at this boutique B&B near Piazza Bellini. Rooms are individually decorated with modern pieces and some have original seventeenth-century ceiling frescoes. Good location. Free wi-fi in the lobby; cable hook-ups in rooms. **€80**

★Donna Regina B&B Via L. Settembrini 80 ☎081 446 799, ⓦdiscovernaples.net; map pp.48–49. Located inside a former convent next to the MADRE, this welcoming B&B is tastefully furnished with a mixture of family heirlooms and modern art. Each room is spacious and uniquely decorated, and the main lounge is cosy and characterful. The family also rents out small apartments around the city and has a B&B on Procida. Doubles **€90**, triples **€120**, quads **€150**

Purgatorio No. 2 Palazzo Spinelli, Via dei Tribunali 362 ☎081 551 6625; map pp.48–49. Artist and provocateur Nathalie St-Phalle's boho B&B, a handful of rooms off a big rug-strewn gallery. Not the most orthodox place to stay perhaps, but full of atmosphere, and a chance to stay in one of the Centro Storico's grandest palaces. **€110**

Tribù Via dei Tribunali 339 ☎081 454 793 or ☎338 409 9173, ⓦtribunapoli.com; map pp.48–49. Behind the decrepit walls of the medieval Palazzo d'Angiò, two architects have created a peaceful artistic oasis of four white rooms, each decorated with original ceramics, contemporary paintings and antiques. In fine weather, breakfast is served on an outdoor terrace in the courtyard. Doubles **€80**, triples **€90**

HOSTELS

Naples Pizza Hostel Via San Paolo ai Tribunali 44 ☎081 1932 3562, ⓦnaplespizzahostel.com; map pp.48–49. Run by the same owners as the *Bella Capri*, this hostel is a bit cheaper than its sister and very well located right in the heart of the old centre. They don't serve pizza, but they do have wi-fi. Dorms **€18**, doubles **€60**

PIAZZA GARIBALDI, FORCELLA AND THE PORT

Many of Naples' budget options are around Piazza Garibaldi, conveniently close to the train station but a rather insalubrious and noisy district and not great for going out at night – although you're only ten minutes' walk from the heart of the Centro Storico. Some of the port area options are very handy for catching ferries.

HOTELS

Casanova Via Venezia 2 ☎081 268 287, ⓦhotel casanova.com; map pp.48–49. Perhaps the best of the budget options near the station, this creeper-clad hotel, run by an affable team, is quiet and has pleasant rooms (most of which are en suite) and a communal roof terrace. **€45**

H2C Via Nuova Marina 8 ☎081 1980 8650, ⓦh2c.it; map pp.48–49. Not a bad stab at a boutique hotel in what cannot be described as the city's best neighbourhood. Nonetheless it's handy for the station and port, and to some extent the Centro Storico too. Good thing they have a reasonable restaurant as there's not much on the doorstep. Rooms are bright, contemporary and comfy, though a bit on the bland side. **€100**

Hotel Naples Corso Umberto I 55 ☎081 551 7055, ⓦhotelnaples.it; map pp.48–49. Unusually the rooms here are actually better than the unpromising lobby – they've been refurbished in contemporary style and have good-sized bathrooms. There's a magnificent curving Art Deco staircase, and the location is handy for the port, Centro Storico and modern centre, and two minutes from Universita metro station. Free wi-fi, a decent buffet breakfast thrown in and large enough – 80 rooms – to often have availability. **€120**

★Palazzo Caracciolo Via Carbonara 112 ☎081 016 0111, ⓦaccorhotels.com; map pp.48–49. In one of the busiest parts of Naples, two minutes from Piazza Garibaldi and handy for the Centro Storico, this place is a bit of a haven; it's a conversion of a venerable old palace with very comfortable rooms in contemporary style. The palace courtyards make a nice lounging and dining space, and the atmosphere is peaceful and restorative – just as well given the mêlée that faces you immediately outside. Free, reliable wi-fi. Doubles can be very good value. **€120**

Romeo Via Cristoforo Colombo 45 ☎081 017 5001, ⓦromeohotel.it; map pp.48–49. Something of a standout on this grungy stretch of waterfront opposite the cruise-ship terminal, this is the ultimate Naples boutique hotel, complete with weird-looking furniture and a sushi bar on the ground floor. Upstairs there's a range of well-appointed rooms, the best of which have views over the bay. Standards of service are high, though at these prices you might wish for a better location. That said, you can virtually fall out of bed into a ferry for one of the islands. Free wi-fi. **€225**

HOSTELS

Hotel Bella Capri Via Melisurgo 4 ☎ 081 552 9494, ⓦ bellacapri.it; map pp.48–49. This upper-floor hostel is virtually a neighbour of the swanky new *Romeo* a few doors down and enjoys an equally handy location right opposite the ferry terminal. It has a mixture of dorm beds and private rooms, and offers wi-fi and a large, light and airy breakfast room. Dorms **€20**, doubles **€65**

Hostel of the Sun Via Melisurgo 15 ☎ 081 420 6393, ⓦ hostelnapoli.com; map pp.48–49. Almost opposite the *Bella Capri*, just off the main waterfront, this is perhaps the best and friendliest hostel in Naples – well placed for going out and with no curfew. Breakfast is included, and it has a range of nicely furnished doubles, both en suite and with shared bathrooms, a couple of floors down. Free wi-fi. Dorms **€20**, doubles **€60**

VIA TOLEDO AND THE QUARTIERI SPAGNOLI

You're not far from anything when you stay on or near Via Toledo: sights like the Palazzo Reale and Castel Nuovo are on your doorstep and the Centro Storico is a mere ten minutes' walk, as are Chiaia and Santa Lucia.

HOTELS

Il Convento Via Speranzella 137/A ☎ 081 403 977, ⓦ hotelilconvento.it; map p.61. Occupying a good position in the Quartieri Spagnoli, just a block from the bottom end of Via Toledo, this rustic mid-range hotel has cosy rooms furnished in a dark, old-fashioned style. A couple of top-floor rooms have private terraces. Free wi-fi throughout. **€100**

NH Ambassador Via Medina 70 ☎ 081 410 5111, ⓦ nh -hotels.it; map p.61. This landmark tower bang in the centre of Naples can certainly claim the best views from its 100+ rooms; be sure to ask for one facing the sea. It's a 1960s period piece inside, with a sleek lobby overlooked by a bar and restaurant, and rooms that are large and well appointed, with free wi-fi, large bathrooms and separate showers. It's a business hotel at heart, but very comfortable and friendly, and the views are the best in the city. **€150**

Palazzo Turchini Via Medina 21–22 ☎ 081 551 0606, ⓦ palazzoturchini.it; map p.61. Once home to an orphanage and a musical conservatory, this building sits on a busy street overlooking the port and Piazza Municipio. Rooms are cosy with all mod cons, and there's a lovely roof terrace. Request a room that faces onto the internal garden for a tranquil night's sleep. Decent value and includes free wi-fi. **€120**

MONTESANTO, LA SANITÀ AND CAPODIMONTE

Not only is Montesanto one of central Naples' most vibrant quarters, it's only a five-minute walk from the Centro Storico and close to Via Toledo, and its train and funicular stations provide good connections. Capodimonte is somewhat apart from the city centre, perhaps it's greatest appeal – along with the art collection at the Museo Nazionale di Capodimonte, of course.

HOTELS

Correra 241 Via Correra 241 ☎ 081 1956 2842, ⓦ correra.it; map p.68. Between Piazza Dante and the archeological museum, this three-star is decorated in primary colours, giving it a fresh, contemporary look. The rooms are a decent size, although the en-suite bathrooms are rather irritatingly up a separate staircase on a mezzanine level. There's a nice little roof garden, and internet access, though the breakfast is frugal, even by Naples standards. **€80**

Villa Capodimonte Via Moiariello 66 ☎ 081 459 000, ⓦ villacapodimonte.culturehotel.it; map p.68. Ideally sited for seeing the Palazzo Reale di Capodimonte, this recently opened modern option is very comfortable, and attractively located, surrounded by its own private park. Some rooms have views over the city's roofs to Vesuvius. **€100**

SANTA LUCIA AND CHIAIA

A number of hotels cluster along the seafront of Santa Lucia, close to the Castel dell'Ovo, making the most of the sea views and charging for the privilege. Just behind, Chiaia is an appealing part of town to hole up in, and perhaps the best place to stay for shops and nightlife.

HOTELS

Chiaia Hotel De Charme Via Chiaia 216 ☎ 081 415 555, ⓦ hotelchiaia.com; map p.74. An old-fashioned and rather quaint very central hotel, with 21 rooms fashioned from an eighteenth-century patrician home – and with lots of antique furniture and old-world style, along with free wi-fi and flatscreen TVs. **€129**

Excelsior Via Partenope 48 ☎ 081 764 0111, ⓦ excelsiornapoli.com; map p.74. Occupying a prime spot on the corner of Via Partenope, with views in both directions across the bay, the *Excelsior* is the *grande dame* of Naples hotels, and makes the most of its wonderful location, not only with the rooms, which are generously sized and comfortable with marble bathrooms, but also with the public areas, best of which is the ground-floor corner salon with its floor-to-ceiling windows and spacious graciousness. There couldn't be a cooler or more restful spot in Naples on a hot summer's day. The rooftop restaurant, too, is lovely, and if you don't want to blow your budget on

1

food you can just sneak up for a drink or a laze on one of its loungers. Check the website for offers. **€240**

Grand Hotel Parker's Corso Vittorio Emanuele 135 ☎ 081 761 2474, ⓦ grandhotelparkers.it; map p.74. The oldest hotel in Naples, or so it claims, which has hosted Oscar Wilde and Virginia Woolf, as well as King Vittorio Emanuele himself. The views from the bay-facing rooms and the top-floor restaurant are superb; there's wi-fi (not free) and service and facilities are excellent. The only slight drawback is its location, which is a bit detached from the main sights and neighbourhoods, although there's a Chiaia-Vomero funicular station five minutes' walk away. **€200**

Miramare Via N. Sauro 24 ☎ 081 764 7589, ⓦ hotel miramare.com; map p.74. This Art Nouveau gem is the less obvious – and cheaper – alternative to the giant and slightly more impersonal palaces on this stretch of the waterfront, with a more homely feel and a warmer welcome. **€200**

Palazzo Alabardieri Via Alabardieri 38 ☎ 081 415 278, ⓦ palazzoalabardieri.it; map p.74. In the heart of Chiaia, this hotel is geared towards business travellers and discerning tourists looking for luxury and courteous service. The well-appointed rooms are decorated with parquet floors, marble and rich fabrics. **€145**

Pinto-Storey Via Martucci 72 ☎ 081 681 260, ⓦ pintostorey.it; map p.74. An evocative Art Nouveau building in a pleasant part of Chiaia, near Naples' most elegant shopping area and a short walk to the Villa Comunale and the sea. Rooms are attractively furnished and many have views of the bay. **€78**

Rex Via Palepoli 12 ☎ 081 764 9389, ⓦ hotel-rex.it; map p.74. In a striking Art Nouveau-style building designed by the renowned Italian architect Coppedè, this family-run hotel in Santa Lucia has some of the friendliest staff around. There's a large sitting room in the reception area frequented by the owner's family and friends, and the rooms are simple and tidy. **€120**

★**San Francesco al Monte** Corso Vittorio Emanuele 328 ☎ 081 423 9111, ⓦ sanfrancescoalmonte.it; map p.74. Occupying a commanding position on the slopes above the Quartieri Spagnoli, five minutes' walk from the Vittorio Emanuele funicular station, this converted sixteenth-century monastery is one of the nicest places to stay in the city, with each of its 45 rooms beautifully decorated and offering panoramic views of Naples. Modern art adorns the walls and chapels are used as dining and conference rooms. There is a beautiful if small pool amid gloriously tranquil roof gardens and a lovely terrace restaurant serving breakfast, lunch and dinner. **€145**

Vesuvio Via Partenope 45 ☎ 081 764 0044, ⓦ vesuvio .it; map p.74. Sister hotel to the *Excelsior* next door but one, and providing the latter's pool and spa facilities, this has equally sumptuous rooms and views of the Castel dell'Ovo opposite. Its *Caruso* restaurant makes the most of its rooftop location, with the entire, glinting bay spread

before you while you eat. Overall service is impeccable, and nothing is too much trouble. If you really do have money to burn you can take a turn on their Vesuvietta powerboat, which provides a way of reaching the islands without having to rub shoulders with the public. **€225**

B&BS

Morelli 49 Via Domenico Morelli 49 ☎ 081 245 2291, ⓦ bbmorelli49.it; map p.74. This small B&B enjoys an excellent location not far from the seafront on the edge of Santa Lucia. Its three spacious rooms are nicely decorated and comfortable. Free wi-fi, flatscreen TVs and a reasonable continental breakfast in the morning. **€75**

MERGELLINA AND POSILLIPO

Mergellina is a nice part of town in which to stay, as is posh Posillipo, and although both are outside the main action of the city centre, they have good restaurants and are well connected with the rest of town.

HOTELS

Ausonia Via Caracciolo 11 ☎ 081 682 278, ⓦ hotelausonianapoli.com; map p.74. A two-star hotel neatly placed in Mergellina, and decorated with a nautical theme. Ask for one of the rooms with bay views. **€80**

Mergellina Via G. Bruno 115 ☎ 081 248 2142, ⓦ hotelmergellina.it; map p.74. This homely budget option is situated just off Piazza Sannazzaro near Mergellina's port. Most of its spick-and-span rooms have balconies and all have free internet access. Excellent value. **€95**

HOSTELS

Ostello Mergellina Salita della Grotta 23 ☎ 081 761 2346, ⓦ ostellonapoli.com; map p.74. A popular official youth hostel with a view of the bay, and conveniently located not far from the Mergellina metro station. Dorms are six-bed maximum and breakfast is included, though there's a three-day maximum stay in July & Aug. Dorm **€18**

OUTER NAPLES
CAMPSITES

There are a number of campsites within a feasible distance of Naples. When *Vulcano Solfatara* is closed, head to one of the other sites around the bay – at Pompeii (see p.127), or, rather nicer, Sorrento (see p.139) both within an hour of the city.

Vulcano Solfatara Via Solfatara 161 ☎ 081 526 7413, ⓦ solfatara.it. Excellent and beautifully landscaped campsite at the entrance to the Solfatara (p.102). As well as tent pitches, there are double bungalows, a large swimming pool, a grocery store and a snack bar-restaurant. Perhaps the best base for Naples if you're camping. Take the Metropolitana to Pozzuoli and walk 10min up the hill. Closed Nov–March. Camping (€10 for each additional person) **€18**, bungalow **€80**

EATING

Nowhere else in Italy is **food** so much part of the culture as it is in Naples. The city bursts with pizzerias, markets, cafés, restaurants, *pasticcerie* and *friggitorie* (fried-food vendors), and nearly every aspect of social life involves food in some way; even the city's famous nativity scenes feature markets, fishmongers and people eating heaped plates of spaghetti.

As Naples is not primarily a tourist-geared city, most **restaurants** are family-run places frequented by locals and as such generally serve good, traditional Neapolitan food at very reasonable prices. You can eat well pretty much everywhere, but inevitably certain districts do certain things best: the **Centro Storico** and **Quartieri Spagnoli** are still home to many simple places that serve a limited menu of daily specials based on what is fresh in the market; **Chiaia** and **Vomero** host more formal restaurants that serve a greater selection of regional specialities; for pricey fish meals with a view, there's the **Borgo Marinaro** in Santa Lucia and **Posillipo**.

Cheap, affordable **snacks** are a Neapolitan staple. Most bars sell food – **pastries** in the morning or all day and sandwiches or light meals in the afternoon, and Neapolitans take their **desserts** and **coffee** seriously and consume them often. Throughout the city, it is still possible to find places that roast their own coffee beans, make their own pastries on the premises, and even manufacture their own ice cream. This painstaking dedication to tradition produces some stellar results – and, arguably, contributes to obesity rates that are well above the national norms. Finally, the city's great **friggitorie**, selling pizza by the slice and all manner of deep-fried treats, make a tempting option for snacky lunches (see p.29).

CENTRO STORICO
RESTAURANTS AND PIZZERIAS

Antica Osteria Pisano Piazza Crocelle ai Mannesi 1–4 ☏ 081 554 8325; map pp.48–49. A small and very traditional trattoria with a reasonably priced menu of well-loved local standards – a few pasta dishes, mainly with fish and seafood, and a short menu of meaty mains for €6–10. Mon–Sat noon–4pm & 7.30–11.30pm.

Bellini Via Santa Maria di Costantinopoli 79/80 ☏ 081 459 774, ⓦ ilbelliniristorante.it; map pp.48–49. This historic establishment, all the more conspicuous given the area's slick contemporary spots, has been here forever. The service is formal and sometimes entertaining, provided by cummerbunded, occasionally cranky waiters. The house speciality, *linguine al cartoccio* (pasta with seafood baked in paper) is really good for €12, but they also serve decent fish, and pizzas in the evening from €5. Nice convivial outside terrace, too. Tues–Sat noon–3.30pm & 8–11pm, Sun noon–3.30pm.

Di Matteo Via dei Tribunali 94 ☏ 081 455 262, ⓦ pizzeriadimatteo.it; map pp.48–49. The crowded *friggitoria* outside announces this terrific and well-located pizzeria, one of the best – and best-known – in the city. (President Clinton famously dropped in for one when he was in town.) For table service, walk in and take a left, then head upstairs with authority and ask for a table. The spartan decor may be reminiscent of a hospital cafeteria, but the enormous pizzas, from €4, more than make up for it. *Pizzette*, *arancini* and other cheap Neapolitan street food (€1 each) to take away are sold at the entrance. Mon–Sat 9am–midnight.

★ **I Decumani** Via dei Tribunali 58–61 ☏ 081 557 1309; map pp.48–49. One of several excellent pizzerias along this stretch, and we reckon one of Naples' best. Freshly remodelled and warmly tiled, *I Decumani* has come a long way since it was a hole-in-the-wall *friggitoria* (still active next door). The *fritti misti* are a must, as are the huge, delicious pizzas, which

average €4–5. It's one of the few places in the Centro Storico open on Sundays. Daily noon–2am.

★ **La Campagnola** Via dei Tribunali 47 ☏ 081 459 034, ⓦ lacampagnolaviatribunali.it; map pp.48–49. This small, busy trattoria serves up great seafood starters – *spaghetti alle vongole* or *frutti di mare* for €8, *sauté di vongole* and hearty mains like *salsiccia e friarielli* (sausage with seasonal greens). Nothing fancy, but full of people happily scoffing delicious, well-priced Neapolitan grub. You may have to wait for a table. Wed–Sat noon–midnight, Sun & Mon noon–4pm. Closed Tues.

★ **La Cantina di Via Sapienza** Via Sapienza 40–41 ☏ 081 459 078, ⓦ cantinadiviasapienza.it; map pp.48–49. Proprietor Gaetano's no-nonsense food and service draw a busy lunch crowd from the nearby hospital and university. *La Cantina* dishes up hearty home-cooked classics like *polpette fritte* (fried meatballs), *melanzane parmigiana*, lovely octopus salad and a staggering array of seasonal vegetable side dishes like *caponata* (sweet-and-sour aubergine) and *peperoni fritti* (fried peppers). Most dishes €4–6. Mon–Sat noon–3pm.

La Locanda del Grifo Via Francesco del Giudice 14 ☏ 081 557 1492, ⓦ lalocandadelgrifo.com; map pp.48–49. With tables on a ramshackle square just off Via dei Tribunali, this place has a short menu of just half a dozen pasta dishes (€10–12) and around the same number of mains (€10–15) – mainly fish – plus pizzas from €4. Great location, good food and excellent . Daily noon–3pm & 7pm–midnight.

★ **La Stanza del Gusto** Via Santa Maria di Costantinopoli 100 ☏ 081 401 578, ⓦ lastanzadelgusto .com; map pp.48–49. Chef Mario Avallone was one of Naples' first culinary innovators, originally based in Chiaia, and with a dedication to creative, seasonal dishes that use only local and sustainable ingredients. The menu here changes regularly but is always full of good stuff – traditionally based, but unlike anything else you'll find in the city. Tasting menus go for €35–65 but you can just as easily order a la carte. It's also known for its downstairs Squisitezze

1

TOP 5 PIZZA JOINTS

Acunzo Not very well-known to tourists, but it's definitely Vomero's best pizza joint. See p.85.

Antica Pizzeria del Borgo Orefici Down a little side street not far from the port, and as yet relatively undiscovered by tourists. Nonetheless some of the city's best pizzas. See p.86.

I Decumani Right in the heart of the Centro Storico, and not quite as widely lauded as its better-known competitors, but definitely among the best pizzas in the city. See p.86.

Sorbillo Yes, it's always got a mob of tourists outside, but this might be the one place that's worth the wait. Extra big pizzas too. See p.86.

Starita a Materdei Tucked up above the Museo Archeologico, this long-standing neighbourhood pizzeria is well worth seeking out. Good *fritti* and great bases. See p.88.

or "cheese bar", which focuses just on local *formaggi* and *salumi* – a five-cheese tasting costs €12 and can be paired with a glass of one of a number of excellent wines, or even the restaurant's decent selection of beers. Tues–Sat 10.30am–midnight, Sun 11am–3pm. Closed Mon.

Lombardi a Santa Chiara Via B. Croce 59 ☏ 081 552 0780; map pp.48–49. Located on Spaccanapoli near the church of Santa Chiara, this well-respected place is known for its pizzas, though there is a moderately priced menu of Neapolitan dishes on offer as well. It's pretty basic, but the upstairs room a little less so than other Centro Storico pizzerias. Pizzas from €4. Mon–Sat noon–3pm & 7pm–1am.

Sorbillo Via dei Tribunali 32 ☏ 081 446 643, ⓦ accademiadellapizza.it; map pp.48–49. In business since 1935, this place has a die-hard cult following that snubs the family's newer pizza joint a few doors down in favour of this, the original. Its popularity means that it's a scrum most nights and you may have to give your name and wait for a table. But the pizzas are great, and use the highest-quality ingredients – the best mozzarella from nearby Agerola, sweet Vesuvian tomatoes and fine olive oil: a novel idea in the pizza business. Pizzas from €4. Mon–Sat 9am–1am.

SNACKS, CAKES AND ICE CREAM

Caffè dell'Epoca Via Santa Maria di Costantinopoli 82 ☏ 081 291 722; map pp.48–49. Excellent coffee and an assortment of pastries and snacks with a few tables outside, offering a front-row seat for the chic bohemian scene in adjacent Piazza Bellini. Mon–Sat 7am–10pm, Sun 7am–2pm.

Capparelli Via dei Tribunali 324–327 ☏ 081 454 310; map pp.48–49. Opposite San Paolo Maggiore, this small *pasticceria* serves hot, flaky *cornetti* and *sfogliatelle* to take away. For a few extra euros, grab a table and an espresso at their bar next door. Mon–Sat 8am–1pm & 4–7pm.

Gay Odin Via Benedetto Croce 61 ☏ 081 551 0794, ⓦ gay-odin.it; map pp.48–49. One of several locations (there are two on Via Toledo alone), the Spaccanapoli branch of this long-established *chocolatier* sells decadent ice cream. Mon–Sat 10am–8pm, Sun 10am–2pm.

Scaturchio Piazza San Domenico 19 ☏ 081 551 6944, ⓦ scaturchio.it; map pp.48–49. This elegant old Naples standard has been serving coffee and pastries in the heart of Spaccanapoli for decades. Elbow your way to the counter or grab a table in the shade of the church of San Domenico. There's another branch right by the Montesanto funicular station. Daily 7.30am–7pm.

PIAZZA GARIBALDI, FORCELLA AND THE PORT

RESTAURANTS AND PIZZERIAS

★ **Antica Pizzeria del Borgo Orefici** Via Luigi Palmieri 13 ☏ 081 552 0996; map pp.48–49. A handful of tables inside, and a little terrace outside, at which you can enjoy some of the city's best pizza at this little-known joint just off busy Corso Umberto. The very large pizzas more than make up for the lack of ambience, starting at €4 and stopping at around €6 for the delicious *salsiccia e friarielli* (sausage with seasonal greens), and they do decent pasta dishes and main courses, too. Mon–Sat noon–10pm.

Da Michele Via Cesare Sersale 1–3 ☏ 081 553 9204, ⓦ damichele.net; map pp.48–49. Tucked away off Corso Umberto I in the Forcella district, this is the most determinedly traditional of all the Naples pizzerias, though has now become so well-known you'll most likely find yourself surrounded by other tourists. *Da Michele* serves just two varieties – *marinara* and *margherita* – for about €4. Don't be surprised if you are shuttled to a communal, marble-topped table and seated with strangers; and don't arrive late, as they sometimes run out of dough. Mon–Sat noon–3pm & 7pm–midnight.

★ **Europeo di Mattozzi** Via Marchese Campodisola 4–10 ☏ 081 552 1323, ⓦ mattozzieuropeo.com; map pp.48–49. Just off Piazza Bovio, Alfonso Mattozzi acts as the consummate host at this reassuringly old-fashioned restaurant, serving up great fish, juicy and succulent *mozzarella di bufala* and lovely seafood starters like *alici fritti* (fried anchovies). *Primi* around €10; main courses €10–15. The home-made *babà* is not to be missed. Mon–Sat 12.30–3.30pm & 7.30–11.30pm.

Mimì alla Ferrovia Via A. d'Aragona 21 ☏ 081 553 8525, ⓦ mimiallaferrovia.it; map pp.48–49. An old-fashioned restaurant that is something of a haven in the none-too-desirable streets off Piazza Garibaldi, and serving traditional

TOP 5 RESTAURANTS FOR CUCINA NAPOLETANA

Cantina di Sapienza Only open for lunch, but as close to a Neapolitan grandma's home-cooking as it's possible to get. See p.85.

Da Dora We reckon this is one of the best places in the city to eat fresh fish and seafood – both staples of Neapolitan cuisine for centuries. See p.88.

Europeo di Mattozzi A consistently good place to try all the most delicious Neapolitan specialities. See p.86.

La Stanza del Gusto Neapolitan and Campanian food, but cooked and served with a modern twist in an informal contemporary environment. See p.85.

Nennella Old-fashioned Spanish Quarter restaurant that serves up the same hearty Neapolitan grub it has done for years. See p.87.

Neapolitan food at reasonable prices – good fish and seafood, including seafood stuffed ravioli, but also earthier fare like pasta with chickpeas. Pasta dishes go for around €7, mains for €10. Mon–Sat noon–3pm & 7–11pm.

Trianon da Ciro Via P. Colletta 44/46 ☎081 553 9426, ⓦpizzeriatrianon.it; map pp.48–49. Across the street from the historic theatre of the same name, in the Forcella district, *Trianon da Ciro* serves pizzas and nothing but (no fritti, no pasta), and has done for a century. You may have to queue, but the magnificent pizzas are worth the wait. All the classics from around €4. Daily 11am–3.30pm & 7pm–11pm.

SNACKS, CAKES AND ICE CREAM

★**Attanasio** Vico Ferrovia 1/4, off Via Milano ☎081 285 675, ⓦsfogliatelleattanasio.it; pp.48–49. This bakery, tucked away on a backstreet near the train station, specializes in delectable *sfogliatelle* – both types, either *frolla* (with shortbread crust) or *riccia* (with a shell-shaped crunchy crust), both served warm, fresh from the oven. Tues–Sun 6.30am–7.30pm.

VIA TOLEDO AND THE QUARTIERI SPAGNOLI

RESTAURANTS AND PIZZERIAS

Ciro a Santa Brigida Via Santa Brigida 71/73 ☎081 552 4072, ⓦciroasantabrigida.it; map p.61. This stalwart of the central Naples restaurant scene is looking a bit tatty these days, and the service can vary from slapdash to fawning. But the food is great: try the pasta in a Neapolitan meat sauce, rich with melting meat and onion, or one of the seafood pastas or fish mains. The pizzas are pretty good too. Starters around €10–12; mains around

€12–15. Mon–Sat 12.30–3pm & 8–11pm, Sun 12.30–3pm.

Fiorenzano Via Pignasecca 14 ☎081 551 1993, ⓦlezendraglie.it; map p.61. Not for the faint of heart, but this is genuine Neapolitan cuisine. This *tripperia* and takeaway-cum-*osteria*, with strips of tripe hanging at the entrance, serves Neapolitan classics like *o' muss* (pig muzzle with a squeeze of lemon) and *trippa al pomodoro* (tripe in tomato sauce) at a handful of tables. Good pasta too and dead cheap. Mon–Fri 1–2.30pm, Fri & Sat also 7–11pm.

Kukai Via C. de Cesare 52 ☎081 425 888, ⓦkukai.it; map p.61. This stylish sushi bar is about as far away from downtown Naples as you can get. It's rather dark inside, but its simple and delectable sushi, sashimi, soups and noodle dishes provide a nice break from pizza and pasta. Sushi from €3 for 2 pieces, noodle dishes €9–13 and great tempura mista for €12. Daily 12.30–3.30pm & 7.30pm–1am.

Leon D'Oro Piazza Dante 48 ☎081 549 9404; map p.61. On the eastern side of the wide-open Piazza Dante, *Leon D'Oro* has been going strong since the 1950s. It serves great pizza and pasta and the vast plates of seasonal vegetable and meat *antipasti* are a meal in themselves. Pasta dishes €8-12, pizzas from €4, most main courses around €12. Tues–Sun noon–11pm.

★**Nennella** Vico Lungo Teatro Nuovo 103–105 ☎081 414 338; map p.61. Born as a cheap cafeteria, *Nennella* still serves up authentic Neapolitan cuisine like *pasta e fagioli* (soup with pasta and beans) and sauteed *friarielli*. The very basic decor has changed little since the cafeteria days, but this only adds to the charm. There are queues at lunchtime – get there before the 1.30pm rush. A full 3-course meal will cost just €10–15. Mon–Sat noon–4pm & 7pm–midnight.

★**Osteria da Carmela** Via Conte di Ruovo 11/12 ☎081 549 9738, ⓦosteriadacarmela.it; map p.61. Bang next door to the Teatro Bellini, one-room *Osteria da Carmela* serves variations on traditional Neapolitan cuisine – great fish, excellent antipasti and tasty pasta and meat too, in an intimate and friendly environment. Quite a find, and moderately priced, with most *primi* around €10, *secondi* €12–20. Daily noon–4pm & 7pm–midnight.

Osteria della Mattonella Via Nicotera 13 ☎081 416 541; map p.61. Uphill from Piazza del Plebiscito, this family-run institution covered in wall-to-wall majolica (*mattonella* means tile) oozes with old-fashioned charm, with an open kitchen that has few airs and graces. The offerings are simple and rustic, served with big baskets of chewy fresh bread. Try the *pasta alla genovese* (pasta with meat and onions) for €5 and various mains – *baccalà*, meatballs, fried squid – for €8–10. Mon–Sat 12.30–3pm & 7–11pm, Sun 12.30–3pm.

SNACKS, CAKES AND ICE CREAM

Gambrinus Via Chiaia 1–2 ☎081 417 582, ⓦgrancaffegambrinus.com; map p.61. The oldest and

1

TOP 5 SPOTS FOR SNACKS AND PASTRIES

Attanasio The best *sfogliatelle* and pastries in the city, bar none, usually served warm from the oven. See p.87.

Friggitoria Vomero You can't come to Naples without eating at one of its classic takeaways or *friggitorie*, and this is one of our favourites, for delicious deep-fried snacks that are as Neapolitan as it gets. See p.90.

Pintauro Right on Via Toledo and great for a savoury snack or delicious pastry on the run. See p.88.

Sfogliatella Mary Despite or perhaps because of its central location right on the corner of Via Toledo and the Galleria, this place continues to turn out some of the city's best *sfogliatelle*. See p.88.

Vaco 'e Presse Close to the Centro Storico and Museo Archeologico, this is a trove of delicious things to eat on the move, both savoury and sweet. See p.88.

best known of Neapolitan cafés, founded in 1861. Not cheap, but its aura of chandeliered gentility and outside seating on Piazza Trieste e Trento makes it worth at least one visit, and the pastries, cakes and snacks on offer are worth the slightly inflated prices. Daily 7am–1am.

La Scimmia Piazza Carità 4 ☎ 081 552 0272; map p.61. One of two locations (the other is in Piazzetta del Nilo in Spaccanapoli), this *gelateria* serves a wide selection of ice creams, though the traditional flavours like chocolate and *stracciatella* (chocolate chip) are by far the best. Specialities include bon-bons and chocolate-covered banana ice cream on a stick. Daily 11am–midnight.

Mexico Piazza Dante 86 ☎ 081 549 9330; map p.61. Famous for its rich and aromatic espresso, *Mexico* sells its own special blends of slow-roasted beans to coffee aficionados seeking to re-create *caffè napoletano* at home. There is also a fine selection of coffee-based confectionery. There's another branch opposite the station on Piazza Garibaldi and in Vomero at Via Scarlatti 169. Daily 6.30am–8pm.

Pintauro Via Toledo 275 ☎ 081 417 339, ⓦ pintauro.it; map p.61. A famous *pasticceria* near Galleria Umberto I whose founder is credited with inventing the *sfogliatella* in 1818. They are also known for their *caprese* (chocolate and almond cake), but they do lots of savoury snacks too. Mon–Sat 9am–8pm, Sun 9am–2pm.

Sfogliatella Mary Galleria Umberto I 66 ☎ 081 402 418; map p.61. Delicious *sfogliatella* pastries. Queue up with the locals to get your sugar fix at the Via Toledo entrance to the Galleria Umberto shopping complex. Tues–Sat 9am–8pm, Sun 9am–2pm.

Vaco 'e Presse Piazza Dante 87 ☎ 081 549 9424; map p.61. True to its name ("I'm in a hurry"), this *friggitoria* on Via Toledo sells cheap, delicious Neapolitan street food like *zeppole* (fried doughballs) and *arancini* (rice balls) to a hungry university crowd. Mon–Sat 9am–9pm.

MONTESANTO, LA SANITÀ AND CAPODIMONTE
RESTAURANTS AND PIZZERIAS

'O Core 'e Napule Via Misericordiella 23/24 ☎ 081 292 566, ⓦ ristoranteocoreenapule.it; map p.68. A short walk from the Museo Archeologico, this moderately priced restaurant serves up delicious pizza, pasta and fish. A speciality is the *tronchetto*, a folded pizza filled with mozzarella and ricotta baked to perfection and draped with *prosciutto*, tomatoes, mozzarella and rocket. There is a shaded patio outside for summer dining. Pasta from €4.50, pizzas from €4, main courses €7–9. Daily 12.30–2.30pm & 7–10.30pm.

★**Starita a Materdei** Via Materdei 27–28 ☎ 081 557 3682, ⓦ pizzeriastarita.it; map p.68. The Starita family has been serving pizza and *fritti* in the Materdei neighbourhood, uphill from the Museo Archeologico, since 1901, and along the way have created unique classics like the *montarana*, pizza dough that is deep-fried before being garnished with tomato and cheese then baked (around €5). For dessert, try the *angioletti*, deep-fried dough slathered in Nutella. It's popular, and although the long main room seems to absorb people you may have a bit of a wait. Mon–Sat noon–3.30pm & 7pm–midnight, Sun 7pm–midnight.

SNACKS, CAKES AND ICE CREAM

Mignone Piazza Cavour 146 ☎ 081 293 074; map p.68. A stone's throw from the Museo Archeologico, this pastry shop turns out some of Naples' best *sfogliatelle frolle*, made fresh on site and displayed with other local treats behind a glass case. They also have a vast assortment of cakes and cookies. Mon–Sat 7am–7pm, Sun 7am–2.30pm.

SANTA LUCIA AND CHIAIA
RESTAURANTS AND PIZZERIAS

Anhelo Via Bisignano 3 ☎ 081 402 432; map p.74. This sleek, small restaurant and café is an all-day affair, serving up excellent coffee and pastries in the morning, and lunch and dinner too. You can also just drop by for a glass of wine – they have an excellent list – and a couple of items from their menu of snacky starters or one of their classy sandwiches. Full dinner options include pasta dishes for €8–10 and modern-style mains like seared tuna fillet with sesame and soy sauce for €12. Quite a rarity in this area of loud bars and *aperitivo* buffets. Mon–Sat 8am–11pm.

★**Da Dora** Via Palasciano 30 ☎ 081 680 519; map p.74. Not cheap, but perhaps the best place in the city to eat seafood and fish. One room, more or less, tiled and decorated in nautical fashion, and presided over by the implacable Dora in her pink pinny, who serves up wonderful seafood linguine and mixed fried fish, and gives you a silly bib to save you from messing up your finery. Moderately priced starters and mains, and fixed price three-course menus for €35. Mon–Sat 12.30–4pm & 8pm–midnight.

Da Ettore Via Santa Lucia 56 ☎081 764 0498, ⓦristoranteettore.it; map p.74. In the heart of Borgo Santa Lucia, this casual and lively neighbourhood restaurant is famous for its *pagnotielli* – sort of pizza sandwiches stuffed to bursting with mozzarella, ham and mushrooms, or *salsicce* and *friarelli*, for €8–9. There is a wide selection of pizza and pasta dishes, and a decent choice of mains too. Good quality and value in a neighbourhood not especially known for either. Mon–Sat noon–3.30pm & 7–11pm.

★**Da Tonino** Via Santa Teresa di Chiaia 47 ☎081 421 533; map p.74. This tiny, two-roomed restaurant with red-and-white checked tablecloths is mainly open for lunch and serves a cheap menu of half a dozen pasta starters and a selection of meat dishes for €4–5 and €6–7 respectively. It's all very simple (great pasta with fresh tomatoes and basil), with friendly, brisk service and a lot of devoted regulars. Daily noon–3pm, Fri & Sat also 7pm–midnight.

Marino Via S. Lucia 118/120 ☎081 764 0280; map p.74. A warm and welcoming family-style place in Santa Lucia with good pizzas (served at lunchtime too) and reliable Neapolitan dishes like *scialatielli* (long home-made pasta) with aubergine, tomato and mozzarella for €8. Great value, and one of the area's few really worthwhile restaurants. A good antipasti table too, and great service. Tues–Sun 12.30–3.30pm & 7.30–11.30pm.

Mattozzi Via Filangieri 16 ☎081 416 378; map p.74. Long-standing Chiaia pizzeria that does great *fritti*, big chewy-crusted pizzas (from €6, so not the cheapest) alongside pasta and main-course meat and fish dishes (around €10). Do try one of the desserts, which are many, varied and excellent. Mon–Sat noon–4pm & 8pm–2am.

Stella Via Partenope 2/A ☎081 764 4086, ⓦristorantepizzeriastella.it; map p.74. A comfortable modern restaurant and bar in a great position, lined up with all the other would-be cool joints along the seafront. Prices here are quite keen for the location, with very good pizzas from €5 and pasta and mains for around €10. Often the quality of the food decreases in inverse proportion to the quality of the views, but happily *Stella* is an exception to this rule. Daily noon–2.30pm & 7.30pm–midnight.

Umberto Via Alabardieri 30 ☎081 418 555, ⓦumberto .it; map p.74. For more than ninety years Umberto has been serving good food to the well-heeled of Chiaia. Quite brightly lit and quite formal, but the food is always reliable and not over priced. Pizza from €8, pasta dishes €8–10. Tues–Sun 12.30–2.30pm & 7–10pm, Mon 7–10pm.

SNACKS, CAKES AND ICE CREAM

Caffettiera Piazza dei Martiri 30 ☎081 764 4243, ⓦgrancaffelacaffettiera.com; map p.74. This elegant Chiaia institution is a fine place both for a leisurely early-morning coffee and an evening aperitif, with good coffee, tables outside on the square and tasty cakes and snacks. Mon–Sat 8am–midnight, Sun 8am–11pm.

L.U.I.S.E. Via Santa Caterina a Chiaia 68 ☎081 417 735, ⓦluisenapoli.it; map p.74. Just off Piazza dei Martiri, this is the perfect place to drop after you've shopped, with *piazzette*, salads, *timballo di pasta* (baked pasta) and *peperoni imbottiti* (stuffed peppers), and rather good *arancini* and other deep-fried delights, plus a few tables in the back at which to enjoy them. There's another branch, with seating, at Via Toledo 269, right outside the Augusteo funicular station. Mon–Sat 7.30am–8.30pm, Sun 9am–3pm.

MERGELLINA AND POSILLIPO

RESTAURANTS AND PIZZERIAS

Al Faretto Via Marechiaro 127 ☎081 575 0130, ⓦalfaretto.com; map p.74. Very atmospheric, romantic and smart, and offering both pizza and fish, this Posillipo wine bar and restaurant provides sweeping views over the bay from its airy dining room. Pizza is on offer too, but most people come for the exceptionally fresh local fish served with great style. In summer, phone ahead to reserve a place on the veranda, suspended over the sea. Expect to pay at least €50 a head, excluding wine. Tues–Sun 12.30–3.30pm & 7.30–11.30pm.

Ciro A Mergellina Via Mergellina 21 ☎081 681 780, ⓦciroamergellina.it; map p.74. Not to be confused with the pastry shop of the same name nearby, this popular ristorante-pizzeria is known for its huge *antipasto della casa* – mozzarella, fried vegetables, *melanzane parmigiana*, seafood salad and *polipetti affogati* (octopus in tomato sauce) – but save room for a classic pizza or fish dish. Pizzas start at around €8, and there are lots of good pasta dishes for €10. Crowded at weekends, so best to call ahead. Tues–Sun 12.30–3.45pm & 8pm–1am.

Da Cicciotto Calata Ponticello a Marechiaro 32 ☎081 575 1165, ⓦtrattoriadacicciotto.it; map p.74. Reservations are essential at this small Posillipo trattoria, with tables outside overlooking the bay. The place might have a rustic feel, but the food is anything but – think *carpaccio di pesce crudo* and raw shellfish. To get here, follow Via Marechiaro to the end, where it opens out onto a small piazza. Take the steps off the far end that lead down to the sea and turn right at the bottom of the first flight. Starters €10–15, mains €15–20. Daily 12.30–3pm & 8–11pm.

Da Pasqualino Piazza Sannazaro 79 ☎081 681 524, ⓦpizzeriadapasqualino.com; map p.74. In the business of serving locals since 1898, this old-school Mergellina trattoria does great *primi* – spaghetti alle vongole, *zuppa di cozze* – lots of fish mains for around €10, and excellent pizzas made in a wood-burning stove. Located right on the square in Mergellina, you can sit outside and watch the traffic. Daily except Tues noon–3pm & 7–10pm.

SNACKS, CAKES AND ICE CREAM

Chalet Ciro Via Caracciolo 1 ☎081 669 928, Ⓦchaletciro.it; map p.74. Right by the Mergellina port, Ciro is a Neapolitan institution known for its *babà* (spongy dough soaked in rum and syrup) and *bignè di San Giuseppe* (cream-filled pastries made around the saint's day – March 19). Its marathon opening hours make it a dependable early-morning or after-dinner pit stop for sweets or ice cream. Daily except Wed 7am–2.30am.

Chiquitos Via Mergellina 31, ☎081 663 197; map p.74. A great *frullati* place, with fruit shakes for around €3, right on the waterfront at Mergellina, where the buses stop. Mon–Thurs 9am–midnight, Fri & Sun 9am–1am, Sat 9am–2am.

Remy Gelo Via F. Galiani 29/A ☎081 667 304; map p.74. Near the Mergellina hydrofoil terminal, this place does superb ice creams and *granite*. Their speciality is *remygnon*, miniature portions of *gelato* covered in chocolate. Mon–Thurs 4–10pm, Fri & Sat 4pm–1am, Sun 4pm–midnight.

VOMERO

RESTAURANTS AND PIZZERIAS

Acunzo Via D. Cimarosa 60–62 ☎081 578 5362, Ⓦpizzeriaristoranteacunzo.com; map p.80. Opened by the Acunzo family in 1936, and owned by Michele and Caterina since 1964, this low-key trattoria has a bustling atmosphere and friendly staff and is upmarket Vomero's best pizza joint. Locals crowd into its spartan interior for the wonderful pizza, available in more than forty varieties, best enjoyed after a plentiful serving of *fritti* or their excellent *parmigiana melanzane*. Pizzas from €5; pasta from €8. Mon–Sat noon–3pm & 7pm–midnight.

Cantina di Sica Via Bernini 17 ☎081 556 7520, Ⓦcantinadisica.it; map p.80. This long-established Vomero restaurant, with its narrow main dining room just

off Piazza Vanvitelli, has a well-priced menu – *primi* from €8, *secondi* from €10–12 – that pulls in a little bit of everything: good seafood, *baccalà alla Siciliana*, *melanzane parmigiana* and a good selection of steak and beef dishes. Good lunchtime specials too. Tues–Sat noon–3.30pm & 7.30–11.30pm, Sun 12.30–3.30pm.

Donna Teresa Via Kerbaker 58 ☎081 556 7070; map p.80. One of the few vestiges of simple dining left in Vomero. Business folk flock here at lunchtime when looking for a home-cooked meal like *sartù di riso* (rice baked with vegetables and meat) or *polpette al sugo* (meatballs in tomato sauce). Little English is spoken so come armed with a dictionary. Expect to pay €15–20 for as much as you can eat. Daily except Sun 1–3pm & 8–10.30pm.

Gorizia Via Bernini 29/31 ☎081 578 2248, Ⓦgorizia1916.com; map p.80. Not far from the Centrale and Chiaia funicular stops, *Gorizia* offers a full menu, but follow the lead set by the locals and skip it in favour of some of Vomero's best pizza (though not quite as good as nearby *Acunzo*, see above), served in a casual and unpretentious setting. Pizzas from €6, fish and meat *secondi* from €10. There are outdoor tables too. Daily except Mon 12.30–3pm & 7.30–11pm.

SNACKS, CAKES AND ICE CREAM

Fantasia Gelati Piazza Vanvitelli 22 ☎081 578 8383, Ⓦfantasiagelati.it; map p.80. Set in Vomero's busiest square, this *gelateria* serves home-made ice cream in some unique flavours – try the "Benevento" (dark chocolate, almond and nougat) – and an assortment of *frutta farcita* (frozen fruit stuffed with ice cream). There are four other locations, including one at Via Toledo 381. Daily 8am–midnight.

Friggitoria Vomero Via Cimarosa 44 ☎081 578 3130; map p.80. A fried-food snack bar opposite two of Vomero's funicular stations. Their deep-fried aubergines and potato croquettes are wonderfully light. Mon–Sat 8am–8pm.

NIGHTLIFE AND ENTERTAINMENT

Neapolitan **nightlife** is largely concentrated in two neighbourhoods: the Centro Storico around Piazza Bellini and the vibrant, humming streets of the Chiaia district. The old part of the city centre is crammed with bars appealing to budget-conscious students and a chic bohemian crowd – there are a half-dozen decent choices in or near Piazza Bellini alone. Chiaia is home to a young professional crowd that prefers the upscale district's see-and-be-seen lounge bars, as well as a few good wine bars and pubs, which tend to put on an "*aperitivo*" hour", opening around 6pm for an after-work happy-hour buffet. Later on, the action moves to the city's **clubs** (see p.91) and **live music venues** (see p.92).

Bar essentials Bear in mind that things don't really get going until at least 10pm, and most bars are closed in the hot summer months, when everyone congregates in the open air in Piazza del Gesù Nuovo and Piazza San Domenico Maggiore, or on Piazza Bellini instead.

Club essentials Owing to licensing laws, some nightclubs require a *tesserino* or membership card to gain entry, which

costs from €10 and can be bought at the door. Others charge a flat cover charge, generally from €15 to €35, which includes the price of a drink. Things get going around midnight or 1am, but it's worth remembering that in July and August most clubs close for the summer and move out to towns around the bay, such as Posillipo, Bacoli and Pozzuoli.

BARS, PUBS AND WINE BARS

Baik Via A. Falcone 372 ☎333 049 4405, ⓦ baikamericanbar.com; map p.74. A mainstay of Naples' nightlife, this chilled-out lounge bar's *aperitivo* buffet heaves with ethnic food to match its exotic decor. Outside, a leafy patio is perfect for summer drinks. Extensive wine list. Daily 7.30pm–3am.

Barcadero Banchina Santa Lucia 2 ☎081 222 7023; map p.74. The perfect place for an evening *aperitivo*, right on the harbour by the Castel dell'Ovo. There's quite a scene here early evening – take the steps down from the causeway to the castle. Daily 6pm–2am.

B-Side Via A. Falcone 275 ☎333 596 8162; map p.74. A cool and unpretentious pub with a popular *aperitivo* buffet, good cocktails, temporary art exhibitions and nightly DJ sets. Tues–Sun 8pm–1am.

★ **Enoteca Belledonne** Vico Belledonne a Chiaia 18 ☎081 403 162, ⓦ enotecabelledonne.com; map p.74. Right in the heart of the Chiaia bar scene, this unpretentious *enoteca* serves an exhaustive collection of Italian wines and delicious selections of cheeses and cold cuts, and doesn't have quite the full-on noise of its nearby rivals. Daily 10am–1.30pm & 5pm–2am.

Intra Moenia Piazza Bellini 70 ☎081 451 652, ⓦ intramoenia.it; map pp.48–49. One of several trendy haunts on Piazza Bellini, where tables spread across the square. A lovely place to sit and read under the wisteria on a sunny day, or for an early-evening aperitif. Substantial snacks and fancy ice creams are served, and there's free wi-fi too. Daily 10am–2am.

Lontano Da Dove Via Bellini 3 ☎081 549 4304; map pp.48–49. A bookshop, tearoom and literary café all rolled into one, with live performances of mostly jazz and blues, held three nights a week. Very comfy – lots of cushions and low-level tables. Mon–Thurs 11am–1pm & 5–8pm; Fri & Sat 11am–1pm & 5pm–1.30am.

★ **Nais** Via G. Farrigui 29 ☎081 658 0466; map p.74. More laidback and less posey than many of the other bars in the area and as a result one of our favourites. Book-lined walls and a good buffet. Daily 6pm–2am.

Perditempo Via San Pietro a Maiella 8 ☎081 444 958; map pp.48–49. Around the corner from Piazza Bellini, this tiny muso-literary café's well-stocked bar serves beer and cocktails and draws an arty and intellectual crowd. Hosts book presentations, live music and DJs, and stocks new and used books, CDs and LPs. Mon–Sat noon–midnight.

Seventy Via Bisignano 19 ☎339 288 0214; map p.74. The bar is loaded with a decent early-evening buffet at this cool, white glitter-ball bar, playing thumping garage to a cool or just plain hungry clientele. Collapse into a white leather sofa and try not to make a mess. Daily 6.30pm–2am.

S'move Vico dei Sospiri 10 ☎081 764 5813, ⓦ frala27 .wix.com/smovelab; map p.74. The dark, industrial interior is more suited for small-hours carousing, although the evening festivities at this self-described "musicfoodbar" get started earlier. Later, a smart Chiaia crowd arrive for acid jazz, techno and funk. Mon–Sat 11am–3am, Sun 7pm–3am.

Trip Via Martucci 64 ☎081 1956 8994, ⓦ tripnapoli .com; map p.74. Located in Chiaia near Piazza Amedeo and dripping in 1950s kitsch, *Trip* is a café by day and a cocktail bar at night, hosting a wide range of cultural events, art exhibitions and lectures for the intellectually curious. Light meals are served and there is a Saturday brunch too. Tues–Sun 11am–11pm.

★ **Vinarium** Vicolo Santa Maria a Cappella Vecchia 7 ☎081 764 4114, ⓦ vinariumnapoli.com; map p.74. Busy wine bar just off Piazza dei Martiri that has a good selection of wines and is not just a place to drink, serving good food from an ever-changing menu – steaks, salads, maybe a burger or *baccalà*. Can get very crowded later on, especially Sunday nights when it often shows *Serie A* football on TV. Mon–Sat noon–3.30pm & 7pm–1.30am, Sun 7pm–1.30am only.

CLUBS

Arenile Via Coroglio 10 Bagnoli ☎081 019 9156, ⓦ arenilereload.com. White cabanas line the volcanic-sand beach, pool and gardens of this ultra-hip *stabilimento* (beach club) in Bagnoli. After dark, the hip-hop, Latin and house beats take over and the clubbers dance on the sand

NEAPOLITAN SOUNDS

Trends in Neapolitan music have been influenced in the modern age by the city's strange, harsh dialect, and to some extent by the American jazz and swing that were introduced by the US military in World War II, bringing an international flavour to traditional Neapolitan songs. The 1970s saw one of Italy's most concentrated musical movements in the urban blues scene of **Pino Daniele** and in the music which developed around the **Alfa Romeo factory** out at Pomigliano d'Arco, which had a radical reputation at the time, and now plays host to an annual jazz festival.

Rap and **hip-hop** exploded onto the scene in the 1990s, a fusion of traditional Neapolitan sounds and African and American influences, with groups such as Almamegretta, Bisca and 99 Posse using their music to comment on the state of Naples and Italian society in general. More recently, Spaccanapoli, an offshoot of the workers' groups at Pomigliano, had a hit album, *Aneme Perze* ("Lost Souls"), combining serious social critique, modern dance music and age-old Neapolitan forms.

1

until the early hours. Bus #R7 from Piazza Municipio. June–Sept daily 9am–4am.

Momah Via Fornari 15 ☎081 422 334, ⓦmomah.it; map p.74. Descend the stairs near the corner of Via dei Mille in the posh Chiaia district, and immerse yourself in *Momah*, a small and exclusive club where house, techno and trance attract Naples' beautiful people. Thurs–Sun 10pm–4am. Closed June to mid-Sept.

Virgilio Club Via Lucrezio Caro 6 ☎081 575 5261, ⓦvirgilioclub.it; map p.74. High up in the Parco Virgiliano on the slopes of Posillipo, this fun club gets jam-packed on summer nights when they open a leafy terrace overlooking the bay. June to mid-Oct Wed–Sun 10pm–4am; rest of year opening variable.

LIVE MUSIC

The live music venues of the Centro Storico host mostly local and Italian bands, although the jazz clubs do pull a wider European playlist. Big international pop and rock artists usually bypass Naples, though once a year at the end of July the Neapolis Rock Festival – ⓦneapolis.it – draws important acts and huge crowds to the Mostra d'Oltremare convention centre in Fuorigrotta.

Bourbon Street Via Bellini 52/53 ☎338 825 3756, ⓦbourbonstreetjazzclub.com; map pp.48–49. A premier venue for Italian and international jazz acts, bringing a slice of American jazz culture to the heart of Naples. Even the walls are authentic – the bricks were imported from New Orleans. Tues–Sun 9pm–3am. Closed June–Aug.

Kestè Largo S. Giovanni Maggiore Pignatelli ☎081 551 3984, ⓦkeste.it; map p.74. Bar, café, gallery and live music venue opposite the university. Go early for the *aperitivo* buffet and stay for the band or DJ set. Tues 7.30am–8pm, Wed–Fri 7.30am–2.30am, Sat & Sun 9pm–2.30am. Closed Aug.

Kinky Bar Via Cisterna dell'Olio 21 ☎335 547 7299; map p.61. Contrary to what the name suggests, this popular Centro Storico bar is Naples' prime venue for reggae, rock steady, dancehall and ska, with DJs and live acts from

---

THEATRICAL NAPLES

Naples is the home of performance, with an innate exuberance and a flair for drama that stretches back for millennia. The city is perhaps best known for its opera, with a suitably ornate venue in the Teatro di San Carlo (see p.62), which also hosts classical concerts and ballet, but it doesn't stop there. From the slapstick of *commedia dell'arte* to the flamenco-style *tarantella*, the city's long tradition of boisterous entertainment is ingrained in its inhabitants, whose love of theatrics is one of their defining and most appealing characteristics.

COMMEDIA DELL'ARTE

With its origins in Roman farce, *commedia dell'arte* has always enjoyed disproportionate popularity in Naples, which is why you see trinkets of one of its main characters, **Pulcinella**, for sale everywhere. It started as a form of street theatre in the sixteenth century, when masked troupes performed all over the city, with a set cast of characters who would play out a variety of plots on the fundamental themes of love, jealousy and revenge but always with a strong anti-authoritarian streak. The equivalent to Britain's Mr Punch, Pulcinella is a hunchbacked, beak-nosed wife beater and an outlaw, optimistic one minute and plunged into melancholy the next. He takes his place alongside the other popular figures: **Arlecchino**, or Harlequin, the forebear of the modern-day clown with his diamond-shaped costume; **Colombina**, Arlecchino's girlfriend; **Il Dottore**, an insufferable old bore; and **Scaramuccia**, a cowardly rogue, among others. Master puppeteer Bruno Leone keeps the tradition alive in Naples with performances involving the whole cast of characters; see ⓦguarattelle.it for details of shows.

OPERA

Many of the stock characters that appear in *commedia dell'arte* were the inspiration for a peculiarly Neapolitan form of comic opera or **opera buffa**, a genre which burgeoned in the eighteenth century when Naples was one of Europe's cultural centres. **Alessandro Scarlatti** was one of its greatest exponents, whose works were distinguished both for their memorable music and their preposterous plots, often involving low-life characters and servants interacting with members of the aristocracy. The prestigious **Teatro di San Carlo** (see p.62; tickets on ☎842 002 008) is the obvious place to catch an opera in the city; as well as staging the old favourites, they are also committed to reviving eighteenth-century comic operas by the likes of Domenico Cimarosa and Giovan Battista Pergolesi.

NEAPOLITAN SONG

Further evidence of the locals' passion for music is the enduring popularity of the **canzone**

Europe and the Caribbean. There's also a 200-strong cocktail list. Tues–Sun 9pm–4am. Closed mid-June to mid-Sept.

Lanificio 25 Piazza E. De Nicola 46 ☎081 658 2915, ⓦlanificio25.it; map pp.48–49. Beside the Porta Capuana, this former nineteenth-century wool factory has been transformed into a venue for experimental music and contemporary performance art. The stark interior hosts pianists, DJs and artists from around the world. Hours vary

– see the website for the most up-to-date details.

New Around Midnight Via Bonito 32/A ☎081 742 3278, ⓦnewaroundmidnight.it; map p.80. A popular jazz club in Vomero that intermittently dips a toe into blues. There are live performances every night, mostly by Italian musicians, although the occasional international star graces the stage. Light meals are also served. Tues–Sun 8pm–1am, most shows start around 9.30pm.

SHOPPING

The character of Neapolitan neighbourhoods is often defined by the **shops** that are found there. It would be hard to imagine the **Centro Storico** without its industrious Via San Gregorio Armeno, the epicentre of nativity-scene production, where handmade wood and terracotta figures are crafted by local artisans. The old centre is also the place for books and prints, especially around Port'Alba off Piazza Dante, while nearby on Via Santa Maria di Costantinopoli is a plethora of antique dealers, art restorers and carpenters. The entire length of **Via Toledo** from Piazza Dante to Piazza del Plebiscito is dominated by mainstream and chain stores, while big-name designer clothes stores and antiques shops populate **Chiaia**, amplifying the district's upmarket feel.

ANTIQUES, ART, CRAFTS AND GIFTS

Aleph Design Via dei Tribunali 309 ☎081 454 793,

ⓦalephdesign.info; map pp.48–49. Alessandra D'Aniello's handcrafted terracotta ceramics are inspired by

---

napoletana, almost the archetypal Italian serenade, sung in Neapolitan dialect and one of the city's most cherished traditions. The genre grew out of an annual song-writing competition held for the Festival of Piedigrotta in the mid-nineteenth century, the first of which was won by Donizetti's *Te Voglio Bene Assaje* ("I love you lots"), an instant hit. You'd be surprised how many of these folksy tunes you recognize: *O Sole Mio* and *Funiculì Funiculà* are among the multitude of songs whose fame spread around the world as Neapolitans left their homeland to seek their fortunes abroad. The great tenor Caruso chose Neapolitan songs as encores; Luciano Pavarotti and Placido Domingo both recorded albums of Neapolitan favourites; and the local singer Roberto Murolo was one of the leading lights of the scene, devoting his life's work to the *canzone napoletana*, and recording new songs right up until his death in 2003. Even if you don't catch a performance at one of many venues around town, you're unlikely to leave Naples without hearing a hearty rendition of one of the classics: buskers angling for small change belt out Neapolitan favourites all over the city.

THE TARANTELLA

Another Neapolitan tradition with ancient roots is the gypsy-style *tarantella*, a 2000-year-old folk dance found in the Naples region and throughout Southern Italy. Performances involve strident singing, as well as the driving, hypnotic keening of traditional musical **instruments**: the *putipù* (a kind of "burping" drum), the *triccaballacco* (a wooden clacker with small cymbals), the *siscariello* (whistle) and more.

The origins of the dance are much debated. One local legend has it that the muses taught it to the women of Capri to enhance their allure and ability to compete with the Sirens; others believe it derives from the ancient Greek cult of Dionysus, imitating the frenzied ecstasies of the Bacchante – a cult that even the pleasure-seeking Romans banned for its excesses; while some ancient authorities claim it originated in Libya, as a fertility ritual mimicking the mating behaviour of the partridge, considered the most lascivious of all animals – making it the original "lemme see you shake your tail feather" dance. Perhaps the most widespread theory is that it was a hypnotic dance invented to cure a tarantula's bite; the writhing movements are in imitation of the delirium and contortions of the supposed victim.

The *tarantella* was brought to the Bourbon court in Naples between the seventeenth and eighteenth centuries, and became a more formalized courtship dance. In this version, dancers move alternately, growing ever closer to each other but not quite touching, and twisting their arms and wrists, flamenco-style. Today, the dance is best witnessed at one of the many local saints' days in the small towns north of Naples.

1

Naples, its landscape and textures. The showroom is in the historic Palazzo d'Angiò and you can watch her work in her atelier nearby on Via S. Paolo 11. Open daily by appointment.

Antichità Ciro Guarracino Via V. Gaetani 26 ☎ 081 599 2000, Ⓦ antichitaguarracino.com; map p.74. Not far from Piazza dei Martiri in Chiaia, this third-generation antiques dealer sells furniture, objets d'art and paintings from the Baroque era through to the early twentieth century. Mon 4–8pm, Tues–Sat 10am–2pm & 4–8pm.

Bowinkel Via Santa Lucia 25 ☎ 081 764 0739; map p.74. Great choice of vintage prints of Naples and the bay, and this old store predates some of them. Another shop, owned by a different branch of the family, is at Piazza dei Martiri 24. Open Mon–Fri 9am–1.30pm & 4–7.30pm, Sat 9am–1pm.

Di Virgilio Via San Gregorio Armeno 18 ☎ 081 552 4064, Ⓦ divirgilioart.com; map pp.48–49. Craftsmen have been producing handcrafted terracotta figures here for three generations, ranging from the traditional holy family to surreal pop-culture figures such as Barack Obama and Diego Maradona. Daily 9am–8pm.

La Smorfia Via Anticaglia 23 ☎ 081 293 812, Ⓦ laboratoriolasmorfia.it; map pp.48–49. Young artisan Fabio Paolella employs eighteenth-century traditions when creating his handmade terracotta Nativity figurines for his Centro Storico shop. A trained art restorer, he also repairs and sells antique Nativity characters and church decorations. Mon 4–8pm, Tues–Sat 10am–1.30pm & 4–8pm.

Maestranze Napoletane Via Conte di Ruvo 7/8 ☎ 081 544 8836, Ⓦ maestranzenapoletane.com; map pp.48–49. Near Piazza Bellini, this is one of the few places left in the city where you can still see the once ubiquitous art of marble *intarso*. The studio specializes in marble-inlaid furniture and art pieces. Mon 4–8pm, Tues–Sat 10am–2pm & 4–8pm.

Maurizio Brandi Antiquariato Via D. Morelli 9–11 ☎ 081 764 3882; map p.74. Maurizio Brandi offers a stellar selection of antiques near Piazza dei Martiri in Chiaia. He specializes in furniture but has a fine collection of ceramics, porcelain and silver as well. Mon 4–8pm, Tues–Sat 10am–2pm & 4–8pm.

BOOKS

Colonnese Via S. Pietro a Maiella 32–33 ☎ 081 459 858, Ⓦ colonnese.it; map pp.48–49. Just off Piazza Bellini, this publishing house and bookshop sells a vast array of new, used and out-of-print books and specializes in eighteenth- and nineteenth-century Neapolitan literature and books on the city's language and culture. Mon–Fri 9am–1.30pm & 4–7.30pm, Sat 9am–1.30pm.

Feltrinelli Via S. Caterina a Chiaia 23 ☎ 081 240 5411, Ⓦ lafeltrinelli.it; map p.74. A busy three-storey bookshop

with a selection of English guidebooks, fiction and magazines. There is a café for lingering, and the Concerteria box office is handy for concert or theatre tickets. There are also branches at Via S. Tommaso D'Aquino 70–76 and inside the main railway station. Mon–Fri 10am–9pm, Fri 10am–10pm, Sat & Sun 10am–10pm.

CLOTHES, SHOES AND ACCESSORIES

Coin Via Scarlatti 86/100 ☎ 081 578 0111, Ⓦ coin.it; map p.80. Large by Italian standards, this department store in Vomero sells name-brand clothing, handbags, underwear and cosmetics. Mon–Fri 10am–8pm, Sat 10am–8.30pm, Sun 10am–2pm & 4.30–8.30pm.

La Reggia 80125 Marcianise ☎ 082 351 0244, Ⓦ mcarthurglen.com/it/la-reggia-designer-outlet. Adjacent to the Naples–Rome *autostrada*, 8km from Caserta, this vast designer fashion outlet has well over 100 boutiques selling all the big labels – both high end and more mainstream brands – at discounts of up to 70 percent. Shuttle buses run every day starting at 9.30am from Piazza Municipio. Daily 10am–7pm.

Marinella Riviera di Chiaia 287 ☎ 081 245 1182, Ⓦ marinellanapoli.it; map p.74. This atelier has been making fine silk ties in original prints for a discerning Chiaia crowd and foreign heads of state since 1914. They sell shoes and other formal accessories as well. Mon–Sat 7am–1.30pm & 4–8pm.

Mario Valentino Via Calabritto 10 ☎ 081 764 4262, Ⓦ mariovalentino.it; map p.74. This Chiaia institution, once a favourite of Sophia Loren, Jackie Kennedy and Ava Gardner, produces custom-made shoes and ready-to-wear clothing and accessories for women. Mon 4–7.30pm, Tues–Sat 10am–1.30pm & 4–7.30pm.

Talarico Vico Due Porte a Toledo 4/B ☎ 081 407 723, Ⓦ mariotalarico.it; map p.61. Delicately worked umbrellas in chestnut, bamboo and horn, made in the Quartieri Spagnoli since 1860. Mon–Sat 6.30am–8pm.

Tramontano Via Chiaia 143/144 ☎ 081 414 837, Ⓦ tramontano.it; map p.74. The flagship store of the Naples-based business, which has been producing beautiful handmade leather handbags, luggage and accessories since 1865. There's a second location at Via Luca Giordano 25/B. Mon–Sat 10am–1.30pm & 4–8pm, Sun 10am–1.30pm.

FOOD AND WINE

Arfè Via Santa Teresa a Chiaia 45 ☎ 081 411 822, Ⓦ gastronomiaarfe.it; map p.74. A posh delicatessen in Chiaia offering the highest-quality cheeses, cured meats, olive oils, pâtés, vinegars and other celebrated products from Campania and across Italy. Look out for the local *capocolla* from Agerola and of course fabulous fresh *mozzarella di bufala*. Open Mon–Sat 8am–2pm & 4.30–8pm.

1

NAPLES' BEST MARKETS

The street-level commerce of Naples is such that the whole city can sometimes seem like one vast market, but there are some places that are worth seeking out – for specific bargains, specialities or just for their atmosphere. Here are some of our favourites.

Pignasecca Map p.61. The streets of Montesanto around Via and Piazza Pignasecca are a riot of food, clothes and household stalls – Naples at its glorious, vibrant best. Daily from 8am.

Poggioreale Map pp.48–49. The city's largest market, held in a down-at-heel neighbourhood near the train station that's better known for its prison. Over 500 stalls, mostly selling clothes and fashion, and more shoes than

you can shake a stick at. Mon, Fri & Sun from 8am.

Porta Nolana Map pp.48–49. Just off Piazza Garibaldi, this legendary fish market is an archetypal Naples experience. Daily from 7am.

Via Pasquale/Via Imbriani Map p.74. Chiaia's Via Pasquale and Via Imbriani are given over to fruit and vegetable hawkers and clothes stalls most weekday mornings. Mon–Sat from 8am.

Gay Odin Via Toledo 214 ☎ 081 400 063, ⓦgayodin.it; map p.61. Originally from Piedmont, Italy's chocolate capital, this family has been whipping up artisan chocolates and handmade confections for Neapolitans since 1922. Look for their signature *foresta*: milk chocolate moulded to resemble a tree branch. Eight other locations in Naples, including one nearby at Via Toledo 472 and another, selling mainly ice cream, at Via Benedetto Croce 61. Mon–Sat 9.30am–8pm, Sun 10am–2pm.

Limonè Piazza San Gaetano 72 ☎081 299 429, ⓦlimoncellodinapoli.it; map pp.48–49. *Limoncello*, the potent liqueur and nearby Sorrento's most famous export, is the focus of this shop, which also sells lemon-infused *grappa* and sweets, and a range of other liqueurs like *crema di melone*. Daily 11am–8pm.

Sogni di Latte Via Kerbaker 13 ☎081 1951 4909, ⓦsognidilatte.com; map p.80. A welcome addition to the busy Vomero shopping scene, this is arguably the best place to buy Campanian and Italian cheese in the city. A turophile's dream indeed. Mon–Sat 10am–1pm & 4–8pm.

Timpani e Tempura Vico della Quercia 17 ☎081 551 2280; map p.61. This deli and *tavola calda* near Piazza del Gesù specializes in classic Neapolitan dishes and *fritti*, and sells a well-chosen selection of cheeses, *salumi* and

Campanian wines. They will pack your purchases for travel and deliver to your hotel. Mon–Sat 9.30am–8.30pm, Sun 9.30am–2pm.

JEWELLERY

Brinkmann Piazza Municipio 21 ☎081 552 0555, ⓦbrinkmann.it; map p.61. Founded in 1900 by a German jeweller, the Brinkmann family continues the century-long tradition of making and repairing high-quality watches and designing elegant jewellery. Mon 3.30–7.30pm, Tues–Sat 10am–1.30pm & 3.30–7.30pm.

Caso Piazza Via Bisignano 8/9 ☎081 403 940, ⓦcaso .it; map pp.48–49. Exquisite grand tour- and belle epoque-era jewellery, including delicately carved corals and cameos and rare micromosaics inspired by works uncovered in Pompeii. There's another branch on Piazza Domenico Maggiore in the heart of the Centro Storico. Mon 4.30–7.30pm, Tues–Fri 9.30am–1.30pm & 4.30–7.30pm, Sat 9.30am–1.30pm.

De Paola Via A. Caccavello 67/69 ☎081 5782 2910; map p.80. On a quiet street near Castel Sant'Elmo, De Paola sells stunning antique and contemporary cameos in shell, coral and agate, as well as attractive coral jewellery. Mon–Sat 9am–8pm, Sun 9am–2pm.

DIRECTORY

Consulates Canada, Via Carducci 29 ☎081 401 338; South Africa, Via Stendhal 23 ☎081 552 5835; UK, Via dei Mille 40 ☎081 423 8911; USA, Piazza della Repubblica 2 ☎081 583 8111.

Hospitals To call an ambulance, dial ☎118. Emergency hospital numbers include ☎081 254 2111, ☎081 254 5111 and ☎081 254 7111. The most central hospitals with A&E departments are Ascalesi, Via Egiziaca Forcella 31 ☎081 563 221; Cardarelli, Via Cardarelli 9 ☎081 747 1111; Santa Maria di Loreto (otherwise known as "Loreto Crispi"), Via Schipa 135 ☎081 254 7111; and Santa Maria di Loreto (otherwise known as "Loreto Mare"), Via Vespucci 86 ☎081 254 2711.

Pharmacies The pharmacy at Napoli Centrale is open 24hr and there's a list of those open at night in the newspaper *Il Mattino* or posted on pharmacy doors.

Police ☎112 or 113; you can speak to an operator in English. The main police station *(questura)* is at Via Medina 5 ☎081 794 1111; you can also report crimes at the small police station in the Stazione Centrale. To report the theft of a car call ☎081 794 1435.

Post office The main post office is in the enormous building on Piazza Matteotti, just off Via Toledo (Mon–Sat 8.15am–7.20pm).

Taxis ☎081 8888; ☎081 0101; ☎081 2222; ☎081 556 4444.

The Campi Flegrei

POZZUOLI WATERFRONT

2

The Campi Flegrei

The area around Naples is one of the most geologically unstable in the world, with Vesuvius only the best known of the many and varied examples of seismic activity in the province. To the west of the city is a head-spinning concentration of volcanic craters, hot springs and fumaroles, known as the Campi Flegrei (literally Fiery Fields). These are the mysterious Phlegraean Fields of classical times, mythologized by Homer as the entrance to Hades, and by Virgil as the Forum of Vulcan, god of fire, as well as being the site of several of the Greco-Roman world's most mystical holy places. It was also eulogized as the Elysian Fields for the sheer gorgeousness of its landscape, which in those days was prime real estate for the movers and shakers of Roman society.

These days the Campi Flegrei's ancient mysteries require some determination to imagine, as suburban blight masks much of the natural beauty of the area. The volcanic activity is dormant for the moment (though, like Vesuvius, not completely extinct), but some of the features that drew the ancients in the first place are still here, and there are substantial and fascinating remains of their presence. Pretty much everything is easily accessible on a day-trip from Naples; most places can be reached on either the Cumana railway or Metropolitana line 2, with buses between Fusaro and Torregaveta via Bacoli and Miseno, filling in the gaps.

   Pozzuoli is easiest to reach and the first place to head for, home to an array of different sights and a departure point for the islands of Ischia and Procida (see Chapter 5). It's also easy to reach the ancient sites at **Baia** and **Cumae** from here, neither of which you will want to miss if you're spending any time at all in the area. Just outside Baia, the regional **archeological museum** is also worth a look – but if you need some respite from dusty relics, head for the beaches at **Bacoli and beyond**.

Pozzuoli

The first town that can really be considered free of Naples' direct sprawl is **POZZUOLI**, which sits 14km to the west of the city on a stout promontory jutting out into the sea from the slender crescent of volcanic hills behind. It was the main port of the Roman Empire – entry point for the all-essential grain from Egypt – until Emperor Trajan expanded the port of Ostia, at the mouth of the Tiber. The name derives from the Latin original Puteoli, meaning "little wells" (although there are also claims that it means "stinking"), probably a reference to the many thermal springs that have been a feature of the area for all of recorded history. Pozzuoli was also the source of – and gave its name to – pink pozzolana volcanic sand. The Romans discovered that adding fine, hard-grained pozzolana to the usual mix of lime, sand, water and gravel resulted in an extra-hard concrete that resisted erosion. Roman buildings of pozzolana concrete

SIBYL'S GROTTO, CUMAE

Highlights

❶ The Solfatara A seething, semi-active volcano that's top of Pozzuoli's must-see sights. **See p.102**

❷ Baia Once the chicest of imperial Roman resorts, now a monumental and atmospheric set of ruins. **See p.104**

❸ Cumae The earliest Greek settlement on the Italian mainland was home to the enigmatic

and profoundly influential oracle, the Cumaean Sibyl. **See p.107**

❹ Cratere degli Astroni This WWF nature reserve occupies the crater of an extinct volcano and is fantastic birdwatching territory, most of it easily accessible by way of a circular track. **See p.109**

HIGHLIGHTS ARE MARKED ON THE MAP ON P.100

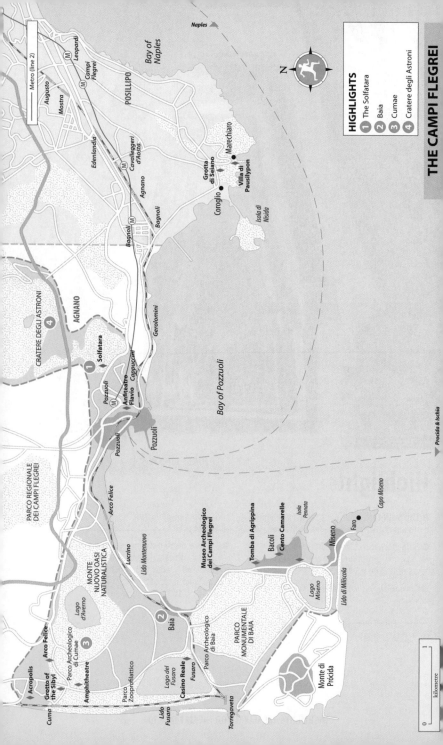

THE CAMPI FLEGREI

HIGHLIGHTS

1 The Solfatara
2 Baia
3 Cumae
4 Cratere degli Astroni

N

Metro (line 2)

Naples

Bay of Naples

POSILLIPO

Leopardi
Augusto
M
Mostra
M
Campi Flegrei

Edenlandia

Cavalleggeri d'Aosta
M

Agnano
M

Bagnoli
M
Bagnoli

Marechiaro
Villa di Pausilypon
Grotta di Seiano
Coroglio
Isola di Nisida

CRATERE DEGLI ASTRONI
4

AGNANO

Solfatara
1

Pozzuoli
Anfiteatro Flavio
Cappuccini
M
Pozzuoli
Pozzuoli

Gerolomini

Bay of Pozzuoli

PARCO REGIONALE DEI CAMPI FLEGREI

Arco Felice

MONTE NUOVO OASI NATURALISTICA

Lucrino

Lido Montenuovo

Museo Archeologico dei Campi Flegrei

Tomba di Agrippina

Bacoli
Cento Camerelle
Isola Pennata

Miseno
Faro
Capo Miseno

Lido di Miliscola

Lago Miseno

PARCO MONUMENTALE DI BAIA

Parco Archeologico di Baia

Baia
2

Lago d'Averno

Parco Zooprofilattico

Lago del Fusaro

Casino Reale

Fusaro

Lido Fusaro

Lido del Fusaro

Torregaveta

Monte di Prócida

▶ Prócida & Ischia

Cuma
Acropolis
Grotto of the Sibyl
Arco Felice
Amphitheatre
Parco Archeologico di Cumae
3

0   1
kilometre

POZZUOLI ON THE MOVE

Pozzuoli has suffered more than most of the towns around here from the area's **volcanic activity**, and subsidence is still a major – and carefully monitored – problem. Almost all of the ancient town is now under water – as with other significant parts of the Campi Flegrei – because of a phenomenon called bradyseism (from the Greek words for "slow" and "movement"), a rare, large-scale rippling effect of volcanic activity deep under the earth's crust, which results in perpetual "slow earthquakes", causing continual rising and lowering of the land. Parts of the place have been slowly rising for the last five hundred years or so, while others are gradually sinking – in some spots up to 2cm a year.

survive throughout the world, the most famous being the vast cast-concrete dome of Rome's Pantheon.

Despite achieving a measure of contemporary glamour as the home town of screen goddess Sophia Loren, modern Pozzuoli is an ordinary little place, friendly and likeable enough, and one that in recent years has attracted local artists, although for most visitors it's mostly of use for its **ferry connections** to the islands of Procida and Ischia. However, there are a few sights of archeological importance, and it makes a good base from which to take in the rest of the Campi Flegrei. One of the best times to visit is on a Sunday, when the whole town turns out for the morning fish market, afterwards eating lunch in one of several waterfront **restaurants**.

Temple of Serapis

Just beyond the Cumana station, between Via Roma and Via Sacchini, the so-called **Temple of Serapis** sits enclosed within a small park. It is sometimes flooded in winter, and thus often closed, but is easy enough to see in its entirety from outside. Its name derives from the unearthing here in 1750 of a statue of the Pluto-esque Egyptian god, Serapis (now in Naples' Museo Archeologico Nazionale), but the structure has since proved to be not a temple but a richly embellished produce market from the first to the third centuries AD, one of the largest to have been excavated. It's pretty decrepit, but you can still make out the shape of the buildings: most of the shops were arranged around the perimeter portico and courtyard, while the tholos, the temple-like circular structure in the centre, was where fish was sold. At the northern end, occupying a large apse, was a sacellum (shrine) dedicated to the worship of the imperial family and of the market's divine protectors. Among these were Serapis – hence the presence of the god's image here – for many Alexandrians lived in ancient Pozzuolo, bringing with them their gods and cults as well as their grain. For hundreds of years much of the site lay underwater, and if you look closely at the shrine's three freestanding columns of cipollino marble, you can see they have been eaten away by marine molluscs – yet another example of how the elevation of this unquiet land ceaselessly shifts.

Rione Terra

Largo Sedile di Porta • Currently closed to the public

On the other side of the port, the **Rione Terra** provides the chance for a slightly more accessible look at Pozzuoli's Roman past – an extensive if sometimes erratically open excavation, accessible by way of an entrance above the tourist office, off Via Marconi. The name originated in the Middle Ages, when what was the ancient acropolis of the Greek town and the heart of the Roman port served as the citadel (*terra* in local dialect). The site stretches over some 2 square kilometres in all, and encompasses a set of ancient Roman streets, lined with structures that are considered to have been apartments (*insulae*), taverns (*tabernae*), millers-bakers (*pistrina*), warehouses (*horrea*), brothels (*ganea*) and other establishments, as well as tunnels and the remains of the

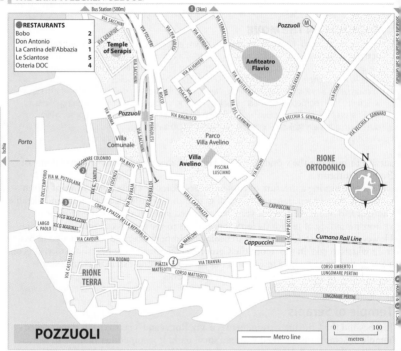

majestic Corinthian-columned *Capitolium*, itself founded on an earlier Greek temple. There are also several extant frescoes and mosaics, and some textbook examples of *opus reticulatum* walls, the distinctive diamond pattern achieved by pushing pyramid-shaped blocks of tufa into wet concrete – a type of construction used only from the first century BC until the second century AD, after which regular horizontal brick construction became the norm.

Anfiteatro Flavio

Via Terracciano 75 • June–Sept Mon & Wed–Sun 9am–1hr before sunset; Oct–May Mon & Wed–Sun 9am–2pm • €4 combined ticket with Sito Archeologico di Cumae, Parco Archeologico delle Terme di Baia and Museo Archeologico dei Campi Flegrei in Baia (valid 48hr)

The best of Pozzuoli's Roman sights is the **Anfiteatro Flavio**, just north of the centre, which was one of the largest in Italy, holding some twenty thousand spectators. It was begun under Nero and completed by Vespasian, and it's still reasonably intact, though visitors are not allowed in the seating area. The subterranean chambers for gladiators and wild beasts are in especially good shape, and lying around are abundant beautifully carved architectural fragments retrieved from various shrines and other structures that were associated with the vast entertainment venue.

The Solfatara

Via Solfatara 161 • Daily 8.30am–1hr before sunset • €7 • solfatara.it • 10min walk up the hill from the Metropolitana/FS station; buses #152 and #M1 also stop outside

You can smell the **Solfatara** well before you see it: the exposed crater of a semi-extinct volcano, into which you can walk. What you walk out onto is actually the plug or cap of cooled-off magma that for the moment blocks the cone – the volcano hasn't erupted for a couple of thousand years at least – a weird, lunar landscape, where the grey-yellow ground is hot to the touch and sounds hollow underfoot, emitting eerily silent jets or fumaroles that leave the air pungent with the odour of sulphur. Solfatara was a major tourist attraction in Roman times too, and it's little wonder the ancients thought the entrance to Hades was nearby. If you bring matches and set paper alight near the fumes, the earth itself seems to respond, with billows of thick smoke all around – a favourite trick caused by the condensation of sulphur in the vicinity. In the nineteenth century some of the fumaroles were covered with brick, creating a nearly unbearable heat (90°C) in a sauna-like box in which you can crouch if you can bear it, while elsewhere bubbling, grey, gloopy mud is fenced off – though it might make an excellent mineral bath in theory. Locals, in fact, still swear by the salutary effects of the rotten-egg ambience the place emits, suggesting that those with respiratory ailments breathe deeply of the brimstone stench for an hour or so. By the time you're finished, you'll be hot, and it's worth knowing about the café and shop by the exit selling drinks, meals and snacks.

Santuario di San Gennaro

Via San Gennaro alla Solfatara 8 • Daily 9am–noon & 4.30–7pm • Free • ⓦ santuariosangennaro.it

A three-minute walk further up the hill from the Solfatara is the sixteenth-century **Santuario di San Gennaro**, built on the supposed site of the final martyrdom of Naples' patron saint under the merciless Diocletian; some accounts say Gennaro first faced wild beasts in the amphitheatre, which he somehow survived, only to be executed anyway. There's an engraved stone niche here, kept behind glass in a chapel off to the right, stained with splashes of the saint's blood (he was beheaded) that reputedly glows at the same time that his blood liquefies in Naples (see box, p.43).

ARRIVAL AND INFORMATION

POZZUOLI

By train You can get to Pozzuoli from Naples on the Metropolitana, or on the Ferrovia Cumana rail line from Montesanto station; both take about 20min. The Cumana station is in the centre of town, not far from the Temple of Serapis, so the train makes more sense if you're visiting the town only. The Metropolitana/FS station is situated above the main part of Pozzuoli, off Via Solfatara, a 10min walk from the port, and so is better if you're just going to see the Solfatara.

By bus Buses #152 and #M1 also run direct to Pozzuoli from Piazza Garibaldi, stopping right outside the Solfatara before descending to the town centre.

Tourist office A five-minute walk from the harbour at Largo Matteotti 1 (Mon–Sat 9am–3pm; ☎ 081 526 6639, ⓦ infocampiflegrei.it).

EATING AND DRINKING

Bobo Via Cristoforo Colombo 20 ☎ 081 526 2034, ⓦ ristorantebobo.com. Moderate- to high-priced harbourside restaurant which does great fish and has an excellent wine list. Try the pasta with sea urchins or with mussels and broccoli, or a host of other great pasta and fish dishes. Not particularly cheap, but the perfect end to a morning at the market. Wed–Sat noon–3pm & 7–10pm, Sun noon–3pm.

★**Don Antonio** Vico Magazzini 20 ☎ 081 526 7941. Perhaps the best-value fish restaurant in Pozzuoli, an unpretentious place without the outside tables and views, specializing in excellent fresh fish and seafood including great *fritti misti* and seafood pasta dishes at very reasonable prices. Follow the quayside round the ferry dock and it's on the left, just past the *Toscano gelateria*. Tues–Sun 1–3pm & 7.30–10pm.

CAMPI FLEGREI FESTIVALS

In addition to its celebrations associated with the blood of San Gennaro (see p.43) – the main one here being on September 19 – Pozzuoli also goes in for a significant **Ferragosto** event (the Assumption, August 15). At the port, youths compete in the Gara del Palo, which involves balancing on a long, soapy wooden pole out over the water to try to snag a banner. Most end up taking a dive, of course. In Bacoli, a feast worth showing up for is the **Sagra delle Cozze** (Mussels Festival), around July 26, when boatloads of the shellfish are boisterously consumed.

La Cantina dell'Abbazia Via Pianura 4/5, Località San Martino ☎081 526 3750, ⓦlacantinadellabbazia.com. A little way inland, just beyond the Astroni nature reserve, *La Cantina dell'Abbazia* is located in the former stables of the San Martino monastery – a summer residence for the monks from the monastery in Naples. It serves a lovely, moderately priced menu, with a few dishes for each course that are either meat-based – di *terra* – or fish or seafood – di *mare*. Tues–Sat 1–2.30pm & 8–10.30pm, Sun 1–3.30pm.

★**Le Sciantose** Via Napoli 55/59 ☎081 526 5380, ⓦlesciantose.it. Right on the seafront just out of the centre, *Le Sciantose* has a traditionally fishy theme but is one of Pozzuoli's more moderately priced choices – reckon on about €30–35 a head for a complete meal. Daily for lunch and dinner.

Osteria DOC Corso Umberto I 181 ☎081 526 2835, ⓦosteriadoc.blogspot.com. This wine bar offers creative cuisine with seasonal specials (the menu changes monthly) and offers set menus for €22–25. You'll usually find pasta dishes – lasagne, gnocchi – along with *frittate*, ham, salami and cheese platters, and the like. Tues–Sat 7.30pm–midnight.

Baia

BAIA, 7km along the coast from Pozzuoli, is a small seaside town with a set of imperial-era Roman ruins piled up on the hill above. The name is said to derive from one of Ulysses' companions, who died here. Ancient Baiae was one of the bay's most favoured spots in Roman times, a fashionable resort where the most powerful of Rome's patricians had villas: Emperor Hadrian died here in 138 AD, and Nero was rumoured to have had his mother Agrippina murdered nearby. The port area of Baia is nice enough in a workaday way, and has a couple of decent restaurants and a small beach, but the real draw is the extensive remains of an important Roman palace, whose enormous baths (not temples as was once thought) leave little doubt that the ancient town was full of preening imperial fat cats and phalanxes of hapless slaves.

Parco Archeologico delle Terme di Baia

Via Sella di Baia 22 • Daily 9am–1hr before sunset • €4 combined ticket with Sito Archeologico di Cumae, Museo Archeologico dei Campi Flegrei in Baia and Anfiteatro Flavio in Pozzuoli (valid 48hr) • ☎081 868 7592, ⓦcir.campania.beniculturali.it/archeobaia

You can follow the steps up from the main street to the entrance to the **Parco Archeologico** or you can reach the entrance from the opposite direction (it's a shortish walk from Fusaro Cumana station). The excavated buildings, dating from the first century BC to the fourth century AD, are evocatively structured across some seven terraced levels. Follow the steps down from the entrance level south to the first terrace of the palace, where the so-called Rooms of Venus contain patches of Roman stuccowork, depicting birds and mythical creatures, and a statue of Mercury, beheaded by vandals. In the centre, there are the remains of a theatre that was later converted into a fountain, as well as an open space – thought to be a *piscina* (pool) – with a pretty garden portico on one side. Perhaps the most impressive structure is to the east, the misnamed Temple of Mercury, actually part of the palace's gigantic baths complex, the

---

WATERY ARCHEOLOGY: THE PARCO ARCHEOLOGICO SOMMERSO DI BAIA

Glass-bottomed boat tours are a good way of exploring the ruined substructures of the now totally submerged villas and the facilities of Agrippa's Portus Iulius along Baia's coast — the work again of relentless bradyseism (see box, p.101). How much you can actually make out depends a great deal on the state of the water on the day you make the trip, but you will at least be able to discern walls and floor plans, plus a few columns, and with a little luck some mosaic pavements. Tours are organized by BaiaSommersa (☎349 497 4183, ⓦbaiasommersa.it) and leave Saturday and Sunday at 10am, noon and 3pm; they cost €10 per person, and you must book in advance. For scuba enthusiasts, BaiaSommersa also runs guided dives of the same sites.

circular domed form (late first century BC) echoed by later monuments, including the Pantheon in Rome. To the north, the so-called Temple of Diana, also part of a baths complex, has marble reliefs and a large octagonal chamber.

Museo Archeologico dei Campi Flegrei

Via Castello 39 • Tues–Sun 9am–2.30pm • €4 combined ticket with Sito Archeologico di Cumae, Parco Archeologico delle Terme di Baia and Anfiteatro Flavio in Pozzuoli (valid 48hr) • ⓦ cir.campania.beniculturali.it/museoarcheologicocampiflegrei • An unexciting 15min walk up the hill from Baia towards Bacoli, or take the Torregaveta bus from Lucrino or Fusaro to Bacoli

2

Many of the finds from Baia and around have found their way into the **Museo Archeologico dei Campi Flegrei**, housed in part of the town's mammoth fifteenth-century Aragonese castle – high above and giving wonderful views back over the bay to Baia, Pozzuoli and beyond. The collection is frequently rearranged, so it's hard to say what will be on show, but one of the highlights is a sacellum or the remnants of a shrine dedicated to the Imperial cult, which deified emperors and even members of their family, from the forum of ancient Misenum on Capo Miseno; among other things it contains an equestrian statue of Nerva (previously thought to be Domitian) and Vespasian and Titus in heroic poses. There's also a partially reconstructed *nymphaeum* or monumental fountain, which was discovered underwater off a nearby cape and includes sculptures of Ulysses and his stalwart Baio, two winsome figures of Dionysus and others of various imperial figures. In another part of the museum are ancient plaster casts or *gessi* of original classical Greek bronzes that were used as models by marble sculptors in ancient Baiae to supply the grand villas. Also noteworthy among numerous rooms devoted to both Cumae and Pozzuoli's Rione Terra are an elegant standing *Persephone* and the exquisite marble head of *Athena Lemnia*, one of only two copies known of the celebrated fifth-century BC work by Phidias.

Lago del Fusaro

A ten-minute walk inland from Baia (take the road from the entrance to the ruins), the train tracks skirt around the bottom of **Lago del Fusaro** – actually a lagoon rather than a real lake. Though densely populated in former times, the entire area became a royal hunting preserve in the eighteenth century, which explains the little Rococo jewel-box of a building set out in the lake on a tiny islet, a couple of minutes from Fusaro station. The **Casino Reale**, accessible through a small park but permanently closed to the public, was built as a royal hunting and fishing lodge, and is now an elegant octagonal folly, the work of Carlo Vanvitelli, the son of the king's favourite architect, who was also responsible for the English Garden at the palace in Caserta (see p.192). Over the years, guests here have included Sir William Hamilton, Mozart, Rossini, a tsar or two and many other crowned heads of state. Following the king's predilection, Lago del Fusaro remains a popular spot for fishing, as the locals lined up along the concrete pier of the village of Torregaveta beyond testify.

ARRIVAL AND DEPARTURE   BAIA

By bus You can get to Baia by taking a SEPSA bus from Pozzuoli, which takes about 10min.

By train Take the the Cumana rail line to Fusaro, from where it's a 10min walk to the ruins.

EATING AND DRINKING

Il Gabbiano Via Cicerone 21 ☎081 868 7969, ⓦilgabbianohotel.com. This plush hotel, just outside the centre of Baia towards Lucrino, has a superb modern Italian restaurant featuring a garden terrace with stunning views, and wonderful fresh fish. Prices are moderate to high. Daily for lunch and dinner.

La Tortuga Via Molo di Baia 11 ☎081 868 8847. Excellent portside restaurant serving reliable Neapolitan food with a smile – great mussels and calamari, seafood pasta dishes and suchlike for moderate prices. Tues–Sat 1–3pm & 8–11pm.

Bacoli and around

Immediately below Baia's castle, **BACOLI** (ancient Bauli, a name associated with one of the Twelve Labours of Hercules, the muscle-bound demigod also credited with single-handedly creating nearby Lago Lucrino) sprawls right round to the adjacent settlement of Miseno and has several ancient ruins, as well as a small stretch of beach by a small harbour.

2

Tomba di Agrippina

Via Spiaggia 36 • Daily 9am–1hr before sunset • Free • ☎ 081 523 4368 if it's not open

Down by the beach and Bacoli's easiest ruin to find, the **Tomba di Agrippina** is actually a small theatre or *odeon* that was transformed into a *nymphaeum* (fountain). The name derives from the belief that it was here that Nero had his mother assassinated and interred in a large mausoleum. It's often locked, but you can get a good view of it from outside.

Cento Camerelle

Via Cento Camerelle • Closed for restoration • Free

Following Via Sant'Ana from the main square in Bacoli, and making a left onto Via Cento Camerelle, the so-called **Cento Camerelle** are literally one hundred small rooms – in fact two large, complex cisterns carved largely out of a tufa cliff, with passageways between them, built in Roman times to service the many villas along here, most of which remain unexcavated. It's an impressive sight, but unfortunately is currently closed for restoration.

Piscina Mirabalis and Lago Miseno

Piscina Mirabalis Tues–Sat 9am–1pm & 3–7pm, Sun 9am–1pm • ☎ 081 523 5174 if the site is closed, or ring the bell for the custodian

Walking from the Cento Camerelle in Bacoli, follow Via Ambrogio Greco from Via Sant'Ana to the end where you'll come across the "marvellous pool" or **Piscina Mirabilis**, a massive and elegantly arched reservoir with 48 pilasters built out on a promontory that commanded the port. The tank – some 70m long, 15m high and 26m wide – provided for the needs of the fleet and was fed by the Serino aqueduct, also built under Augustus.

Below the *piscina*, **Lago Miseno** was once a reservoir serving the nearby imperial port of **Misenum** – the name is said to derive either from that of another companion of Ulysses or from Aeneas's trumpeter – and was created by cutting a canal through to allow access to the inland basin. Nowadays silting has isolated the water here from the

---

BEACHES IN THE CAMPI FLEGREI

Some of the best of the area's **beaches** are at Bacoli, to one side of Capo Miseno, and at **Lido di Miliscola**, on the other. There are some nice *scoglie* (rocky coves and reefs) to explore, and beach services are provided by a number of establishments along the seashore. Be warned, however: the limited sandy area gets packed during high season, not only with sun-worshippers but also with rows and rows of lounge chairs and umbrellas – for which you'll pay the usual charges. **Lido Montenuovo** at Lucrino is a nice stretch of sand and is handily placed right by the Cumana station, while the patch of beach below the castle housing the Museo Archeologico dei Campi Flegrei is only accessible by boat (walk out of Baia on the main road and make a left at the sign) and as such can be quieter than other locations. There's also **Lido di Licola**, which is a long stretch of sandy beach just to the north of Cuma, which you can reach direct on the Circumflegrea from Naples or walk to in ten minutes from Cumae.

open sea, and it is now known as the Mare Morto or Dead Sea, but in the first century AD, under Augustus, Misenum was a major naval base. Not much has been excavated, but there are a few ruins – of a small amphitheatre and shrine – mixed in with the housing that surrounds the lake.

Capo Miseno

Finally, don't miss the view from the top of **Capo Miseno** itself, the lofty outcrop at the very tip of the Phlegraean peninsula. Easily walkable from the far end of Via Miseno, its commanding position, controlling both the Gulf of Pozzuoli and the Procida Channel, made it a perfect strategic location. Today, there's an important lighthouse at its summit, and from here you can take in the nearby islands of Procida and Ischia and the expanse of the entire Bay of Naples.

2

ACCOMMODATION AND EATING   BACOLI

Hotel Cala Moresca Via del Faro 44, Capo Miseno ☏ 081 523 5595, ⓦ calamoresca.it. A nice place to eat lunch or dinner, but also to stay, with a hilltop garden and pool, and private access to the sea. The restaurant is white, bright and elegant. It's moderately priced, and enjoys lovely views of Procida and Ischia from its terrace. **€85**

★**Osteria Da Caliendo** Via Mozart 67, Bacoli ☏ 081 523 4073, ⓦ dacaliendo.it. Rustic, family-run restaurant on the main street near the Mare Morto, specializing in fresh seafood antipasti and pasta dishes as well as pizza. Mon, Tues, Thurs & Fri 4pm–1am, Sat & Sun noon–1am.

Cumae

About 6km up the coast from Torregaveta, the eighth-century BC town of **CUMAE** has lain in ruins since the ninth century AD. It was the first Greek colony on the Italian mainland, a source of settlers for other colonies (Naples – Neapolis – was originally settled by Greeks from Cumae) and a vital centre of Hellenistic civilization. It was home to an important soothsaying priestess of Apollo, the so-called **Cumaean Sibyl**, from whom Tarquinius purchased the Sibylline Books (see box, p.108) which became the guiding inspiration for the Republic.

Sito Archeologico di Cumae

Via Monte di Cuma 3 • Daily 9am–1hr before sunset • €4 combined ticket with Parco Archeologico delle Terme di Baia, Museo Archeologico dei Campi Flegrei in Baia and Anfiteatro Flavio in Pozzuoli (valid 48hr) • ☏ 081 804 0430

The ruins of Cumae, a short walk from the bus or Circumflegrea stop, are spread over a large area and not at all comprehensively excavated. Still, the only part you're likely to want to see forms a tight nucleus close to the entrance. The best-known feature is the **Grotto of the Sibyl**, discovered only in 1932, and considered by some to be the long-sought temple seat of one of the most famous of all ancient oracles (though wet-blankets say the structure served some military purpose). The entrance is a spooky 131m-long gallery (*dromos*) excavated out of a solid mass of volcanic tufa. Trapezoidal and vaguely anthropomorphic in shape, it is reminiscent of many Creto–Mycenaean tomb corridors, and penetrates deep under the side of the acropolis high above. Strips of light enter from a series of tall slits in the seaward wall, creating a striking visual rhythm of dark and light that can be hypnotic as you walk along. At the end of the passageway, from the dim obscurity of an alcove with stone benches, the Sibyl would dispense her cryptic prognostications, allegedly in perfectly metrical verse.

Steps lead up from here to the main part of the site, the fortified acropolis. You pass a constructed belvedere (on the left) and the fairly scanty ruins (on the right) of an archaic fifth-century Greek **temple of Apollo**, overlain by Roman

2

ANCIENT ROMAN PROPHECIES

The tale of the acquisition of the **Sibylline Books** by Lucius Tarquinius Superbus, or Tarquinius Priscus, the semi-legendary last king of Rome, is one of the most enduring of Roman myths. Around the time of the founding of the city of Rome, an old woman arrived in the city and offered nine books of prophecies to King Tarquinius. Because she was demanding an extortionate sum, the king refused. The woman then burned three of the books and offered the remaining six to Tarquinius at the same price, which he again declined. She then burned three more and repeated her offer. Tarquinius finally relented and bought the last three at the original steep price, and the woman – afterwards held to be none other than the Cumaean Sibyl – promptly vanished. The books, which were believed to contain unparalleled wisdom within their pages, were kept thereafter in the Temple of Jupiter on Rome's Capitoline Hill, to be consulted in times of crisis.

The **Cumaean Sibyl** features most famously in Virgil's *Aeneid*, book VI, when Aeneas, princely demigod, offspring of Venus and Anchise, and heroic refugee from defeated Troy, comes to Cumae to consult the Sibyl. The relevant lines from Virgil are now posted on either side of the entrance to the grotto. The seeress is said to have conducted him on a bracing tour of the Underworld (the opening to which was, of course, considered to be nearby) where the spirit of his father showed him visions of founding a "New Troy" further north, and naming it Rome. It is certain that Virgil, Augustan Rome's official epic poet and propagandist, largely fabricated his *Aeneid*, weaving an incongruous range of earlier sagas into a new tale designed to provide the Latins with a high-flown pedigree (the Julian line were treated as direct descendants of Aeneas and therefore of Venus) and an exalted foundation myth. Thus imperial Rome's inclination to world conquest appeared to be divinely mandated and linked by magic to the supreme glories of Homeric Greece.

---

modifications, and then by a sixth-century Christian basilica, on the way to the highest point of the site, where you'll find the remains, mostly just the base and a couple of arches, of a **temple of Jupiter**, which acquired similar accretions over nearly a thousand years. Colossal marble cult statues and other artefacts found here, such as Egyptian statuary from a temple of Isis and eighth-century BC Greek tomb furnishings, are now preserved in Naples' Museo Archeologico Nazionale. The lower part of the site has now been excavated too, revealing a forum, the remains of a baths complex and other more workaday buildings. But the **views** from the top remain one of the best reasons to come here: south across the Lago del Fusaro to the bottom corner of the peninsula's coast, and on the other side of the temple the curving shore north up to the Gulf of Gaeta.

Arco Felice and the Lago d'Averno

There are more ancient traces inland, most notably the **Arco Felice**, a grandiose triumphal gate about 2km east of Cumae. Standing some 20m high, it marks a point where the Romans cut through a mountain in order to connect Cumae by road with Puteoli. Just 1km from the arch, on the eastern shore of **Lago d'Averno**, there's the ruined shell of a second-century hall that was originally as big as Rome's Pantheon, and, like it, domed. The structure is commonly called the **Temple of Apollo**, though it was most likely part of an important baths complex. The lake itself is the Lake Avernus of antiquity, a volcanic crater that the Greeks believed to be the **entrance to Hades**: sacrifices were regularly made here to the chthonic deities that lurked beneath the murky surface, and birds flying over were said to suffocate instantly from the noxious miasma given off by the lake's infernal waters. Indeed the name may derive from a Greek word meaning "without birds". Despite such beliefs and the deeply rooted sanctity of the spot, it was here that Agrippa constructed a military harbour, the Portus Iulius, in 37 BC, joining it to Lago Lucrino by a canal, and, in turn, joining that lake by a canal to the open sea. The military installations on Avernus were also linked by

EXPLORING CAMPI FLEGREI'S EXTINCT VOLCANOES

There are two **nature reserves** in the Campi Flegrei: the craters of **Monte Nuovo** and **Astroni**, both of them extinct volcanoes that have been taken over by rampant vegetation.

MONTE NUOVO OASI NATURALISTICA

Mon–Fri 9am–1hr before sunset, Sat & Sun 9am–1pm • Free • ☎ 081 804 1462

Monte Nuovo is Europe's newest mountain and one of its smallest volcanoes, which sprang up on September 29–30 1538, when violent seismic activity buried the village of Tripergole and sent all the Puteolani fleeing to Naples. It's now a verdant cone in the midst of white houses at the Pozzuoli end of Lago Lucrino. It is just 140m high, with a switchback path up to the rim and then more pathways down into the steep-sided crater. Most of the interior is also thickly forested and makes a fine spot for a picnic.

LE CRATERE DEGLI ASTRONI

Via Agnano agli Astroni • Fri–Sun 9.30am–1hr before sunset in high season; during other periods phone ☎ 081 588 3720 • €5 • Bus #C14 from either Bagnoli or the Circumflegrea stop of Pianura; bus #P6 from Pozzuoli; alternatively bus #C2 from Naples arrives within 2km of the entrance

Now a World Wildlife Fund Nature Reserve, this volcano 3km northwest of Pozzuoli is much the older of the two, having arisen some four thousand years ago. The Romans are known to have had a thermal spa here, though no traces have yet been discovered and the springs vanished after the nearby eruptions of 1538. Since the reserve was established in 1987, flora and fauna have made an impressive advance, and Astroni is an especially rich site for birdwatchers. The oval caldera is 2km by 1.6km wide, circumscribing small mountains of up to 255m in height, a large lake on the southern side, near the entrance, and two small ponds towards the centre. There's a good dirt road (the old royal hunt road), which affords an approximately two-hour circuit around the central Colle dell'Imperatrice, and there are several sixteenth-century towers too – lookouts for what was once the royal hunting preserve – although the paths around the rim of the crater itself are open only for scientific research

tunnels to the port of Cumae, thus completing the strategic scheme. However, when Augustus later had Agrippa build the military port at Misenum, sacred Avernus reverted to its tranquil, if gloomy, inviolability.

ARRIVAL AND DEPARTURE   CUMAE

By bus and train The best way to reach Cumae is to take the Cumana train to Fusaro and a bus from there.

ACCOMMODATION

Averno Damiani Via Montenuovo Licola Patria 85 ☎ 081 804 2666, ⓦ averno.it. An all-purpose and very attractive tourist complex with a hotel, independent bungalows and a campsite; amenities include a large restaurant, a club, a thermal spa and tennis courts. Camping (add €10 for each additional person) €20, doubles €110, bungalows €135.

Santa Marta Via Licola Patria 28, Arco Felice ☎ 081 804 2404, ⓦ santamartahotel.com. A simple, modern, comfortable hotel featuring a good restaurant with terrace seating, just 100m from the sea. €80

South of Naples

MOUNT VESUVIUS

South of Naples

It's home to the most famous Roman sites of all – Pompeii and Herculaneum – but the coast to the south of Naples is otherwise the least attractive stretch of the bay, the Circumvesuviana train squeezing out of Naples through a demoralizing cityscape of derelict industrial buildings and scruffy jerry-built housing. You're on the train for around twenty minutes before you begin to feel anything like free of the city, and even then the train tracks and main *autostrada* south pick their way through a dense grid of apartment blocks and market gardens that stretch all the way down to the sea. Behind, Vesuvius glowers over it all, suburban sprawl peppering its slopes like a rash. Most people come here to see Herculaneum and Pompeii, or to scale Vesuvius, all easy day-trips from Naples – or they skip the lot for the resort town of Sorrento (see Chapter 4). But there are one or two other places and attractions that are worth getting off the train for: lesser-known ancient sites like the Villa Poppea at Oplontis in Torre Annunziata and the magnificent Stabiae villas at Castellammare, as well as more recent examples of grand houses at Portici, Ercolano and around.

Herculaneum

The first real point of any interest on the coast south of Naples is the town of **Ercolano**, the modern offshoot of the ancient site of **HERCULANEUM**, which was destroyed by the eruption of Vesuvius on August 24, 79 AD. The new town is a bit ragged, but the historic site is smaller and somewhat quieter than Pompeii, an ancient residential area rather than bustling port city. A little closer to Naples than Pompeii, it's also the best departure point for Vesuvius, making it possible to see the site and to scale the volcano on the same day.

The site

Corso Resina 187 • Daily: April–Oct 8.30am–7.30pm, last entry 6pm; Nov–March 8.30am–5pm, last entry 3.30pm • €11; combined ticket for 5 sites including Pompeii, Oplontis, Stabiae and Boscoreale €20 (valid for 3 days) • ☎ 081 857 5347, ⓦ pompeiisites.org

Situated at the bottom end of Ercolano's main street, the site of **Herculaneum** was discovered in 1709, when a well-digger accidentally struck the stage of the buried theatre. Excavations were undertaken throughout the eighteenth and nineteenth centuries, during which period much of the marble and bronze from the site was carted off to Naples to decorate the city's palaces, and it wasn't until 1927 that digging and conservation began in earnest. Ancient Herculaneum was a residential town, much smaller than Pompeii but more well-to-do, and as such it makes a more manageable site, less architecturally impressive perhaps, but better preserved and more easily taken in on a single visit. Archeologists believed for a long time that most of the inhabitants of Herculaneum had in fact managed to escape. However, recent discoveries of

Highlights

❶ Herculaneum The quieter and arguably easier-to-discern alternative to Pompeii. **See p.112**

❷ Vesuvius Mainland Europe's only active volcano, visible from just about everywhere in the Bay of Naples; no trip to the region is complete without making the hike to its summit. **See p.118**

❸ Pompeii No introduction needed – the ancient Roman resort buried and partially preserved by ash in Vesuvius's 79 AD eruption, and one of the greatest ancient sites you'll ever visit. **See p.122**

HIGHLIGHTS ARE MARKED ON THE MAP ON P.114

entangled skeletons found at what was once the shoreline of the town suggest otherwise, and it's now believed that most of the population was buried by huge avalanches of volcanic mud, which later hardened into the tufa-type rock that preserved much of the town, including some wooden structures that don't usually survive. In early 2000 the remains of another 48 people were found; they were carrying coins, which suggests they were attempting to flee the disaster.

At the ticket office pick up one of the excellent free maps to the site, before you enter the city proper, and look in at the pavilion housing the remains of a boat that archeologists have surmised was thrown onto the beach by the force of the earthquake and smashed against the ruins of houses. As well as the boat, and a

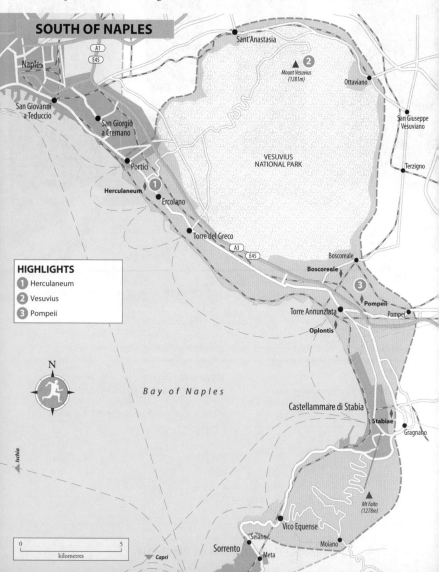

SOUTH OF NAPLES

Naples

Sant'Anastasia

San Giovanni
a Teduccio

San Giorgio
a Cremano

▲ 2
Mount Vesuvius
(1281m)

Ottaviano

San Giuseppe
Vesuviano

Portici

VESUVIUS
NATIONAL PARK

Terzigno

1

Herculaneum

Ercolano

Torre del Greco

Boscoreale

Boscoreale

3

HIGHLIGHTS

1 Herculaneum

2 Vesuvius

3 Pompeii

Pompeii

Torre Annunziata

Pompei

Oplontis

N

Bay of Naples

Castellammare di Stabia

Stabiae

Gragnano

Ischia

Mt Faito
(1278m)

Vico Equense

Seiano

Moiano

0   5
kilometres

Sorrento

Meta

Capri

serpent prow, finds include a coil of rope and a leather sheet (with signs of stitching) fused to scorched wooden planks.

Cardo III

Because Herculaneum wasn't a commercial town, there was no real central open space or forum as there was in Pompeii, just streets of villas and shops in a grid based on three very straight main thoroughfares. The bottom end of Cardo III is a good place to start, where you'll see one of the largest properties of the ancient town, the **Hotel** – you can get a good impression of its size from the rectangle of stumpy columns that made up its atrium. Across the street, the **House of the Argus** is more complete, a very grand building judging by its once-impressive courtyard. On the upper storey excavators found terracotta jars containing spelt, olives, almonds and dried fruit, and – a sign that life was going on as normal until the eruption struck – loaves of bread left to rise before being baked. Further up on the right, there's the **House of the Skeleton**, named after a skeleton that was discovered by nineteenth-century archeologists on the upper floor, with a mosaic-covered *nymphaeum*, and a **thermopolium** or café on the corner, where there's a well-preserved counter with sunken jars.

The most interesting house on Cardo III is a little way up on the right, however – the **Hall of the Augustals** – basically a temple dedicated to the worship of the cult of the Emperor Augustus. It's one of the site's most impressive large rooms, with four giant columns holding up the blackened remains of the wooden frame of the house and everything focusing on the wall paintings that face each other in the apse-like space on the right. The frescoes are from the first century AD, and show on one side Hercules with Juno and Minerva, and on the other Hercules with an Etruscan god.

Cardo IV

If you go back to where Cardo III meets the Decumanus Inferior, you'll see the large **Thermae** or bath complex stretching across to Cardo IV. There are two entrances to the baths: one just off the atrium on Cardo III and the other on Cardo IV. The first entrance takes you into the domed *frigidarium* of the men's section, decorated with a floor mosaic of dolphins, and with a *caldarium* containing a plunge bath and a scallop-shell apse. Still intact are the benches where bathers sat and the wooden, partitioned shelves for clothing. On Cardo IV is the entrance to the women's section, which has a well-preserved black-and-white mosaic of Triton and sea creatures, and original glass shards in its window.

Across Cardo IV there's the **Samnite House**, which has an attractive atrium, with a graceful loggia all the way round and a hole in the roof decorated with animal spouts. Three doors up, the **House of Neptune and Amphitrite** holds sparklingly preserved wall mosaics featuring the gods on one wall, hunting dogs and deer on a vibrant blue background on another, richly ornamented with shells, lava foam and theatrical masks. Adjacent is the **House of the Beautiful Courtyard**, so called for its central atrium, which unusually has steps up one side with a balcony at the top. It also has a perfectly preserved mosaic floor, beyond which another room displays skeletons of bodies under glass still lying in the positions in which they fell.

In the opposite direction down Cardo IV, on the corner of the Decumanus Inferior and across from the Thermae, the **House of the Wooden Partition** still has its original partition doors (now under glass) – evidence that it was the home of a poorer class of person than many of the buildings here. The **Trellis House** next door was a plebeian boarding house, originally divided into separate apartments, and with an upper-storey balcony overhanging the streetfront that was built using so-called *opus craticium*, a building method that used poor-quality material held together by wooden frames – making it ironic that this very well-preserved example should still be standing.

Across the road is the **House of the Alcove**, where you can follow a perfectly preserved mosaic-paved passage right round to the back of the house, while beyond, the **House of**

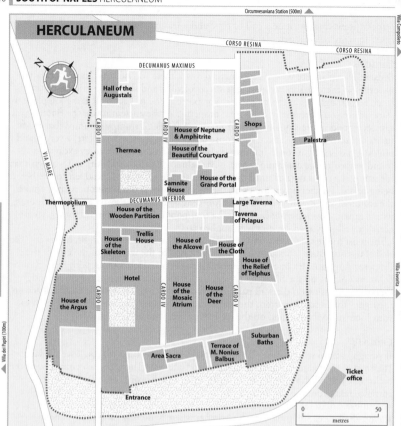

HERCULANEUM

Circumvesuviana Station (500m)

Villa Campolieto

CORSO RESINA

CORSO RESINA

N

DECUMANUS MAXIMUS

Hall of the Augustals

CARDO III

CARDO IV

CARDO V

VIA MARE

House of Neptune & Amphitrite

Shops

Palestra

Thermae

House of the Beautiful Courtyard

House of the Grand Portal

Samnite House

Thermopolium

DECUMANUS INFERIOR

House of the Wooden Partition

Large Taverna

Taverna of Priapus

House of the Skeleton

Trellis House

House of the Alcove

House of the Cloth

House of the Relief of Telphus

Hotel

CARDO III

CARDO IV

House of the Mosaic Atrium

House of the Deer

CARDO V

House of the Argus

Villa dei Papiri (100m)

Area Sacra

Terrace of M. Nonius Balbus

Suburban Baths

Ticket office

Entrance

Villa Favorita

0   50
metres

the **Mosaic Atrium** was a grand villa in its day and retains its mosaic-laid courtyard, corrugated by the force of the tufa.

Cardo V

A block across from Cardo IV lies Cardo V and most of the rest of the town's **shops**, which include a baker's, complete with ovens and grinding mills, a weaver's, with loom and bones, and a dyer's, with a huge pot for dyes. Behind the shops on the left you can see the **Palestra**, where public games were held, and accessible by way of a monumental gateway halfway down, beyond which there's a large colonnade and an apsidal hall, along with a terrace of rooms up above, giving an impression of just how large a structure this was.

Back on Cardo V, opposite the entrance to the Palestra, the **House of the Grand Portal**, close to the corner of the Decumanus Inferior, is so called for its doorway with Corinthian columns, still very much intact. Opposite here, the **Large Taverna** has a well-preserved counter, while another shop down Cardo V, the **Taverna of Priapus**, has a faint but still suggestive painting above the counter. Next door to this is the **House of the Cloth** with blackened steps (behind glass), while next door the **House of the Deer** was another luxury villa, its two storeys built around a central courtyard, its corridors decorated with richly coloured still lifes. It would have occupied one of the most sought-after locations in town, with a central sitting room leading to a terrace with what would have been a commanding sea view. Opposite, the **House of the Relief of**

THE VESUVIAN VILLAS

It wasn't only during Roman times that Ercolano was considered a desirable place to live. In fact the town and its neighbours only really took on their present unprepossessing appearance during the last half-century. In the late eighteenth century and into the nineteenth century they were home to some of the most chi-chi residences on the bay – indeed, unbelievable as it might seem now, this stretch was once known as the Miglio d'Oro or "Golden Mile". In fact Italy's first ever train line, built in 1839, ran from Naples to Portici, which gives you some idea of how different this stretch of coast was in those days. Known collectively as the Vesuvian Villas, many of the properties that were built here during that time are still standing; some are occasionally open to the public, while others are used for hotels, conferences, exhibitions and concerts, and a few venues host an arts festival in June. For more details go to Ⓦ villevesuviane.net.

The **Reggia di Portici**, in Portici (best accessed on the main train line to Salerno, though you can also walk from Via Libertá on the Circumvesuviana), is probably the most sumptuous of all the villas, designed by Ferdinando Fuga and Luigi Vanvitelli in the late eighteenth century and now home to the agriculture faculty of Naples' university. It was originally used to house the best of the finds from Herculaneum, and although these days there's not a great deal to see inside, it's open from Monday to Friday during office hours, and behind it there's a botanical garden occupying the former royal hunting grounds that is open at weekends too. In Ercolano the **Villa Campolieto** is within walking distance of the Herculaneum ruins, just five minutes away to the right along Via Resina as you exit the site. It's another creation of the Vanvitelli family (Luigi and his son Carlo), built between 1763 and 1773, with a magnificent sea-facing circular courtyard. A small museum here is devoted to the most famous Vesuvian Villas (Tues–Sun 10am–1pm), although the reason most people come is for the concerts and plays that are held during the summer. Finally, the **Villa Favorita**, also in Ercolano, is a ten-minute walk from the ruins – take the exit behind the ticket office, then right, then left and you're there. The villa was built in the 1760s by Ferdinando Fuga and is perhaps the most pleasant to visit because of its park, which stretches down to the waterfront, although most of the main buildings are used for conferences and thus it's not always open to the public. Finally it's worth knowing that you can stay in the Villa Aprile, in Ercolano (see p.118), or in the more intimate Villa San Gennariello in Portici (see p.118).

Telephus is the second-largest villa in Herculaneum, the home, it's thought, of one M. Nonius Balbus, proconsul of Crete and an associate of Augustus himself, and discovered with a collection of sculptures that includes the relief you can see on the wall, showing Telephus, the son of Hercules.

From here, the end of Cardo V, the path descends under a covered passageway down to the so-called **Suburban Baths** on the left: one of the most impressive – and intact – structures in Herculaneum, complete with extremely well-preserved stuccowork and a pretty much intact set of baths; it also has a complete original Roman door, the only one in Herculaneum that wasn't charred by fire. If you find it open, its damp mustiness makes it certainly the most evocative stop on a tour of the site. Next door, the **Terrace of M. Nonius Balbus** is so called for the funerary altar in the centre, which remembers the good deeds and great works of the proconsul, while beyond, the two temples – the **Sacellum of Venus** and **Sacellum of the Four Gods** – which together make up the Area Sacra, are decorated respectively with a marble altar and reliefs of Minerva, Neptune, Mercury and Vulcan.

Villa dei Papiri

Closed at the time of writing • ☎ 081 857 5347, Ⓦ pompeiisites.org for up-to-date information

Situated just to the north of the main site, the **Villa dei Papiri** is the best-known of all the Herculaneum villas, and the model that J. Paul Getty used for his Malibu California museum. It was the home of Julius Caesar's father-in-law, Lucius Calpurnius Piso, a learned man who was an enemy of Cicero and a consul of the Republic before his son-in-law. His villa supposedly stretched for more than 200m along what would have been the waterfront here, and was by far the most luxurious residence in the vicinity. Built on several levels, it housed a vast library of around two thousand scrolls as well as a large collection of sculptures (including the stunning bronze runners now in Naples' Museo Archeologico Nazionale, which also has an archive of what was left of the carbonized scrolls). A relatively new technique known as multi-spectral imaging has made it possible to read many of the charred scrolls for the first time in almost two thousand years, but, as far as the site is concerned, excavations have been suspended for some years and there is no sign of them re-starting. As such, it's hard to say when the Villa dei Papiri might be open to the public. But don't hold your breath.

MAV (Museo Archeologico Virtuale)

Via IV Novembre 44 • Tues–Sun 9.30am–5.30pm • €7.50, €11.50 including the film • ☎ 081 1980 6511, ⓦ museomav.it

You pass this multimedia museum as you walk down the hill from the station to Herculaneum. Basically Herculaneum and Pompeii-lite, **MAV** displays CGI images of villas and other buildings both in ruins and as they might have looked before the disaster, plus a film (optional) detailing the eruption of Vesuvius. It's not badly done, and some of the images and holograms do help you to piece it all together, though to be honest it's the ruins themselves that win the day.

ARRIVAL AND DEPARTURE
HERCULANEUM

By train Herculaneum is very easy to reach from Naples or Sorrento; its most central station, Ercolano Scavi, is on the main Circumvesuviana line between the two about 20min from Napoli Centrale and 45min from Sorrento. Once in Ercolano, the site is a 10min walk down the hill from the train station. Pompeii Scavi station is about 20min away on the same line, so you can, if you have the energy, do both sites in a day.

ACCOMMODATION

Miglio d'Oro Corso Resina 296, Ercolano ☎ 081 739 9999, ⓦ migliodoroparkhotel.it. This four-star hotel with all the trimmings is housed in the pink eighteenth-century Villa Aprile, one of Ercolano's royal villas, which was renovated as a hotel a few years ago. It's only a few minutes' walk from the site, and the gardens are a peaceful respite from the grime of the bay. The rooms are decent, predictably large and well kitted out in a mostly contemporary style, plus there's a swimming pool, solarium and a good restaurant. €145

Villa San Gennariello Via Madonnelle 5, Portici ☎ 081 776 1220, ⓦ villasangennariello.com. Housed in a lodge in the grounds of the Portici Royal Palace not far from Via Libertà Circumvesuviana station and 20-minutes' walk from the Herculaneum site, this is a simpler option than the Villa Aprile. It has got to be the best bargain in the area, with large, simply furnished rooms looking over the park. Free wi-fi too. €80

Mount Vesuvius

Daily: Jan, Feb, Nov & Dec 9am–3pm; March & Oct 9am–4pm; April, May, June & Sept 9am–5pm; July & Aug 9am–6pm • €10 • ⓦ parconazionaledelvesuvio.it

Since its first known eruption in 79 AD, when it buried the towns and inhabitants of Pompeii and Herculaneum, **MOUNT VESUVIUS** has dominated the lives of those who live on the Bay of Naples, its brooding bulk – often snow-capped in winter and even spring – forming a stately backdrop to the ever-growing urban sprawl clogging its lower slopes. There have been more than a hundred **eruptions** since then, and the people who live here still fear the reawakening of the volcano, and with good cause – scientists calculate it should erupt every thirty years or so, and it hasn't since 1944. Vesuvius is carefully monitored, of course, and there is apparently no reason to expect any movement for some time, although local government has been relocating residents on the slopes to housing elsewhere for years. But the subsidence in towns like Ercolano is a continuing reminder of the instability of the area, which is one of southern Italy's most densely populated.

Making the **ascent** to the crater from the car park takes twenty to thirty minutes depending on how fit you are. It's a medium-to-strenuous stroll across reddened, barren

VESUVIUS: WILL SHE BLOW?

The only active volcano in mainland Europe, **Mount Vesuvius** dominates the Bay of Naples from almost wherever you stand, a huge and menacing presence that overlooks the most densely populated volcanic region in the world. It's much smaller than Sicily's more active Etna, but is considered by experts to be much more dangerous and unpredictable. The crater and summit have changed with almost every eruption, and it's likely that the profile of Vesuvius you're looking at now is nothing like the one the ancients would have seen. It's almost the classic volcano shape, but not quite, owing to the fact that its main summit and caldera – Monte Somma – was blown off in an earlier eruption and is now separated from the current summit by a 5km-wide valley. The main summit today is 1281m high, and the crater 650m wide and 230m deep, and it's this that you can visit – a bare, cindery expanse from which it's possible to see the calcified lava flows of the previous eruptions, but below which the fertile soil is lushly forested and intensively cultivated with vines and market gardens.

Vesuvius has had plenty of **eruptions** over the years, most famously in 79 AD, when it buried Pompeii and Herculaneum and most of the towns around with hot ash (not lava), and most recently in 1944, when part of the rim of the crater was blown away and the nearby towns of San Sebastiano and Massa di Somma were destroyed – an event memorably described by Norman Lewis in his war memoir *Naples '44*. In between those two events there have been many other violent eruptions – among them one in 472 AD, when ash from the volcano could be seen as far away as Constantinople, and another in 1036, when lava flows were seen for the first time. In the Middle Ages the volcano was largely dormant until a massive eruption in 1631 which killed three thousand people, since when there has been an eruption at least four times each century. The first eruption of the twentieth century, in 1906, sent more lava down the mountain than ever before – after which Vesuvius was 100m shorter. Everything has been quiet since 1944, which, chillingly, is the longest period of dormancy in recorded history; indeed, most experts agree that not only is Vesuvius well overdue another eruption, but because of the way volcanoes work, when it does blow it may well be the most violent eruption for some time – not much comfort to the million or so people who live in its potential danger zone.

It's nothing new that the slopes of Vesuvius are heavily populated: the volcano's flanks have always drawn settlement thanks to their fertile soil and mild climate – a lushness that is particularly evident as you make your way up to the top. The mountain has been monitored closely since the first observatory was built on its slopes in 1841, and the authorities remain as alert as ever. There is a detailed **evacuation plan**, which assumes two weeks' notice of a major eruption, and which would be capable of shifting half a million out of the biggest danger zone, where they could be in the way of pyroclastic flows of ash and rock. Nonetheless, Vesuvius is prone to sudden, extremely intense eruptions, and if this happens the chances of a mass evacuation of its very densely populated slopes are remote in the extreme. The authorities are trying to discourage construction on the volcano – hence the rather derelict nature of many of the buildings near the top – and have even offered financial incentives to people to move away; and the mountain is also protected within its own national park (W parconazionaledelvesuvio.it), which has a rich variety of flora, some quite rare or unusual this far south. For the moment the volcano is quiet – but looking at its history and the massively developed straggle from Naples that encircles it, you can't help feeling that it is a very large accident waiting to happen. Indeed, if anything is responsible for the sunny fatalism that characterizes so many Neapolitans, it's this.

gravel and rock along a marked path that is roped off to minimize the chance of stumbling and falling down the sheer drop. At the top is a deep, wide, jagged ashtray of red rock swirled over by midges and emitting the odd plume of smoke, though since the last eruption effectively sealed up the main crevice this is much less evident than it once was. A small kiosk sells drinks and trinkets, and the path continues halfway around the crater so you can get a view from the other side – a further fifteen minutes or so on foot. The climb is well worth it, not only for an eerie glimpse inside the volcano, but also for a stunning panorama of Naples' bay.

ARRIVAL AND DEPARTURE   MOUNT VESUVIUS

There are several ways of getting to Vesuvius, or at least the car park and huddle of souvenir shops and cafés which sit just above the greenery among the bare cinders of the main summit and crater. If you have your own car perhaps the best way is to drive and simply pay a small fee – currently €2.50 – for parking. But there are lots of public transport options if you don't.

From Ercolano Perhaps the most direct route to Vesuvius from Naples is to take a Circumvesuviana train to Ercolano Scavi station, from where there are regular shuttle buses run by Vesuvio Express (ⓦ vesuvioexpress.it); buses leave from right outside the station, taking about half an hour to reach the car park near the summit (€10 return). Groups can also take a taxi, though this will cost at least €50 return and won't be much quicker.

From Pompeii There are more options for reaching Vesuvius from Pompeii, though do bear in mind it's a lot further from the summit so altogether more time-consuming. EAV Bus public buses run twice a day from Piazza Anfiteatro (€10 return); the journey takes just over an hour and the last bus back is at 2.30pm. Busvia del Vesuvio (ⓦ busviadelvesuvio.com) runs excursions that leave every hour between 9am and 3pm from

Pompeii-Villa dei Misteri, from where you take a truck to within 600m of the summit (3hr in all). A third way is to take one of the Tramvia bus services (€12 return), which leave from Camping Zeus, next door to Villa dei Misteri station, three times a day (the last bus back is at 5.30pm). Finally, various operators around town offer tours (€22 per person, including entrance fee); they run every hour in high season and last for 2 hours in total, giving you about an hour at the site.

From Naples If you're in Naples and want to do things the easy way, you can take a taxi all the way from Naples city centre to Vesuvius. There is a fixed fare of €90, which includes a two-hour wait. Make sure you've agreed the rate beforehand, otherwise it will be one of those rare occasions when the driver prefers to switch on the meter, and it will cost you much more.

Oplontis

Via Sepolcri, Torre Annunziata • Daily: April–Oct 8.30am–7.30pm; Nov–March 8.30am–5pm • €5.50, includes Boscoreale and Stabiae; €20 for 5 sites including Pompeii, Herculaneum, Stabiae and Boscoreale (valid for 3 days) • ☏ 081 857 3457, ⓦ pompeiisites.org

Ten minutes or so beyond Ercolano on the Circumvesuviana line, the hardscrabble coastal town of **Torre Annunziata**, famous for its pasta-making factories, is home to the **Villa Poppea**, a well-preserved Roman patrician villa that's part of a complex of Roman buildings known as **Oplontis**. The site is a short walk from the Circumvesuviana station in a not particularly nice area. It probably belonged to Nero's second wife Poppea, and is remarkable for the scale and elegance of its architecture, wall paintings and gardens. Because of the proximity of Herculaneum and Pompeii, it's often ignored, and parts have been under restoration for a while, but the villa would have been a sumptuous residence in its day, and is worth visiting if you have already seen its better-known neighbours.

From the atrium, adorned with intricate architectural paintings of columns and shields, the vista extends right through the house, to the colonnaded portico surrounding it and the restored, formal gardens bordered with box hedges. It had its own sun terrace and swimming pool, and bones discovered under the lawn suggest that a goat kept the grass in check. **Inside**, some of the highlights include the frescoed *salone* or sitting room, where frescoes show peacocks and theatrical masks, and the bright-red and tawny-yellow *caldarium* of the villa's baths complex, where a pastoral painting portrays Hercules, draped in lion skin, in the garden of the Hesperides, while above him, astride a sea horse, sits a sultry Nereid. In the other direction is a frescoed *triclinium* or dining room and, just behind it, the villa's kitchens, from where you can stroll through various **courtyards** and **inner gardens** – a small one with a fountain, facing what would have been the villa's main entrance hall or atrium (the building faced the sea), followed by a small peristyle with a fountain, edged by servants' quarters, and a larger peristyle that served as a peaceful internal garden. Close by, the latrines show the easy genius of Roman plumbing, while a frescoed corridor leads to the **swimming pool**, a huge affair some 60m long, deliberately tilted towards the sea to allow drainage.

CLOCKWISE FROM TOP LEFT POMPEII (P.122): TEMPLE OF APOLLO; WALL PAINTING, VILLA DEI MISTERI; THE RUINS AND VESUVIUS >

Boscoreale

Via Settetermini, Boscoreale • Daily: April–Oct 8.30am–7.30pm, last entry 6pm; Nov–March 8.30am–6.30pm, last entry 5pm • €5.50, includes Oplontis and Stabiae; €20 for 5 sites including Pompeii, Herculaneum, Stabiae and Oplontis (valid for 3 days) • ☏ 081 857 5347, ⓦ pompeiisites.org • Take the Circumvesuviana 2 stops from Torre Annunziata or 1 stop from Pompeii Santuario, to Boscoreale station, from where it's a 15-minute walk.

The **Antiquarium of Boscoreale**, a small archeological museum displaying finds from a group of nearby villas also buried in the 79 AD eruption, is located in a modern purpose-built structure, rather incongruously plonked in the middle of a housing estate. Unlike the villas at other sites, these were rustic farmhouses rather than upscale holiday homes, and most of the finds here reflect that. There are vast terracotta pots (the sort that pantomime villains hide in), wine and oil presses, the calcified bodies of farm animals – a pig and a dog coiled in a tortured pose – food (figs, nuts, loaves of bread) along with agricultural tools, cowbells and horses' bridles, even a primitive drinking vessel for pets. Outside, you can visit one of the farmhouses, **Villa Regina**, although sometimes access is only permitted as far as the balcony above. The old farm specialized in the production of wine and despite the built-up location vines still grow around it. If you're lucky, you can view rooms that would have been used for grape-pressing, a wine cellar and barn, and even see the calcified tracks from a cart that was found in the vicinity.

Pompeii

Famously destroyed by Vesuvius in 79 AD, **POMPEII** was a much larger town than Herculaneum and one of Roman Campania's most important commercial centres. After a spell as a Greek colony, Pompeii came under the sway of the Romans in 200 BC, later functioning as both a moneyed resort for wealthy patricians and a trading town that exported wine and fish products, notably its own brand of fish sauce. A severe earthquake destroyed much of the city in 63 AD, and the eruption of Vesuvius sixteen years later only served to exacerbate what was already a desperate situation.

The site

Daily: April–Oct 8.30am–7.30pm, last entry 6pm; Nov–March 8.30am–5pm, last entry 3.30pm • €11; €20 for 5 sites including Herculaneum, Oplontis, Stabiae and Boscoreale (valid for 3 days); audio guides €6.50 • ☏ 081 857 5347, ⓦ pompeiisites.org

The **site** of Pompeii covers a huge area, and seeing it properly takes half a day at the very least; really you should devote most of a day to it and take plenty of breaks – unlike Herculaneum there's little shade, and the distances involved are quite large: comfortable shoes are a must. There is a **bar-restaurant** on site for when you really flag, but the best thing to do is to bring lots of supplies, including a picnic lunch. Early morning is best on hot days, although usually a sea breeze picks up about 3pm or so.

All of this makes Pompeii sound a bit of a chore – which it certainly isn't. But there is a lot to see, and you should be reasonably selective: many of the streets aren't lined by much more than foundations. Look for the site map, which you'll find at every entrance. To see as much as possible you could take a tour (around €10 per person), although one of the pleasures of Pompeii is to escape the hordes (some 2.5 million visitors a year or five thousand a day) and absorb the strangely still quality of the town, which, despite the large number of visitors, is quite possible.

As regards a **route**, there are two main entrances to Pompeii: Porta Marina, right by the Pompeii-Scavi-Villa dei Misteri Circumvesuviana station, and Piazza Anfiteatro, on the other side of the site in modern Pompei. You can take either, but given its proximity to the station where you'll most likely arrive, the Porta Marina entrance makes most sense and is the way we've written our account – from west to east, with a side trip to the **Villa dei Misteri** at the end.

AUGUST 24, 79 AD: THE END OF POMPEII

Vesuvius had been spouting smoke and ash for several days before the eruption and in fact most of Pompeii had already been evacuated when disaster struck: out of a total population of twenty thousand it's thought that only two thousand actually perished, asphyxiated by the toxic fumes, scorched by thermal blasts, or buried under metres of volcanic ash and pumice.

Pliny, the Roman naturalist, was one of the casualties – he died at nearby Stabiae (now Castellammare). His nephew, Pliny the Younger, described the full horror of the scene in two vivid letters to the historian Tacitus, who was compiling a history of the disaster, writing that the sky turned dark like "a room when it is shut up, and the lamp put out".

In effect the eruption froze the way of life in Pompeii as it stood at the time – a way of life that subsequent excavations have revealed in precise and remarkable detail. Indeed Pompeii has yielded more information about the ordinary life of Roman citizens during the imperial era than any other site: its social conventions, class structure, domestic arrangements and its (very high) standard of living. Some of the buildings are even covered with ancient graffiti, either referring to contemporary political events or simply to the romantic entanglements of the inhabitants. The full horror of their deaths is apparent in plaster casts made from the shapes their bodies left in the volcanic ash – with faces tortured with agony, or shielding themselves from the dust and ash.

The first parts of the town were discovered in 1600, but it wasn't until 1748 that **excavations** began, continuing more or less through to the present day. Indeed, exciting discoveries are still being made. New funds have been dedicated to excavating a further fifty acres of the site, and this may reveal whether or not survivors attempted to resettle Pompeii after the eruption. A privately funded excavation some years ago revealed a covered heated swimming pool, whose erotic wall paintings were deemed by the Vatican to be unsuitable for children. And, in a further development, a luxury "hotel" complex was uncovered in 2000 during the widening of an *autostrada*, slabs of stacked cut marble suggesting it was still under construction when Vesuvius erupted.

Bear in mind that most of the best mosaics and murals (from Herculaneum too) are in Naples. You can only see a small proportion of the finds *in situ*, and to comprehend their sheer variety and richness, as well as the lifestyles of the residents of the ancient city, you should definitely make a visit to Naples' Museo Archeologico Nazionale (see p.67).

The western sector: from the Forum to the House of Caccia Antica

Entering the site from the western, Pompeii-Villa dei Misteri side, through the Porta Marina, the first real feature of significance is the **Forum**, a long, slim open space surrounded by the ruins of what would have been some of the town's most important official buildings – a basilica, temples and a market hall. The rectangle of huge column slabs on the right of the site entrance marks the **basilica**, a courtroom basically, where the judges would sit at the far, still-columned end, in front of the only bit of wall that survives. At the opposite end of the Forum, steps lead up what would have been a **Temple of Jupiter**, on the left of which are literally hundreds of amphorae recovered from the site, along with some examples of the calcified bodies for which Pompeii is famous. Walking north from here takes you towards some of the town's more luxurious houses. The **House of Pansa** is a large villa around two courtyards, the second of which has most of its columns intact. Turn left out of here and you reach the **House of the Tragic Poet**, named after its mosaics of a theatrical production and a poet inside, though the "Cave Canem" (Beware of the Dog) mosaic by the main entrance is more eye-catching; it also has a pretty courtyard and some painting fragments, accessible by way of an entrance on the side street. Next door, there's the **Thermopolium Caupona**, a tavern where you would have chosen and purchased what you wanted at the counter and eaten it at tables in the back. Further along the same street the residents of the **House of the Faun**, the largest house in Pompeii, had a friendlier "*Ave*" (Welcome) mosaic outside their house, beckoning you in to view the atrium and the copy of a tiny, bronze, dancing faun (the original is in Naples) that gives the villa its name, not to mention the extensive garden behind. Here, too, you can see a copy of the damaged mosaic of Alexander the Great in battle (the original is in Naples' Museo Archeologico

▲ Sorrento

POMPEII

■ ACCOMMODATION
Camping Pompei 2
Camping Zeus 1

0   200
metres

N

Pompei-Santuario Station

Pompei FS Station

VIA DUCA D'AOSTA

VIA PIAVE

PIAZZA BARTOLO LONGO

VIA SACRA

VIA SAN GIUSEPPE

PIAZZA SCHETTINI

Santuario della Beata Vergine del Rosario

VIA ROMA

VIA VITTORIO EMANUELE

VIA NOLANA

VIALE GIUSEPPE MAZZINI

VIA COLLE SAN BARTOLOMEO

PIAZZA ANFITEATRO

PIAZZA IMMACOLATA

Porta di Sarno

Amphitheatre

House of Venus in a Shell

Palestra Grande

Porta di Nocera

VIA DI NOCERA

VIA ALTEATRI

VIA PLINIO

House of Octavius Quartio

SCAVI DI POMPEII

Thermopolium of Vetutius Placidus

House of the Celi

House of Menander

Lararium of Achilles

House of Asclepius

Little Theatre

Quadroporticus dei Teatri

Porta di Stabia

Fullonica Stephani

House of the Cithara Player

Temple of Isis

Grand Theatre

VIA DELL'ABBONDANZA

Porta di Capua

House of the Golden Cupids

Stabian Baths

VIA STABIANA

VIA DI NOLA

Sammite Palestra

Doric Temple

VIA DEI TEATRI

TRIANGULAR FORUM

VIA ALTEATRI

VIA PLINIO

House of Caccia Antica

Brothel

Porta di Vesuvio

House of the Vettii

House of the Dioscuri

House of the Faun

Thermopolium Caupona

VIA DI MERCURIO

VICOLO DEL TORNO

VICOLO DEL FAUNO

VICOLO DEL MERCURIO

VICOLO DI VESUVIO

Cafeteria

Temple of Jupiter

FORUM

Temple of Apollo

Basilica

Porta Marina

VIA MARINA

House of the Tragic Poet

House of Pansa

VIA DELLA FORTUNA

Porta Ercolano

Pompei-Scavi-Villa dei Misteri Station

VIA VILLA DEI MISTERI

Villa dei Misteri

AUTOSTRADA NAPOLI-SALERNO

A3

E45

SS18

2

VIALE ALTEATRI

● RESTAURANTS & CAFÉS
De Vivo 1
Il Principe 2
Todisco 3

▼ Napoli

Nazionale), where it was found. A bit further down, on the opposite side of the street, the **House of Caccia Antica**, has paintings of hunting scenes among others around its main courtyard, as well as a round sunken bath in the columned courtyard behind.

The western sector: from the House of the Dioscuri to the House of the Golden Cupids

On the street behind the **House of the Faun** (there's an exit at the back), the **House of the Dioscuri** is another grand place, with a large atrium, where many more of the paintings now in Naples were unearthed. On the same street in the opposite direction, the **House of the Vettii** is one of the most delightful and best maintained villas in Pompeii, a merchant's house ranged around a lovely central peristyle that gives a good impression of the domestic environment of the city's upper middle classes. The first room on the right off the peristyle holds some of the best Pompeii murals actually viewable on site: the one on the left shows the young Hercules struggling with serpents; another, in the corner, depicts Ixion tied to a wheel after offending Zeus, while a third shows Dirce being dragged to her death by the bull set on her by the sons of Antiope. There are more paintings beyond here, through the villa's kitchen in a small room that's normally kept locked – erotic works showing various techniques of lovemaking (Greek-style, woman on top; Roman-style, man on top) together with an absurdly potent-looking statue of Priapus from which women were supposed to drink to be fertile; phallic symbols were also, it's reckoned, believed to ward off the evil eye. Along the street from here, on the next block, the **House of the Golden Cupids** holds a wall painting of Jason, just about to depart on his quest to find the golden fleece, as well as lots of other paintings, both decorative and figurative, and a very pleasant garden.

3

The eastern sector: Via dell'Abbondanza and Via del Teatro

Cross over to the other side of the site for the so-called **new excavations**, which began in 1911 and actually uncovered some of the town's most important quarters, stretching along and beyond the main **Via dell'Abbondanza**. On the corner of Via dell'Abbondanza, the **Stabian Baths** is Pompeii's oldest baths complex, with a still partially arcaded courtyard and various other bath interiors, all remarkably intact, with excellently preserved stucco work on the barrel-vaulted ceilings, and more calcified unfortunates in their perpetual death throes, their togas and sandals clearly discernible.

Just behind the baths, and perhaps appropriately situated down a small side street called Vicolo Lupanare, is the town's principal **brothel**, the *lupanare*. Whereas most brothels required membership, this one was open to anyone in search of a *lupa* (prostitute or "she-wolf"). The walls inside show the graffiti of some 150 customers and about an equal number of workers, and above each doorway a fresco illustrates the prostitute's speciality, presumably performed inside the room on the stone bed – shorter in length than a modern bed but long enough to permit the promised activity. Back in front of the baths, take Via dei Teatri south off Via dell'Abbondanza to a relatively peaceful part of the site, where a columned portico gives way to the **Triangular Forum**, which opens out to the steps of a very ruined **Doric Temple**, originally from the sixth century BC, and beyond that to what would have been a lovely small circular temple around an ancient well. Immediately below the Triangular Forum is the small, grassy, column-fringed square of the **Quadroporticus dei Teatri** – a refectory and meeting place for spectators from the nearby **Grand Theatre**, which is very well preserved and still used for performances. Walk around to the far side of the Grand Theatre, down the steps and up again, and you're in front of the **Little Theatre** – a smaller, more intimate venue also still used for summer performances and with a better-kept corridor behind the stage space.

On the corner, beyond this complex of buildings, there's a small **Temple of Asclepius**, with a short flight of steps leading up to a central podium, and a slightly more intact **Temple of Isis** next door. Follow the road east from here and you're in front of the **House of the Ceii**, on the left, where there's a painting of a hunting scene showing wild boar and other animals in one of the rooms behind the main courtyard. Opposite, the **House of Menander** is one of the most complete of Pompeii's large villas, with a small atrium in the front and a large, columned one behind, and wonderful paintings, including one of the Greek dramatist from which the house takes its name.

The eastern sector: Via dell'Abbondanza to the Amphitheatre

Back on Via dell'Abbondanza, the **Lararium of Achilles** has a niche with a delicate relief depicting scenes from the Trojan War – tiny figures, showing Achilles and Hector doing battle; like so much else here, it's amazing they have survived. Next door, the **Fullonica Stephani** is a well-preserved laundry, with a large tiered tub for washing, while the **House of the Cithara Player**, a few steps back in towards Porta Marina, is a vast complex on several levels with a number of leafy courtyards that for some reason are often devoid of other visitors – you could spend quite a while poking around here. Further east, past the well-preserved shop counter and mural of the **Thermopolium of Vetutius Placidus**, stop off at the **House of Octavius Quartio**, a gracious villa fronted by great bronze doors. Paintings of Narcissus gazing rapt at his reflection, and of Pyramus and Thisbe frame a water cascade in the back, where once water flowed down a channel and into the villa's lovely garden, which has been replanted with vines and shrubs. Roughly opposite here, the so-called **House of the Chaste Lovers** is currently under excavation, and you can watch the archeologists at work from a series of walkways, while next door, the **House of Venus in a Shell** is of interest for its pretty courtyard with one of the site's best-preserved paintings on its back wall, showing Venus reclining in a giant floating clam shell surrounded by cupids, as well as little architectural studies around the main courtyard.

Make a right turn from here to the **Amphitheatre**, one of Italy's most intact and accessible, and also its oldest, dating from 80 BC. It once had room for a crowd of some twelve thousand – well over half the town's population. Next door, the **Palestra Grande** is a vast parade ground that was used by Pompeii's youth for sport and exercise – still with its square of swimming pool in the centre. It must have been in use when the eruption struck Pompeii, since its southeast corner was found littered with the skeletons of young men trying to flee the disaster.

Villa dei Misteri

One last sight you shouldn't miss at Pompeii is the **Villa dei Misteri**, a suburban mansion that is probably the best preserved of all Pompeii's palatial houses. Located half a kilometre from the Pompeii-Villa dei Misteri station or just outside the Porto Ercolano exit from the site, it's an originally third-century BC structure with a warren of rooms and courtyards that derives its name from a series of paintings in one of its larger chambers: depictions of the initiation rites of a young woman into the Dionysiac Mysteries, an outlawed cult of the early imperial era. Not much is known about the cult itself, but the paintings, set on a vivid red background, are marvellously clear, beautifully executed and still bright in tone and colour. They follow a narrative, starting with the left-hand wall and continuing around the room with a series that shows sacrifice, flagellation, dancing and mysterious rituals, all under the serene gaze of the mistress of the house.

ARRIVAL AND DEPARTURE   **POMPEII**

By train You can take the Circumvesuviana from Naples to Pompei-Scavi-Villa dei Misteri, a 40min journey, which leaves you right outside the western, Porta Marina entrance to the site; left-luggage facilities are available at the station and at the entrance. Alternatively, take the roughly hourly mainline train (direction Salerno) to the main Pompei FS station, on the south side of the modern town; this is only a better bet if you want to enter the site from the opposite side or you are staying in modern

Pompei. From the FS station, it's around a 10min-walk to the site. Finally, central Pompei also has a stop on the Poggiomarino/Sarno branch of the Circumvesuviana line, Pompei-Santuario, which is just one stop from Boscoreale and three from Torre Annunziata, making it useful if you're combining a trip to Pompeii with Oplontis or Boscoreale.

By car To reach Pompeii from the A3 *autostrada*, heading south, exit at Pompei Ovest; heading north toward Naples, exit at Pompei Est.

INFORMATION

Tourist office Via Sacra 1, just off Modern Pompeii's main square (Mon–Sat 9am–6pm; ☎ 081 850 7255). Has maps of the site, town plans and details of accommodation.

ACCOMMODATION

Most people visit Pompeii on day-trips from Naples or Sorrento, but in case you want to make the town an overnight stop, there are plenty of hotels and a couple of convenient campsites, one of which offers rooms.

Camping Pompei Via Plinio 113, south of the main entrance ☎ 081 862 2882, ⓦ campingpompei.com. Well placed for exploring Pompeii and a decent enough camping and caravan site, with self-catering bungalows and villas for rent too. Camping (add €4 for each additional person) **€11.50**, caravan plots **€7.50**, bungalows for two **€40**, villas for 4 **€65**

Camping Zeus Via Villa dei Misteri 3 ☎ 081 861 5320, ⓦ campingzeus.it. Right by Porta Ercolano and very handy for excursions to Vesuvius (see p.118), this complex has shady pitches for tents, a number of basic rooms and more luxurious hotel-style en suites, along with a restaurant and café. Camping (add €5 for each additional person) **€10**, caravan plots **€7**, basic doubles **€40**, en-suite doubles **€70**

EATING AND DRINKING

De Vivo Via Roma 38/42 ☎ 081 863 1163, ⓦ lapasticceriadevivo.it. Close by the Anfiteatro entrance to the Pompeii site, this long-established café is perfect for a coffee, pastry or *gelato*, with a few seats outside and a bright airy interior. Daily 6am–midnight.

Il Principe Piazza Bartolo Longo 8 ☎ 081 850 5566, ⓦ ilprincipe.com. Conveniently located on the corner of the town's main square, this place is one of Pompeii's top restaurants, serving a moderately priced menu of exquisite dishes based on ancient Roman recipes. Pasta *primi* start at around €12, main courses go for €16–20. The cheaper wine bar serves up equally good food in a more relaxed environment with outside tables. Tues–Sun noon–3pm & 7–11pm.

★**Todisco** Piazzale Schettini 19 ☎ 081 850 5051. Situated across a scruffy square from the tourist office, cheap and very cheerful self-service *tavola calda* dishes up great food – lovely stuffed aubergines and zucchini, fresh, succulent balls of mozzarella, roast chicken and pork, tasty chunks of polenta and various salads and veggie dishes. Perhaps the best place for lunch in central Pompei, and very affordably priced. Daily noon–4pm & 7–10pm.

Castellammare di Stabia and around

By the time you reach **CASTELLAMMARE DI STABIA**, a few kilometres further around the bay, the urban shadow of Naples has started to lift a little, though the cranes and containers of its portside areas don't make you any more likely to want to stop. There are, however, a couple of reasons to jump off the Circumvesuviana: a minor and relatively under-visited ancient site, **Stabiae**, which is perhaps the best choice after Pompeii and Herculaneum, and, if it is running again, the cable-car trip to nearby **Monte Faito**.

Stabiae

Daily: April–Oct 8.30am–7.30pm; Nov–March 8.30am–5pm • €5.50, includes Boscoreale & Oplontis; €20 for 5 sites including Pompeii, Herculaneum, Stabiae and Boscoreale (valid for 3 days) • ☎ 081 857 5347, ⓦ pompeiisites.org • Bus #1 runs to Stabiae from outside Castellamare di Stabia Circumvesuviana station, or it's a 10min walk to Villa Arianna and a further 10min to Villa Marcos

The best-known attraction of Castellammare itself is the site of **Stabiae**, a grouping of ancient villas located in the hills above the modern town. Stabiae was a seaside resort in 79 AD, and a wealthy one at that, before being buried like everything else under Vesuvius's hot ash – the most famous victim was the Roman historian Pliny the Elder, who set out from the naval port of Misenum across the bay to better observe the eruption, and just managed to make it here, only to die of a heart attack (see box, p.123). The villas were in fact discovered and partially excavated earlier than Pompeii, in the mid-eighteenth century, but they soon lost out to the larger and more alluring digs nearby and fell into relative obscurity. Certainly there is less to visit, but at Stabiae you're getting a peak at the lifestyles of the super-rich.

Villa Arianna

Bus #1 from the Circumvesuviana station, or to walk (10min) turn right out of the station and follow the road to the end. Turn right and walk up the hill for 100m, and then cross the road and take the small road that doubles back up the hillside. Villa Arianna is on the left after 200m.

Of the villas, the closest to Castellammare station is Villa Arianna, a sprawling complex of buildings, with a large courtyard on the landward side and a series of rooms opening out onto a terrace, with mosaic floors still pretty much intact and fragments of wall paintings, one of which depicts Ariadne – hence the villa's name – being rescued by Dionysus. There's a kitchen area with an enclosed pool for keeping fish and a large central atrium with more fresco fragments. Best of all though are the views, as magnificent as those originally described by Pliny the Elder when he wrote about the rich resort of Stabiae. Ironically it was here that he died, while attempting to rescue friends from the 79AD eruption, having uttered the memorable lines, "Fortune favours the brave".

Villa San Marco

From Villa Arianna, Villa San Marco is around 800m further down the main road, on the left (10min). From here you can walk 1km to Via Nocera station on the same line, saving yourself the walk back.

Villa San Marco is an even larger and grander affair than Villa Arianna, and includes an imposing internal atrium, complete with mosaic floor and central pillars, and a bath complex built around a small atrium with a plunge pool. Perhaps most impressive is the large open courtyard flanked by columns and a series of *dietae* or "leisure rooms", decorated in Fourth Pompeiian Style with frescoes of Perseus and Iphygenia and other tranquil figures, including a delightful young girl on a swing. Best again, though, are the views across the Bay of Naples, which more than anything else tell us what it meant to be rich and Roman in 79 AD.

Vico Equense

The small resort town of **Vico Equense** marks the end of Naples' urban sprawl and the beginning of the brighter, lighter, more pleasure-driven delights of the Sorrentine peninsula. Down at the bottom of a winding road there are a couple of stretches of sandy **beach** here to keep you occupied. In the main part of 129), but that's not Vico's only foodie attraction: its *provolone del monaco* goat's cheese, soaked in brine, dried, then aged 4–18 months, is delicious, as is *riavulillo* – smoked *scarmorza* or *caciocavalino* cheese that has been stuffed with black olives and *peperoncino* (hot chilli peppers).

ARRIVAL AND DEPARTURE   CASTELLAMMARE AND AROUND

By train Castellammare and Vico Equense are both on the main Naples to Sorrento Circumvesuviana railway line; their stops are just 5min apart.

ACCOMMODATION

Capo la Gala Via Luigi Serio 8, Vico Equense ☎ 081 807 5758, ⓦ hotelcapolagala.com. Jutting out from boulders above the sea, this elegant hotel doesn't have thermal waters, so it created an aquarium spa with a heated seawater pool. Rooms are bright and contemporary, and continue the blue sea theme. Its *Maxi* restaurant (open Tues–Sun) earned a Michelin star in 2009 for chef Danilo Di Vuolo's imaginative updates of Neapolitan cuisine, including menus for vegetarians and children. **€350**

Sant'Angelo Piazzale dei Capi, Monte Faito ☎ 081 879 3042, ⓦ santangelofaito.it. A short walk from the Monte Faito *funivia* station, this is a lovely place to stay, with a fresh, Swiss chalet-style feel, pleasant rooms and a good

restaurant. It's perfectly placed for the hike down to Positano the next day. **€60**

Vesuvian Institute Via Salario, Castellammare di Stabia 12 ☎ 081 871 7114, ⓦ vesuvianinstitute.it. This much-renovated former convent on the hillside now houses the *Vesuvian Institute*, which organizes educational trips to the ancient sites of the bay. The hotel has almost 100 rooms, and the views are lovely, plus there's a restaurant and bar on the premises. The Institute runs tours of Stabiae and makes a good base for exploring other sites like Pompeii and Herculaneum. Open all year. **€100**

Villa Giusso Astapiana Via Camaldoli 51, Vico Equense ☎ 081 802 4392. This former monastery was a place of

WALKS FROM MONTE FAITO

At 1100m, **Monte Faito** is the highest peak on the Sorrentine peninsula and provides a bucolic and delightful escape from the congestion below, along with access to a whole host of **walking opportunities**, including a route on foot down to Positano and the Amalfi Coast. Unfortunately the cable car or *funivia* which would normally whisk you to the top was closed at the time of writing, but due to open again in 2015. It runs from the station next door to the Circumvesuviana station. The journey takes just eight minutes, and, even though it's maybe not for those of a delicate disposition, is worth doing for itself, giving as it does increasingly stupendous views of the bay. At the top, there are a couple of bars selling drinks and sandwiches and, if you really can't face the trip back down, there's a bus stop nearby. If the *funivia* is still closed, then you can take a bus to the top of Monte Faito from Vico Equense station, and from Sorrento there's a shuttle service run by Sorrento Shuttle (Ⓦ sorrentoshuttle .com). From the *funivia* station at the **summit**, paths lead off in two main directions: if you're feeling lazy you can take the one off to the right (west), which in a short while descends to Piazzale dei Capi and the *Sant'Angelo* hotel (see p.128), walkable in about fifteen minutes or so. You can have a drink or eat lunch in the hotel's restaurant, which has views right up the coast to Sorrento and across the peninsula to the Bay of Salerno. Outside of high season at least, a more peaceful or airy spot you couldn't hope to find.

Walking in the opposite direction from the *funivia* station, it's more of a hike to the **Santuario San Michele**, at 1278m the second-highest spot on the mountain. The sanctuary is a small chapel built on the site of a tenth-century original, and the walk there takes around ninety minutes; taxis go there too, for €10 a head, and the panorama over the bay once you're there is magnificent. Beyond the sanctuary, a path climbs steeply up to Monte Faito's highest point at 1444m, **Monte San Michele**, where the view takes in everything on both sides of the peninsula from Naples to Salerno. This leg takes about another hour, and you'll know when you're more than halfway there when you pass the **Sorgente dell'Acqua Santa** spring, which has gushed forth in its little grotto ever since St Michael blessed it with his sword.

Walking from the *funivia* station to Monte Faito's summit at Monte San Michele and back is a good day's hike, stopping for a picnic on the way. But if you're feeling particularly energetic, and are suitably prepared, you could trace your steps back a short way from the summit and pick up the main path all the way to **Monte Pertuso** or **Santa Maria al Castello**, each a signposted two-hour walk away up above the Amalfi Coast, and from there down to **Positano** – a further hour or so's descent.

3

meditation for Camaldalese monks until 1807, when Napoleon's rule suppressed the order. It is still in the family of the duke that purchased it soon after, and beautiful family antiques furnish the public areas and ten guest rooms. It's back in the hills above an olive grove and vineyards, with a stone terrace that is perfect for enjoying the view of the bay and the Sorrento coast. Breakfast and dinner are served in the original kitchen, decorated with Vietri ceramics. **€100**

EATING AND DRINKING

Antica Osteria Nonna Rosa Via Privata Bonea 4 Loc. Pietrapiano, Vico Equense ☎ 081 879 9055, Ⓦ osteria nonnarosa.it. Sophisticated and imaginative dishes, beautifully presented but often using humble local ingredients and complemented by a fine range of Campanian wines. Try the fish soup with lemon and camomile, spaghetti with anchovies and pecorino, or ravioli filled with cheese and topped with pear sauce. Moderate to high prices – starters €16–20, mains €20–30, or try the €70 tasting menu for a really memorable dining experience. Daily for dinner only.

★ **Da Gigino** Via Nicotera 15, Vico Equense ☎ 081 879 8309. The birthplace of "pizza by the metre" is probably Vico's most famous attraction, a giant restaurant that buzzes with people who have come from far and wide to eat pizza, sliced by the length you wish to eat. There are other dishes too, and it's inexpensive and generally excellent. Prices start at €28 for a metre of pizza, pasta dishes are €8 upwards and regular *secondi* cost €10–15. Follow the main road out of the harbour to the main square/roundabout, turn left and then left again and it's right there. Open daily for lunch and dinner.

★ **La Torre del Saracino** Via Torretta 9 Loc. Marina d'Aequa, Vico Equense ☎ 081 802 8555, Ⓦ torredel saracino.it. A little way west of Vico Equense, with a beautiful setting in a watchtower, you get both atmosphere and gourmet food at Gennaro Esposito's restaurant – one of the best fine dining experiences around. Not cheap, though; tasting menus go for €110–150. Tues–Sat 12.45–2.30pm & 7.45–10.30pm, Sun 12.45–2.30pm.

Sorrento and its peninsula

VIEW FROM SORRENTO

Sorrento and its peninsula

Topping the rocky cliffs close to the end of its peninsula, Sorrento is solely and unashamedly a resort, its inspired location and mild climate drawing foreigners from all over Europe for close on two hundred years. Ibsen wrote part of *Peer Gynt* in Sorrento, Wagner and Nietzsche had a well-publicized row here, and Maxim Gorky lived for over a decade in the town. Nowadays it's strictly package-tour territory, but really none the worse for it, a bright, lively place that retains its southern Italian roots and celebrates the art of doing nothing much in particular – with lots of streets to aimlessly stroll and views to admire. It's not hard to find decent and affordable restaurants too, or, if you know where to look, reasonably priced accommodation, making this an excellent, easy and economical base from which to explore the rugged Sorrento peninsula, the islands of the bay and even parts of the Amalfi Coast. Indeed, if you're after an Italian seaside holiday, with a bit of walking, some ancient Roman sites, and maybe even a bit of urban life thrown in, it's hard to beat.

Sorrento and around

Built around a deep gorge that cuts through the town, and perched on the top of high cliffs, **SORRENTO** is a place to enjoy more for its dramatic location than for specific sights. It's one of southern Italy's premier and most attractive resort towns, a bright and breezy place that is more or less given over entirely to the pursuit of pleasure – an activity that is very, very easy here. Not only is it pleasant to wander the small grid of streets that make up its **old town**, Sorrento also makes a great base for nearby beaches and walks in the countryside, and has long been popular with British and American tourists in particular.

East along the bay, the town's ribbon of settlement blends almost seamlessly into a number of coastal villages – Sant'Agnello, Piano di Sorrento and Meta – whose small and densely populated centres are skirted by the main coast road. This is all many travellers see of them, though there are one or two things that might draw you here from Sorrento, not least some marginally better beaches.

The old town

Sorrento sprawls into its neighbouring villages in both direction, but at its heart is the tight-knit grid of streets that makes up its **old town**, anchored by Piazza Tasso and Via Capo at each end, and nestled between Corso Italia and the sea. Most of the area is pedestrianized and the streets lined with restaurants, cafés and shops selling tourist gear, souvenirs and *limoncello*. Right in the centre of the old town, the arched **Sedile Dominova** at the junction of Via San Cesareo and Via Giuliani, a seventeenth-century loggia that was once the meeting place of local nobles and now a veteran's club, is a historical focal point. From here you can stroll down to the shady gardens of the **Villa**

Walks from Sorrento p.142   Best spots for a swim p.143

CORAL, PUNTA CAMPANELLA MARINE RESERVE

Highlights

❶ **Sorrento** The Bay of Naples' archetypal seaside town – the perfect quick escape from Naples and a great complement to nearby Pompeii and Herculaneum as well as the Amalfi Coast. **See p.132**

❷ **Marina del Cantone** A pleasant beach village in a great location, with a tempting array of marvellous restaurants too. **See p.143**

❸ **Punta Campanella** This protected marine reserve has the coastal area's best dive sites. **See p.143**

❹ **Sant'Agata sui Due Golfi** Come up here for the unsurpassed views and to eat at its legendary restaurant. **See p.143**

HIGHLIGHTS ARE MARKED ON THE MAP ON P.134

Comunale (daily: April–Oct 7.30am–midnight; Nov–March 7.30am–8pm; free), whose terrace has lovely views out to sea. There's a lift as well as a path down to the town's main beach from here (see p.137). Off to the right, the small thirteenth-century cloister of the church of **San Francesco**, planted with vines and bright bougainvillea, is a peaceful escape from the bustle of the rest of Sorrento, while the triangular square beyond, Piazza Sant'Antonino, is named after the town's patron saint, a seventh-century hermit who lived in a nearby grotto. The basilica of **Sant'Antonino**, on the far side of the square, is the town's most frequented place of worship, with a crypt full of votive offerings with a nautical theme.

Piazza Tasso
Piazza Tasso is the effective centre of Sorrento, sitting astride the gorge and named after the wayward sixteenth-century Italian poet to whom the town was home. It has a statue of Tasso in the far corner, while on the opposite side of the square the church of **Santa Maria del Carmine** is an eighteenth-century confection, of little interest except on the saint's feast day of July 16, when fireworks light up the facade and there's music and carousing on the square.

Corso Italia
Piazza Tasso is about midway down Sorrento's main artery of **Corso Italia**, which runs from beyond the train station to the far eastern edge of town. It's a busy commercial thoroughfare, lined with some of the best of Sorrento's shops, and is pedestrianized every evening after 7pm for the lively *passeggiata*. There's a small-scale historical attraction too, the **Bastioni di Parsano**, between Corso Italia and Via degli Aranci (daily 10am–1pm & 7–11pm; free), where you can walk around a small section of the town's originally Roman walls – most interesting at night when they are all lit up.

The Cattedrale
Corso Italia 1 • Daily 8am–12.30pm & 4.30–9pm • Free
Halfway down Corso Italia on the left, Sorrento's **Cattedrale di San Filippo e Giacomo** has been much rebuilt, and the real challenge of its gaudy interior is how to tell the fake marble from the real. The bishop's throne, on the main aisle, is certainly genuine, dating from the late sixteenth century, as are the inlaid wood scenes on the main doors and choir stalls, which add a proper Sorrentine touch. Take a look also at the large *presepio* nativity scene just inside the main doors, and the chapel in the left aisle, which is dedicated to San Giuseppe Moscati – a Neapolitan doctor who died in 1927 and is venerated in Naples' Gesù church (see p.55).

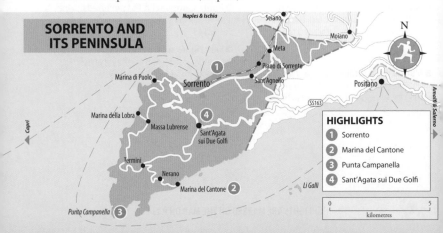

Villa Fiorentino
Corso Italia 59 • Daily 10.30am–1pm & 6–10pm • Free

Just past the cathedral on Corso Italia, the grand white *palazzo* of **Villa Fiorentino** was built for a wealthy local family in 1935. During World War II it was used as a base by General Clark and the US army – an American connection that was continued after the war, with regular visits by the likes of the Rockefellers, Vanderbilts and various New York dignitaries. Subsequently bequeathed to the city, it now hosts a small art gallery that puts on regular temporary exhibitions, while the gardens – with a children's playground – are lovely.

Museo Bottega della Tarsialignea
Via San Nicola 28 • Daily 10am–6.30pm • €8

Appropriately housed in an ancient mansion in the artisanal quarter of the old town, the **Museo Bottega della Tarsialignea** is a shrine to the traditional Sorrentine craft of *intarsio* – inlaid woodwork basically, using different types of wood to decorate furniture and other items with patterns or pictures.

Intarsio work has been around since the 1500s, and is a real craft, although inevitably Sorrento is packed with shops selling not particularly distinguished examples. But don't let the tourist tat put you off: the ground floor of the museum has stylish examples of contemporary local *intarsio* for sale (at a price), while upstairs are works by Sorrento's late nineteenth-century *intarsio* greats – Luigi Gargiulo, Michele Grandville and Giuseppe Gargiulo – beautiful if sometimes overwrought.

Museo Correale di Terranova
Via Correale 50 • Tues–Sat 9.30am–6.30pm, Sun 9.30am–1.30pm • €8

The one sight in Sorrento you probably shouldn't miss is the town's excellent civic museum, the **Museo Correale di Terranova** – though perhaps its greatest charm is the building itself, an aristocratic villa set in a tranquil garden, with a series of lovely views unfolding over orange and lemon groves as you climb its grand staircase.

The museum is home to various Roman finds – busts, sarcophagi, domestic bits and pieces, inscriptions – and, as you might expect, examples of local *intarsio* work, perhaps most notably a fantastic seventeenth-century ebony and ivory inlaid comic strip of Tasso's *Gerusalemme Liberata*. Plenty of paintings by local artists are on display, one of them by the nineteenth-century Meta-born maritime artist Eduardo de Martino, who lived and died in London and was a favourite of Queen Victoria, while upstairs you'll find canvases by seventeenth-century Neapolitan artists, including Andrea Vaccaro and Giovanni Lanfranco, alongside ancient editions of works by Tasso and the poet's death mask. Perhaps the best artwork of them all is the late eighteenth-century roulette game, *Il Biri Bisso*, painted on wood by one Francesco Celebrano (see p.55), which hangs alongside landscapes by relocated eighteenth-century Dutch and Flemish artists who were more inspired here than they were at home – they're worth looking at just to see how much has changed hereabouts. Finally, the attic floor has ceramics, a handful of presepe figures and marvellous views over the entire Bay of Naples from its picture window.

Giardini di Cafaldo
Via Correale 27 • Daily: April–Sept 9am–9pm; Oct–March 9am–6.30pm

Virtually opposite the Museo Correale, the **Giardini di Cafaldo** is a nice place to unwind, an orange and lemon grove cut through with paths, where you can taste and buy delicious home-produced lemon liqueurs at the small outdoor café. They also have a shop on the main road.

4

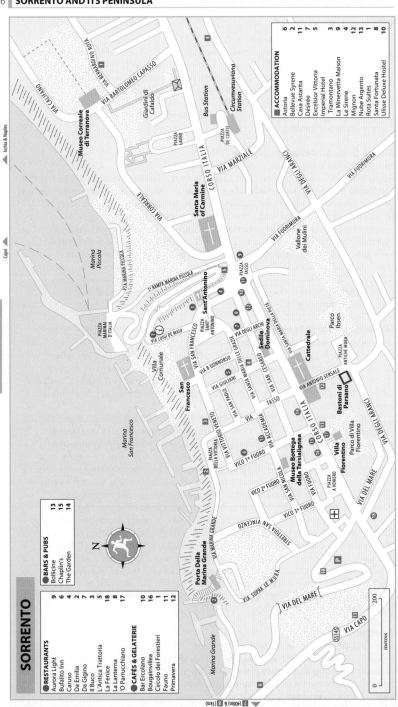

SORRENTO

● RESTAURANTS

Aurora Light	9
Bufalito Inn	6
Caruso	4
Da Emilia	2
Da Gigino	7
Il Buco	3
L'Antica Trattoria	5
La Fenice	18
La Lanterna	8
'O Parrucchiano	17

● CAFÉS & GELATERIE

Bar Ercolano	10
Bougainvillea	16
Circolo dei Forestieri	1
Fauno	11
Primavera	12

● BARS & PUBS

Bollicine	13
Chaplin's	15
The Garden	14

▮ ACCOMMODATION

Astoria	6
Bellevue Syrene	2
Casa Astarita	11
Désirée	5
Excelsior Vittoria	3
Imperial Hotel	7
Tramontano	3
La Minervetta Maison	9
Le Sirene	4
Mignon	12
Nube Argento	13
Rota Suites	1
Santa Fortunata	8
Ulisse Deluxe Hostel	10

The beaches

Strange as it may seem, Sorrento isn't particularly well provided with **beaches**. In the town itself there are several small sandy strips of lido at the **Marina San Francesco** (a couple of which are free while the others charge an entrance fee, usually around €10 including a sun bed), which are accessible from the Villa Comunale gardens by a path or by lift (€1), or from nearby **Marina Piccola** harbour. To get to Marina Piccola take the steps from *Il Buco* restaurant and then follow the steps that shadow Via Luigi di Maio to the bottom.

Alternatively there are the rocks and a tiny, crowded strip of sand (all free) at **Marina Grande**, Sorrento's pleasant fishing harbour, ten minutes' walk or a short bus ride west of Piazza Tasso. If you decide to walk, either follow the city walls from the end of Via San Nicola, or take the road that edges past the *Hotel Bellevue Syrene*, off the Villa Comunale; both end up at the same flight of steps that lead down to the east end of Marina Grande's beach, just above the *Da Emilia* restaurant.

Finally there is another small, stony **beach** a few hundred metres west of town below the *Tonnarella* and *Désirée* hotels – a good choice during the heat of the day as it is quite shady in the afternoon (€4 entry, plus sun beds, etc). Or you can always try the beaches further east, such as Marinella beach at Sant'Agnello (see below) and the strips of sand around Meta (see below), or the beaches to the west near Capo (see box, p.143).

Sant'Agnello di Sorrento

More or less a continuation of Sorrento proper, **SANT'AGNELLO** is the next village east, centred on the main Piazza Matteotti, where you'll find the train station. It's a five-minute walk from here to the sea at Punta San Francesco, where the **Marinella beach** has a nice strip of dark-grey sand that is reachable by lift from the promenade above (daily: May–Aug 7am–10pm; Sept–April 9am–6.30pm; €5 plus €1 for the lift and the usual extras for umbrellas and sunbeds).

Piano di Sorrento

Heading further east from Sorrento, **PIANO DI SORRENTO** has a cliff-top esplanade with beetling views from which a road zigzags down to the **Marina di Cassano**, a refreshingly workaday harbour with a short stretch of dark-grey sandy beach at each end. At the western end of the esplanade, **Villa Fondi** makes the most of its excellent location by hosting weddings, concerts and other functions in its lush gardens and sumptuous terraces. The small **Museo Georges Vallet** archeological collection is also housed here (Tues–Sun 9am–7pm; free), made up mostly of finds from the Sorrentine peninsula, including some beautiful marble reliefs from a seaside villa near Massa Lubrense, as well as a scale model of the now partially submerged Ruderi Villa Romana di Pollio at Capo di Sorrento (see p.143).

Meta

Occupying the far end of Sorrento's plain, before the road rises to bend around the cliffs of the peninsula, **META** has a long-standing nautical history and is known for both its shipbuilding industry and the sea captains it has provided to the Italian navy over the years, including the unfortunate Francesco Schettino, who notoriously steered the Costa Concordia onto the rocks off the coast of Tuscany in 2010. Meta is worth visiting for **Alimuri beach**, two decent-sized stretches of grey sand on a small spit sticking out from the high-sided cliffs of the bay. A lift can deliver you from the road above, or you can drive down to a small car park. A little further along, a few small stretches of beach, each with parking, are tucked right up against the cliff-face.

4

ARRIVAL AND DEPARTURE

By train Sorrento's train station is in the centre of town, a 5min walk from the main Piazza Tasso along busy Corso Italia. Most local buses and buses to the Amalfi Coast also leave from here. Sant'Agnello, Piano and Meta each have stops on the Circumvesuviana line.

By bus Blue SITA buses run to the bus station next to the

train station from Massa Lubrense, Sant'Agata, Termini, Nerano, Marina del Cantone, Positano and Amalfi. Buses also run from here to Naples' Capodochino airport.

By ferry Ferries to and from Capri, Ischia and Positano arrive and leave from the little harbour of Marina Piccola.

GETTING AROUND

By mini train You can walk pretty much everywhere in Sorrento, but if you want a bit of easy orientation, it's worth taking one of the mini train tours that leave every 35min from Piazza Tasso (daily 9am–midnight; €6, children €3); tours last about half an hour.

By bus There are several (orange) bus routes around the town and surrounding area, including line A between Meta, Piano, Sant'Agnello, Sorrento itself and out to Massa Lubrense; lines B and C from Meta to Piano,

Sant'Agnello, Sorrento train station, Piazza Tasso and Marina Piccola; and line D between Marina Grande and Piazza Tasso.

By scooter You can rent scooters and mopeds at Jolly Service & Rent, just outside the old town at Corso Italia 3 (☎ 081 878 2403) and also just off the eastern end of Corso Italia at Via degli Aranci 180 (☎ 081 877 3450) – ⓦ jollyrent.eu, though you're best off phoning or calling in. Rates start at €22/day, €185/week.

INFORMATION AND ACTIVITIES

Tourist office The main tourist office on Via Luigi de Maio 35, just off Piazza Sant'Antonino in the large yellow Circolo dei Forestieri building (July & Aug daily 8.30am–7pm, Sept–June Mon–Sat 8.30am–4.15pm; ☎ 081 807 4033, ⓦ sorrentotourism.com), has free maps and bus and ferry timetables, and information about excursions. During the summer info points are scattered around town, including just off Piazza Tasso, outside the train station and by the ferry ticket offices at Marina Piccola.

Tours City Sightseeing Sorrento & Amalfi Coast run

hop-on-hop-off trips every day between April and October around the town and main sights of the Sorrentine peninsula. Four tours a day leave from outside the train station and cost €12 per person for a ticket that is valid for 6 hours. The same company also runs hourly buses to Positano and Amalfi (€8 one way).

Diving Sorrento Diving Futuro Mare (Via Marina Piccola 63 ☎ 349 653 6323, ⓦ sorrentodiving.it), organizes dives for beginners and qualified divers at various spots around the bay, including the protected marine park of Punta Campanella (see p.143).

ACCOMMODATION

Sorrento has more **hotel** beds than anywhere else in the Bay of Naples, and you should have no problem finding somewhere to stay, though you'd be well advised to book ahead at any time of year to secure the best options. There are some truly splendid places to splurge, both in **Sorrento** itself and in next-door **Sant'Agnello** (see p.137) – grand places with fantastic views and venerable histories, as well as a couple of cool boutique alternatives – but there are decent **budget options** too, both in the old town itself and further out on the road leading to Massa Lubrense. Bear in mind that the small places may shut down entirely between November and March, although the larger hotels tend to be open all year.

SORRENTO

HOTELS AND B&BS

★**Astoria** Via Santa Maria delle Grazie 24 ☎ 081 807 4030, ⓦ hotelastoriasorrento.com. It's unusual to find a hotel right in the heart of old Sorrento, and this place is quite special, with reasonably sized doubles that have been nicely furnished and equipped, the best of which overlook a peaceful garden; prices include an excellent buffet breakfast. €130

Bellevue Syrene Piazza della Vittoria 5 ☎ 081 878 1024, ⓦ bellevue.it. This lovely nineteenth-century hotel, built on the remains of a Roman villa, boasts glorious views and has lifts down to the bathing facilities below, free to

hotel guests. Most of the rooms have been recently renovated and are very spacious. Deals are often available. €300

Casa Astarita Corso Italia 67 ☎ 081 877 3991, ⓦ casastarita.com. Cosy, friendly, and in a good position, *Casa Astarita* is one of Sorrento's best options at this price. Six nice rooms overlook the street, each with a bathroom, a flatscreen TV and a fridge, plus there's free wi-fi and rates include a good breakfast around a communal table. €90

Désirée Via Capo 31/B ☎ 081 878 1563, ⓦ desireehotelsorrento.com. About 700m from the end of Corso Italia, this is a nice small hotel with friendly management and twenty-odd good-sized doubles (triples and quads also available), some with balconies overlooking the sea, though they vary a bit in size and style. There's a roof terrace and café, and breakfast, parking and access to the stony beach below are all included. **€95**

Excelsior Vittoria Piazza Tasso 34 ☎081 807 1044, ⓦexvitt.it. This fabulously grand hotel set atop tufa cliffs has been owned by the same family since 1834, and its grand entrance is right in the centre of town. Its lovely formal garden with a lemon and orange grove has a large pool; the lift from the swish terrace bar plunges straight down to the seafront; and the service is immaculate yet friendly. The rooms are gorgeous, and you can choose from a garden or sea view. **€500**

Imperial Hotel Tramontano Via V. Veneto 1 ☎081 878 2588, ⓦhoteltramontano.com. A pilgrimage of sorts for literary visitors, this has been a hotel since 1812, and once upon a time hosted Byron, Shelley, Keats, Ibsen and Longfellow. Even Milton is said to have stayed here in its days as a private residence. Rooms are grand without being overpowering and the views are stunning. **€240**

La Minervetta Maison Via Capo 25 ☎081 877 4455, ⓦlaminervetta.com. Sorrento's only real boutique hotel is something special, perched on the cliff overlooking Marina Grande, designed and decorated with flair by the family's architect son. There's a plunge-pool and lounge-terrace overlooking the sea, and rooms are decorated in cool blues and whites. One of Sorrento's best options for a splurge. **€330**

Mignon Via Sersale 9 ☎081 807 3824, ⓦsorrentohotelmignon.com. Rooms here are well appointed and come with satellite TV, a/c and free wi-fi. They either have balconies, or open onto a shared terrace overlooking the garden at the back. Parking is available near the hotel (€10/night) and there are beach discounts too. **€110**

Rota Suites Via B. Rota 25 ☎081 878 2904, ⓦrotasuites.com. A 5min walk from the centre of town, this sharply furnished suite hotel is a great choice for self-caterers. Suites for 2–4 people come with a/c and a kitchenette. Five-day minimum stay in summer. **€200**

HOSTELS

Le Sirene Via degli Aranci 160 ☎081 807 2925, ⓦhostellesirene.com. A private youth hostel which is a bit spartan but decent enough. To get there from the train station, turn right on the main road and Via degli Aranci is 200m down on the left. Room rates include breakfast. Dorms **€20**, doubles **€65**, quadruples **€100**

Ulisse Deluxe Hostel Via del Mare 22, ☎081 877 4753, ⓦulissedeluxe.com. They call themselves a hostel, but *Ulisse* is really more of a hotel, and a well-situated one at that, on the edge of the old town and on the road to the beach at Marina Grande. Fifty comfortably furnished rooms – doubles, family rooms, triples – with free wi-fi and en-suite bathrooms, plus two dormitories (1 male, 1 female) with 14 beds each. Discounted rates on the attached gym, spa and pool too. Dorms **€18**, doubles **€100**

CAMPSITES

Nube d'Argento Via del Capo 21 ☎081 878 1344, ⓦnubedargento.com. Scenic site on the western side of the town centre, 100m from the end of Corso Italia. Camping **€10**, bungalows for 2 **€85**

Santa Fortunata Via del Capo 41 ☎081 807 3579, ⓦsantafortunata.com. Just over 1km out of Sorrento on the way to Massa Lubrense, this site has a private beach and superb sea views. Open April–Oct. Camping (add €12.50 for each additional person; €6 for a car) **€20.50**, cabin **€98**

SANT'AGNELLO

Corallo Rione Cappuccini 12 ☎081 807 3355, ⓦhotelcorallosorrento.com. In a great position overlooking Sant'Agnello's beach, this 1920s-style hotel was renovated a few years ago and has large modern rooms, painted white with splashes of colour, overlooking the sheer drop below. **€180**

Grand Hotel Cocumella Via Cocumella 7 ☎081 878 2933, ⓦcocumella.com. A former monastery with a vaulted hall, antique furniture in many rooms, a frescoed ceiling in the bridal suite, plus a swimming pool, tennis courts and even its own luxuriously appointed tall ship. **€375**

Mediterraneo Via Crawford 85 ☎081 878 1352, ⓦmediterraneosorrento.com. Right opposite the Marinella beach (and with its own lift to reach it), this place has a boutique feel, with clean, contemporary rooms – the best with balconies and sea views – a garden and pool, and a cool almost completely white bar and rooftop restaurant. Just a 10min walk from the centre of Sorrento too. **€225**

Parco dei Principi Via Rota 1 ☎081 878 4644, ⓦgrandhotelparcodeiprincipi.net. Designed by Giò Ponti in 1962, this hotel is a classic of the era and enjoys one of the best views going over the Bay of Naples. The rooms maintain a deliberately cool minimalism, and overall the hotel's blue ceramic tiles and stylish lounge furniture boast a unique of-its-time elegance. A lift descends to the hotel's own "*spiaggia*" where dinner is served, a memorable location for a romantic evening. **€250**

Seven Hostel Via Iomella Grande 99 ☎081 878 6758, ⓦseven.eu. This smart hostel has been ingeniously adapted from an old monastery, and boasts a combination of private rooms, dorms, triples and quadruples. Wi-fi is free throughout and the fab terrace on the roof has amazing views over the bay. Spotless, well-run and all in all a great place to stay whatever your budget, just 15min walk from the centre of Sorrento or a short stroll from Sant'Agnello's Circumvesuviana station. Dorms **€15**, private rooms per person **€30**

4

EATING AND DRINKING

Sorrento has no shortage of **restaurants**, and most of them are of reasonable quality, although inevitably in a town so devoted to tourism you can come across places where the service is slow and the food not up to scratch. The places below are some of the better options. The town also has a lively after-dark scene, kicking off with the *passeggiata* along the Corso. There are plenty of decent spots for a **drink** around town, from down-to-earth pubs to swanky lounge bars.

CAFÉS AND GELATERIE

Bar Ercolano Piazza Tasso 28 ☎081 807 2951. The friendlier and less self-important of the two main bars on Piazza Tasso – with not such good views of the parading crowds, but a lot shadier when it's hot. A good place to start the day with a pastry. Daily 8am–midnight.

Bougainvillea Corso Italia 16 ☎081 878 1364, ⓦbougainvillea.it. This always busy and convivial joint has one of old Sorrento's widest choices of ice creams – around eighty flavours at the last count – and a garden to enjoy them in. Daily 10am–midnight.

Circolo dei Forestieri Via Luigi di Maio 35 ☎081 877 3263, ⓦcircolodeiforestieri.com. Tucked away behind the tourist office, many miss out on the fancy, old-world charm and wonderful views at this place. They do food and it's a nice venue for a pre-dinner aperitif. Daily noon–10pm.

Fauno Piazza Tasso 13/15 ☎081 878 1135, ⓦfaunobar .it. *The* place to watch the crowds drift by during the evening *passeggiata*, if you can bear the thinly disguised contempt the waiters have for tourists. Food includes the usual pasta dishes, burgers and omelettes. Daily 8am–1am.

Primavera Corso Italia 142 ☎081 807 3252, ⓦprimaverasorrento.it. There's a great choice of flavours at this veteran *gelateria*, just off Piazza Tasso. Check out the photos of the famous and infamous who have stopped by for a quick *cono*. Daily 10am–1am.

RESTAURANTS

Aurora Light Piazza Tasso 3 ☎081 877 2631, ⓦauroralight.it. Sister restaurant to the pizzeria next door, and as central as you can get, *Aurora Light* is a nice place to eat decent food while watching the crowds on Piazza Tasso. A perfect spot to stop by for a quick snack or a full meal at any time of day: club sandwiches and burgers for €10, pasta dishes for €10–12, salads for €8 and heftier fare €12–16. Daily noon–midnight.

★**Bufalito Inn** Vico 1e Fuoro 21 ☎081 365 6975, ⓦinnbufalito.com. A great, relaxed and busy restaurant specializing mainly in buffalo dishes – mozzarella naturally, but also steaks, sausages and the like. Delicious *antipasti misti*, good pasta dishes, inventive mains and interesting cheese platters. Moderately priced, with *primi* going for €10–14, *secondi* €10–16. The owners also run a small shop on Piazza Tasso selling buffalo goodies to take home. Daily noon–midnight.

Caruso Via Sant'Antonino 12 ☎081 807 3156, ⓦristorantemuseocaruso.com. A must for opera buffs, bursting with memorabilia of the famous tenor, but locals like it too – for the food, which is high-end and among Sorrento's best, but also for a special night out. Menus for around €70, otherwise a la carte dishes go for €15–20 for starters, €25–30 for main courses. Daily noon–midnight.

Da Emilia Via Marina Grande 60 ☎081 807 2720. With a menu as short as the menus in the upper town are long, this restaurant serves simple food in perhaps Sorrento's best location – on the waterfront of Marina Grande, with tables out on a stilted terrace over the water. It's very good for pasta dishes, with half a dozen great seafood and tomato-based *primi*, and the same number of principally fishy *secondi*. No credit cards. Open daily for lunch and dinner.

Da Gigino Via degli Archi 15 ☎081 878 1927. A great, no-nonsense choice, with a menu of the usual standards – decent pasta dishes for €8–11, main courses including good *saltimbocca* and *saute di cozze* for €10–15 and excellent pizzas from €6. Daily noon–11.45pm.

Il Buco 2a Rampa Marina Piccola 5, Piazza Sant'Antonino ☎081 878 2354, ⓦilbucoristorante.it. Housed in the wine cellar of a former monastery, this is Sorrento at its gastronomic best, with a real variety of creative antipasti and *primi* that focuses on local ingredients, sea or turf. You can order a la carte and pay around €20 for a pasta dish, €25 for a main course, or choose from set menus that cost €60–90 for three courses. Mon, Tues, Thurs–Sun 12.30–3pm & 7.30–11pm.

L'Antica Trattoria Via P. R. Giuliani 45 ☎081 807 1082, ⓦlanticatrattoria.com. This elegant venue with a vine-covered terrace is one of the best and longest-established restaurants in Sorrento, serving top-end seasonal food from fixed-price menus starting at around €45 for three. They also serve a great-value three-course set lunch for €19.50. It's popular – best to book ahead. Daily noon–11pm.

La Fenice Via degli Aranci 11 ☎081 878 1652. Just outside Sorrento's immediate centre and, as such, as popular with locals as it is with tourists. It's always busy, and does good fish, served in the covered patio full of plants or outside on the terrace. Pasta dishes €7–14, mains €10–18, plus pizzas from €5, and there's a nice antipasti table too. Tues–Sun noon–2.45pm & 7–11.30pm.

★**La Lanterna** Via San Cesareo 23 ☎081 878 1355. Down a dead end off Via San Cesareo, just off Piazza Tasso, this has long been one of the better restaurants in the centre of town, with tables outside, decent service and consistently good food; it does great fish and seafood but much else besides, and there are nice touches like baskets

WALKS FROM SORRENTO

Not many people come to Sorrento and explore the surrounding countryside, walking up into the **hilly interior**. That's a real shame because the resort's peninsula offers picturesque **walks-a-plenty** amid vineyards and olive groves that look down over the Bay of Naples.

You could walk up into the hills from the village of **Capo**, near the Ruderi Villa Romana di Pollio beach, and accessible on the same bus or by walking along Via del Capo for about twenty minutes. A narrow road leads up from the crossroads to the village of **Pantano** – a roughly fifteen-minute walk, though admittedly uphill most of the way; from here you can take the narrow Via Li Simoni through the village and then drop back down to Sorrento, making a left at Via Paradisello, following the winding path downhill and eventually merging with the main road. Follow this for a short stretch, and then take a left on Via Priora, emerging on the main road out of town opposite the *Nube d'Argento* campsite. This would take a maximum of two hours in all.

To head straight into the hills from the centre of Sorrento itself take the road off Via degli Aranci towards the *Hilton Sorrento Palace*. At the end of this road there's a **church**, from where a steep path leads up to the village of **Crocevia** and the church of Santa Maria. Follow the path from here to the village of **Priora** and then on to **Pantano**, from where you can either take a bus or loop back down to Sorrento following the route of the previous walk, or head on down to the village of Capo.

of home-made bread full of onions, *prosciutto* and olives. It's moderately priced – *primi* €7–14, *secondi* €8–16, pizzas from €6. Mon, Tues, Thurs–Sun noon–3pm & 7pm–midnight.

'O Parrucchiano Corso Italia 67 ☎ 081 878 1321, ⊛ parrucchiano.com. More of a conservatory than a restaurant, this vast place is very popular and although it's a bit of a factory for processing tourists, the food is actually pretty good and decent value. Plenty of Italians come here and the boss is always around for a chat. Mon, Tues, Thurs–Sun noon–3pm & 7–11.15pm.

BARS AND PUBS

Bollicine Via Accademia 7 ☎ 081 878 4616. In the heart of the old town, this small, wood-panelled wine bar has a wide range of fine Campanian wines, good beer, a variety of snacks and a full menu too. Daily from 7pm.

Chaplin's Corso Italia 18 ☎ 081 807 2551. Perhaps the nicest of Sorrento's English pubs, with welcoming owners and live sport on an array of TVs. Check out the wisdom behind the bar dispensed by the legions of inebriated holidaymakers who have passed through over the years. Daily 6pm–2am.

The Garden Corso Italia 50/52 ☎ 081 878 1195, ⊛ thegardenrestaurant.it. A wine shop and wine bar, with beer on tap too, and a few outside tables. A great place to unwind, *The Garden* serves the usual wine-bar fare (cheeses, salads and panini for lunch), and there's a restaurant attached (entrance around the corner). Daily noon–2am.

Southwest of Sorrento

The main coast road – **Via del Capo** – climbs out of Sorrento to head southwest towards **Massa Lubrense**, the small administrative centre and market town for most of the villages at this end of the Sorrentine peninsula. Strictly speaking, you're at the far western end of the Amalfi Coast here, and the landscape and coastal villages bear comparison with that more fabled stretch, most notably the beach village of **Marina del Cantone** and nearby **Punta Campanella** marine park. There's also the hilltop redoubt of **Sant'Agata sui Due Golfi**, whose renowned local restaurant is just one of several superb places to eat in this area.

Massa Lubrense and around

About 5km southwest of Sorrento, **MASSA LUBRENSE** is a pleasant enough market town perched above the sea, but with nothing much in the way of sights. It's the main centre of the local area, and a good place to stay if you're after something quieter, poised between Sorrento itself and the smaller resorts on the south coast of the peninsula. It is also well placed for some great walking in the hills hereabouts. A few kilometres below Massa Lubrense, **Marina della Lobra** is a lovely spot, a quiet harbour village with a marina, a handful of fishing boats, a busy bar and a couple of waterfront restaurants.

BEST SPOTS FOR A SWIM

Five minutes on the bus or twenty minutes on foot from Sorrento's centre, there are a couple of prime swimming spots. The first is the **Ruderi Villa Romana di Pollio**, ten minutes' walk from the bus stop at Capo di Sorrento on the main road (itself about 1.5km from town), where the ruins of a Roman villa lie on and around the seashore rocks, which are fairly flat and swathed with walkways; there's also a lovely enclosed seawater pool. The other is reachable by strolling 100m further along the main road and taking a path off to the right just before the *Hotel Dania*, which short-cuts in ten minutes or so to the **Marina di Puolo**, a short stretch of mainly sandy beach lined with fishing boats and a handful of trattorias, that is perhaps the nicest place to swim in the vicinity of Sorrento. You can also reach this by car by taking a turn-off a few hundred metres beyond the path that winds down to the beach – there are (paid) parking spaces just above the beach and you walk the rest of the way.

Termini and Nerano

Less than 5km south of Massa Lubrense, **TERMINI** is an airy, cheerful place with an almost too perfectly framed view of Capri from its main square. Beyond Termini the road descends to **NERANO**, where there are another couple of good **accommodation** choices and a spectacular place to eat. It also has a diving centre that runs trips out to the choice spots of Punta Campanella (see below).

Marina del Cantone

Down below Nerano, stretched languidly around the beautiful Bay of Ieranto, **MARINA DEL CANTONE** has a strip of pebbly beach lined with parasols and lounge chairs in front of several bar-restaurants. There's a spot in the middle where you can just throw down your towel for free; otherwise it costs the usual €15 or so for a couple of beds and sunshade. Once you've tired of the sun and sea, you could take a boat excursion to Capri or rent a boat from any number of local operators (see p.144). Marina is an unusually good place for foodies too, with a number of excellent **restaurants**, both here and up in Nerano, so you can just skip the beach and come here to eat (see p.145). You can also take a boat around the headland to the right to **Punta Campanella** (see below), though if you want to get into the water here you'll need to contact the diving outfit Nettuno Residence Diving (see p.144).

Punta Campanella

Ⓦ parks.it/riserva.marina.punta.campanella

The further finger of the Sorrentine peninsula is known as **Punta Campanella**, a series of rocky headlands where the cliffs drop vertically into the sea. The name comes from the bell on a fourteenth-century tower that sits on the end of the main headland, which used to ring to warn of the arrival of pirates; nowadays it's a rudimentary lighthouse. You can see the area on boat excursions from Marina del Cantone, but the area is a protected marine reserve, and you absolutely can't enter the water without permission. Nonetheless it's reputed to be a great place to snorkel and dive; if you want to do this you must go with an approved outfit, like Sorrento Diving (see p.138) or Nettuno Residence Diving (see p.144).

Sant'Agata sui Due Golfi

Immediately south of Sorrento, high up in the hills that form the backbone of the Sorrentine peninsula, **SANT'AGATA SUI DUE GOLFI** is a hill-town and provincial capital, so named for its spectacular view of both bays. It's a pleasant, airy place, busy with tour buses going to and from the coast, and a nice place to base yourself both for Sorrento and the Amalfi Coast, with a couple of good places to stay and excellent places to eat. The church of **Sant'Agata** on the main square is worth a peek for its mid-seventeenth-century polychrome altar of marble and mother-of-pearl, and the best place to experience the views is the **Deserto** convent, a short, ten-minute walk from here; the grounds afford good views of the Sorrento side, but for the best views climb the **Belvedere** (April–Sept daily 10am–noon & 5–7pm; Oct–March daily 10am–noon & 3–5pm; free), which gives a jaw-dropping 360-degree panorama: Capri dreaming just off the end of the promontory, Ischia and Procida ghostly presences beyond, and the creamy digits of Naples spread beneath Vesuvius's gloomy form, before you turn to see the whole of the Gulf of Salerno stretching into the distance.

ARRIVAL AND DEPARTURE
SOUTHWEST OF SORRENTO

By bus Local buses run between Sorrento's Circumvesuviana station and Massa Lubrense and Sant'Agata roughly every 45min, though less often at weekends. There are also around 8 buses a day to and from Marina del Cantone, via Termini and Nerano, some of which also stop at Sant'Agata.

INFORMATION AND ACTIVITIES

Tourist office Massa Lubrense's tourist office is right in the centre of town at Via Filangieri 11 (April–Oct daily 9am–1pm; ☎081 533 0135). Sant'Agata also has a tourist office on the main square at Corso Sant'Agata 11/A (☎081 533 0135), but its opening times are erratic.

Diving Nettuno Residence Diving, located on the grounds of the *Nettuno Villaggio* campsite just outside Marina del Cantone (Via Amerigo Vespucci 39 ☎081 808 1051, ⓦ divingsorrento.com), runs dives daily for both beginners and experienced divers, in the nearby Punta Campanella marine park and Bay of Ieranto. You can also dive with Sorrento Diving Futuro Mare (see p.138) among other outfits.

Boat tours Cooperativo Marina della Lobra (☎081 808 9380), based at the harbour in Marina della Lobra, will ferry you around Capri, Positano and nearby beaches for around €40 a head, and will pick you up from your hotel if you wish.

Boat rental Coop San Antonio (☎081 808 1638), right on Marina del Cantone's beach, rents boats for around €100 a day, as do a number of local operators.

ACCOMMODATION

MASSA LUBRENSE

La Primavera Via IV Novembre 3 ☎081 808 9556, ⓦ laprimavera.biz. A 2min walk from the top of the main street in Massa, this is a decent option, with 16 well-furnished rooms, all en suite, and the best of which have balconies with sea views. Also has a good restaurant with a nice seaward-facing terrace. **€95**

TERMINI

Relais Blu Via Roncato 60 ☎081 878 9552, ⓦ relaisblu.com. About 1500m below Termini, this boutique hotel is one of the nicest places to stay in the Sorrento area, with 11 large rooms and suites beautifully furnished in a cool marine style and wonderfully relaxing common areas bathed in white and light. Its rooftop lounge commands as amazing a view of the Bay of Naples and Capri as you'll ever find. Closed Nov to mid-March. **€345**

NERANO

Casale Villarena Via Cantone 3 ☎081 808 1779, ⓦ casalevillarena.com. A small and secluded complex of rooms and self-catering apartments (available per week €770–1950 or by the day) hidden away in the centre of the village within a well-maintained garden. Doubles **€110**, apartments for 4 **€220**

Olga's Residence Piazza Nerano 3 ☎081 808 1013, ⓦ olgasresidence.com. An apartment hotel right in the heart of the village, with a pleasant garden and small swimming pool overlooking the bay below, and clean, nicely furnished apartments available for week-long rentals. Olga runs the village shop opposite, where there's a small reception. Apartments for 3 **€110**, apartments for 6 **€135**

MARINA DEL CANTONE

Le Sirene Marine del Cantone ☎081 808 1027, ⓦ lesirenehotel.it. This place has a nautically themed reception, spruce en-suite rooms, some with beach-facing balconies, wi-fi and a good restaurant with terrace. Rates give you access to the beach loungers right in front of the hotel. It's worth paying a little extra for a sea view. **€120**

Lo Scoglio Piazza delle Sirene 15 ☎081 808 1026, ⓦ hotelloscoglio.com. Known primarily as a restaurant (see p.145), *Lo Scoglio* also has 14 simply decorated rooms upstairs, each one named after a different constellation, and its own beach down below. **€139**

Nettuno Villaggio Via A. Vespucci 39 ☎ 081 808 1051, ⓦ villaggionettuno.it. Located on either side of the road into Marina del Cantone, this campsite and self-catering complex is only a 5min walk from the sea and has its own small stretch of private beach. There are cabins, a shop and restaurant on one side, and tent and campervan pitches on the other, seaward side, along with a handful of apartments in an old Saracen tower. Wi-fi costs €2.50/day and it's also the home of Nettuno Residence Diving (see p.144). Camping **€20**, cabins **€50**, apartments **€145**

Taverna del Capitano Piazza delle Sirene 10/11 ☎ 081 808 1028, ⓦ tavernadelcapitano.it. Nice rooms above a restaurant, with largish balconies and sea views, wi-fi throughout and free loungers on the beach below. **€160**

SANT'AGATA SUI DUE GOLFI

Don Alfonso Corso Sant'Agata 11/13 ☎ 081 878 0026, ⓦ donalfonso.com. Right in the centre of town, yet somehow set apart and very peaceful, this has seven suites in the main building and another on its own in the grounds, in which there's also a small pool, a terrace and the rooms of the hotel's own cooking school. The restaurant is pretty special too (see below). **€350**

Villa Green Paradise Via Deserto 14/c ☎ 081 808 0152, ⓦ greenparadise.biz. A 5min walk from the square on the way to the Deserto convent, this bed and breakfast has three en-suite rooms, including one with its own large terrace. Breakfast is taken in a shady corner of the garden and the welcome is warm and friendly. **€90**

EATING AND DRINKING

MASSA LUBRENSE

La Primavera Via IV Novembre 3 ☎ 081 808 9556, ⓦ laprimavera.biz. One of the best places to eat in Massa Lubrense, with a consistently good menu of local specialities. Both pasta dishes and mains go for €8–15; pizzas from €5. Daily except Mon for lunch and dinner.

MARINA DI LOBRA

Funicoli Funicola Via Fontanella 16 ☎ 081 362 2087. A basic menu with no surprises, but not expensive, and you eat on a terrace overlooking the harbour. Pasta dishes go for €7–14, main courses €10–18 – try their signature *scialatielli* dish, with zucchini, *vongole* and *gamberetti*. Mon, Tues, Thurs–Sun noon–3pm & 7.30–10.30pm.

NERANO

I Quattro Passi Via Amerigo Vespucci ☎ 081 808 1271, ⓦ ristorantequattropassi.com. Just below the main part of the village, on the road down to Marina del Cantone, Antonio Mellino's restaurant is one of the most revered and upscale in the region, serving top-end Italian cuisine using the freshest local ingredients. You'll need to book, and to save up probably – tasting menus go for €120–150, while ordering a la carte will set you back around €30–35 for a pasta dish, €45–50 a main course. They also have a few rooms upstairs. If you really love it, you can visit Antonio's restaurant of the same name in London's Mayfair on your way home. Mon, Tues, Thurs–Sun 12.30–3pm & 8–10.30pm.

MARINA DEL CANTONE

★ **Lo Scoglio** Piazza delle Sirene 15 ☎ 081 808 1026. Quite a well-known restaurant hereabouts, with a reputation earned by serving up great fish and an excellent *spaghetti alle zucchine* on a peaceful terrace jutting out into the sea. Not at all posh in presentation or, for that matter,

prices – most pasta *primi* go for around €13, seafood and fish mains for €16–20. Open daily for lunch and dinner.

Maria Grazie Marina del Cantone ☎ 081 808 1011. Shady beachside terrace restaurant where excellent antipasti really hit the spot at lunch. Open daily for lunch and dinner.

SANT'AGATA SUI DUE GOLFI

★ **Don Alfonso** Corso Sant'Agata 11/13 ☎ 081 878 0026, ⓦ donalfonso.com. Sant'Agata's famed Michelin-starred restaurant is wonderful for lunch or dinner, a temple of Mediterranean cuisine ensconced in cheery, vivid pastels, with the kitchen and its team of Alfonso and sons in full view behind glass. Much of the produce comes from their own garden, including oil from olive trees perched at improbable angles above the sea. Sommelier Livia selects the perfect wines. Menus €130. Wed–Sun 12.30–3pm & 8–11pm.

Lo Stuzzichino Via Deserto 1 ☎ 081 533 0010, ⓦ ristorantelostuzzichino.it. Just off the main square, this place has an attractive garden and serves well-priced local specialities featuring good fish, seafood and mountain fare, such as chestnut and cabbage soup, as well as local cheeses. It's a relaxed and welcoming option, and moderately priced – pasta dishes for €6–10, pizzas €4–7, main courses €12–16. Daily Mon, Tues, Thurs–Sun noon–3pm & 7–11pm.

Tramonto Rosso Via Leucosia 22, Santa Maria delle Neve ☎ 081 808 1045, ⓦ ristorantetramontorosso .com. Situated in the village just below Sant'Agata, and with almost indecently wonderful views of both the Gulf of Salerno and Capri, this is a big, busy local restaurant serving down-at-home country cooking from a blackboard of daily specials – *fritto di paranza*, *carpaccio dei porcini* and other delicious items you might not be able to find so easily down on the coast. Pizzas too if you want them. Tues–Sun for lunch and dinner.

4

The islands

FISHING BOATS MOORED AT PROCIDA

5

The islands

Guarding each prong of the Bay of Naples, the alluring trio of Capri, Ischia and Procida makes up the best-known group of all Italian islands. They're easy day-trips from Naples and other points around the bay, and you'd be mad not to visit at least one while you're in the city. But give them more time if you can: Procida is easily covered on foot in a day or two; Capri deserves at least an overnight stay if only to see what it's like after the tidal wave of day-trippers has left; and you could easily spend a week exploring multifaceted Ischia.

Travelling to and between the islands is a fairly simple matter, with conveniently scheduled **ferries** and **hydrofoils**. The three islands are quite different from each other in terms of landscape and culture. Each has been the stuff of myth, anecdote and, in some instances, international scandal. **Capri** swarms with visitors but is so beautiful that a day or more here is by no means time squandered. The most dramatic by far, it's a small place that has spurred imaginations and incited lavish, as well as lascivious, dreams for millennia. Purported home to the mythical Sirens of the ancient world, it has been much-eulogized as a playground of the super-rich in the years since, and it has now settled down to a lucrative existence as a target for day-trippers. The largest island of the three, **Ischia**, absorbs tourists more readily and is more low-key in its pleasures, a lively and attractive setting in which to while away an entire holiday. Its natural hot springs have always been a target for cure-seekers, although these days, it mostly attracts northern European package tourists and weekenders from Naples. Workaday and self-sufficient, it never feels as crowded as Capri, while the sandy beaches and green volcanic interior are further draws. Pretty **Procida** is the smallest but most densely populated of the islands. It has least to offer in the way of sights but life goes on here much as it has for generations, and, happily, tourism is still an afterthought, making it probably the best venue for peaceful lazing since it's relatively untouched even in high season.

GETTING TO THE ISLANDS

There are regular ferries (*nave* or *traghetto* in Italian), hydrofoils and catamarans (*aliscafo*) to all of the islands throughout the year, though they run more frequently and from more ports between April and October. The principal point of departure for hydrofoils is Naples' **Molo Beverello**, at the bottom of Piazza Municipio; car ferries leave from Calata Porta di Massa, about 200m further east. A free shuttle service links the two ports. Other departure points to the islands for hydrofoils and catamarans are Naples **Mergellina** (for Ischia), **Pozzuoli** (for Procida and Ischia), **Castellammare** (Capri), **Salerno** (Capri and Ischia) and **Sorrento** (Capri). It's also possible to sail between Capri and Ischia, and Ischia and Procida, although, curiously, the islands are not as well connected as you might expect. Whichever route you take, **day-trips** are feasible; usually the last connection delivers you back on the mainland in time for dinner. Note that you can't take a **car** to Capri, nor, in summer months, to Ischia or Procida; there's a useful car park in Naples' Calata di Massa port (daily 6am–10pm; €22 for 24hr; ☎ 081 551 4988, ⊕ tirreniparking.it).

BY FERRY

Schedules Ferry timings are published daily in the newspaper *Il Mattino*, as well as being available from local tourist offices, and online at the island-specific websites as well as those belonging to the ferry lines themselves.

Tickets All of the operators below offer online booking but

Highlights

❶ Villa Jovis, Capri The ruins of Tiberius's city-sized palace overlook a stunning panorama of the Amalfi Coast. **See p.154**

❷ Villa San Michele, Capri The Swedish physician's house and classical collections are a marvellously poetic re-creation of ancient splendours in a tremendous location. **See p.158**

❸ La Mortella, Ischia This verdant garden paradise is a labour of love created by British composer William Walton and his wife. See p.172

❹ Il Sorgeto, Ischia These volcanically heated hot springs on Ischia's tranquil southern side are a novel spot for a sundowner. **See p.174**

❺ Monte Epomeo, Ischia Approached from all sides, the perfect cone of this dormant volcano makes for a memorable hike. **See p.175**

❻ Chiaiolella Beach, Procida The tiny island's most appealing beach includes a picturesque cove, a well-appointed lido and views of the Vivara nature reserve. **See p.183**

HIGHLIGHTS ARE MARKED ON THE MAP ON P.150

5

in general, there's no need to book tickets in advance; just make sure you arrive at the docks 15min before departure. It's usually better to buy a single rather than a return ticket – it's no more expensive and you retain more flexibility on the time you come back, and the service you decide to use. The exception is summer weekends (especially on Capri and Procida, and especially by hydrofoil), when it can be a good idea to buy your return ticket as soon as you arrive, to avoid the risk of finding the last service fully booked.

FERRY LINES

Alilauro ⓣ 081 497 2222, ⓦ alilauro.it. Naples–Ischia (Porto and Forío); Capri–Ischia (Porto); Castellammare–Capri; Sorrento–Capri and Ischia (Porto); Salerno–Capri and Ischia (Porto); Positano and Amalfi–Capri and Ischia (Porto).

Caremar ⓣ 081 551 3882, ⓦ caremar.it. Naples–Capri, Ischia (Porto and Casamicciola) and Procida; Pozzuoli–Ischia (Porto); Procida–Ischia (Porto); Sorrento–Capri.

Gescab ⓣ 081 704 1911, ⓦ gescab.it. Naples, Sorrento, Positano, Amalfi, Salerno and Castellammare–Capri.

Medmar ⓣ 081 333 4411, ⓦ medmargroup.it. Naples and Pozzuoli–Ischia (Porto and Casamicciola); Ischia, Naples and Pozzuoli–Procida.

Metrò del Mare ⓦ metròdelmare.it. Cilento–Capri (high summer only).

NLG ⓣ 081 552 0763, ⓦ navlib.it. Naples, Sorrento, Positano, Amalfi, Salerno and Castellammare–Capri.

SNAV ⓣ 081 428 5555, ⓦ snav.it. Naples–Capri, Ischia (Casamicciola) and Procida; Procida–Ischia (Casamicciola); Castellammare–Capri; Sorrento–Capri.

ALTERNATIVE TRANSPORT

By water taxi and helicopter For most people the plentiful public services should be enough, but you could splash out on a water taxi, departing from Naples Beverello (ⓣ 081 837 8781, ⓦ capriseaservice.com; €790 for the 50min one-way ride, carrying up to six people), or a private helicopter (ⓣ 0828 354 155 or 800 915 012, ⓦ capri-helicopters.com), taking up to six passengers on the Naples–Capri trip of about twenty minutes for a cool €1650 one-way.

USEFUL WEBSITES

ⓦ **capri.com**, ⓦ **capritourism.com** A wealth of information on the island, from ferry schedules to helicopter rental.

ⓦ **ischiaonline.it**, ⓦ **ischia.it** Full of useful details on the island's main settlements, plus a hotel booking service and events calendar.

ⓦ **procida.it**, ⓦ **isoladiprocida.it** Ferry timetables, weather reports and much besides.

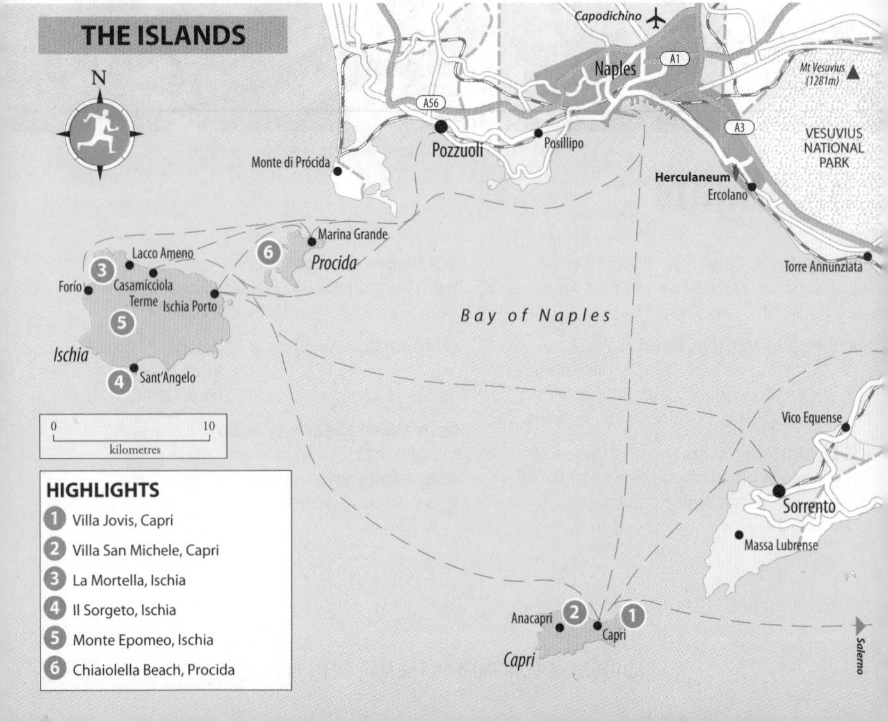
THE ISLANDS
N
Capodichino
Naples
A1
Mt Vesuvius (1281m)
A56
A3
Pozzuoli
Posillipo
VESUVIUS NATIONAL PARK
Monte di Prócida
Herculaneum
Ercolano
Marina Grande
Procida
Torre Annunziata
Lacco Ameno
Forío
Casamicciola Terme
Ischia Porto
Bay of Naples
Ischia
Sant'Angelo
0
10
kilometres
Vico Equense
Sorrento
Massa Lubrense
Anacapri
Capri
Capri
Salerno
HIGHLIGHTS
1 Villa Jovis, Capri
2 Villa San Michele, Capri
3 La Mortella, Ischia
4 Il Sorgeto, Ischia
5 Monte Epomeo, Ischia
6 Chiaiolella Beach, Procida

Capri

The island of **CAPRI** has long been the most sought-after destination in the Bay of Naples. No place is more glamorous than this tiny isle of immense, weatherworn crags, jutting out of the deep blue waters just off the Sorrentine peninsula. Composed primarily of softly gleaming white limestone, Capri is a mostly perpendicular environment, presenting tall rock faces around much of its perimeter. Still, where vegetation does grow across the island's jagged surface, it is lush, dense and fragrant – nearly a thousand species of flowers and plants grow here – helped along by the agreeable climate.

Capri tends to get a mixed press, the consensus being that while undoubtedly an attractive place, it's overrun by crowds and prices are high. It's certainly busy, to the degree that in July and August, and on all summer weekends, you should probably give it a miss. But at most other times of year the crowds are bearable and relatively easy to escape, and these days there is reasonably priced and attractive accommodation in both Anacapri and Capri town. Day-trippers arrive year-round, most of them to see the **Blue Grotto**, the early nineteenth-century rediscovery of which fed the rise of tourism. But most are gone by sunset, when the real Capri comes out of hiding. Indeed, despite the island's petite size – a mere 6km long and 2.7km wide – and its inevitably touristy centre, the island retains a degree of unspoiled charm that is worth a leisurely walk up a steep hill to find.

Brief history

Capri has been inhabited since Paleolithic times, and Greek colonists from Cumae and, later, Neapolis are known to have used it as an outpost as early as the eighth century BC. The island's illustrious reputation dates back about two thousand years, to the days when it served as the private pleasure enclave of Roman emperors. It entered the history books in 29 BC when soon-to-be Emperor Augustus persuaded the local Greek rulers to trade him Capri for Ischia, which belonged to Rome at the time. Then, most famously, in 27 AD the island was chosen by **Emperor Tiberius** as the spot where he wanted to live out the remainder of his days: in effect, making Capri the empire's de facto capital. Literary gossipmonger Suetonius, in his *Twelve Caesars*, claims that Tiberius got up to all sorts of debaucheries while ensconced here, including throwing tiresome lovers off the island's sheer cliffs, to be harpooned by servants below should

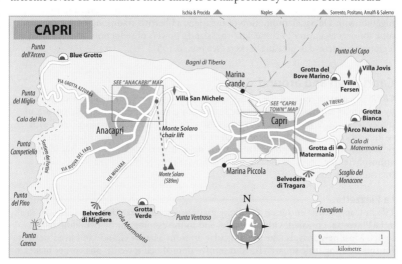

5

WATER WORSHIP

What little accessible shoreline Capri has is primarily rocky and pebbly. The island nevertheless offers plenty of opportunities for a swim and for watersports, as it is encircled by some of the deepest waters in the Bay of Naples. The following are the most promising spots for a dip. In some places a pair of plastic slip-on shoes is a good idea, or you risk scraped feet from the sharp rocks, and possibly sea-urchin spines. Note that in recent years swimming in the Blue Grotto has been banned as a result of bacterial and other pollution from heavy boat traffic.

Marina Grande Beyond the port area and the bus terminal is a sand and shingle beach of mixed quality. It's often crowded but is possibly the easiest place to swim on the island. There are lots of free spots too, though you can pay for the usual facilities if you prefer.

Marina Piccola Small, pebbly strand on the south side of the island, with a full complement of seaside services. One of the most kid-friendly beaches in the area, with a shallow, calm lagoon and plenty of cheap beach toys for sale.

Via Krupp More daring souls can try their luck down beyond the lowest point of this precipitous road, where a rough trail cuts off and down to the left. At the bottom, there are huge, flat stones lying right along the shore, facing I Faraglioni. Bring water and snacks.

Baths of Tiberius Follow signs to *Da Paolino* restaurant, and then take Via Palazzo a Mare down to a sheltered turquoise bay overlooked by the ruined walls of one of Tiberius's villas. If you are feeling lazy, the little lido here has a boat service shuttling to and from Maria Grande (kiosk next to the ferry ticket booths; €10). There are free patches of sand here as well, and it is a safe place to swim or paddle.

Faro/Punta Carena Exciting swimming in a rocky cove (accessed by little ladders), or lazy swimming in a pool belonging to the *Lido del Faro* (with a great restaurant to boot).

---

they survive the fall into the sea. Tiberius had some twelve sumptuous palaces built on the island, one dedicated to each of the Olympian gods – most notably **Villa Jovis**, the House of Jove (Jupiter), the vast ruins of which still dominate the eastern peak. Following the fall of Rome, Capri went about its modestly bucolic business for some fifteen hundred years, well out of the international limelight. Finally, in 1776, it was none other than the **Marquis de Sade** who visited the island and discovered its potential for personal freedom – and, judging from his letters, sex tourism. He was filled with admiration for the classical beauty of the Capri natives of both sexes and wrote enthusiastically about their charms. Ancient tradition held the island to be the home of the Sirens, whose ravishing, maddening song lured men to their doom, and this, together with De Sade's promotion of the island's libertine tradition, set the dominant tone for over a century to come, and the island's powers of seduction have attracted a legion of modern-day pleasure-seekers (see box, p.155).

Capri town and around

CAPRI is the main town of the island, nestled between two mountains. Once peopled by fishermen and farmers, it has long since been given over entirely to the pursuit of pricey pleasure. Winding alleyways fragrant with flowers and lemons are lined with whitewashed houses and clustered with cafés, hotels and shops, all with an air of polished Mediterranean grace. There aren't many historic sights as such, but it's the atmosphere that provides the allure: it's rich with history and fascination, but unassumingly so.

La Piazzetta

Life in Capri town centres on the dinky main square of **Piazza Umberto I**, known to all as **La Piazzetta**, crowded with café tables and in the evenings lit by twinkling fairy lights. Most new arrivals take the funicular up from Marina Grande and head straight for this bustling little square. The diminutive domed bell tower in one corner makes a modest landmark, and although La Piazzetta is really nothing more than a cluster of cafés, surrounded by quaint arcades, the square nevertheless evokes the glamour that makes Capri unique, fizzing with gossip and preening glitterati – at least when the day-trippers have gone home. On one side of the square, steps lead up to a series of covered walkways and the domed seventeenth-century parish church of **Santo Stefano** (daily 9am–1pm & 4–7pm), worth a look for its marble floor made up of remains from the Villa Jovis and other Tiberian ruins.

Museo del Centro Caprense "Ignazio Cerio"

Via Ignazio Cerio 5 • April–Sept Tues–Sun 10am–2pm; Oct–March Tues–Sat 10am–1pm • €2.50 • ☎ 081 837 6681, ⓦ centrocaprense.org

Directly across from the church, the modest **Museo del Centro Caprense "Ignazio Cerio"** was founded in honour of the Cerio family, who were hugely influential in Capri in the nineteenth and early twentieth centuries. It houses archeological remains, artefacts of the island's prehistory and various zoological and botanical finds, the product of Ignazio Cerio's studious efforts upon his arrival here in the mid-nineteenth century.

Certosa di San Giacomo

Via Certosa 11 • Tues–Sun 8.30am–1.30pm • €4 • ☎ 081 837 6218, ⓦ polomusealenapoli.beniculturali.it

Through elegant, shop-lined lanes and on across to the far side of town, the recently restored fourteenth-century monastery, **Certosa di San Giacomo**, is recognizable by the distinctive Moroccan-style vaults forming a series of little domes. During the nineteenth century the monastery served alternately as barracks, hospice and as a prison for anarchists and disgraced soldiers, while nowadays it's home to the

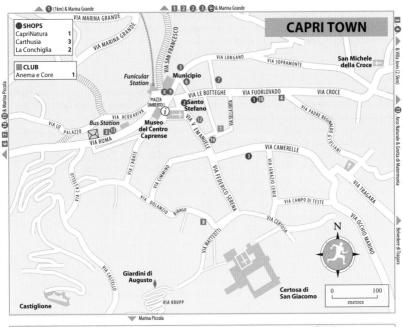

■ ACCOMMODATION			● RESTAURANTS		Da Paolino		● CAFÉS & GELATERIE	
'A Paziella	4	Quattro Stagioni	6	Aurora	10	Lemon Trees	1	Bar Caso	8
Belvedere		Villa Sarah	3	Buca di Bacco		Da Tonino	4	Bar Onda d'Oro	15
& Tre Re	1	Weber		"da Serafina"	5	L'Approdo	2	Bar Tiberio	9
Da Giorgio	5	Ambassador	7	Canzone del Mare	14	Le Grottelle	11	Buonocore	
JK Place Capri	2			Capri Pasta	6	Scialapopolo	7	Gelateria	12
La Tosca	8			Da Giorgio	13	Villa Verde	16	Il Gelato al Limone	3

5

Diefenbach collection of 31 paintings and five sculptures by quirky German Symbolist painter Wilhelm Diefenbach, who arrived in Capri in 1900 and spent the remaining thirteen years of his life here. A couple of shapeless Roman statues dredged up from the deep, a chapel frescoed by Florentine Niccolò di Tommaso, and two cloisters complete the visit.

Giardini di Augusto

Daily 9am–7.30pm • €1 (March to mid-Nov)

Past the monastery of San Giacomo, taking Via Matteotti to the far side of the island, the **Giardini di Augusto** afford astonishing panoramas of the rocky coast below and the towering jagged cliffs above. These lushly green terraced gardens are dotted with benches, flowers and marble statuary, making it a very pleasant place to while away an hour or two. They were once part of the estate of German steel industrialist **Friedrich Alfred Krupp**, who ran Europe's largest company and was one of the most notorious of the island's nineteenth-century thrill-seekers, but he was eventually forced to leave Capri under a cloud of shame due to his sexual liaisons with local fishermen and other young men. He was obliged to return to Germany, where he shortly afterwards committed suicide. Krupp also bequeathed to the island the dramatic, zigzagging pathway down, still known as **Via Krupp**, which you can see from the gardens. You walk under a high archway to get to it, and from there follow the picturesque switchbacks down, either all the way to the bottom and beyond to a beach of large flat rocks, or around to **Marina Piccola** (see p.156).

Belvedere del Cannone

Heading out of Capri town along Via Castello, which starts at Via Roma, a pleasant fifteen-minute walk leads you to the **Belvedere del Cannone**, which offers marvellous views, especially overlooking **I Faraglioni** rock stacks to the left and Marina Piccola to the right.

Villa Jovis

Via Tiberio • March–Oct daily 9am–1pm; 1st to 15th of the month closed Tues, 16th to end of the month closed Sun; currently closed Nov–Feb but check with the tourist office for the latest details • €2 • From the Piazzetta take Via Le Botteghe, followed by Via Fuorlovado and Via Croce, then take Via Tiberio up the hill and all the way to its end

Further out of town, there's a more demanding walk to the eastern summit of the island, where you can visit the ruins of Emperor Tiberius's villa, **Villa Jovis** – a steep forty-minute hike from La Piazzetta. It was here that Tiberius retired in 27 AD, to the grandest of his twelve imperial Capri villas, dedicated to the king of the gods. According to Suetonius and Tacitus, he came to lead a life of vice and debauchery and to take revenge on his enemies, many of whom he apparently had thrown off the overhanging cliff-face, known infamously as *Il Salto di Tiberio* (Tiberius's Leap). You can see why he chose the site: it's among Capri's most dazzling, with incredible **views** stretching across the bay to the Sorrentine peninsula and the Amalfi Coast; on a clear day you can even see to Salerno and beyond. There's not much left of the **villa** – which was almost a town in itself, covering some 7000 square metres – but you can get a good sense of the shape and design of its various parts. Arched halls and narrow passageways survive, though to the untrained eye much of it remains inscrutable. Some of the artistic treasures that were unearthed here are now part of the collection in Villa San Michele in Anacapri (see p.158).

Villa Fersen

Via Lo Capo • Tues–Sun 10am–6pm; closed Nov–April • Free • ☎ 081 838 6111

Just down from Villa Jovis is the much more recent **Villa Lysis**, known to locals as **Villa Fersen** after Count Fersen-Adelsward, a somewhat dissolute gay French-Swedish writer who built the house in the early 1900s. The house is empty now, but the location is amazing, and its echoing rooms and panoramic terraces retain a pungent atmosphere,

CAPRI'S THRILL-SEEKERS

It was the Marquis de Sade who "discovered" Capri, but the divine madness only really got under way about a century after his time, when more and more northern Europeans of a nonconformist stripe discovered that they could let it all hang out, at least more easily, in this southern, sunlit Arcadia. From the late 1800s until World War II, Capri was awash with all sorts of exiles, almost all of them seeking the sexual emancipation denied to them in their starchier home countries.

The very long list of mostly wealthy and/or aristocratic Capri **visitors and residents** includes Oscar Wilde and his partner Lord Alfred Douglas, who visited Capri in 1897 – to the outraged consternation of some of those present – not long after he was released from Reading Gaol. W. Somerset Maugham knew Capri well, too, even setting one of his most famous short stories, *The Lotus Eater*, on the island. Among the international writers who resided for a time on Capri was **D.H. Lawrence** – who called the isle "a gossipy, villa-stricken, two-humped chunk of limestone" – as well as Henry James, George Bernard Shaw, Joseph Conrad and Graham Greene, who wrote several of his novels here.

Capri's allure drew devotees of all professions, including British entertainer **Gracie Fields**, who bought a villa here in 1933, in which she died 46 years later. In her memoirs she recalled, "I knew that if only one small blade of grass of this gentle, wonderful place could belong to me, I would be happy." Even radical politicos in exile found their way here, including **Maxim Gorky** and Vladimir Illich **Lenin**, no less, who visited in 1910 and is said to have remarked that "Capri makes you forget everything."

The end of World War II and the rise of Hollywood brought a new breed of star to Capri, most notably movie-goddess **Rita Hayworth** who disembarked in 1949. That same year fashion designer Emilio Pucci created pencil-thin "Capri pants" and suddenly Capri was the place to be. Now everyone who was anyone was showing up here to be photographed strolling the quaint, whitewashed lanes: film stars, royalty and anyone rich and famous enough who wanted to make their mark. **Aristotle Onassis'** floating palace, the *Christina*, was often seen, first bearing opera diva **Maria Callas** and later **Jacqueline Kennedy** and her entourage; and **Princess Grace of Monaco** put in an appearance most years, too. In the early 1960s Pozzuoli-born **Sophia Loren** shot a romantic comedy on Capri, *It Started in Naples*, co-starring **Clark Gable**, while the Malaparte villa played a supporting role to Brigitte Bardot's behind in Jean-Luc Godard's acclaimed 1963 film *Le Mépris* (Contempt). The island had become a powerful symbol of style.

with a handful of photos of the count with various friends and lovers. You can see the upstairs bedrooms with what would have been at the time state-of-the-art fitted bathrooms, and a basement den where the count used to smoke opium, a habit he acquired on a trip to Ceylon. He died in style here in 1923 after overdoing it on a cocktail of champagne and cocaine – a fitting end to a hedonistic life.

Arco Naturale

The **Arco Naturale**, an impressive natural rock formation at the end of a high, verdant valley, is a leisurely, signposted 25-minute stroll from Capri town, following Via Le Botteghe out of the square and branching off up Via Matermania after ten minutes or so. Towards the end of the trail, a series of rustic stairways offers some precipitous panoramas. Finally you reach the arch itself, where the plummeting views can only be described as vertiginous: a huge arc of limestone amid lush greenery, with the glittering sea far below.

Grotta di Matermania

Just before the path begins to descend to the Arco Naturale, past the restaurant *Le Grottelle*, steps lead down to the right to the **Grotta di Matermania**, a ten-minute steep trek down through a rocky overhang to a dusty cave that was converted to house a shrine to the goddess Cybele (Matermania is a corruption of "Magna Mater" or the Great Mother) by the Romans. Looking at it now, it is difficult to imagine Cybele's frenzied priests, who

5

would ritualistically castrate themselves in an ecstasy of devotion, although according to island gossip the cave is occasionally used for neo-Pagan rites of dubious nature.

Belvedere di Tragara and the Via Tragara

From the Grotta di Matermania, steps continue on down through the trees, before flattening into a fine path that you can follow all the way round to the **Belvedere di Tragara**, comprising some of the island's best views. From here, follow the panoramic **Via Tragara** back to Capri town – reachable in about half an hour from the belvedere. Along the way, take time to admire **I Faraglioni**, the picturesque rock stacks just off the island, as well as the **Villa Malaparte** nearby (not open to visitors), built for the eponymous eccentric Italian writer in 1937. Like a giant red anvil plonked unceremoniously down on one of the island's most scenic promontories, it's an extreme, and utterly incongruous, piece of minimalist architecture.

Marina Piccola

Buses from Capri town drop off at Marina Piccola, or you can walk, either following Via Mulo from Via Roma, via a series of stairways, or taking Via Krupp (see p.154); either way takes about 20min

Directly across the lowest central point in the island's "saddle", **Marina Piccola** has a lagoon-like harbour and a modest group of houses, restaurants and shops clustered round an even more modest pebble beach. It's reasonably uncrowded out of season, though in July or August you'd be advised to steer well clear. You can pay for the usual facilities or just lay your towel on the arc of pebbles – not all that comfortable, but the swimming is good and there's diving from the small rock stacks just offshore in the middle of the lagoon. This is also the one spot on the island where you can rent **kayaks**: the best way to explore the island's coastline, or even to go for a complete circumnavigation (see box, p.162).

Anacapri and around

The island's other main settlement, **ANACAPRI**, is more sprawling than Capri town and less obviously picturesque, though quieter and greener. The prefix *ana* is Greek, indicating "an elevated place", and it's certainly true that getting to the island's second town is a rather hair-raising ride up a lofty and sheer cliff, to a point some 300m higher than Capri town. The minuscule switchback road, the only way to get there, seems hardly wide enough for two of the island's diminutive buses to pass, and when two do encounter each other, passengers on the seaward side stifle gasps of awe and horror at the sight of the rocky seashore below.

Piazza Vittoria

Anacapri's main square, **Piazza Vittoria**, is pleasant enough, ascending in broad terraces with flowers, and larger than Capri's La Piazzetta. It's flanked by souvenir shops, nondescript fashion boutiques and restaurants decked with multilingual tourist menus – Capri without the chic.

WATERSPORTS AT MARINA PICCOLA

Taking a **kayak** around the island is a memorable experience. You can rent single and double kayaks (about €15/hr) at Marina Piccola; make sure you take water and something to eat, though be aware that there's not room for carrying very much. Count on about five hours to make the circuit, including stops for ducking into the many grottoes and for pulling up on beaches for a swim. You could also consider disembarking on **I Faraglioni**, where a unique species of lizard lives, brilliantly cobalt blue in imitation of the surrounding sea; the middle rock stack is pierced by a 60m-long tunnel, wide enough for small boats to pass through. **Windsurfers** can also rent gear at Marina Piccola at about the same rate, although the water, facing the open sea, can often get too choppy for smooth sailing.

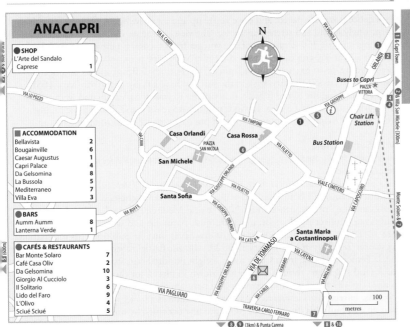

Casa Rossa

Via G. Orlandi • May–Oct Tues–Sun 10am–5pm • €3

A short walk from Piazza Vittoria, the distinctive and eclectically styled **Casa Rossa** was the eccentric home of nineteenth-century American writer and archeologist John Clay MacKowen. The red-hued, crenellated building nowadays houses a small collection of local art, mostly paintings of the island, along with a handful of Roman statues.

San Michele

Piazza San Nicola • Daily: April–Oct 9am–7pm; Nov–March 9.30am–3pm • €2

A short walk from Piazza Vittoria, down shop-lined Via G. Orlandi, the church of **San Michele** is one of Anacapri's star attractions. The entire floor consists of thousands of tiles painted with a delightful depiction of the *Earthly Paradise*, completed in 1761 by one Leonardo Chiaiese, a majolica tilemaker. To view the work in its entirety, you climb a narrow, rickety staircase to an upstairs balcony. Taken from a drawing by the prolific Baroque Neapolitan painter Solimena, it's executed in clear blues and honey yellows, portraying cats, unicorns and other creatures, enjoying their jungle-like world in surrealistic harmony with Adam and Eve, though with the serpent at the centre of the scene. The fallen pair, displaying repentance at their crime, are no longer nude, though animal hides rather than fig leaves preserve their modesty. A smug Archangel Michael straddles a cottony cloud, sword raised, pointing the transgressors to the nearest exit. The animals – who presumably get to stay – watch them go with apparent indifference.

Monte Solaro

Piazza Vittoria • Daily: March–Oct 9.30am–5.30pm; Nov–Feb 10.30am–3pm • €7.50 one-way, €10 return • ⓦ capriseggiovia.it • The chair lift takes 12min; hiking up takes 1hr 30min, or it's around 1hr downhill

Off Piazza Vittoria, there's a **chair lift** (*seggiovia*) station, operating regular services up to **Monte Solaro**, the island's highest point (596m). The ride seems precarious, but the whole

5

experience is well managed, and once you're up and away, swinging out into space, it's a surprisingly restful and serene experience. The views of the sea on the way up are dazzling, and the 360-degree panorama you get from the top is perhaps the bay's best, and on a clear day you can easily see the entire Sorrentine peninsula and Vesuvius. Pause before going down to check out the ruins of the Fortino di Bruto and its photogenic assembly of classical statuary, bask in the sun and have a drink at the bar (see p.165). Instead of taking the chair lift back, many prefer to **walk** the pleasant and well-marked path down to the main piazza. It winds past old stone walls and through the unique vegetation thriving in the intensely humid pre-dawn fog that enshrouds the mount.

Villa San Michele

Via Axel Munthe 34 • Daily: March 9am–4.30pm; April & Oct 9am–5pm; May–Sept 9am–6pm; Nov–Feb 9am–3.30pm • €7 • ☎ 081 837 1401, ⓦ villasanmichele.eu

At the top of Piazza Vittoria, turn left at the *Capri Palace Hotel* and continue on past a gauntlet of souvenir boutiques and stalls to the **Villa San Michele**, a ten-minute walk. This rambling, nineteenth-century Neoclassical Mediterranean villa, built by Swedish physician, pioneer psychiatrist, philanthropist, naturalist and writer **Axel Munthe** (1857–1949), has been a popular tourist draw ever since he published his international bestseller *The Story of San Michele* in 1929. Munthe first climbed up the long, steep Scala Fenicia staircase from Capri town – eight hundred-odd steps carved from the rock (and still there, though a bit tumbledown in places, for those who want to give it a try) – in 1874 and was immediately and permanently captivated by Anacapri's serene charms. Fifteen years later, after making his fortune as a society physician in Paris, he was able to build his dream home, on a site first occupied by one of Tiberius's villas, later by a monastery. It's a light, airy dwelling with luxuriant and fragrant gardens and splendidly plunging panoramas – one of the real highlights of the island. About his beloved creation, Munthe said, "My house must be open to the sun, to the wind, to the light of the sea, like a Greek temple, with light, light, light everywhere!" He lived here for a number of years, until, ironically, it was the light that became too overwhelming for his failing eyesight. He was finally obliged for health reasons to leave the island forever in 1943 and return to Sweden.

The interior

The legacy Munthe bequeathed to Anacapri, managed by the Swedish government, boasts a wonderful **interior** full of his furniture and knick-knacks, as well as Roman artefacts and columns plundered from ruined villas on the island, including that of Tiberius over which it is built. It's an appealing hotchpotch of ancient Etruscan, Roman, Egyptian, Romanesque, Renaissance and Moorish styles, some of the pieces being imitations dating from the seventeenth to the nineteenth centuries. Notable objects include the much-photographed granite sphinx looking out over the isle at the far end, a head of Medusa and a marble bust of Tiberius himself. Elsewhere, Corinthian capitals serve as coffee tables, surfaces are formed of intricate medieval Cosmati mosaic-work and bronzes on marble plinths adorn every arcaded breezeway.

The gardens and bird sanctuary

The terraced **gardens** with their pergolas and balconies are magnificent, and give wonderful views over Marina Grande and Capri town. The bronze resting Hermes (a copy of the original from the Villa dei Papyri at Herculaneum) was given to Munthe by the city of Naples in gratitude for his healing work during the devastating cholera epidemic of 1884. The villa's belvederes are especially lovely, affording some of the best views on the island, and the arboured gardens also hold an attractive natural history exhibition, which fills you in on local flora and fauna, to the (recorded) accompaniment of the golden oriole and the nightingale. Munthe's famous book

FROM TOP ISCHIA'S ARAGONESE CASTLE (P.169); LA PIAZZETTA, CAPRI TOWN (P.152) >

5

– more an autobiography than anything – has been translated into dozens of languages and is well worth a read. It encompasses all of his interests, passions and projects, including that of establishing an island bird sanctuary in the ruins of the **Castello Barbarossa**, a fortress on the mountain peak above the villa that dates at least to the eleventh century, perhaps all the way back to Tiberius. Guided **tours** take in the fortress according to demand between April and October; call in advance to book.

The Blue Grotto

Daily 9am–1hr before sunset, but closed in bad weather • Boat from Marina Grande €12 (10min), rowing boat into the grotto plus admission €13.50 • Some round-island excursions include the Grotto (see p.162); you could also hike from Anacapri (a good 45min), starting off down Via Lo Pozzo, or take the bus (every 20min from Piazza Vittoria; 15min)

The most famous of all Capri's sights is the **Blue Grotto**, or Grotta Azzurra. Its renown means that it is also the island's most exploitative sight, the boatmen whisking visitors onto boats and in and out of the grotto in about five minutes flat. It's best to plan a visit in the **morning**, as it's more likely to be closed after 1pm due to high tide.

In use since Roman times – it was Tiberius's own personal *nymphaeum*, decorated then with marble statues of gods and goddesses – it has been the island's most celebrated attraction since its legendary rediscovery some time in the eighteenth century by a poor fisherman named Zoccolone (roughly translated as "big clog"). Others claim, however, that islanders always knew of its existence but that it was German writer August Kopish who created the first international buzz in 1826, putting Capri firmly on the tourist map.

Perhaps surprisingly, despite the hype and brevity of the experience, the grotto manages to live up to its reputation well enough. It isn't by any means the only sea-grotto of the sort – there are more around the island and along the Amalfi Coast too – but it is certainly the largest, and seeing it does give you an undeniable thrill. Part of the fun is the system of boats and oarsmen, all bobbing chaotically about the tiny entrance. People enter in twos; when the boatman instructs you to duck, in order to enter the low opening, one person will need to lean back into the other one's lap to make it through and avoid scraped heads. Instantly, all is a uniquely glowing blue; the radiance and intensity are caused by sunlight entering the cave from beneath, up through the water. In the past you could swim into the cave but that is now prohibited due to the pollution from boats.

ARRIVAL AND DEPARTURE   CAPRI

All hydrofoils and ferries arrive at Marina Grande, roughly in the middle of Capri's northern coast, with the island's main town perched up the hill.

GETTING TO CAPRI TOWN

If you've booked a hotel, you can arrange for a porter to meet you at the pier. Otherwise, you can generally bypass the hubbub of the port and take the funicular or bus; tickets for both need to be bought at the kiosk.

By funicular The funicular runs directly up to Capri town (daily 6.30am–8.30pm; departures every 15min; €1.80

one-way; wait in line at the kiosk to get tickets).

On foot To walk up the steep hill, go to the fountain at the centre of Marina Grande's semicircular port and turn right. The steps start on the left a few metres up and are clearly marked. They number about 300 in all and take from 20min to 45min to climb, depending on your stamina and your urge to stop and admire the views.

GETTING AROUND

By bus Capri's main bus station is on Via Roma, near the Piazzetta. The bus service runs from end to end and from side to side of the island, connecting all the main centres – Marina Grande, Capri town, Marina Piccola, Anacapri – every 15min. Buses run every 20min down to the Blue Grotto from Anacapri, and also to Punta Carena. Tickets cost €1.80 for a single trip, €2.70 for an hour and €8.60 for a day,

and they're available from ticket booths, newsstands and *tabacchi*, as well as upon boarding.

On foot You can get almost everywhere on foot – and sometimes Capri's overcrowded buses make this the most appealing option. Capri town to Anacapri is about an hour's walk uphill, while Capri town to Marina Piccola is a lovely 15min walk down Via Krupp (longer on the way back up).

CAPRI WALKS

Once you get away from the tourist centres, Capri abounds in easy-to-mildly-challenging **hikes**. The walk to the **Arco Naturale** (see p.155) is one of the island's most popular; the hikes below take in most of the major panoramas and form complete circuits.

ANACAPRI

Time about 2hr **Level** moderate

From Anacapri's Piazza Vittoria, walk down Via Tommaso, in the opposite direction to Capri town, until you get to the bus terminus. Turn left here and take the short walkway, Viale Cimitero, up to the town **cemetery**. Turn right onto the paved pathway, called both Via Caposcuro and Via Migliara. Walk along this pleasant ridge with sea views to the right for about twenty minutes until you come to *Da Gelsomina* hotel and restaurant, which enjoys a panoramic perch. If the timing is right, this makes a good spot for lunch.

Directly across from *Da Gelsomina* is the **Parco Filosofico** (daily sunrise–sunset), the brainchild of a Swedish economics professor and part-time resident of the island. It's basically a patch of untamed vegetation, crisscrossed with rudimentary pathways and set about with benches, meant to provide a place of contemplation and meditation. The significant feature here is the tiles placed all around, hand-painted with pithy quotes by important Western thinkers ("Know thyself" and "I think, therefore I am" among them) to get your ruminations going.

Continuing, you soon reach the end of the walkway, at the **Belvedere di Migliera**, an elevated spot from which you can take in one of the island's most astounding views, of wild crags and pinnacles of wind-sculpted limestone, and of the turquoise sea below. From here, stone steps lead down to the right into a pine forest, with a path that continues along the ridge for about a quarter of an hour, eventually coming to some buildings and then leading out onto the paved road. At the road, turn left and go down the hill about 100m. Look for a sign marked "Punta Carena" (viewable only coming up the hill, in the opposite direction, so keep looking back), indicating concrete steps going down. Take the series of stairways all the way down the steep hillside until you get to **Punta Carena** and the **Faro** (lighthouse). Here you'll find swimming facilities and all services, as well as the beginnings of the **Sentiero dei Fortini**, a much longer nature walk (4–5hr) past old forts, which eventually arrives at the Blue Grotto. From Punta Carena, there are buses to take you back to Anacapri.

SENTIERO DEI FORTINI: PUNTA CARENA TO THE BLUE GROTTO

Time 4–5hr **Level** moderate

The Sentiero dei Fortini path begins at **Punta Carena** and the **Faro** (see above) and meanders along Capri's west coast to **Punta dell'Arcera** and the **Blue Grotto**, passing a series of *fortini*, blockhouses built by the British to defend against French invasion in 1806. The path covers a distance of 4.5km and can be done in reverse.

Beginning at Punta Carena, follow Via Nuova del Faro for around 500m until a fork in the road curves left towards the **Cala del Tombosiello**. From here, there is a steep concrete path that leads past the first of three *fortini*, the **Forte del Pino**, a circular building 60m in diameter clinging to the cliff 40m above sea level. Before the fort, a dirt path leads to a worthwhile detour, a belvedere with breathtaking views over the **Cala di Limmo** and the Faro. This area was once a military outpost where cannons defended against Napoleon's fleet. Back on the Sentiero dei Fortini, and past the Forte del Pino, follow the marked path along the steep cliffs trimmed with artemisia and juniper bushes. Around 600m on, stone steps lead to an unsightly wood-and-iron bridge built to traverse the **Cala di Mezzo**. After another 600m, head off the main trail to the right to reach the **Fortino di Mesola**, a circular structure, on the wild **Punta Campetiello**. Return to the main trail and continue up towards the valley to cross the Rio Cesa and Rio Chiuso, then walk up along the cliff. After a few hundred metres, head downhill, pass a side path, and continue to the final fort, the semicircular **Fortino Orrico**. It was here, on the **Punta del Miglio**, that French troops disembarked in October 1808, breaching the British fortifications to take the island. Back on the Sentiero, the path continues for around 500m until you reach Via Grotta Azzurra, the curving road that hugs the Punta dell'Arcera before descending to the **Blue Grotto**.

5

By boat Capri Boat, located to the right of Marina Grande as you arrive, next to the ferry ticket booths (☎ 081 837 5188), rents boats for a minimum of 3hr (mid-April to mid-Oct 9.30am–6.30pm; €90 per boat for a maximum of five people). Kayak rental is available at Lo Scoglio delle Sirene, Via Mulo 63, Marina Piccola (from €15/hr for a single; ☎ 081 837 0221), along with other watersports equipment too. There are also operators at Marina Grande offering boat excursions around the island, taking in the Blue Grotto on the way, for €17, not including entrance to the grotto; trips last 2hr, or 1hr if the Blue Grotto is closed.

By scooter Although roads are narrow and often very steep, scooters are a possibility, but plan on doing as much

on foot as you have time for. You can rent scooters in Marina Grande from Oasi, at Via Provinciale Marina Grande 208 (☎ 081 837 7138 or ☎ 334 353 2975), and Capri Scooter (☎ 081 837 7712), at various locations including Via Marina Grande 280, just up from the port to the right, and Piazza Barile 26, Anacapri. Reckon on paying around €50 a day.

By taxi Non-residents' cars are not allowed to disembark on Capri from mid-March to November, and you can't hire a car, so the island's stylish convertible taxis are the only private option; they are, however, expensive–the journey from the port to the centre of Capri will cost around €20. There's a taxi rank up to the right as you leave the port (☎ 081 837 0543), and one in Anacapri (☎ 081 837 1175).

INFORMATION

TOURIST OFFICES

Marina Grande Just on the left at the beginning of the quay (April–Oct Mon–Sat 9am–1pm & 3–6pm, Sun 9.30am–1.30pm; Nov–March Mon–Sat 9am–3pm; ☎ 081 837 0634, ⓦ capritourism.com). They sell a handy map (€1) and offer free promotional materials.

La Piazzetta Up in Capri town, in the famed Piazzetta (Mon–Sat 9.30am–1.30pm & 4–6.45pm, Sun 9.30am–1.30pm; closed Sun Oct–April; ☎ 081 837 0686), offering the same services.

Anacapri Via G. Orlandi 59, two minutes from Piazza Vittoria (Mon–Sat 9am–3pm; ☎ 081 837 1524).

ACCOMMODATION

Due to its world-class cachet, Capri **accommodation** prices are uniformly inflated. Still, there are relative bargains – and if you can afford to splurge, the luxury options are well worth it. Around Capri town the hotels have always tended to be the island's priciest, while just up from Marina Grande there are a few budget options, as well as in Marina Piccola and Anacapri, though the latter is also home to some of the island's chicest hotels. In any case, real bargains are just about impossible to find, and you'll need to book very early if you want to snag even a moderately priced room. Many hotels require bookings of at least two nights on summer weekends.

CAPRI TOWN AND AROUND

★ **'A Pazziella** Via Fuorlovado 36 ☎ 081 837 0044, ⓦ royalgroup.it. Cool and breezy even on the hottest day, this place has a palpable serenity, yet it's located in the middle of town. The rooms are elegant and comfortable, many with private balconies and sea views, and there are lovely gardens and free use of the next-door *Sirene* hotel's pool (May–Sept). Closed mid-Oct to April. **€251**

Belvedere & Tre Re Via Marina Grande 264 ☎ 081 837 0345, ⓦ belvedere-tre-re.com. Just steps from the port, this hotel offers an extensive terrace and fine views, as well as easy private access to the beach just below. The rooms are fresh and clean, some with balconies, and all have views of the Bay of Naples. Closed Nov to mid-April. **€156**

Da Giorgio Via Roma 34 ☎ 081 837 5777, ⓦ dagiorgiocapri.com. With gracious rooms affording views of the bay, this modest little hotel is an excellent choice, not least because it also boasts one of the island's best restaurants (see p.164). Closed Nov–March. **€150**

JK Place Capri Via Marina Grande 225 ☎ 081 838 4001, ⓦ jkcapri.com. Capri's top blow-the-budget choice is this stylish bolthole that lords it over Marina Grande from its own clifftop perch, a safe distance from the hustle and bustle of the port below. The rooms are perfumed with

freshly cut blooms, the decor is chic and breezy, and the wrap-around terrace has dazzling views. The restaurant, pool and on-site spa are top-notch too. It's the perfect place to unwind – so long as someone else is paying. Closed mid-Oct to mid-April. **€900**

★ **La Tosca** Via Dalmazio Birago 5 ☎ 081 837 0989, ⓦ latoscahotel.com. Genuine bargains on Capri are few and far between, but this place is a real find. A short walk from the Giardini di Augusto on a quiet lane, this whitewashed house has 11 en-suite doubles, some with sea views, kept in spick-and-span condition. Ultra-friendly service and thoughtful extras – such as free use of an iPad – are a bonus, and breakfast on the tiny terrace overlooking I Faraglioni is a treat. Closed Nov–March. **€130**

Quattro Stagioni Via Marina Piccola 1 ☎ 081 837 0041, ⓦ hotel4stagionicapri.com. In a pretty location, a little way out of Capri town at the fork of the roads to Marina Piccola and Anacapri, this place has friendly staff, and offers a 10 percent discount to carriers of this book from mid-March to Oct. **€125**

Villa Sarah Via Tiberio 3a ☎ 081 837 7817, ⓦ villasarahcapri.com. A bit of a walk from Capri town, this historic villa with magnificent views has been lovingly restored and retains much of its old-world flavour – an

5

ancient stone well graces the terrace – without skimping on modern comforts. Gracious gardens complete the quintessential Capri experience. Closed Nov to mid-March. **€220**

Weber Ambassador Via Marina Piccola ☎ 081 837 0141, ⊛ hotelweber.com. This quiet, comfortable choice offers great views from its multi-levelled terraces, particularly of the iconic Faraglioni rocks. The decor is cosy and elegant, with warm terracotta accents, and steps lead directly down to the Marina Piccola beach. The frequent shuttle to Capri town is a bonus. Closed Nov–March. **€140**

ANACAPRI AND AROUND

Bellavista Via G. Orlandi 10 ☎ 081 837 1463, ⊛ bellavistacapri.com. Gardens and spectacular views greet new arrivals to this hotel boasting some of the island's most photogenic trellised walkways and terraces; the rooms meanwhile are spacious and comfortable. Discounts for guests are available at nearby restaurants, and in summer it's possible to use the pool at the hotel over the road for a €10 daily charge. Closed Nov–Easter. **€180**

Bougainville Viale Tommaso de Tommaso 6 ☎ 081 837 3641, ⊛ hlb.it. A comfortable choice, set in a lush flower garden, which some rooms overlook, just a few minutes' walk down the main road from the centre. Rooms are comfortable and nicely furnished and amenities include a good restaurant, a solarium and guest pick-up/drop-off at Marina Grande. Closed Nov to mid-April. **€169**

★ **Caesar Augustus** Via G. Orlandi 4 ☎ 081 837 3395, ⊛ caesar-augustus.com. The terrace of this luxury mansion has always been a major attraction, touted as having the most beautiful panorama in the world. In one sweeping vista, it takes in the entire Bay of Naples, overlooked by a statue of the Emperor Augustus. Inside, too, the hotel offers a truly imperial experience, from the refurbished rooms to the infinity pool – which seems to merge with the distant sea – to the manicured gardens. Closed Nov–mid-April. **€460**

Capri Palace Via Capodimonte 14 ☎ 081 978 0111, ⊛ capripalace.com. One of the top choices on the entire

island: rooms are decorated in tasteful, luxurious fabrics in light neutral tones, surrounded by gardens and with hill views of Mount Solaro or sea views of the Mediterranean and Bay of Naples. Several suites have private pools. Its concept store has a shoemaker and dressmaker, as well as designer threads in case you arrive without luggage. **€528**

Da Gelsomina Via Migliara 72 ☎ 081 837 1499, ⊛ dagelsomina.com. The location is stunning, but getting there with luggage may dampen your enthusiasm: it's a good 20min walk from Piazza Vittoria along a paved, pedestrian-only path. However, it does offer a pool, an excellent restaurant and a stupendous setting, with plenty of hiking trails nearby. Rooms are simple and fresh, and each has its own terrace. It's always full in high season, so it's worth knowing that they have a sister hotel, the similarly priced *Villa Ceselle* in the centre of town, at which you get access to the *Gelsomina* restaurant and pool. **€150**

★ **La Bussola** Via Traversa la Vigna 14 ☎ 081 838 2010, ⊛ bussolahermes.com. This boutiquey hotel is a true oasis of peace, a 10min walk from the centre of Anacapri. Cool, stylish rooms, all with balconies – the upper-floor ones are best – and a friendly, welcoming vibe. Closed Oct–March. **€150**

Mediterraneo Via Caposcuro 12 ☎ 081 837 2907, ⊛ mediterraneo-capri.com. Down the curving staircase from the pedestrian-only lane is a garden courtyard decorated with classical statuary and terracotta pots. The airy, fresh feel is maintained throughout, and the rooms evoke understated elegance. Friendly service. Closed mid-Nov to March. **€252**

Villa Eva Via La Fabbrica 8 ☎ 081 837 1549, ⊛ villaeva .com. For a long time now, Villa Eva has been the cult budget option of the island, and the legend only gets better. It has a wide choice of individually styled rooms to choose from, most of them spacious and light, in the main building, as well as others scattered around the gardens, and a grand-piano shaped pool. No dinner, but there are snacks available by the pool, where breakfast is served too. Take the Grotta Azzurra bus and ask to be let off at *Villa Eva*. Closed Nov–March. **€140**

EATING AND DRINKING

Dining on Capri can mean anything from indifferent tourist rations to a true gourmet experience. The island is known, of course, for its signature dish, *insalata caprese*: fresh tomatoes and whole basil leaves just plucked from the volcanic soil, which gives them an unparalleled rich flavour, and *mozzarella di bufala*, made from local buffalo milk, known for its complex taste and juicy texture, topped off with pungent extra-virgin olive oil. Lemon specialities are favourites, as is *torta caprese*, a dense chocolate cake made with ground almonds, bittersweet chocolate and a splash of liqueur. Quality is generally good, so it's difficult to go wrong, although as in any tourist spot standards are prone to slip at busy times of year. The places below offer consistently tasty food and good value, within the parameters of the island's high prices.

Capri town has a few small *salumerie*, which make up panini for a few euros and sell all you'll need for a picnic. Try Da Brioches at Via Fuorlovado 5, near La Piazzetta (Mon–Sat 7.45am–9pm, Sun 9am–8pm) or Salumeria da Aldo in Marina Grande (daily 7am–9pm). Tucked away just a few metres back down towards Marina Grande from the island's little roundabout, there's also a sizeable supermarket.

5

CAPRI TOWN AND AROUND

CAFÉS AND GELATERIE

Bar Caso Piazza Umberto I 4, Capri town ☎ 081 837 0600. Of the quartet of bars on La Piazzetta, this one is traditionally the gay favourite. In any case, it has the same smart service, refreshing treats and extortionate prices as anywhere else in on the glitzy square. Daily 7am–1am.

Bar Onda d'Oro Marina Piccola ☎ 081 837 0698. A beach bar (and popular pizzeria), well sited for taking a break from the sea and sun and cooling down in the shade, with I Faraglioni as part of your panoramic view. Daily 9am–11pm.

Bar Tiberio Piazza Umberto I 18, Capri town ☎ 081 837 0268. This is supposedly where Neapolitans go when they want to while away an hour or two, while Capri natives are said to favour the rival *Piccolo Bar* on the same square. Which one you choose depends on whether you prefer to people-watch in the direction of the new arrivals up from the marina, or to keep an eye on who's wending their way along from the chic hotels. Daily 6am–2am.

Buonocore Gelateria Via Vittorio Emanuele 35, Capri town ☎ 081 837 7826. A fantastic family-run *gelateria* serving up the creamiest ice cream in town, made with fresh fruit – figs, prickly pears, mandarins – from their own garden. Specialities include the sinfully rich *fantasia di Capri* (vanilla with Nutella and almonds) and cones are made to order from a generations-old family recipe. Daily 8am–8pm; closes 2am in high season. Closed mid-Nov to mid-March.

Il Gelato al Limone Piazzetta Fontana 63, Marina Grande ☎ 081 838 9403. Whether arriving or waiting for a ferry, this is a good place to indulge in some Caprese *limoncello* ice cream. Lemons are harvested at the foot of the Scala Fenicia and all other ingredients are of the highest quality. Sweets and cakes for sale as well. Daily 8.30am–8.30pm.

RESTAURANTS AND PIZZERIAS

Aurora Via Fuorlovado 18–22 ☎ 081 837 0181, ⓦ auroracapri.com. This attractive place is the longest-established restaurant on the island, featuring Neapolitan and Caprese cuisine, with tables outside and a crunchy speciality called *pizza all'acqua* (€12–14 depending on topping) made in its wood-burning oven. Full meals are much pricier, easily racking up €55 a head. Daily noon–3pm & 5pm–midnight. Closed Dec–Feb.

Buca di Bacco "da Serafina" Via Longano 35 ☎ 081 837 0723. This old favourite is rated by locals and visitors alike as one of the best; try the *spaghetti alla pescatora* for €17, or fresh fish mains from €15. It's located just behind La Piazzetta, with a cosy, whitewashed interior decorated with copper pans. Some tables have sea views. Daily noon–3pm & 7pm–midnight. Closed Jan & Feb.

Canzone del Mare Via Marina Piccola 93 ☎ 081 837 0104, ⓦ lacanzonedelmare.com. This bathing establishment and restaurant is a top choice on the island's southern side, with the freshest fish and meat, and wines from Campania, which you can enjoy in the more formal restaurant (reckon on at least €40 a head); the comfy bar and pool areas serve bar snacks. Daily Easter–Oct noon–4pm.

Capri Pasta Via Parroco Roberto Canale 12 ☎ 081 837 0147. A family-run, hole-in-the-wall takeaway serving delicious, crispy pizza, as well as a handful of hot dishes – the likes of spinach pie, meatballs or *melanzane alla parmigiana* – for a few euros. Everything's home-made, delicious and very cheap. Mon–Sat 9am–8pm, Sun 9am–2pm. Open all year.

Da Giorgio Via Roma 34 ☎ 081 837 0898, ⓦ dagiorgiocapri.com. This popular local hangout has a great, very central yet picturesque location on Capri town's main street, with lovely views through its picture windows. Service is brash but efficient and the prices moderate by Capri standards (pasta dishes around €15) – try the *linguine ai frutti di mare* or fish with artichokes. The restaurant also offers good-value hotel rooms (see p.162), with optional half or full board. Daily noon–3pm & 7pm–midnight. Closed Tues in low season and from mid-Oct to March.

Da Paolino Lemon Trees Via Palazzo a Mare 11 ☎ 081 837 6102, ⓦ paolinocapri.com. It's hard not to succumb to the allure of lemon trees so laden with lemons that it seems the owner, Lino, must be busy gluing any back on that fall off. He'll guide you to the tempting buffet for antipasti, then help you choose fresh fish or meat for the main course. Celebrity tracking is part of the Capri game, and they've all been here – Richard Gere, Nicolas Cage, Tom Cruise, you name them. Yellow tablecloths, ceramic plates, majolica lamps and handcrafted candles complete the very yellow experience – a sure bet to charm anyone. A full meal with wine will set you back around €60 per person. Daily 7pm–midnight. Closed mid-Oct to April.

★ **Da Tonino** Via Dentecala ☎ 081 837 6718. Tucked away in the hills above Capri town near the Arco Naturale (it's about a 15-minute walk from the Piazzetta), *Da Tonino* is worth the trek. Campanian cuisine with a gourmet twist – such as risotto in a beer reduction, or courgette-flower tempura (€15) – is on the menu, and the wine list is exceptional. Ask for a tour of the cellar, which holds over 15,000 bottles from all over Italy. Daily 11.45am–3pm & 6.45pm–midnight. Closed Mon in April, May & June, and closed Nov–March.

L'Approdo Piazza Angelo Ferraro 12 ☎ 081 837 8990, ⓦ approdocapri.com. A reliable option in Marina Grande, at the quieter end of the quay beyond the more touristy restaurants and the pushy touts, this place is renowned for its crispy pizza but it also offers a tempting selection of pastas, risottos and grilled fish (two courses with wine around €40). Right on the water, it has a good view of the comings and goings in the port too. Daily noon–4pm & 6.30pm–midnight.

Le Grottelle Via Arco Naturale 13 ☎ 081 837 5719.

Almost all the way down to the Arco Naturale, the appeal of this family-run place is its stunning position, set amid lush greenery and with precipitous views down to the sea. The traditional cookery is generally good – pastas tend to be the most reliable – and the service amiable. Prices are high (at least €40 per person) but it's still worth a visit. Mon & Wed–Sun noon–3pm & 7.30–10.30pm. Closed mid-Nov to March.

Scialapopolo Via Gradoni Sopramonte 6/8 ☎ 081 837 9054. A well-priced lunch option just a short walk from the Piazzetta, this friendly family-run place serves good pizza and reasonably priced pastas, meat and fish mains and salads (around €11). Daily noon–4pm & 7–10.30pm. Closed one month in winter.

★**Villa Verde** Vico Sella Orta 6a ☎ 081 837 7024, ⓦ villaverde-capri.com. Great antipasti and creatively presented seafood cuisine are the culinary delights here, as well as traditional fare and excellent *focaccia*, in a soothing and intimate garden setting, complete with grotto and fountain. Dinner will set you back about €60 without wine. Daily noon–3.30pm & 7pm–12.30am. Closed Nov to early Dec and Jan to mid-March.

ANACAPRI AND AROUND

CAFÉS

★**Bar Monte Solaro** Monte Solaro, Anacapri ☎ 081 837 1877. Probably the island's ultimate café experience, good for cooling drinks and tasty snacks while you catch some sun, ogle the international clientele and take in the stupendous views. Daily 9.30am–5.15pm.

Café Casa Oliv Viale Axel Munthe 34, Anacapri ☎ 081 837 1401. If you can bear to drink without people-watching, this treetop terrace oasis nested amid maritime pines is a fine alternative for a drink. You have to pay the *Villa San Michele* entry fee (see p.158), but you can savour the good life and sea views while sipping a coffee or cocktail (around €10), and also enjoy a simple but lovely lunch in this private, tranquil setting. Mon–Thurs, Sat & Sun 10am–6pm, Fri 10am–9pm. Closed Dec–March.

RESTAURANTS AND PIZZERIAS

★**Da Gelsomina** Via Migliara 72 ☎ 081 837 1499, ⓦ dagelsomina.com. This excellent restaurant with lovely views makes a wonderful lunch option. The food is traditional

Capri fare and consistently delicious, with lunch going for about €30 per person. Try the spicy, "hunter-style" rabbit with tomatoes (*coniglio alla cacciatora*). The attached hotel is equally good (see p.163). Daily noon–3.30pm & 7.30–11pm. Closed Tues in April & Sept and closed Oct–March.

Giorgio Al Cucciolo Via La Fabbrica 52 ☎ 081 837 1917. This rather pricey choice has a terrace overlooking the sea and distant Ischia. If you're based in Anacapri, phone ahead and they'll come and pick you up from your hotel, and take you back again. Daily noon–3pm & 7pm–midnight. Closed Wed in low season and closed Nov–March.

★**Il Solitario** Via G. Orlandi 96 ☎ 081 837 1382, ⓦ trattoriailsolitario.it. Take the little walkway back from the street and discover an arboured garden patio setting decorated with appealingly kitsch statues and coloured fairy lights. A family-run restaurant where the food is excellent – they do a very generous *spaghetti alle vongole* with home-made pasta, and great pizzas too; the prices are moderate, and the service very friendly. Mon, Tues & Thurs–Sun noon–3pm & 7pm–midnight. Closed two months in winter.

L'Olivo Via Capodimonte 2/b ☎ 081 978 0560. The only restaurant on Capri to be awarded two Michelin stars, this plush pad in the *Capri Palace Hotel* is renowned for its creative nouveau Mediterranean cuisine (7-course tasting menu €120, or a la carte dishes around €40). Natural textiles in neutral tones, Murano glassware and handmade dishes complete a very luxurious picture. Daily 7.30–10.30pm. Closed Nov–March.

Lido del Faro Località Punta Carena ☎ 081 837 1798, ⓦ lidofaro.com/it/ristorante. Set above the dramatic rocky cove below Anacapri's lighthouse, this is a great place for lunch; ladders lead down into the cove for sea-swimming, but there is a pool as well (no children after 3pm). The food is expensive – you could easily spend €60 on three courses, without wine, but the food (tender octopus salad, crisp fried *baccalà*) is really good, and the setting is gorgeous. Daily noon–sunset. Closed end Oct–Easter.

Sciué Sciué Via G. Orlandi 73 ☎ 081 837 2068. This friendly joint does triple duty as a *rosticceria, pasticceria* and pizzeria, and turns out delicious pizza by the slice and other traditional snacks. Great for when time is short and you need a pick-me-up. Daily 9am–midnight. Closed Nov–March.

NIGHTLIFE

Capri's main square, La Piazzetta, is always bustling, but after dark it begins to show its true colours. Everyone, sooner or later, will pass through, on their way back from dinner, or out for a night on the tiles. Most of the bars here stay open until everyone goes home. Otherwise nightlife revolves around the island's hotel bars and a handful of good clubs.

Anema e Core Via Sella Orta 39e, Capri town ☎ 081 837 6461, ⓦ anemaecore.com. The "Soul and Heart" was and still tries to be the epitome of the *dolce vita* lifestyle. Ideally located right in the poshest of the posh areas – across from

the sumptuous *Hotel Quisisana* – this club is frequented by a very self-consciously fashionable set. Live Neapolitan and Italian music and some Latin American acoustic sets. Admission €40, includes 1 drink. Daily 11.30pm–4am.

5

Aumm Aumm Via Caprile 18, Anacapri ☏ 081 837 3000. This good-sized bar doubles as a pizzeria, and, with its huge screen, as a sports bar whenever there's a big game on. Locals love it, and it's open till late. The antidote to the glamour of Capri. Tues–Sun 7pm–1am.

Lanterna Verde In the Hotel San Michele, Via G. Orlandi 1, Anacapri ☏ 081 837 1427, ⌨ lanternaverdecapri.it. A long-established bar and occasional live-music venue (it opened in Capri's heyday in 1952), in a cavernous space carved out of the rock. The atmosphere is a little cheesy but huge windows with sea views remind you of where you are. Daily 5pm–1am.

SHOPPING

Capri is known for its sun-kissed local produce, above all the prized lemons and *limoncello*, but there are handmade crafts of all sorts, too, including sandals. Capri town's famous **boutiques** are, of course, on the pricey side, and include a hefty sprinkling of international designer labels. Below are a few of the more artisanal enterprises, most of which will open every day during summer, less often in spring and autumn, and a few may even close altogether during the depths of winter.

CapriNatura Concessions in food shops across the island: Piccolo Bar, La Piazzetta; Salumeria Ferraro, Via Le Botteghe; and Ristorante Aurora, Via Fuorlovado ☏ 0825 520 170, ⌨ caprinatura.com. This micro-producer of Mediterranean digestive liqueurs near Avellino sells flavours including lemon, mandarin, laurel and basil, made from local citrus and herbs using traditional recipes.

Carthusia Various locations, including Via Camerelle 10, Capri town, and Via Axel Munthe 26, Anacapri ☏ 081 837 0529, ⌨ carthusia.it. Back in 1380, a bunch of wildflowers picked by a monk and left in water for a few days was the starting point for Capri's now-thriving perfume business. The monk used the scented water to create a perfume, and went on to concoct formulas that went undiscovered until 1948, when the prior of the monastery discovered the monk's scribblings and, with the pope's permission, passed them to a perfumer. The perfumes are still made according to the monk's original methods; *fiore di Capri* is the bestseller, with lily of the valley, wild carnation and sandalwood. Daily 9am–6pm. Closed Nov–March.

L'Arte del Sandalo Caprese Via G. Orlandi 75, Anacapri ☏ 081 837 3583, ⌨ sandalocaprese.it. Getting sandals made to fit is a Capri tradition. Or try a pair of moccasins. Unless you choose one of the most elaborate models, chances are Antonio Viva will have your made-to-order pair ready within the hour. Daily 9am–10pm.

La Conchiglia Via Le Botteghe 12 & Piazza Umberto 1, Capri town ⌨ laconchigliacapri.com. This publisher also has a bookshop that specializes in Capri literature, including writings in several languages about the island, and the bizarre assortment of people who have frequented it. There's also a selection of reproductions of antiques, as well as original paintings and prints. They hold readings and other events in local hotels and piazzas. Daily 9am–9pm; the store in the Piazzetta closes 1.30–2pm.

DIRECTORY

Festivals Two main events commemorate the island's patron saints: San Costanzo on May 14 in Capri town, and Sant'Antonio on June 13 in Anacapri. The Settembrata Anacaprese in the first week of September celebrates the grape harvest in Anacapri, while September 8 sees a costumed procession up Monte Solaro. The Capri film festival takes place late December. On January 1 and 6, New Year and Epiphany celebrations include the *tarantella* dance in La Piazzetta.

First aid ☏ 081 838 1239; emergency at sea ☏ 1530.

Hospital Via Provinciale Anacapri 5, Capri town (☏ 081 838 1205).

Internet Il Gabbiano, Via C. Colombo 76, Capri town (☏ 081 837 6531), charges €5/hr. At the time of writing a free wi-fi scheme was being trialled in the Piazzetta; check with the tourist office for the latest.

Left luggage Closest to the port is in the unnamed souvenir shop opposite the entrance to the dock (daily 9am–6pm). There's another left-luggage facility at the top of the funicular, on Via Acquaviva (daily 8am–8pm; July & Aug open till 10pm). Both charge €3 per bag per day.

Post office Branches at Via Roma 50, Capri town, and Via De Tommaso 8, Anacapri.

Ischia

Largest of the islands in the Bay of Naples, **ISCHIA** rises out of the sea in a series of pointy green hummocks. Its perfect cone shape is the giveaway to its geological roots: the island is essentially a long-inactive volcano (last known eruption 1301), although in this notoriously seismic area, perpetual slumber is no certainty. The main port is defined by the nearly perfect rim of an extinct crater, opened up to the sea only in 1855, when part of the ring was ordered to be cut away by Ferdinand II.

ISCHIA

5

Procida, Pozzuoli, Naples & Sorrento

Capri & Salerno

Punta Caruso

Spiaggia di San Montano

Negombo

La Colombaia

Spiaggia di San Francesco

La Mortella

Lacco Ameno

Spiaggia di Chiaia

Casamicciola Terme

SEE "ISCHIA PORTO & ISCHIA PONTE" MAP

Ischia Porto

Monterone

Forio

Monte Toppo (390m)

Monte Trippodi (502m)

Ischia Ponte

Castello Aragonese

Spiaggia di Cava dell'Isola

Giardini Ravino

Cuotto

Monte Epomeo (789m)

Fontana

Fiaiano

San Michele

I Pilastri

Spiaggia di Cartorama

Spiaggia di Citara

Giardini Poseidon

Ciglio

Piedimonte

Buonopane

BARANO D'ISCHIA

Molara

Punta del Soccorso

Panza

Serrara Fontana

Vatoliere

Spiaggia di San Pancrazio

Succhivo

Testaccio

Punta San Pancrazio

N

Il Sorgeto

Sant'Angelo

Spiaggia dei Maronti

Punta Sant'Angelo

0   2
kilometres

A sure sign that all has far from cooled off underground is the plentiful **hot springs**, which are part of the island's long-standing allure, offering everything from luxury spas to moonlit skinny-dipping in coves with natural steam-heated rock pools. The island's thermal spas, some of them radioactive, claim cures for almost anything that ails you, be it "gout, retarded sexual development, or chronic rheumatism", to quote one old brochure. Sometimes called the Emerald Island, Ischia is also studded with pine groves and surrounded by sparkling waters that lap its long sandy beaches. German, Scandinavian and British tourists, in particular, flock to its beach resorts in droves during peak season. The island's reputation has always been less glamorous than Capri's, and it is perhaps not so dramatically beautiful. But you can at least be sure of being alone in exploring many parts of the mountainous interior, which rises to the peak of **Monte Epomeo** (793m) at its centre. It's at its most developed along its northern and western shores. The majority of ferry connections are to **Ischia town** on the northeastern side of the island, a sprawling small town made up of Ischia Porto and quieter Ischia Ponte to the east. West of Ischia Porto, Casamicciola Terme and Lacco Ameno are spa centres known for their restorative radioactive waters. Nearby, **La Mortella** is a unique draw, an exotic garden cultivated by the British composer William Walton and his Argentine wife Susana, while workaday **Forío** has plenty to offer in the way of beaches, as does **Sant'Angelo** beyond, a former fishing village that's now one of the island's most appealing places to rest up for a few days.

Brief history

The island's history is probably the area's most ancient, having known habitation since about 2000 BC. From the eighth to the fifth centuries BC, this area became an important part of **Magna Graecia** (Greater Greece) when colonists from Greek city-states in Euboea

5

established themselves on Ischia, which they called Pithekoussai (in reference to the abundance of potting clay, *pithos*) until the eruption of Montagnone made them decide to settle Cumae on the mainland instead. The Greeks evolved a myth to explain the island's volcanic nature, saying that Zeus had imprisoned the monstrous giant Typhon, creator of volcanoes, beneath the island and that the hot springs and steam were his tears of frustration and huffs of rage. Archeological evidence shows that there was a significant disturbance in the second century BC, too, which again drove island inhabitants away. The last time Typhon grumbled was in 1883, causing an earthquake. During most of the Roman period, the island was of oddly little importance – the archeological record showing mostly signs of humble peasant life – probably due to the pronounced seismic activity. Following the fall of the Roman Empire, the island was little more than a political football, and in the Middle Ages was plagued by natural catastrophes and attacks by Saracen corsairs. The high point was the early 1500s, when Renaissance humanist Vittoria Colonna resided in the Castello Aragonese. Much later, the island (like Capri) attracted its share of artistic foreign residents: the Norwegian playwright Henrik Ibsen penned *Peer Gynt* here in the nineteenth century, and later the locals of Forío were at once honoured, puzzled and scandalized by the antics of gay English poet W.H. Auden and his circle.

Ischia Porto and Ischia Ponte

Ischia's main town, **ISCHIA PORTO**, or simply Ischia, is the arrival point for most hydrofoils and ferries, inside the protective ring of the uniquely circular little port. It's an appealing enough stretch of hotels, wannabe ritzy boutiques and beach shops along lanes planted with lemon trees and prickly pear. Beyond a few churches, Ischia Porto has no special sights, and amounts to pretty much what first meets the eye – a stretch of low-key resort commercialism and hotels, with plenty of gardens and greenery. The best way to occupy your time here is to window-shop, slurp a *gelato* and stroll along the mostly pedestrianized Corso Vittoria Colonna and parallel lanes.

But Ischia Porto is really just the snootier, parvenu half of a two-part urbanized spread. Follow Corso Colonna past the Baroque extravaganza

Map

ISCHIA PORTO & ISCHIA PONTE

VIA IASOLINO
Porto
Punta San Pietro
Bus Station
Ferry Terminal
San Pietro
VIA PORTO
ISCHIA PORTO
LUNGOMARE IA SOLINO
VIA ROMA
VIA BUONOCORE
VIA TERME
VIA MORGIONI
S. Maria delle Grazie
Spiaggia del Lido
VIA ALFREDO DE LUCA
VIA R GIANTURCO
LUNGOMARE
VIA D'ALVOS
VIA DELLO STADIO
PIAZZA D'EROI
VIA EDGARDO CORTESE
Villa Nenzi Bozzi
San Girolamo
VIA GIANTURCO
COLOMBO CRISTOFORO
VIA MICHELE MAZZELLA
VIA SOGLIUZZO
CORSO VITTORIA COLONNA
VIA ANTONIO SOGLIUZZO
San Antonio
Spiaggia dei Pescatori
N
VIA MIRABELLA
VIA PJ NAMO
VIA SEMINARIO
VIA LUIGI MAZZELLA
Museo del Mare
ISCHIA PONTE
Ponte Aragonese
Immacolata
Castello Aragonese
Tempio di San Pietro

Procida, Naples, Pozzuoli, Sorrento & Capri

ACCOMMODATION

Eurocamping dei Pini	6
Il Monastero	8
Il Moresco	5
La Marticana	3
Locanda sul Mare	2
Macrí	1
Terme Oriente	4
Ulisse	7

CAFÉS & RESTAURANTS

Alberto a Mare	2
Calise Caffè	3
Da Coco'	4
Gennaro	1

0   400
metres

5

of the colourful tile-domed church that goes by two names, **San Pietro** and **Santa Maria delle Grazie**, alongside the shaded plantings of the Villa Nenzi Bozzi and then on past the impressive park of umbrella pines. This is the woodsy line of demarcation between Ischia Porto and **ISCHIA PONTE** (3km away from the port at its furthest tip; also reachable by bus #7) – the quieter, centuries older and generally less touristy half of the island's main settlement. Despite signs of gentrification, such as one or two elegant antiques shops and several art galleries, things are just a bit more run-down here, a bit earthier – home to the less crowded **Spiaggia dei Pescatori** ("Fishermen's Beach"), as well as the island's major landmark, the **Castello Aragonese**.

Castello Aragonese

Ischia Ponte • Daily 9am–sunset • €10 • ⓦ castelloaragonese.it

The dominant focus of Ischia Ponte is indubitably the island's emblem, the regal **Castello Aragonese**. The Castello crowns an offshore volcanic outcrop about 113m high – affording stupendous views – accessible by Ischia Ponte's causeway of 220m, built by Alfonso of Aragon in the fifteenth century. The hulking structure's distinctive pyramid shape acted as a backdrop in the film *The Talented Mr Ripley* and serves almost daily as the picturesque setting for wedding photos, usually complete with classic car.

A fort of some sort has crowned this rock since at least the fifth century BC, and has belonged to the Greeks, the Romans, the Goths, the Arabs and others, though its most famous occupant was the Renaissance poet **Vittoria Colonna** (see box, p.170). The citadel itself where she lived is a mere shell now, part of so much that was destroyed by British bombardment in the early nineteenth century. At one time the entire mount was covered with buildings, forming a sizeable town boasting a population of some eight thousand souls. Now the only extant structures lie landward from the abandoned citadel, constituting a ramble of buildings. You arrive by stairs or lift in the midst of these, and you can stroll freely around, admiring the stunning **views** at every turn. To the right, you'll find the graceful sixteenth-century **Tempio di San Pietro**, like a mini-Pantheon, and, further up, the remains of the fourteenth-century *carcere* that once held political prisoners during the upheavals of Italian Unification. To the left is the weird open shell of the ruined **cathedral**, built in 1301 but reworked in the eighteenth century in Baroque style; the largely intact crypt holds Giotto-inspired frescoes painted in the fourteenth century. Close by is the fairly undamaged eighteenth-century **Immacolata** church, noted for its imposing dome. You can also explore the grim remains of the **convent of the Poor Clares**, many of whose inmates were not here by choice, but were sent by their families. A couple of dark rooms ringed with a set of commode-like seats used to serve as a macabre open cemetery for the dead sisters – propped up here to putrefy and eventually mummify in full view of the living members of the community, a practice that continued until the early nineteenth century.

Two café-restaurants offer plenty of shady spots to enjoy the stunning views; the rest of the convent has been turned into a hotel (see p.177).

Museo del Mare

Via Giovanni Da Procida 3 • Daily: April–June, Sept & Oct 10.30am–12.30pm & 3–7pm; July & Aug 10.30am–12.30pm & 6.30–10pm; Nov–Jan & March 10.30am–12.30pm • €3 • ⓦ museodelmareischia.it

Ischia Ponte is home to the island's **Museo del Mare**, which traces the community's seafaring roots. Housed in the modest Baroque Palazzo Orologio, the fascinating displays explore Ischia's maritime connections over the millennia. They include ancient, barnacle-encrusted pottery retrieved from the sea, exhibits of marine fauna, navigation instruments ranging from sextants to sonar, along with displays of nautical and fishing gear. Perhaps most appealing are the meticulously detailed models of typically Ischian sailing vessels, though the colourful collection of sea-themed stamps is also eye-catching and includes some blocks depicting the amphibious dinosaurs and other monstrous denizens that plied these waters aeons ago.

VITTORIA COLONNA

Vittoria Colonna, Renaissance poet, humanist luminary and close friend of Michelangelo, lived out much of her life in the Castello Aragonese, banished here following the seizure by Pope Alexander VI of her family's land in and around Rome. In 1509, she was married in the castle's cathedral to the scion of the d'Avalos family, Ischia being one of their feudal fiefdoms. Vittoria created a brilliant court here – one of the most renowned of a sparkling era – while her husband Ferrante was away fighting wars. After his death in the Battle of Pavia in 1525, she continued to maintain her intellectual circle and life of spiritual retreat here until 1536. Her close friendship with Michelangelo was a lifelong platonic affair – including dedications of works of art and mutual exchanges of high-flown poems – ending with her death in 1547, in Rome.

The beaches

Ischia Porto has some good **beaches**, once you get past the buildings hugging the shoreline. The **Spiaggia San Pietro** and **Spiaggia del Lido** are to the right of the port – follow Via Buonocore off Via Roma – while the **Spiaggia degli Inglesi**, its name hailing back to the brief British hegemony in the early nineteenth century, is on the other side of the port; take the narrow path that leads over the headland from the end of Via Iasolino. In Ischia Ponte there is the more proletarian, dark-sand **Spiaggia dei Pescatori**.

Casamicciola Terme

The first village you reach heading west from Ischia Porto is **CASAMICCIOLA TERME**, a spa centre with an array of hotels and a crowded beach. The village's claim to fame is that Ibsen spent a summer here, writing *Peer Gynt*, but most people stop off here for its spa waters, which are said to be full of iodine (reputedly beneficial for the skin and the nervous system).

The sea can be quite rough here, but if you must take a dip, there's a **beach** with facilities around the Spiaggia dei Bagnitelli on the road heading east towards Ischia Porto. For **spa treatments**, the **Terme Belliazzi** (mid-April to Oct; ☎081 994 580, ⓦtermebelliazzi.it) is a bathing complex built above a hot spring prized by the Romans: you can soak in pools beneath ancient brick arches. Dedicated to medicinal cures – the radioactive waters are thought to help respiratory disorders – it also offers the usual pampering treatments; a massage or mud treatment costs from €30.

Lacco Ameno

Less than 3km west of Casamicciola is **LACCO AMENO**, a brighter, altogether more stylish little town, with a beach and spa waters that are reputedly the most radioactive in Italy, a property that is said to ease a host of ailments. A 10m-tall tufa rock sprouting out of the sea is the town's most distinctive landmark, affectionately nicknamed **Il Fungo**, which is likely to have been spewed from the erupting cone of Mount Epomeo millennia ago and does indeed vaguely resemble a mushroom. Nowadays Lacco Ameno is simply an attractive place to pass some time, and its appeal is preserved thanks to a curve in the main road just before it reaches the town centre, leaving the area along the waterfront pedestrian-only, with gurgling fountains in piazzas, low-key shops and waterside cafés.

Lacco Ameno is a resort above all, but the town also has a strong sense of place and a colourful history. Legend holds that the martyred body of fourth-century Tunisian virgin **Santa Restituta** was borne to this spot by lilies, and there's a sugary pink-and-white confection of a church in Piazza Santa Restituta decorated with a nineteenth-century painting cycle remembering those events. Archeological excavations have revealed that it's built on top of a fourth-century paleo-Christian basilica, a second-century BC Roman town, and even more ancient remains – such as a pottery kiln – of what was once the Greek colony of Pithecusae. There are a few artefacts exhibited in the **Area Archeologica di Santa Restituta**, under the church (daily: April, May, Sept & Oct 9.30am–12.30pm & 4–6pm, closed Sun afternoon; June–Aug 9.30am–12.30pm & 5–7pm, closed Sun afternoon; suggested donation €3), including votive amphorae and *ex voto* objects accumulated over many centuries, as well as Byzantine, Roman and Greek ceramics, coins, toys and statuettes dating as far back as the fifth century BC.

Museo Archeologico di Pithecusae

Villa Arbusto, Corso Angelo Rizzoli • Tues–Sun: June–Oct 9.30am–1pm & 4–7.30pm, Nov–May 9.30am–1pm & 3–6.30pm • €5 • ☎ 081 333 0288, ⓦ pithecusae.it

Above the main square, in a panoramic spot across from where the ancient Greek acropolis once stood, the eighteenth-century Villa Arbusto houses the **Museo Archeologico di Pithecusae**, consisting of well-displayed finds from the acropolis of Monte di Vico, in continuous use from the eighth to the first centuries BC. The island was the first and northernmost Greek settlement in the West, a thriving and vital staging post at the western end of routes from the Aegean and the Levant; in addition to local artefacts, the museum preserves locally excavated burial paraphernalia imported from Syria, Egypt and Etruria.

The most celebrated piece is the so-called **Coppa di Nestore** (Nestor's Cup; display case XX), a typical eighth-century BC pottery drinking cup (*kotyle* in Greek) in the so-called late geometric style, probably made on the island of Rhodes. There's a famously puzzling three-line verse incised on the humble vessel (scratched in, actually, at some point well after its fabrication), which reads something like "I am Nestor's cup, good to drink from. Whoever drinks from this cup, straightaway desire for beautiful-crowned Aphrodite will seize him." Scholars disagree on exactly what the poem signifies, though some say it was most likely the consequence of a drinking game, while at least one authority claims it's meant to be a humorously ironic comparison to the splendour of the legendary golden cup of Nestor described in Homer's *Iliad*. In any case, the inscription is one of the earliest known examples of writing in the Greek alphabet. Elsewhere in the collection, a catastrophic shipwreck scene whimsically depicted on a locally made pot (*krater*, display case XVI, also dating to the eighth century BC) is judged to be the oldest example of figurative painting in Italy.

Negombo

Baia di San Montano • Mid-April to mid-Oct 8.30am–sunset • €30 for a day pass, €32 mid-June to mid-Sept; €25 for a half-day pass (from 12.30pm), €26 mid-June to mid-Sept; €17 for an evening pass (from 3pm), €22 mid-June to mid-Sept (from 4pm); spa treatments from €45 for a massage • ☎ 081 986 152, ⓦ negombo.it

Walk on through town, up and over the hill and follow the signs (for about 20min) to **Negombo** on the Baia di San Montano, whose namesake is a renowned bay in Sri Lanka. Billing itself as a "thermal garden", the spa covers 22 acres, is home to some five hundred species of flowers and plants, and is dotted with modern sculpture. Amenities consist of fourteen mineral bathing pools – hot, cold, cascading, wading and more – laid out amid lush vegetation on a hillside overlooking a private beach and an unspoiled bay. For the price of admission you get the use of all facilities; spa treatments are extra. There are restaurants on site too.

Spiaggia di San Montano

It's about a 20min walk from Negombo, or take the CS bus, or the #1 or #2 bus to Via San Lorenzo and walk the last 250m downhill along Via San Montano

You can take a dip at one of the paid beach clubs along Corso Rizzoli next to Lacco Ameno's marina, but not far out of town lies one of the island's best sandy beaches, the **Spiaggia di San Montano**, on the crystalline bay of the same name. Most of the crescent shore is dominated by Negombo's spa and beach club, but there is a small public beach at the bay's western end.

5

La Mortella

Via Francesco Calise 39 • April–early Nov Tues, Thurs, Sat & Sun 9am–7pm • €12; concerts including garden visit €20 • ☎ 081 986 220, ⓦ lamortella.org • Bus #CS from Ischia Porto, Casamicciola and Lacco Ameno, or CD from Forío – ask the bus driver to drop you off; taxis from Forío or Casamicciola cost about €10; free parking at upper entrance, in Via Zaro

Nestled in the hills halfway between Forío and Lacco Ameno is one of Ischia's highlights: the ravishingly beautiful gardens of **La Mortella**, whose name derives from the Neapolitan dialect and translates as "The Place of the Myrtles", the flower sacred to Aphrodite, goddess of love, and worn by brides in ancient Greece. The gardens are the creation of the English composer Sir William Walton and his Argentinian wife Susana, who lived here and tended the garden until her death in 2010. The Waltons moved to Ischia, then sparsely populated and little known to tourists, in 1949, forerunners of a coterie of writers and artists, including W.H. Auden and Terence Rattigan. With the help of garden designer Russell Page they created La Mortella from an unpromising volcanic stone quarry, the first phase of landscaping alone taking seven years to complete.

Paths wind up through the profusely luxuriant site, home to hundreds of species of rare and exotic plants, most of them clustered around the fountain and the large rock pool up to the left from the main entrance. The emphasis in the lower garden, known as the Valley, is on water plants, and further still to the left is a glasshouse, the Victoria House, sheltering the world's largest water lily, *Victoria amazonica*, a gender-bending giant that flowers as a female with white petals, imprisons beetles for pollination purposes, and reopens later in the day with male organs and deep crimson petals. Above here sits a charming terraced tearoom, a birdhouse, and a memorial to Susana Walton, while, beyond, a pyramid-shaped rock holds Walton's ashes. There's a cascade guarded by a sculpted crocodile, surrounded by heavy-headed purple agapanthus and serene pink lotus, and at the garden's summit, the upper area known as the Hill, a pretty Thai pavilion provides superb views across the island.

Devotees of Walton's music also shouldn't miss the prettily theatrical **museum** above the rather genteel English tearoom, which shows a video about the composer and features portraits by Cecil Beaton, a bust by Elisabeth Frink, paintings and set designs by John Piper and even an Italian puppet theatre by Emanuele Luzzati.

It's also well worth combining your visit to the garden with one of the **concerts** held here (see the website for upcoming events). Chamber music recitals take place in the recital hall on Saturdays and Sundays in spring and autumn, while symphonic concerts performed by young musicians are held on summer Thursdays in the Greek-style **theatre** at the centre of the gardens – surely one of the best backdrops ever for Walton's music.

La Colombaia

Via F. Calise 142 • ☎ 348 512 7762 • Mid-April to early Nov Tues–Sun 10.30am–sunset • €6

If you're visiting La Mortella, another sight worth a stop, especially for cinema buffs, is **La Colombaia**, the summer retreat of the Italian film and theatre director **Luchino Visconti**, whose stylishly epic films included *The Leopard*, *Death in Venice* and *The Damned*. The striking house dates to the late nineteenth and early twentieth centuries and is a whitewashed, neo-Moorish pseudo-castle with exotic Art Nouveau flourishes, ensconced in thick forest and gardens and affording splendid views. It was here that Visconti entertained his lovers of both sexes, threw legendary parties, and consoled his close friend and opera diva Maria Callas when Greek tycoon Ari Onassis ditched her to marry Jackie Kennedy. The building is now a public trust and houses not only a foundation dedicated to Visconti but also a **museum** bringing together photographs and multimedia images, costumes and an array of memorabilia relating to the director's exceptional life. Music and theatre **performances** take place in the villa's natural amphitheatre in the summer months.

Forío

At the opposite side of the island from Ischia Porto, on the west coast, the island's most populous town, **FORÍO**, possesses none of the polish found elsewhere in Ischia but is definitely not without its charms. A bustling, down-to-earth port town, it sprawls around the bay, with a seafront of bars, pizzerias and cheerful chaos, focusing on the attractive, pedestrianized Corso Umberto.

The Torrione and Museo Civico

Via del Torrione 30 • Usually open the following hours, but call to check: March–Nov Mon, Wed, Fri, Sat & Sun 9am–sunset • €3 • ☏ 348 512 7762 or ☏ 081 333 2126

Forío's main landmark is the late fifteenth-century **Torrione**, the gnarly stone cylinder that dominates the town's modest skyline, one of over fifty watchtowers built around the coast to keep a fearful eye out for invading Saracen corsairs. Inside the tower, the former jail houses the **Museo Civico**, which preserves portraits and busts by the local late nineteenth-century Realist sculptor, painter and poet Giovanni Maltese. Much more interesting are his scenes of everyday Ischian life and his true-to-life, if rather sentimentalized, sculptures of island dwellers.

Chiesa Soccorso

There's not much else to see in Forío, but the twisting medieval alleyways of its old town are worth a wander, full of little votary niches with colourfully painted tiles of the Virgin, with the odd bunch of flowers offered in an old jam jar. Make your way out to the point on the far side of the old centre (turn right at the far end of Corso Umberto) to the simple **Chiesa Soccorso**, a bold, whitewashed landmark that looks more Spanish than it does Italian. It's worth the short walk to stand on the majolica balustrade, from which there's a good view back towards the town and out across the sea.

The beaches

There are good **beaches** either side of Forío: the **Spiaggia di Chiaia**, a short walk to the north, followed immediately by the **Spiaggia di San Francesco** (both bus #1, #2 or #CS); to the south, **Cava dell'Isola**, popular with a younger crowd; and the **Spiaggia di Citara**, a somewhat longer walk south along Via G. Mazzella (both bus #2).

Giardini Ravino

Via Provinciale Panza 140b • March–Nov Mon, Wed, Fri, Sat & Sun 9am–sunset; tours Sun at 11am • €9 • ☏ 081 997 783, ⓦ ravino.it • Bus #1, #2 & #CS from Ischia Porto and Forío

In a scenic setting overlooking the Spiaggia di Citara, the **Giardini Ravino** are a labour of love created by botanist Giuseppe D'Ambra. A sailor in the 1960s, D'Ambra collected rare plant specimens on his travels and dreamed of having a garden in which they could flourish. Today, his garden is bursting with exotic species, most notably the collection of cacti and succulents – one of the largest and most diverse in Europe – and is home to a pride of friendly peacocks.

Giardini Poseidon

Via Giovanni Mazzella 87 • Mid-April–Oct daily 9am–7pm • €32 per day (€34 in Aug); €27 per half-day (€29 in Aug), beginning at 1pm; €5 evening visits, from 6pm; towels €4 per day plus €6 deposit • ☏ 081 908 7111, ⓦ giardiniposeidonterme.com • Bus #2 from Ischia Porto and Forío or #14 from Lacco Ameno and Casamicciola Terme

At the far end of the Spiaggia di Citara is the venerable **Giardini Poseidon**, an extensive garden complex of relaxing thermal and mud baths, jacuzzis and saunas – twenty pools in all – on its own white-sand beach. There are three places to eat on site: a self-service restaurant; a garden café by the sea, which also has a piano bar; and a so-called wine grotto, which has outdoor picnic tables with tiki-style umbrellas.

5

Il Sorgeto

Bus #1 or #CS to Panza; ask the driver to let you off at Il Ritrovo, then walk down the steep steps to the beach

South of Forío, below the sleepy town of Panza, is **Il Sorgeto**, an appealing alternative to Ischia's pricey spas. This pretty cove is home to natural hot springs that bubble up in a series of rocky pools at different temperatures – some so warm that people bring their lunch and heat it up in the water. It's a popular spot after dark: canny locals take a bottle of wine and make a night of it.

Sant'Angelo

Buses CS and CD stop outside the town, about 5min away, and cars have to be left in the car park at the entrance to the village

Ischia's restful southern side, divided into the Serrara Fontana (west) and Barano d'Ischia (east), is quieter and greener. **SANT'ANGELO**, probably Ischia's most attractive coastal settlement, is a tiny former fishing village, clustered evocatively around a narrow isthmus linking with a humpy islet topped with the ruins of a watchtower. Inevitably, the clutch of mostly white cubic buildings has been developed since the access road was first built in 1948, and, centring on the harbour and a square crowded with café tables and surrounded by pricey boutiques, it has a gentrified feel. But if all you want to do is laze next to the sea on a whitewashed terrace or beach, it's one of the island's most appealing spots to do so.

Spiaggia dei Maronti

Take bus #5 from Ischia Porto (25min); from Sant'Angelo hop on a taxi boat (€5) or walk 25min along the steep path to the right from the top of the village

There's a reasonable **beach** lining one side of the isthmus that connects Sant'Angelo to its islet, or you could head to the **Spiaggia dei Maronti**, perhaps the island's finest, longest stretch of beach, with both paid and free areas. The broadest sands lie at the eastern end of Maronti, but taxi boats will drop you at one of a number of specific sites. One, the **Fumarole**, at the Sant'Angelo end, is a kind of outdoor sauna, where steam emerges from under the rocks, and is popular on moonlit nights.

Terme Cavascura

Via Cavascura • Mid-April to mid-Oct daily 8.30am–6pm • Swim and sauna €12; treatments €10–47 • ☎ 081 999 242, ⓦ cavascura.it

About halfway up the Spiaggia dei Maronti, a path cuts inland through a mini-gorge to the **Terme Cavascura**, one of the most historic hot springs on the island, used since Greek times. Its waters are reported to be particularly effective in treating conditions related to joints, lungs and skin, as well as gynaecological problems. Treatments offered include thermal soaks, mud packs, massage and more, but don't expect the luxury and comfort of the larger establishments: facilities are all natural, simple and basic.

Fonte delle Ninfe Nitrodi

Via Pendio Nitrodi, Barano • Daily: April 9am–6.30pm; May–Aug 9am–7.30pm; Sept 9am–7pm; Oct 9am–6pm; Nov 9am–5pm • €12 per day (€13 July & Aug); €9 per half-day (€10 July & Aug) from 4.30pm • ☎ 081 990 528, ⓦ fonteninfenitrodi.com • Bus #CS or #CD, or #11 from the Spiaggia dei Maronti

Towards the eastern end of the Spiaggia dei Maronti and about 1km inland, there's another ancient spa, the **Fonte delle Ninfe Nitrodi**, a humble little place these days but once sacred to the Greeks, as attested by the many carved votive images unearthed here, now in the Museo Nazionale Archeologico in Naples and St Petersburg's Hermitage Museum. Nitrodi is legendary for its warm sulphate mineral waters, officially recognized as therapeutic by the Italian Ministry of Health.

The southeast corner

The coastal areas east of the Spiaggia dei Maronti present almost entirely unscalable cliffs until just before Ischia Ponte. The **Spiaggia di San Pancrazio** is a tiny pebble beach accessible only by boat, and further around the curve of coast, the **Spiaggia di Cartaromana** is easily reached on foot from Ischia Ponte, although bus #C12 and #C13 from Ischia Porto can get you pretty close. It's a pleasant sandy beach with thermal springs, as well as submerged ancient ruins, which make it a draw for snorkelling archeologists.

I Pilastri

Bus #CD, #5, #6, #15 or #C12 from Ischia Porto

Beaches aside, this quadrant of the island is pretty much without interest for the average tourist, with only one sight of note, **I Pilastri**, the beautiful stone double-arches of an aqueduct which snake through the hamlets and villages of the Barano valley. The aqueduct dates back to the sixteenth century when it was built to transport mountain spring water from the Buceto source down to Ischia Ponte.

Monte Epomeo

Buses CD and CS regularly stop at Fontana; you can drive to within twenty minutes' walk of the summit, leaving your vehicle by the signs for the military exclusion zone

There are plenty of opportunities for **walks and hikes** in the pastoral wilderness of southern Ischia, the least frequented part of the island, though perhaps the best of

---

HIKING IN ISCHIA

There's almost no limit to the number of **walks and hikes** you can take on Ischia, of varying degrees of difficulty. The populated areas are generally clustered along the coast, and most of the island is still wild and rocky, broad areas of it swathed in dense forest. The hikes below are just a sample of the possibilities, and they make complete circuits. Along both recommended trails, routes are **colour coded**, with arrows indicating the main route, and one-way detours in another colour. The tourist office in Panza (see p.176) is a good source of **information** on hiking.

MONTE TOPPO, THE SORGENTE DI BUCETO AND IL FONDO FERRARO

Time 2hr 15min **Level** moderate

Take bus #6 from Ischia Porto to Fiaiano and ask to get off at *Bar Nik*, well before the bus heads down a steep gradient to the end of the line. The route is very well marked all the way; follow the directions indicated by the lizard and arrow on red. From the *Bar Nik*, where there is a helpful sign, head up the road, follow the signs up the rustic stairs and then onto the trail proper. You'll walk into thick forest, mostly chestnut trees, with several clearly marked side trails that lead to viewpoints. At several places along the way, the canopy of oak trees opens up and you can take in splendid panoramas of the Castello, the sea and Procida. The top of the hike skirts the base of **Monte Toppo** (390m), and then the trail proceeds on to the **Sorgente di Buceto**, finally descending into the leafy extinct crater – the island's largest – known as **Il Fondo Ferraro**. Eventually you wind up back on a paved road, passing old stone houses as you walk back down to the starting point.

THE CRATER OF VATOLIERE AND THE SANCTUARY OF MONTEVERGINE

Time 2hr **Level** moderate to difficult

Take bus #5 (make sure it's marked "via Vatoliere") to Vatoliere. The trail begins at the scruffy and overgrown old volcanic crater that is now home to the hamlet of **Vatoliere**; throughout, follow the directions indicated by the lizard and arrow on violet. This is an altogether rougher and rockier hike than the one above, little forested and so open to the sun, with vineyards and chestnut copses as nearly the only significant vegetation except for grasses and cacti. You'll do a bit of trudging and even scrambling up and along dusty ridges, with steep drop-offs to one side, and you should keep an eye out for troglodytic dwellings cut into the rock here and there. The trail follows the coast for a while, affording great views out to the south, until you arrive at the splendid whitewashed **sanctuary of Montevergine**, an island pilgrimage site in a superb position, at nearly 230m. From here, the trail continues north through similar terrain until it rejoins the road for a while, winding down again to Vatoliere.

5

the hikes is towards the centre, to the craggy summit of Ischia's now dormant volcano, **Monte Epomeo**. Buses stop at the small village of **Fontana**, the usual departure point for hikes to the top, and it's a superb ride, with wonderful views back over the coast. To climb up to the summit of the volcano from here, follow the signposted road off to the left from the centre of Fontana; after about five minutes it joins a larger road. After another ten to fifteen minutes take the left fork, a stony track off the road, and follow this up to the summit – when in doubt, always fork left and you can't go wrong. It's a steep hour or so's climb, especially at the end when the path becomes no more than a channel cut out of the soft rock. At the summit, there are two terraces. One holds a little **church** dedicated to San Nicola di Bari, built in 1459, with an attractive majolica floor; a governor of the island fled here in the eighteenth century, eschewing politics for a hermit's existence. On the other terrace, there's a scenically placed **café** (March–Oct; lunch only).

ARRIVAL AND DEPARTURE ISCHIA

By ferry Ferries and hydrofoils from various points around the bay arrive at the main port, Ischia Porto (from Naples, Capri, Procida, Pozzuoli, plus Sorrento and the Amalfi Coast in high season); at Casamicciola Terme (from Naples, Procida and Pozzuoli); and on the western end of the island at Forío (from Naples). If you arrive at the main port of Ischia Porto, you will need to walk up to the main road to find the bus terminal, where there is a kiosk for purchasing tickets before boarding. If you arrive at another port town, you'll find bus stops at several points along the main ring road – the stops are easy to spot as you leave the quay.

GETTING AROUND

The island is fairly large and has some two-dozen towns, villages and hamlets, spread around in a ring, with the cone of the dormant volcano in the centre, and the more reasonable order for a visit is anticlockwise, given the way the towns are clustered. If you don't want to bring or rent a car or scooter (see below), you can rely on the efficient bus system to get to all of the major towns and some of the other popular spots, such as the Spiaggia dei Maronti and the various points of departure for hikes. Outsiders are prohibited from bringing cars from Easter to the end of summer.

By bus The bus system is run by EAV Bus (☎081 991 808, ✆eavbus.it). At the ports, the bus stops are near the port area and on the same side of the street as the port, except at Ischia Porto, where you have to walk around the port to the main bus stop. The main buses, CS (anticlockwise) and CD (clockwise), circle the entire island at 30min intervals; a round trip would take around 1hr 30min. Twenty lesser lines gain access to various byways and smaller settlements; the tourist office can provide you with timetables. Tickets cost €1.90 and are valid for 1hr 30min; day tickets are available for €6, two-day tickets for €10.
By boat Rental at Nautica De Angelis, Via Iasolino 100, Ischia Porto (☎081 981 500); Noleggio Barche Monti Angela, next to the docks in Forío (☎339 751 4876 or

☎338 226 8720). Craft with skipper also available for fishing trips or excursions.
By car and scooter Rental at Autonoleggio Ischia, Via Iasolino 27, Ischia Porto (☎081 992 444, ✆autonoleggioischia.it); In Scooter, Via Monsignor Filippo Schioppa 69, Forío, 200m from the port (☎081 998 513, ✆autonoleggioinscooter.it). Expect to pay around €40/day for a car or scooter.
By taxi There are fixed rates for journeys, with a minimum cost of €12. Ischia Porto–Fontana (for Monte Epomeo), for example, costs €30. A three-hour taxi tour of the island costs €80. Ischia Porto: ☎081 984 998, ☎081 992 550 or ☎081 993 720; Forío: ☎081 997 482; Casamicciola Terme: ☎081 994 800.

INFORMATION

Ischia Town Ischia Porto's tourist office is right by the quayside ferry ticket offices in the old Terme Comunali building (March–Oct daily 9am–2pm & 3–8pm; ☎081 507 4231, ✆infoischiaprocida.it).

Panza The information office in the small town of Panza, between Forío and Sant'Angelo (Tues–Sun 9.45am–1pm & 6.30–8.30pm; ☎081 908 436, ✆prolocopanzaischia.it), has lots of information on local walks.

ACCOMMODATION

There's no lack of **accommodation** in Ischia Ponte and Porto, though many places close from November to Easter, opening only for a short time between Christmas and New Year. Of the two parts of Ischia town, Ischia Porto makes a livelier base, but Ponte is decidedly more charming, and preferable for long-term stays. As for other parts of the island, Sant'Angelo is maybe the most scenic spot, but Forío and Lacco Ameno are both good bases, and very handy for the island's main attractions. If you decide to make Casamicciola your base, you'll have over sixty hotels to choose from, from sumptuous five-star palaces to simple *pensioni*, but the best options take advantage of the thermal springs and panoramic views, while Lacco Ameno's accommodation focuses on quality rather than quantity. Finally a point on **spas**. If visiting a spa with thermal waters is important to you, be sure to read the hotel's fine print, as many claim to have a "spa" or "*trattamenti*", but may not actually have thermal waters, which is one of Ischia's special features. Generally there is a distinction between aesthetic treatments and "*cure termali*", the latter of which are cures prescribed by doctors who are available on site.

ISCHIA PORTO AND PONTE

Eurocamping dei Pini Via delle Ginestre 28, Porto ☎081 982 069, ⓦischia.it/camping; map p.168. A pleasant campsite with nice stands of trees a short walk from the port. To get there, follow Via Mazzella away from the sea and turn right several roads after the football fields. Bungalows accommodating two to four guests are available, as well as tent pitches. €10 per person plus €10 per tent

★**Il Monastero** Castello Aragonese, Ponte ☎081 992 435, ⓦalbergoilmonastero.it; map p.168. Located on the upper floors of the Castello Aragonese, this is the place to stay in Ischia Ponte, with twenty-odd guestrooms in former nuns' cells, which are suitably spare but coolly and stylishly furnished. The hotel has a broad, sunny terrace overlooking the sea and a picturesque café and restaurant with sweeping views. It also has a beauty centre with massages and hosts the occasional art exhibition or concert. There's a 5 percent discount if you pay cash and half board is available for €35 per person. Closed Nov to mid-April. €135

Il Moresco Via E. Gianturco 16, Porto ☎081 981 335, ⓦilmoresco.it; map p.168. This plush and luxurious hotel is housed in a quirky 1950s villa in the heart of Ischia Porto, but still manages to feel secluded thanks to its high walls and lush garden. The spacious rooms and suites feature traditional tiles and botanical prints, some with private balconies and terraces, and there's a grotto, thermal pools and a spa, as well as a private beach, an excellent restaurant (half board €30 per person) and pool bar. Closed mid-Oct to mid-April. €170

La Marticana Via Quercia 48–50, Porto ☎081 333 4431, ⓦlamarticana.it; map p.168. An easy walk from Ischia Porto, this B&B offers 13 comfortable, airy rooms, set in a tranquil garden filled with lemon, orange and fig trees. It's worth paying an extra €20 for a room with a terrace or balcony. Hosts Giancarlo and Anna are very welcoming, and discounts for the island's best spas are available too. €120

Locanda sul Mare Via Iasolino 80, Porto ☎081 981 470, ⓦlocandasulmare.it; map p.168. Near the port (ask for a room with a view to enjoy the comings and goings of the boats), this tiny, idiosyncratically decorated and very pleasant hotel is a bargain, and has a decent restaurant too. Closed Nov–March. €125

Macrí Via Iasolino 78/a, Porto ☎081 992 603, ⓦalbergomacri.it; map p.168. Just steps from the arrival docks of Ischia Porto, this prettily furnished and simple place has its own bar, parking and garden, and is handy for a night out in lively Porto. The hotel prefers to take bookings by telephone. Open all year. €110

Terme Oriente Via delle Terme ☎081 991 306, ⓦorientehotel.it; map p.168. The decor may be a little dated but this is a good budget option in a convenient location in the heart of Porto, a few minutes' walk from the port. There are two swimming pools, a spa and a restaurant (half board an extra €18 per person). Open all year. €73

★**Ulisse** Via Champault 9, Porto ☎081 991 737, ⓦhotelulisse.com. A laidback family-orientated choice at the eastern end of Porto's centre with two swimming pools and extensive gardens. Locally crafted tiles give the spacious rooms a homespun touch, and some have balconies with views of the sea and the Castello. Optional half board is reasonable. Closed Oct–Easter. €64

CASAMICCIOLA TERME

★**Ape Regina** Via Cretaio 59 ☎081 994 813, ⓦhotelaperegina.it. A pleasant villa nestled in greenery, with a thermal pool, inspiring views and an excellent restaurant (half board is a very reasonable €15 per person); having your own car is recommended, as it's about 2km up from the port. Closed Nov–March. €100

Terme Manzi Piazza Bagni 4 ☎081 994 722, ⓦtermemanzihotel.com. The immaculate *Terme Manzi* is one of Ischia's leading hotels, and from its marble-floored reception to its luxurious guest rooms, it doesn't disappoint. The restaurant, *Il Mosaico*, boasts two Michelin stars and offers excellent cookery classes, and in addition to a top-notch spa, the hotel has a heated rooftop pool. The free shuttle to the port and other local points is a bonus. €270

LACCO AMENO

Covo dei Borboni Residence Via Cava Scialicco 2 ☎081 994 333, ⓦcovodeiborboni.it. For those who prefer to self-cater, this complex has 12 apartments off Via Borbonica for weekly rental. Apartments sleep 2–6, each with kitchen, TV, phone and garden patio. A swimming pool overlooks the sea. Guests may use the spa facilities at *Hotel Grazia Terme*. Closed Nov–April. €900 per week

Hotel Grazia Terme Via Borbonica 2 ☎081 994 333, ⓦhotelgrazia.it. A hotel designed for both relaxation and sport, it has two thermal water pools (one indoors, one out), red clay tennis courts, jacuzzi, billiards, a beauty centre and two restaurants, one outside near the pool

5

(June–Sept). A free shuttle runs several times a day to Lacco Ameno and back. Closed Nov–March. **€180**

San Montano Via Nuova Montevico 26 ☎ 081 994 033, ⓦ sanmontano.com. If you want to treat yourself, this is the place: the discreetly luxurious *San Montano* caters for every whim, with several pools of different temperatures, a swanky spa-with-a-view offering alfresco treatments, a private stretch of beach and an excellent restaurant (half board available). It enjoys an isolated position above the bay of San Montano, and the panoramic views from all over the hotel are second to none. **€365**

Villa Angelica Via IV Novembre 28 ☎ 081 994 524, ⓦ villaangelica.it. Standing in whitewashed modesty just above the little harbour, *Villa Angelica* offers lush gardens and a thermal rock pool, along with spa services. The rooms have terracotta floors and some have balconies with views. Half board also available for an extra €15 per person. Closed Nov to mid-April. **€120**

FORÍO AND AROUND

Casa Lora Via Costa 16 ☎ 335 584 9988, ⓦ casaloraischia.it. Pretty much the perfect Ischian hideaway, this whitewashed country house is set in its own lush grounds (with pool, Turkish bath and a shady lemon grove slung with hammocks), high up away from the coastal crowds yet just a short drive or bus ride from Forío or Sant'Angelo. Seven rooms, two with kitchens, furnished with family antiques and enjoying sweeping views of the coast. Dinner, eaten at a long table with other guests on the terrace, is an option every night. Open all year. **€90**

★**Paradise Beach Backpackers Hostel** Via Provinciale Panza 387, Cuotto Forío ⓦ paradisebeachhostel.com. Just a 5min walk from Forío and 10min from Citara beach, this scenically sited hostel is hemmed in by vineyards and has lovely sea views from the simple, spotless rooms. Hosts Andrew and Shaun are passionate about the hostel, planting herbs for guests to use in the communal kitchen and organizing events such as barbeques in the sunny garden (complete with fumaroles), beach parties and trips to nearby Il Sorgeto. There's a bar and a good-sized pool too. Open all year. Dorms **€21**, doubles **€75**

Il Vitigno Via Bocca 31 ☎ 081 333 4789, ⓦ ilvitigno .com. About 1.5km south of town and 0.5km inland is this wonderfully rustic agriturismo with grape-arboured terraces, bucolic views and a pristine rocky pool, plus delicious meals prepared from proprietor Giuseppina's own home-grown produce (dinner €20). Closed Nov–Easter. **€100**

★**La Rotonda sul Mare** Via Aiemita 29 ☎ 081 987 546, ⓦ larotondasulmare.com. At the start of the Spiaggia di San Francesco, about a 20min stroll from the centre of Forío, this is a rental property offering comfortable holiday-let apartments that sleep up to six. It's a bit isolated from the shops, but there are restaurants and cafés handy, and it's in an ideal position for catching sunsets – plus it has its own swimming platform. Guests can use the pool at sister hotel *Poggio del Sole*. Open all year. Two-person apartments **€100**

La Scogliera Via Aiemita 27 ☎ 081 987 651, ⓦ hotellascogliera.it. On the Spiaggia di San Francesco north of Forío, this hotel offers gardens, three swimming pools and softly lit comfort in public rooms and guestrooms, which all have either sea or mountain views from private balconies or terraces. The buffet breakfast is fresh and tempting, and the sea is only a short walk away. Guests get 50 percent discount on some cures at the nearby Terme Castaldi, with free shuttle. Minimum stay 7 nights in Aug. Closed mid-Oct to mid-April. Half board **€190**

Poggio del Sole Via Baiola 193 ☎ 081 987 756, ⓦ hotelpoggiodelsole.it. Above the town proper, towards the foot of Monte Epomeo, the *Poggio del Sole* offers views over this entire stretch of the island, where the sunsets are especially spectacular. The simple, bright, light-filled rooms with balconies are set in greenery and there's a pool too. It's run by a very friendly family, who also have one of the area's best restaurants, *La Casereccia*, here (see p.180). Closed mid-Nov to April. **€90**

Punta del Sole Piazza Maltese ☎ 081 989 156, ⓦ casthotels.com. This charming and centrally located hotel has balconied rooms set in a beautiful garden close to Forío's sandy beaches; plus it offers full health and beauty services in its own spa, and an on-site restaurant. Open all year. **€90**

SANT'ANGELO AND AROUND

Casa Giuseppina Via Gaetano D'Iorio 11 ☎ 081 907 771, ⓦ casagiuseppina.it. Up in Succhivo, a 10min walk from the centre in the direction of Forío (the bus passes right by), this family-run, pleasantly rustic garden villa has a swimming pool and hot tub, and organizes mountain-bike excursions through the surrounding countryside. A/C costs an extra €7/day. Minimum stay 3 nights at weekends. No credit cards. Closed Nov–April. Half board **€100**

Conte Via Nazario Sauro 42 ☎ 081 999 214, ⓦ hotelconteischia.it. Out on the rocky headland facing the town and the long arc of Spiaggia dei Maronti, the *Conte* is excellent value: practically on the water, with simple, well-appointed rooms, some with balconies, and terrace dining. Seven-day minimum stay in Aug. Closed end Oct–Easter. **€157**

La Palma Via Comandante Maddalena 12 ☎ 081 999 215, ⓦ lapalmatropical.it. Well placed in the centre of town, this Moorish-style villa offers great views of Sant'Angelo and the bay and has plushly furnished rooms with tasteful decor, some with balconies, and an inviting garden terrace restaurant, too. Admission to their thermal

5

complex, *Terme Tropical*, is included in the rate. Closed mid-Oct to mid-April. Half board **€210**

★**Punta Chiarito** Via Sorgeto 51, Panza ☎ 081 908 102, ⓦ puntachiarito.it. To the west towards Il Sorgeto, set on a dramatic promontory some 40m above the sea, is this memorable hotel, where gardens and groves add to the lush feel, and there's a thermal spring just for guests. Rooms are handsomely furnished and many have their own terrace with views. Closed Nov–Easter. **€163**

Villa Mario Via Succhivo 46, Panza ☎ 081 907 775, ⓦ villamario.it. A calm, restful retreat with wonderful views of Sant'Angelo, this little hotel is expertly run by Tiberio and his family. There's a thermal pool and a flower-filled terrace, and the restaurant is excellent – dishes are prepared with ingredients from the family's garden. Located in Succhivo, just outside Sant'Angelo, the hotel has direct access to the lovely Cava Grado beach. Closed Dec–Feb. **€90**

EATING AND DRINKING

ISCHIA PORTO AND PONTE

For nightlife, head for the lively run of late-night **bars** and cafés along Via Porto. More laidback entertainment is provided in the gardens of *Calise Caffè* (see below), where there's live music after dark until 3am in summer.

Alberto a Mare Viale C. Colombo 8, Porto ☎ 081 981 259, ⓦ albertoischia.it; map p.168. This upmarket restaurant on stilts over the sea has panoramic views, immaculate service and beautifully presented seafood. The *marinata mista* (fish *carpaccio* marinated in lemon, orange and balsamic vinegar) is a wonderful starter, and *linguine con cozze* (with mussels) is the pasta speciality. The €25 two-course menu at lunch is a good deal. Daily noon–2.30pm & 7–11pm. Closed Nov to mid-March.

Calise Caffè Concerto Piazza degli Eroi 69, Porto ☎ 081 991 270, ⓦ barcalise.com; map p.168. An island institution with many locations, this branch is set in the midst of a veritable jungle oasis and is a truly all-purpose venue, serving up everything from excellent ice cream to scrumptious cakes and sandwiches, *tavola calda* dishes and pizzas. After hours, it becomes a lounge bar and music venue. Daily: 7.30am–3am in summer; 7.30am–midnight in winter. Closed Tues Nov–March.

Da Coco' Piazzale Aragonese, Ponte ☎ 081 981 823; map p.168. In an enviable position just below the Castello Aragonese, this bar-restaurant boasts lovely sea views and great seafood from around €10, with home-made ice cream for afters. Daily 12.30–2.30pm & 7.30–10.30pm. Closed Wed Oct–March.

Gennaro Via Porto 59, Porto ☎ 081 992 917; map p.168. One of a string of restaurants on the harbourfront, but one of the longest-established and best, with great seafood pasta and risottos as well as excellent Ischian specialities such as *spaghetti vellutati* – "velvety" pasta with creamed potatoes and mussels (€12) – all presided over by the ever-attentive Gennaro himself. Wash it down with the local Ischia DOC wine made with white *biancolella* grapes. Daily noon–3pm & 6.30pm–midnight. Closed Nov to mid-March.

CASAMICCIOLA TERME

Calise Piazza Marina 26 ☎ 081 995 555, ⓦ barcalise .com. A branch of the island-wide chain, you'll find all the

same snacks and pastries here, along with simple pizzas from €4. Daily 6am–midnight.

Il Focolare Via Cretajo al Crocefisso 3, Barano d'Ischia ☎ 081 902 944, ⓦ trattoriailfocolare.it. The Casamicciola area's most celebrated restaurant, with a warm welcome and great views of the port from its hilltop perch, is worth the 5min taxi ride from the port. The menu is refreshingly focused on ingredients other than the seafood, with lots of produce from the hills like home-made *pappardelle* with porcini mushrooms, snails in broth, pumpkin lasagne, wild greens and – their speciality – *coniglio all'ischitana* (rabbit stew). Check out the movie posters of films set in Ischia while you wait for your food. Expect to pay about €40 per person for a full meal. June–Oct: Mon–Wed 7.30pm–midnight, Thurs–Sun noon–3pm & 7pm–midnight; Nov–May: Mon, Tues & Thurs 7.30pm–midnight, Fri–Sun noon–3pm & 7pm–midnight.

LACCO AMENO

Indaco Piazza S. Restituta 1 ☎ 081 994 322, ⓦ reginaisabella.com. In a waterside, glass-enclosed setting, this gourmet restaurant is an atmospheric place for a special-occasion meal, all the more so in fine weather, when you can dine outside by candlelight. Chef Pasquale Palamaro – a rising star – justifies his Michelin star with creative, beautifully presented cuisine. Tasting menus cost €90 for six courses. Daily 8–11pm.

Kalinikta Corso A. Rizzoli 210 ☎ 339 577 2690. Sharing the same entrance as the Museo Archeologico di Pithecusae, up a steep path from Lacco Ameno's piazza, this restaurant benefits from glorious sea views from its rustic terrace. Barbequed meat is the order of the day here (though fish can also be arranged if you call in the morning); hamburgers (€11) are a speciality. There's also a good choice of pastas (€7–12), as well as savoury crêpes. Daily noon–2.30pm & 7.30pm–midnight. Closed lunch July & Aug, and Mon in winter.

FORÍO

Da Gisella Località Sorgeto ☎ 081 909 390. Ultra-cheap and friendly, this is a great place to eat if you're heading to Il Sorgeto. The portions are huge and Signora Gisella will pick ingredients fresh from her own garden to fill your

5

order. The decor is appealingly rustic, the views of Il Sorgeto are splendid, and a meal will cost you little more than €10. Daily noon–4pm & 6pm–midnight.

La Bussola Via Marina 36 ☏081 997 645. One of the best of the fish restaurants on Forío's waterfront, *La Bussola* also serves wood-fired pizzas for both lunch and dinner, starting at just €3 for the classic Neapolitan version. Pasta dishes start at about €6, fresh fish at about €10, and there's ample terrace seating for people-watching. Daily noon–3.30pm & 7pm–midnight.

La Casareccia Via Baiola 193 ☏081 987 756, ⓦlacasereccia.com. Above the town, in the foothills of Monte Epomeo, this small hotel has a large garden restaurant where Mamma Tina turns out dish after dish of superbly inventive yet deeply authentic Ischian cookery – home-made pizza, courgette flowers stuffed with mozzarella and fresh mussels in wine sauce, among many others. Full meals from about €20 per person. Since it's rather far from the centre, just call and someone will give you a lift up there and back. Daily 1–2.30pm & 8pm–midnight.

Ristorante Cantina Pietratorcia Via Provinciale Panza 401 ☏081 907 232, ⓦristorantepietratorcia.it. Sample fine Ischian wines, along with island rabbit and local fish, on the lovely terrace of this winery's tasting rooms. A lighter menu of cold meats and cheeses with three wines costs €15. There's also a *Pietratorcia* wine bar in town, just behind the San Gaetano church. Daily: April to mid-June & mid-Sept to Oct 10am–1pm & 4–8pm, open till midnight Fri–Sun; mid-June to mid-Sept 5.30pm–midnight.

Umberto a Mare Via Soccorso 4 ☏081 997 171, ⓦumbertoamare.it. Established in 1936 as an inn, *Umberto a Mare* is set atop a promontory from where the views of clouds and changing light over the sea are dazzling. As for the food, the elegantly presented fish menu changes daily according to the local catch and is accompanied by a large wine selection. It's not cheap – reckon on €65 a head for a meal with wine – but the food is excellent, and although the terrace has only 10 tables, both dining rooms overlook the sea. Rooms are available, and moorings for small boats too, if you plan to arrive by sea. Daily noon–3pm & 7.30–10.30pm. Closed end Oct–Easter.

SANT'ANGELO

Da Pasquale Via Sant'Angelo 79 ☏081 904 208, ⓦdapasquale.it. Restaurants in Sant'Angelo don't come cheap, but you could do worse than stoke up on the fine pizzas they serve at this unpretentious pizzeria up in the old centre of the village. Other simple dishes, such as *melanzane alla parmigiana*, are available too. Expect to pay around €10–20 per person. Daily 12.30–3pm & 7pm–midnight. Closed Dec–March.

Divina Via Nazario Sauro ☏081 999 392. In a picturesque location on Sant'Angelo's waterfront, *Divina* is an excellent spot for lunch where dishes are prepared with great care, using the freshest of ingredients. The octopus salad is a tasty option, or try the *bucatini* with Ischian rabbit. It's not cheap (expect to spend around €40 for a full meal), but the location and quality of the food make up for that. Also a bar, it's an atmospheric spot for an *aperitivo* come sundown. Daily 9am–1am.

★**Enoteca La Stadera** Via Comandante Maddalena 15 ☏081 999 893. Just behind the main piazza, this is a great place to sample a glass of Ischia's prized Biancolella, paired with delicious cheese (dishes around €20). Owner Ivo is a local legend who sources products you won't find elsewhere. Service can be slow, so come to linger over a few glasses of wine rather than for a quick drink. Mon & Wed–Sun 9am–1pm & 5.30pm–midnight; open daily in Aug.

DIRECTORY

Festivals Ischia has a lively festival calendar, with a number of saints' days throughout the year celebrated with processions, concerts and fireworks, including the following: Jan 20 (San Sebastiano; Barano); first Sun in May (San Francesco di Paola; Forío); May 16–18 (Santa Restituta; Lacco Ameno); June 13 (Sant'Antonio; Ischia Porto and Ponte); June 14–17 (San Vito; Forío); July 21–24 (Santa Maria Maddalena; Casamicciola Terme); July 26 (Sant'Anna; Ischia Ponte); Aug 16 (San Rocco; Barano); four days from the first Sun in Sept (San Giovan Giuseppe della Croce; Ischia Ponte); Sept 12 (Santa Maria al Monte; from Ischia and Forío to Monte Epomeo); Sept 29 & 30 (San Michele Arcangelo; Sant'Angelo). There's also a jazz festival (ⓦpianojazz.it) in late Aug/early Sept and a film festival (ⓦischiafilmfestival.it) in late June/early July.

Health The island's hospital, Ospedale Anna Rizzoli, is at Via Fundera 2, Lacco Ameno (☏081 507 9111); for emergency first aid call ☏081 983 292 (Ischia Porto and Ponte) or ☏081 998 655 (Casamicciola, Forío and Lacco Ameno).

Internet Pointel, Via De Gasperi 19, Casamicciola Terme (daily 9.30am–1.30pm & 3.30–7pm; ☏081 333 4711).

Post office Ischia Porto: Via Alfredo de Luca; Ischia Ponte: Via Mazzella; Forío: Via Matteo Verde. Mon–Fri 8am–6pm, Sat 8am–12.30pm.

Watersports The major beaches are geared up for windsurfing, kayaking and canoeing. Associazione di Nemo (☏366 127 0197, ⓦnemoischia.it) organize snorkelling, diving, whale- and dolphin-spotting trips, while Il Regno di Nettuno, at Via Iasolino 106, Ischia Porto (☏081 981 852, ⓦischiadiving.net), offers equipment rental and dives (from €40).

Procida

5

A serrated hunk comprising the remnants of at least four volcanoes, **PROCIDA** is the bay's smallest island, barely 4km long and scarcely half that wide. It's also the most densely inhabited – in fact, with over ten thousand residents it's the most densely populated of any island in the Mediterranean. However, it has so far managed to fend off the tourist onslaughts that have flooded Capri and Ischia, remaining unassumingly immune to mass tourism, except during the height of summer. It may lack the spectacle or variety of the other islands in the trio, but it more than compensates with its easy accessibility and laidback pace, and retains an authentic feel too – something that's obvious on the evening ferry back to Pozzuoli, when it is thronged with working-class commuters who still make their living as fishermen. No wonder that this spot, the closest island to Naples itself, was chosen as a location for the films *Il Postino* and *The Talented Mr Ripley* (see p.242).

The pleasures of minuscule Procida are reliably low-key: visitors arrive at the diminutive main town of **Marina Grande**, which offers warrens of gritty street life behind its surprisingly menacing castle. The next cove over, **Corricella**, is the classic Neapolitan fishermen's enclave, while elsewhere lovely beaches await, the best being around the picturesque little bay at **Chiaiolella**, at the far end of the island.

Marina Grande

The island's main town, **Sancio Cattolico**, commonly called simply **MARINA GRANDE**, is a lived-in, unpretentious place where all ferries dock, and whose gently dilapidated

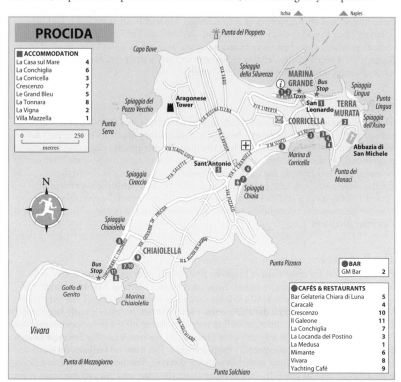

5

state only adds to its allure. As you approach the island from the sea, you'll immediately notice the houses' confetti-like colours – painted, it is said, so that fishermen could recognize their homes from afar. Look closer and you'll also spot the unique elements of the local architecture: arched boat-storage shelters are built into the bottom of many of the fishermen's houses, tall with long external staircases adding to the delicate appeal of this vernacular design. Among the picture-perfect conglomeration of pastel houses lining the port, the twelfth-century **Palazzo Merlato** or Palazzo Montefusco (no visitors) dominates the west end, its broad, pink flatness topped with arches and Venetian-looking finials.

Terra Murata

At the east end of the port, beginning at Via Principe Umberto, multi-hued cubic houses rise from the waterfront to a network of steep streets winding up to the island's fortified acropolis – the so-called **Terra Murata** (91m). It's a wonderful walk up, especially for the slice-of-life glimpse it gives of the town, and the panorama is among the region's best, taking in the whole of the Bay of Naples, from Capo Miseno right in front of you all the way around to the end of the Sorrentine peninsula and Capri on the far right. Part of this summit is the site of a rather forbidding prison-fortress, the **Castello d'Avalos**, only abandoned in 1988. The best view of it is on the promontory's far side, where it looms over Corricella beach.

Abbazia di San Michele

Via Terra Murata 89 • Mon 10am–12.45pm, Tues–Sat 10am–12.45pm & 3–5.30pm • €2 donation expected • ☎ 081 896 7612

The abbey complex of **San Michele** dates from the eleventh century. The ceilings and domes are decorated with paintings by Baroque master Luca Giordano and others, including several stirring scenes of the archangel Michael beating back the Turkish Saracens from Procida's shore. The museum also contains fascinating votive offerings, including cataclysmic depictions of storms at sea donated by sailors who made it back home alive; a wonderfully detailed eighteenth-century nativity scene; and a spooky maze of catacombs, ending in a hidden chapel.

Corricella

The most characteristic spot on Procida and its oldest village, **CORRICELLA** is also known as the "Borgo di Pescatori" because it remains very much a working port for local fishermen. You may recognize it as the quaintly picturesque place that featured so prominently in the Oscar-winning film *Il Postino*. The restaurants here are disarmingly no-nonsense, and provide the island's best bargains, specializing in the freshest catch of the day. Stay a while to take in the view from here back towards the overweening ruined citadel; it's one of Procida's most evocative sights, especially given the stark contrast between the stronghold's sprawling grimness and the gentle whimsy of typical Procidan dwellings.

The beaches

Procida's appeal for most visitors lies in its fine opportunities to laze on one of its half-dozen **beaches** in relative peace. There are two beaches near Marina Grande itself, one of which is to the right as you sail into dock, just on the far side of the jetty (take Via Roma). This is **Spiaggia della Silurenza** – lovely (when it's clean), fairly large and sandy, and offering all facilities, as well as rocks for diving off. In the opposite direction, beyond the marina on the way to Punta Lingua, lies the much smaller **Spiaggia Lingua**, a pebbly beach that boasts especially limpid waters. There are no facilities on this beach, but a small restaurant is within walking distance. Further away but theoretically walkable – at least at low tide – continuing along the coast and around the point is the

5

small rocky beach made famous by Elsa Morante's novel, *L'isola di Arturo*: the **Spiaggia dell'Asino**, below the looming Terra Murata fortress.

Beyond Corricella, reached by 186 steps, is **Spiaggia Chiaia**: an arching strip of grey volcanic sand that wraps around the Cala di Sant'Antonio's serene waters. **Buses** #L1, #L2 and #C1 stop nearby at Piazza dell'Olmo, or you can walk from Marina Grande – uphill then down again – in about half an hour. Follow Via Vittorio Emanuele and head down the flight of nearly two hundred steps from near the Church of Sant'Antonio Abate; once on the beach, you'll find facilities enough to make a day of it.

Chiaiolella and around

On the whole, if you want to swim you're best off making the fifteen-minute bus journey (#L1 or #L2), or the forty-minute walk, from Marina Grande to **CHIAIOLELLA**, where there's a handful of bars, restaurants and hotels around a pleasant, almost circular bay and two long stretches of good sandy beach along the entire western shore, divided by the so-called **Faraglione di Procida**, a large pyramid-shaped rock. The closest of these beaches is **Chiaiolella**, also called Ciraciello or simply the Lido, with full facilities right next to Chiaiolella Marina. Afternoon winds make it a perfect spot for windsurfing. The beach further back to the right as you face the sea, **Ciraccio** (reached by bus #C1) is the island's longest, with facilities and situated near several campsites. Finally, there's the **Spiaggia del Pozzo Vecchio** in a cove at the northwest corner of the island (also accessible by bus #C1), located down a cliff from the island's cemetery. It's sometimes referred to as the Postino Beach, as it was one of the picturesque locations featured in the famous film.

ARRIVAL AND GETTING AROUND   PROCIDA

By boat Ferries and hydrofoils from Naples and Ischia (see p.150) arrive in the port of Marina Grande. Boat rental is available at Blue Dream Sailing Charter, Via Vittorio Emanuele 14, Marina Grande (☎081 896 0579, ⓦbluedreamcharter.com), and Ippocampo, on the west side of Marina di Chiaiolella (☎081 896 7018, ⓦippocampo.biz).

By bus The island's four bus lines crisscross the island. The most useful, #L1 and #L2 (€1.10 single, tickets sold in *tabacchi* – try *Bar Capriccio* in Marina Grande – and newsstands and on board), coincide with all ferry arrivals

and connect Marina Grande with Chiaiolella roughly every 20min.

By car Given the island's tiny size and good transport links, not to mention its challenging traffic, using a car here is not recommended. Non-residents are not allowed to bring a car onto the island between mid-April and September.

By taxi There's a rank in Marina Grande (☎338 433 8644).

By bike and scooter There's bike rental at Autoricambi Todisco, Via Roma 112 (☎081 896 0060); rent scooters from General Rental, Via Roma 134 (☎081 810 1132). Both are by the port.

INFORMATION

Tourist information The travel agency, Graziella Travel, Via Roma 117, Marina Grande (Mon–Sat 9am–1pm & 5–8pm, shorter hours in winter; ☎081 896 9594, ⓦisoladiprocida.it), is a good source of information about

the island, its services and facilities. The website ⓦprocida .net has some useful information, including ferry and bus timetables.

ACCOMMODATION

There's not much choice if you want to stay on the island, but a few decent options are available. Although last-minute bargains can be found in low season, due to the scarcity of options advance booking is a good idea year-round, especially if you're intending to visit during the August peak.

Crescenzo Via Marina Chiaiolella 33 ☎081 896 7255, ⓦhotelcrescenzo.it. Painted a beautiful sky-blue with white trim, this hotel with on-site restaurant-pizzeria near a sandy beach is a family-run, friendly place with plenty of repeat guests. Some of the ten rooms overlook Chiaiolella

harbour and others have a small balcony, while there are also quieter choices, set behind the harbour. Half and full board also available. Open all year. **€120**

La Casa sul Mare Via Salita Castello 13, Terra Murata ☎081 896 8799, ⓦlacasasulmare.it. One of the island's

5

top choices, consisting of ten bright, elegant guestrooms with private balcony and views, in a seventeenth-century villa with gardens and terraces. Free shuttle to beaches. Open all year. **€150**

La Conchiglia Via Pizzaco 10, Spiaggia Chiaia ☎ 081 896 7602, ⊛ laconchigliaristorante.com. This restaurant (see below) also has four simple apartments to rent near the beach, each with a double bedroom, basic cooking facilities, a little terrace and sea views. Closed Nov–March. **€70**

La Corricella Via Marina Corricella 88 ☎ 081 896 7575, ⊛ hotelcorricella.it. Spacious rooms, tastefully decorated, in a lovely position at the heart of this colourful little fishermen's community, with an exotic and almost African beauty. When you get to the port and face the water, look for the pink building up at the left end. It also has its own restaurant, *La Lampara*, offering terrace dining high above the sea. Closed mid-Nov to Easter. **€100**

La Tonnara Via Marina Chiaiolella 51b ☎ 081 810 1052, ⊛ latonnarahotel.it. This handsome building on the marina – which once housed nets used to catch tuna – has fourteen comfortable guestrooms, all with panoramic sea views. Colours are cheerfully kaleidoscopic in the public spaces. Open all year. **€130**

La Vigna Via Principessa Margherita 46 ☎ 081 896 0469, ⊛ albergolavigna.it. With a magical setting – it's in a vineyard, with a tucked-away seating area overlooking the sea – this hotel is a tranquil retreat, with a spa offering an array of treatments, including vinotherapy. The standard rooms are compact and simple, while the superior rooms are more spacious, with the bed on a mezzanine level. The suite (€200) has a four-poster and an in-room jacuzzi. It's about a 15min walk uphill from the port, or a short taxi ride. Closed mid-Nov to mid-Feb. **€150**

Le Grand Bleu Just off the main road, about halfway between Corricella and Chiaiolella at Via F. Gioia 37 ☎ 081 896 9594, ⊛ isoladiprocida.it. An excellent self-catering option, the apartments here are smartly contemporary and each has its own terrace with exceptional views over the island and beyond. Chiaia beach is about 150m away, and there's a bus stop 100m away. Open all year. Seven nights **€550**

Villa Mazzella Via Bartolomeo Pagano 13 ☎ 081 896 7417, ⊛ villamazzella.com. A friendly B&B whose six large rooms, each with its own entrance, overlook a well-tended garden. Breakfast, served in the garden, is a feast of fresh pastries and home-made lemon jam. Open all year. **€110**

Vivara Via IV Novembre 2 ☎ 081 896 9242. Best bet of the five campsites on the island, just 30m from the sea, with no tent spaces but caravans and cabins for rent and a bar. To get there, take the Marina Grande–Chiaiolella bus #L1 and get off at Piazza Olmo. Closed mid-Sept to mid-June. **€60**

EATING, DRINKING AND NIGHTLIFE

Eating well on Procida is generally easier and somewhat cheaper than on the other islands. **Restaurants** line the waterfront along Via Roma in Marina Grande, but atmospheric Marina di Corricella or Marina di Chiaiolella are more scenic spots for a meal. If you're staying for more than a day, explore the narrow lanes of the island's interior, where a number of authentic trattorias can be found. The **café-bars** in Marina Grande are a good option for drinks or ice cream while you're waiting for a ferry.

Bar Gelateria Chiara di Luna Via Marina di Corricella 87 ☎ 333 770 0776. Procida's tastiest ice cream is sold in this little *gelateria* in picturesque Marina di Corricella. They also make delicious aperitifs with fresh fruit and Prosecco. Daily 11am–1am. Closed Nov–Easter.

★**Caracalè** Via Marina di Corricella 62 ☎ 081 896 9192. A refurbished fisherman's hut by the sea is the setting for this fish restaurant, with seating inside or outside on benches. *Fusilli* with seafood, octopus, and swordfish are the specialities here, but there is a nice choice of vegetables too, and rabbit is occasionally on the menu. A full meal costs upwards of €40 a head. Daily 12.30–4pm & 7–11pm. Closed Tues March–June & Sept–Nov, and mid-Nov to mid-March.

Crescenzo Via Marina di Chiaiolella 33 ☎ 081 896 7255. Opened in the 1960s near Chiaiolella harbour, this hotel restaurant serves a wide variety of fish dishes (*primi* €8–16), from fritters to pasta and main dishes, especially fried or grilled. Rabbit is one of the few meat dishes available, and in the evening they also make pizza (from €3.50). A local favourite for decades. Daily 1–4pm & 7.30–11.30pm. Closed Tues in winter.

GM Bar Via Roma 117 ☎ 081 896 7560, ⊛ gmbar.it. Open since 1949, this historic bar in the port area is lively at *aperitivo* time, and becomes an even livelier cocktail bar later on, specializing in whisky and rum cocktails. There's live music on Fridays. Mon & Wed–Sun 5am–3am.

Il Galeone Via Marina di Chiaiolella ☎ 081 896 9622. An unpretentious, attractive restaurant right by the bus terminus between the bay and the beach, offering pizzas from €4 at lunch and dinner, and a tasting menu of fish specialities based on the day's freshest catch for around €12. Mon, Tues & Thurs–Sun noon–3.30pm & 7pm–midnight. Open for dinner only in winter.

★**La Conchiglia** Via Pizzaco 10, Spiaggia Chiaia ☎ 081 896 7602, ⊛ laconchigliaristorante.com. Perched above Chiaia beach and its enchanting bay (there's a handy boat shuttle from Marina Corricella), this restaurant makes an ideal spot for lunch after basking in the sun. Locals come here to tuck into excellent and moderately priced antipasti, pasta dishes like *stracci cozze e broccoli* (strips of pasta with mussels and broccoli) and *cappelletti* filled with provolone cheese and aubergine, or just fish grilled to perfection. A full meal will set you back around €40. It's always busy, so book ahead. Daily 12.30–3.15pm & 8.30–10.30pm. Closed Nov–March.

★**La Locanda del Postino** Via Marina di Corricella 45, Corricella ☎081 810 1887. Set in the fishermen's cove of Corricella, with outside tables under big umbrellas and a charmingly shabby handwritten sign. The delicious fish soup (pre-booking necessary) is prepared in the local way, with bread, and goes for about €25 for two. A plate of pasta will cost €6–12. The interior commemorates the eponymous hit film, with pictures of its beloved star, the late Neapolitan actor Massimo Troisi. Daily 9.30am–10pm; July & Aug open 8am–2/3am.

La Medusa Via Roma 116, Marina Grande ☎081 896 7481. Opposite the ferry terminal and well positioned for an evening *passeggiata*, *La Medusa* offers a house speciality of *pepata di cozze* (mussels in a peppered broth) for €7 and *spaghetti ai ricci di mare* (with sea urchins) for €16. The rest of the menu also draws on the day's catch. Mon & Wed–Sun 12.30–3pm & 7.30–11.30pm.

Mimante Via V. Emanuele 225 ☎081 896 9385. About halfway along the main road from Marina Grande to Chiaiolella, this café-pizzeria-restaurant is also known as the *Giardini di Elsa* because it was this pleasant spot that the author Elsa Morante chose as her base while she lived on the island. The gardens are extensive, the villa and its decor nostalgically atmospheric and the prices reasonable (expect to pay around €20 per person for a full meal). Tues–Sun 12.30–3pm & 7.30–11pm. Closed Jan–March.

Vivara Lungomare Cristoforo Colombo 6, Chiaiolella ☎081 896 0594. Right on Chiaiolella beach, with big windows, this breezy restaurant serves up seafood specials such as gnocchi with cuttlefish and mussels (€13); *secondi* include salmon with courgettes for €13. Daily 12.30–3.30pm & 7.30pm–midnight. Closed Nov–March.

Yachting Café Restaurant Via Marina di Chiaiolella 23 ☎081 896 8074. Right in Chiaiolella's port, this place couldn't be better placed, and it attracts its fair share of hungry yacht-people passing through on flotillas. Food is good and hearty, with lots of good fish and seafood dishes from €8, pizzas from €3 (evening only), and big windows making the most of the pretty harbour view. Daily 8am–midnight.

DIRECTORY

Festivals Easter events include the Procession of the Hooded Apostles on Maundy Thursday, and Procession of the Mysteries and of the Dead Christ at Terra Murata on Good Friday. April brings an artichoke festival. On 8 May a procession honours the island's patron saint San Michele. Corricella in Jazz takes place in Marina Corricella in July and August. The Sagra del Mare (usually last weekend in July) is summer's main event: a beauty contest to choose the island's "Graziella", the novel by Lamartine set in Procida. In September the Elsa Morante Literary Prize is celebrated

with a week of cultural events, while the Sagra del Vino (wine festival), usually in the first week of November, has wine tasting and street performers.

First aid ☎081 896 9058 or ☎118; emergency at sea ☎1530 or ☎081 553 6017.

Hospital Via SS. Annunziata 1 (☎081 810 0510).

Internet *Bar Capriccio* at Via Roma 99, Marina Grande (daily 6am–3am), has free wi-fi, or it's €3/hr to use a computer.

Post office Via Libertà 34, Marina Grande (Mon–Fri 8.20am–1.30pm, Sat 8.20am–12.30pm).

North of Naples

SANT'AGATA DEI GOTI

North of Naples

There are not a great many attractions to draw you to the inland territory north of Naples. Most visitors find plenty to occupy their time along the coast, and only the most dedicated venture into the interior. For one thing, to get here you will have to face the depressing reality of the towns just outside the city. Casoria, Afragola and Acerra are known as the "Triangle of Death", due to their status as Camorra strongholds, and they make up a bleak conurbation of blighted housing, industrial mess and general squalor. Thankfully, no tourist is likely to come into contact with the mafia, and there are places of genuine interest beyond the triangle. Caserta isn't the most charming, but it does have the remarkable royal palace and gardens to draw you here, while the adjoining towns of Santa Maria Capua Vetere and Capua boast some significant ancient sights. Once past Capua, the countryside begins to assert itself, and you can push on to the lovely hill-town of Sant'Agata dei Goti and the pleasant market town of Benevento. Out here, you couldn't feel further from the coast, the Camorra, Naples – or indeed other tourists. And that is precisely the appeal.

Caserta and around

A little further inland, but just barely, from the really nasty Neapolitan suburbs, **CASERTA** is overwhelmingly the most popular destination in this part of Campania. The town is known as the "Versailles of Naples" for its vast eighteenth-century **Palazzo Reale**, generally known simply as **La Reggia**, which is said to have been the largest building constructed in that century – although one waggish historian noted that it was "a colossal monument to minuscule glory", since the kingdom of Naples was at that time far from a major power, and in precipitous decline. However, Grand Tour travellers often lingered in this sophisticated court, and today visitors can either wallow in the pomp of the building or stroll the immense grounds and gardens. The palace is the only reason people are drawn to this lacklustre modern town, and most tend to make a beeline for La Reggia and turn right around again. But if you do come this way, it's worth making time too for a walk through the small medieval town of **Casertavecchia** and the remarkable silk factory town of **San Leucio**, both of which are just a short bus ride away. The province of Caserta also has some good wineries and lovely agriturismi in the countryside, much of which is surprisingly pristine.

La Reggia di Caserta

Viale Giulio Douhet • Mon & Wed–Sun, Tues 8.30am–7.30pm; Gardens: Mon, Wed–Sun: Jan, Feb, Nov & Dec 8.30am–3.30pm, March 8.30am–5pm, April 8.30am–6pm, May & Sept 8.30am–6.30pm, June–Aug 8.30am–7pm, Oct 8.30am–5.30pm • €12 for apartments and gardens, €3 for gardens only • ☎ 0823 277 111, ⓦ reggiadicaserta.beniculturali.it • 5min walk from Caserta train station; underground parking available at Piazza Carlo III in front of the palace

Begun in 1752 for the Bourbon King Charles III to plans drawn up by **Luigi Vanvitelli**, and finally completed by his son Carlo nearly thirty years later, the **Reggia di Caserta** is an

Food and festivals p.193

REGGIA DI CASERTA

Highlights

❶ Reggia di Caserta A vast royal palace with the most mind-bogglingly long water-garden imaginable. **See p.188**

❷ Casertavecchia One of Southern Italy's most intact medieval towns. **See p.192**

❸ The Capuas Bang on the old Via Appia, both ancient – Santa Maria Capua Vetere – and modern Capua have lots to see, including the

ruins of the second largest ancient amphitheatre in Italy. **See p.194**

❹ Museo Provinciale Campano di Capua Capua's star attraction, and worth a visit alone for its unique collection of Madri Dei, ancient fertility figures. **See p.196**

❺ Sant'Agata dei Goti An extraordinary little hill-town, built on a massive table of tufa. **See p.197**

HIGHLIGHTS ARE MARKED ON THE MAP ON P.190

NORTH OF NAPLES

HIGHLIGHTS

1 Reggia di Caserta
2 Casertavecchia
3 The Capuas
4 Museo Provinciale Campano di Capua
5 Sant'Agata dei Goti

Benevento

Sannita
Chianche
Torrioni
Tufo
Altavilla Irpina
San Leucio del Sannio
Summonte
Grottolella
Ceppaloni
Petruro Irpino
Pietrastornina
Sant'Angelo a Scala
Capriglia Irpina
Avellino
Arpaise
Roccabascerana
Sant'Angelo a Cupolo
Apollosa
Mercogliano
Montesarchio
Rotondi
Cervinara
Sirignano
Mugnano del Cardinale
Tocco Claudio
Airola
Sperone
Baiano
Monteforte Irpino
Pago del Vallo di Lauro
Marzano di Nola
Taurano
Sarno
Arienzo
Cicciano
Roccarainola
Domicella
Quindici
Palma Campana
Sant'Agata dei Goti
Cimitile
Nola
San Paolo Belsito
Dugenta
San Giuseppe Vesuviano
Casertavecchia
Maddaloni
Ottaviano
Castel Morrone
Mt Vesuvius (1281m)
Sant'Angelo in Formis
Caserta
Acerra
Sant'Anastasia
San Leucio
Capodichino Airport
San Prisco
Marcianise
Capua
Santa Maria Capua Vetere
Caivano
Afragola
Naples
Aversa
Casal di Principe
Marano
Qualiano
Grazzanise
Pozzuoli
Bàia
Mondragone

N

0 kilometres 2

awesome behemoth, built around four cavernous courtyards, with a facade 247m long. It's an amazing building, and if size and ostentation were everything, it would be perhaps the greatest European palace of all, which was certainly the intent of Charles who planned to transfer his court from Naples to Caserta while he ruled the Kingdom of Two Sicilies. These days the Reggia claims to be the fifth most visited attraction in Italy, and it totally dominates the town as it always has – you see it as soon as you walk out of the station.

The royal apartments

Although its sheer mass lends a staid aspect, the majestic triple staircase up to the **royal apartments** manages to hit exactly the right note (literally, too – the double vaulting enhanced the sound of the musicians who played in niches when the court arrived), while the marble lions remind you that this is a power entrance. At the top, the octagonal-shaped vestibule gives onto the **Palatine Chapel**, designed to resemble that in Versailles and the best bit of the palace, according to Vanvitelli himself, although it wasn't actually completed until 1784, long after his death. From the vestibule you enter **the apartments** – strangely impressive in their own way – a bombastic parade of gilt, coloured marble and stucco, furnished in elaborate Italian Rococo and French Empire style, and with great, overbearing Neoclassical statues. Some of the plush textiles were manufactured in nearby San Leucio, a mill town newly designed not only to produce luxurious fabric but also as a grand sociological experiment that was never fully realized (see p.192). Along the way enjoy the frescoes of the countryside of Campania and Southern Italy, a pastoral mini tour of the kingdom, that makes a welcome counterpoint to the palace's brazen display of wealth, and smug portraits of the Bourbon dynasty and the House of Farnese, especially podgy Francis I with his brat-like children. Other decorative touches include a sumptuous cradle with in-built guardian angel of gold, an ancient Roman-style basin of solid granite serving as the royal bathtub, a very elaborate 360-degree *presepe* or Neapolitan nativity scene and a strange cage clock in Queen Mary Caroline's apartment that encloses an embalmed bird.

Even more than its lavish contents, though, it's the enormous scale of the building that is its most enduring feature. Five storeys high and larger than either Versailles or the Bourbon palace in Madrid, it has a total of 1200 rooms, including, besides the royal apartments, a vast, golden throne-room and a church-sized chapel. Its private **theatre**, on the third floor, was built in the horseshoe shape of Naples' Teatro San Carlo, and has twelve ancient columns from Pozzuoli that support a ceiling vault frescoed with Apollo trampling a python; the back wall of the stage can collapse so that the idyllic royal gardens can appear as the backdrop; and shells, flowers and putti cavort on its five tiers of boxes, the king's decorated with a crown and drapes. The palace's **recent history** is also compelling: it was requisitioned as the centre of operations for the Allied forces in 1943, and it was on this spot that the Germans formally surrendered in 1945. More recently, you might recognize it as the backdrop of the giant Naboo palace in the *Star Wars* films, and from *Mission Impossible II*, when it doubled as the Vatican.

The gardens

Regular shuttle buses (€2.50) make the circuit around the gardens, dropping off at regular intervals and turning round at the top of the main cascade; bike hire €4/hr, auto-rickshaws €13/hr, horse and carriage €50/30min

Behind the palace, the **gardens** are more than a match for the Reggia in scale and formality, stretching behind the palace along a central axis that's a full 3km in length, punctuated by cascades of various heights, rapids and huge fountains based around the myths in Ovid's *Metamorphosis*, such as the Fountain of Aeolus, which sports numerous grottoes. The main promenade is longer than it looks from the palace (a good half an hour's walk), and it climbs to an elevation of 204m, where a grotto spills over to form a series of cascades, the 78m-high **Grande Cascata**, which depicts Diana turning Actaeon into a stag while her nymphs gaze quizzically on. The waterfall was fed by Vanvitelli's purpose-built Carolina aqueduct from mountain sources 40km away, and powered the region's silk mills, then burst into the Reggia here. (Three tiered and nearly 100m high, the aqueduct spans the verdant Maddaloni Valley just 4km to the east; it's an awesome sight and best viewed from the SS265 road, which links Mt Longano with Mt Marzano.)

On the left side as you face back towards the palace is the large **English Garden** (closes 1hr before the rest of the park) – a very pleasant spot for a picnic. The last part of the park to be completed, it's styled according to the principles of English landscape architect Capability Brown and has refreshingly non-rectilinear pathways winding through groves and meadows decorated with would-be ancient ruins, some of them adorned with copies of statuary from Pompeii. Have a wander further down and you'll discover a picturesque pond with swans and a mock Roman temple adorning a grassy islet at its centre, built for the pleasure of young royals.

Casertavecchia

Perched on a precipitous hill and just 20 minutes by hourly bus from Caserta train station, **CASERTAVECCHIA** was founded in the ninth century by the Lombards. "Casa Hirta" (Steep House), as it was then called, actually has a history stretching all the way back to the ninth century BC, when it was Etruscan and went by the name of Galatea or Galizia. The town was completely abandoned with the construction of La Reggia, partly because all hands were needed to carry out the mammoth project, but also because there were ambitious plans to build a model city adjacent to the palace (a dream that was clearly not realized, given the disarray of Caserta today). As a happy result, the old hill-town was marvellously preserved and now stands as one of the most important examples of a medieval settlement in Italy, with narrow stone alleyways that are a delight to wander. The massive, 30m-high, thirteenth-century **keep** (*mastio* in local dialect) of the now mostly vanished castle sits right at the top of the village. It was the place of refuge in times of danger, and a persistent legend tells of a hoard of gold stashed somewhere beneath the tower's broad, sixteen-sided base.

The Cattedrale

Piazza della Cattedrale • Daily 9am–1pm & 3.30–8pm, till 6pm in winter • Free

Casertavecchia's imposing twelfth-century **Cattedrale** was constructed over an earlier church and is built in a very refined Romanesque style, with a great octagonal lantern and sculpted white marble portals with four animals representing the Evangelists, as well as striking Sicilian-Moorish elements, such as the intertwined blind arches adorning the facade's pediment and banding around the drum-like dome. The thirteenth-century campanile, to the right, continues the motifs, its base gracefully spanning the street with a broad Gothic arch. Inside, the delicate, irregularly sized grey-white columns and their capitals are recycled from ancient temples, although they've now been given a setting with an almost Moorish feel, particularly the almost horseshoe-shaped arches they support. Also, don't overlook the exquisite Cosmatesque multicoloured marble floor mosaics, the unusual Gothic baptismal chapel, or the fourteenth-century Sienese fresco of the *Madonna and Child*, the only remnant of what was probably a complete fresco cycle embellishing most of the interior. Just behind the cathedral, the small, mostly Gothic-style church of **Santissima Annunziata**, has a lovely marble portal, and the whitewashed interior is now used for art exhibitions and other cultural events.

San Leucio

Via Atrio Superiore, San Leucio • Mon & Wed–Sun 9.30am–6.30pm, winter 9am–6pm; by appointment only, guided visits only; gardens open weekends only • €6 • ☎ 0823 301 817, ✉ belvedere@comune.caserta.it • Enquire at the Arethusa ticket office at the Reggia for shuttle service

In the opposite direction from Casertavecchia, just 3km outside Caserta, lies one of Europe's largest and most important eighteenth-century royal textile factories,

FOOD AND FESTIVALS

In this expanse of rural Campania, every little town and village honours its patron saint with a procession or festival of some sort, in addition to those for **Carnevale** (especially in Capua and Telese) and all other major religious holidays. However, since this is one of the most fertile farming areas anywhere, abundant **harvest festivals** are also very much in evidence, with all sorts of bounty from the earth, including game. Keep an eye out for signs announcing such festivals, or *sagre*, from the word for "sacred"; there are *sagre* dedicated to *funghi porcini* (porcini mushrooms), *cinghiale* (wild boar), gnocchi, *maiale* (pork) and especially the Nera Casertana, a local black pig that is being brought back from near extinction, *maialetto* (suckling pig), *fichi* (figs), *fico d'India* (prickly pear), *castagne* (chestnuts), *melanzana* (aubergine), *fagiolo* (bean), *carciofo* (artichoke), *cardi* or *gobbi*, which looks like a rustic stalk of celery but tastes like artichoke, 'nfrennula (a kind of biscuit made in Sant'Agata dei Goti, celebrated the second week of Sept) and many more, including, of course, wine and olive oil. Fish was more of a special occasion food, except for anchovies, which are used to enrich a number of recipes.

One of the most original agricultural products here is the **mela annurca** apple, fascinating due to the age-old method used to ripen the fruit. They're picked green and then carefully laid out row upon row for kilometres on *melari*, or ripening beds of straw, which are then covered with netting. Every apple is turned daily until it turns purply-red and is ready to eat. These apple beds line the country roads, and in the autumn you can see dozens of women on their hands and knees, lovingly rotating the precious *mele*. Italians consider the *annurca* the "Queen of Apples", and its *sagra* is held November 7–10 in the Valle di Maddaloni, between Caserta and Sant'Agata dei Goti. Besides savouring the fruit's firm and juicy white pulp, prepared in countless ways – to make cider, sauces and sweets – the festivities involve elaborate mosaics created using only the prized apples.

At the top of this culinary heap, however, belongs the **bufala**, the water buffalo imported some centuries ago for its ability to thrive in swampy areas. So valuable is its milk for the mozzarella industry that locally it's referred to as "white gold". This is definitely a matriarchic society, where the females are pampered with just the right diet, which of course affects the quality of their milk. Each is named and tagged, so that each batch of milk can be traced to an individual *bufala*. Except for the lucky few kept around for breeding, the less valuable males tend to end up as salami. They like to wallow in mud and puddles and to soak in small ponds, so look for them on the landscape where there is more dirt and less grass. Campania has two main *bufala* raising areas, in the province of Caserta and in the province of Salerno near Paestum. The former tends to be softer, the latter chewier. Both are sublime.

Local **grape** varieties, some ancient, produce good local wines in the province of Caserta, among them Asprinio di Averso (DOC), Falerno del Massico (DOC), Galluccio (DOC), Roccamonfina (IGT) and Terre di Volturno (IGT). Try them here, as you may have difficulty finding them elsewhere, even in Campania. A couple of wineries worth visiting are Trabucco and Masseria Felicia. Visit ⓦsagreinitalia.it to find out more about Campania's food and wine festivals.

complete with living quarters for both the king and his privileged workforce – and still in operation. Commonly referred to simply as the **Belvedere**, though officially entitled the **Complesso Monumentale del Belvedere di San Leucio**, it is firmly linked in both spirit and epoch to La Reggia. Besides the commanding hilltop views, the draw here is the **Real Fabbrica della Seta** (the Royal Silk Factory) and its dependent buildings: a converted Royal Hunting Lodge (Casino Reale), the Belvedere itself and houses (Il Borgo) for the employees of the factory. The complex has recently been meticulously restored, and the marvellous cherry-wood contraptions for working the silk reveal the cutting edge of late eighteenth-century technology to spin, weave and dye reams of fine fabric for the insatiable decorating demands of La Reggia, as well as for markets outside Italy.

Perhaps the most interesting aspect of the place, however, is that it was a self-conscious experiment in utopian socialism, the product of the egalitarian Enlightenment philosophy to which the era's Bourbon kings were at least in theory committed. The whole undertaking was the brainchild of Ferdinand IV, who handed

6

down the community's very liberal charter in 1789. The king still ruled here, as is evident in the central courtyard, and the royal apartments are no less self-indulgent than those in La Reggia, especially the queen's salon-size walk-in bathtub. But the row of workers' houses – well away from the royal digs, of course – are comfortable, spacious and even beautiful, evincing a certain awareness of and respect for the collaborative nature of any successful enterprise. Unfortunately the scheme had barely got off the ground when the French Revolution sent the House of Bourbon into serious disarray. But modern-day San Leucio still turns out some of the finest silk in Europe, and you can watch the process at close hand in the factory itself. The complex also has a small café serving drinks and snacks.

ARRIVAL AND DEPARTURE
CASERTA AND AROUND

By train Caserta's train station, right opposite the Reggia, is connected by regular trains from Naples (40min).
By bus There are buses every 20min from Naples (journey time 1hr), stopping right outside the train station.

By car If you drive to Caserta, finding the palace can be a little confusing – the signage is inadequate. Parking is available under the restored formal gardens of Piazza Carlo III in front of the building.

INFORMATION

Tourist offices There is a tourist office inside the palace itself (daily 8am–3.45pm; ☎ 0823 550 011), and a booth – the more helpful of the two – just a block away along

Viale Douhet at the corner of Piazza Dante (Mon–Fri 9.30am–1.30pm & 2–4.50pm, Sat 10am–1pm; ☎ 0823 321 137, ⓦ casertaturismo.it).

ACCOMMODATION AND EATING

There's not much to keep you in Caserta and most people hurry back to Naples after seeing the palace. If you want to stay overnight, the nearby village of Casertavecchia is a decidedly more appealing prospect.

Antica Caffetteria La Reggia Corso Trieste 7–9, Caserta ☎ 0823 456 335. There is a café inside the Reggia but otherwise this is the closest option and as such the most obvious spot for a sit-down and a pastry or sandwich after the rigours of the palace and its gardens. They make a superior *cappuccino*. Daily 8am–8pm.
Antica Osteria Massa Via Mazzini 55, Caserta ☎ 0823 456 527, ⓦ ristorantemassa.it. Just up Via Mazzini on the right from Piazza Dante, this is an excellent choice for a reasonably priced meal in a historic building. Great seafood – octopus, *baccalà*, all beautifully presented. *Primi* around €9, *secondi* €15–20. Daily noon–2.30pm & 7.30–10.45pm.
Da Teresa Via Torre 6, Casertavecchia ☎ 0823 371 201.

The best feature here is the magnificent view, either from window seats or outdoors in the spacious, flower-arboured garden. Main courses, featuring mountain game and other regional highlights, average about €10; the set menus, including wine, go for €15–20. Open daily for lunch and dinner. Closed Wed in winter.
Hotel Caserta Antica Via Tiglio 75, Casertavecchia ☎ 0823 371 158, ⓦ hotelcaserta-antica.it. Just outside the ancient heart of Casertavecchia, this is a modern hotel with a swimming pool in the garden and free parking. The rooms are handsome and simple, the setting quietly rural; ask for a view overlooking the valley. It has a decent restaurant too. **€75**

The Capuas

The twin towns of **Capua** and **Santa Maria Capua Vetere** lie a not especially pleasant bus-ride away from Caserta, past petrol stations and run-down housing, and frankly aren't particularly appealing destinations in themselves. Indeed it's hard to believe now, but Capua was once the third largest city in the Roman world, after Rome and Carthage, a place so famous for its luxury and pleasure that even today there's a popular Italian expression, "*gli ozi di Capua*" or "languid idleness of Capua", referring to a state of sensual idleness. The Romans built the Appian Way through here, emphasizing its strategic importance and establishing a useful route for Romans to conquer the South, and later constructed Capua's first-century AD amphitheatre. Neither town makes for an especially alluring place to stay, although the countryside around has a few beautiful places to laze about, or "*oziare*".

Santa Maria Capua Vetere

Of the two Capuas, **SANTA MARIA CAPUA VETERE** is the more ancient of the two Capuas, though you wouldn't realise it now from the sprawl of modern buildings and roundabouts that greets you. Nonetheless there are a few rewards if you're willing to pick your way through the somewhat blighted townscape, and not just ancient ruins either – believe it or not, there's an excellent vegetarian restaurant too.

The amphitheatre

Via del Lavoro • Tues–Sun 9am–one hour before sunset • €2.50, combined ticket with Mithraeum and Museo Archeologico • The amphitheatre is in a small park, just off Corso Aldo Moro, a 2min walk from the central Piazza San Francesco d'Assisi

6

Capua's **amphitheatre** was once one of the Roman Empire's largest. However, the site has been pillaged as a ready-made rock quarry over the centuries, and is less well preserved than its small counterpart in Pozzuoli (p.102), bereft of almost all of its marble and upper tiers. However, the network of tunnels underneath survives reasonably intact, and you can wander about on your own, getting a pretty good sense of what it must have looked like in its heyday. Adjacent to the amphitheatre was a highly regarded Roman gladiator school and barracks, which was the site of the slaves' and gladiators' revolt, led by Spartacus, in 73 BC – a massive rebellion that was only suppressed after two years of fighting and four lost battles. Amid the heaps of rubble and a handful of artefacts dotted around the area, look for a large fragment of mosaic – the floor of a *terme* (baths complex) – showing sea deities and delightful creatures, some of them mythical. There is also a small museum, the **Museo dei Gladiatori**, which has some fearsome gladiator helmets, a life-size animated diorama of the arena, and a scale model showing how the amphitheatre would have looked in its day. However, many of the treasures found here are now in the Museo Provinciale in nearby Capua (p.196) or the archeological museum in Naples (p.67).

Museo Archeologico dell'Antica Capua

Via Roberto d'Angiò 48 • Tues–Sun 9am–7pm • €2.50, includes amphitheatre and Mithraeum • To get here from the amphitheatre, cross the road, head left, then take the first right

Just off the central Piazza San Francesco d'Assisi, the **Museo Archeologico dell'Antica Capua** houses archeological remains unearthed mostly at other sites around the area. Exhibits, in old-fashioned rudimentary cases, follow chronological order, starting with Bronze Age artefacts, then Etruscan and finally Greek and Roman. Highlights include a statue of a Resting Satyr after Praxiteles; some painted terracotta heads with intense eyes, of both Greek and Etruscan origin; from the Samnites, beautiful funerary articles and painted tombs, which survived World War II bombing; and terracotta pots, jars and votive figurines from the ancient Temple of Diana Tifatina nearby – now incarnated as Sant'Angelo in Formis (see p.196).

The Mithraeum

Vicolo Mitreo, off Via Morelli • Tues–Sun 9am–6pm • €2.50, includes amphitheatre and Museo Archeologico • Notify the museum ticket office so the guard can unlock the site

Perhaps the most significant of the array of ancient sights in town is the **Mithraeum**, an almost two thousand-year-old subterranean temple to the primordial Indo-Persian god Mithras that was discovered in 1922 – a profoundly mysterious place that is redolent of the inscrutable, blood-letting rites which accompanied the secretive monotheistic cult of Mithraism. There were once many thousands of such places of worship throughout the ancient world, from Britain to Asia Minor, all of which were relatively small, accommodating no more than thirty to forty men. This one boasts the best-preserved extant fresco of Mithras himself in action (it's at the far end beyond the altar); he slays the sacred bull while others look on, a dog jumps up and a snake slithers underneath. Other frescoes along the sides, above rudimentary benches and much less well preserved, reveal esoteric details of the various stages of initiation, making this visual record of a once-dominant religion one of the most complete there is still in existence.

Capua and around

Four kilometres further up the Via Appia from Santa Maria Capua Vetere, situated on the broad curve of the Volturno River, **CAPUA** is a more attractive place than its Roman counterpart, with a walled medieval heart that goes some way to making up for its sister town's unruly sprawl. Originally called Casilinum, it became Capua in the ninth century AD, when the Capuans resettled here after Saracen invaders razed their city. While here, you should take the time to head out of town to see the nearby basilica of **Sant'Angelo in Formis**, one of the finest Byzantine sights in Southern Italy.

6

The medieval town

The town centre is small and like most things around here somewhat run-down. But it's a busy place, not entirely without appeal, and among the many historic structures dotted around are the fairly intact **Roman Bridge**, which was destroyed in World War II and rebuilt; the sixteenth-century **Palazzo Municipale**, adorned with seven heads of Roman deities removed from the Capuan amphitheatre; the handsome sixteenth-century **Porta Napoli** gate; and the **Duomo**, which, although completely reconstructed after bombs reduced it to rubble in 1943, preserves its original ninth-century campanile, and some notable works, including the powerfully moving eighteenth-century sculpture of the *Dead Christ* by Bottigliero.

Museo Provinciale Campano di Capua

Via Roma 68 • Tues–Sat 9am–1.30pm (Tues & Thurs 3–6pm), Sun 9am–1pm • €6 • ☎ 0823 961 042

Most of the finds from ancient Capua are now deposited in the excellent **Museo Provinciale Campano di Capua**, housed in the fifteenth-century Palazzo Antignano, which sports a flamboyant Catalonian portal of dark volcanic rock. They include a series of some two hundred "Madri Dei" – vigorously carved tufa votive figures of earth mothers cradling tightly bundled babies in their arms, dating from the sixth to first centuries BC. They were unearthed in 1845 at a nearby ancient shrine to the Mater Matuta, a primordial Italic fertility divinity. Early versions hold two or three *bambini*, while later Roman-era statues are freighted with twelve, deemed by the Romans to be the ideal number. Opinion is divided about the exact purpose of the formidably hieratic statues: whether to ask for children, to give thanks for them, to honour departed parents or simply to glorify the Great Mother. The museum also contains remnants of statuary from the original Porta Federiciana di Capua, the "Gateway to the South", constructed in 1234 during the reign of Federico II, of which two bulky tower-bases still loom outside the town. Fragments from the Porta include a headless statue of Federico on his throne and a bust of the emperor's advisor, Pier della Vigna, and a colossal head of Jupiter, dubbed the *Testa di Capua Fidelis*.

Sant'Angelo in Formis

Via Galatina • Mon–Sat 9am–5pm, Sun 9am–12.30pm & 3–6pm • Free • Daily buses from Caserta and Santa Maria Capua Vetere

Some 4km from Capua, the tenth-century Basilica of San Michele Arcangelo, better known as **Sant'Angelo in Formis**, is considered by some experts to be one of the best-preserved Byzantine churches in Italy, built on the ruins of a reputedly magnificent temple of Diana, and with mismatched ancient columns inside and out. The portico is worth a closer look, with its squat Corinthian columns, a mix of Romanesque and Moorish arches, and, in the four lower lunettes, elegantly stylized twelfth-century frescoes relating the touching mystical bond between St Anthony Abbot and St Paul the Hermit– two Egyptian religious ascetics of the third and fourth centuries who were considered the founders of Christian monasticism. **Inside**, nearly every centimetre is frescoed, and the paintings are very well preserved. They were created during the reign of Abbot Desiderius, who became Pope Victor III in 1084 and died three years later – he's pictured in the lower left of the apse, his halo square rather than round, indicating that the painting was executed during his lifetime. Above him are the archangels, and above them Christ enthroned, the quintessential Byzantine icon. On the wall opposite, the *Last Judgement* shows sinners plunging into demon-infested Hell, while a three-levelled narrative cycle around the nave relates Bible stories, including Noah and the Ark, Cain and Abel and depictions of the life, teachings and passion of Christ. Finally, don't overlook the intricate fragments of original mosaic flooring from the ancient temple to Diana, or the altar, pulpit and fonts, all refashioned from salvaged ancient materials. And don't forget to enjoy the splendidly panoramic view of Vesuvius outside.

6

ARRIVAL AND INFORMATION

THE CAPUAS

By train Hourly trains run from Naples to Capua. The train station is a 10min walk south of the centre of town, at the end of Viale Ferrovia.

By bus Regular buses run from Naples to Capua and drop you on Via Napoli, just outside the walls of the medieval town. From Caserta, buses run to Santa Maria Capua Vetere (15min), either from the train station or from the stop just to the left as you exit the palace. Get off at Piazza San Francesco d'Assisi; Capua is 15min further on.

Tourist office Capua's small tourist office is on the old town's main square at Piazza Giudici 6 (Mon–Sat 9.30am–1pm, 3.30–7.30pm; ☎ 0823 962 279) and doles out town plans and other bits and pieces.

ACCOMMODATION AND EATING

THE CAPUAS

Amico Bio Piazza 1 Ottobre, Santa Maria Capua Vetere ☎ 0823 183 1093, ☓ spartacusarena.it. The Roman arena in Santa Maria Capua Vetere is a surprising place to find a restaurant of this quality, especially bearing in mind its sister restaurants are in central London. Owner Pasquale Amico's roots are in this town – his father ran a bakery nearby – and his excellent café-restaurant serves up organic Italian food just as it does in London, but using ingredients from the nearby family farm. Lots of veggie choices, great pasta, pizzas, fabulous buffalo mozzarella, and interesting soups and starters (€2.50–7.50). Main courses from €9. Daily 10am until late.

NORTH OF CAPUA

Agriturismo il Contadino Via Starze 1, Caianello ☎ 0823 922 043. This rustic restaurant serves its own pork from its own Nera Casertana pigs and other quality meats, all especially good grilled. Food is always fresh and ingredients top-notch. Reckon on about €40 for a full meal. Mon–Sat lunch and dinner, Sun lunch only.

Terre di Conca Fraz. Piantoli Conca della Campania ☎ 0823 953 663. About 30min from Caserta in pristine countryside, in the hollow of defunct and forested Roccamonfina volcano, this agriturismo is worth a detour. The four rooms are tastefully furnished with antiques, the swimming pool is in a lovely setting, and the food is excellent, served outside in nice weather. The owners raise their own pigs to produce excellent *prosciutto*, cultivate vegetables and make their own cheese and jams, so everything is always fresh and seasonal. They also run a restaurant in a separate location – *Il Contadino* (see above).

Villa de Pertis Via Ponti 30 San Giorgio Dragoni ☎ 0823 866 619, ☓ villadepertis.com. A few kilometres north of Capua, this aristocratic 17th-century house has been converted into a cosy B&B with an excellent, good-value restaurant that serves meals for €30. A good base to explore this virtually untouched part of Campania. Open March–Nov. **€75**

Sant'Agata dei Goti

Between Caserta and Benevento is an area frequently referred to as the **Sannio** (Samnium): the province of the ancient Samnites. Mostly mountainous and forested, it stretches all the way across the peninsula to border the region of Puglia. By far the most charming of the towns here is **SANT'AGATA DEI GOTI**, set in the Taburno Regional Park, with the Apennines as a distant backdrop – a richly endowed hill-town, boasting an important papal and feudal past, built on a large, raised flat table of tufa, dropping off on its sides into deep gorges. The town's Romanesque, medieval and Renaissance treasures suffered great damage in the 1980 earthquake but have now been mostly restored, and there are good reasons for an overnight visit if you can manage it.

Most people arrive in the fairly conventional new part of town, where the first thing to do is stroll over the bridge spanning the Martorano River to take in the **view** – a much-photographed sweep of colourful domes above narrow stone houses on the edge of a cliff, which plunges into a lushly verdant ravine. What you're looking at is the **old town**, 1km in length and around 200m in width, its cobblestones shiny with centuries of foot traffic. You can spend a happy few hours just wandering around, but there are a few sights worth building your stroll around.

Castello

On the main piazza across the bridge is the **Castello**, which is currently being used as the offices of a law firm, but whose grand rooms you can peek into if you're discreet. Go up the broad stone staircase to take in the entrance hall of the *piano nobile*, frescoed from floor to ceiling mostly with images in imitation of works found at Pompeii, including cornucopias, gardens, Pan and his nymphs and a scene of Diana being discovered at her bath by the ill-fated Actaeon.

Duomo

Via Roma 1 • Daily 8am–noon & 4–6pm • Free

Nearby, the **Duomo**, on Piazza Sant'Alfonso, is notable for its handsome portico of ancient columns, the walls inset with imperial epigraphs, among other Roman artefacts, although its main draw is the crypt – all that remains of the original twelfth-century Romanesque structure. Its harmonious multi-vaulted ceilings are supported by a curious mix of slender recycled columns and an even odder assortment of capitals, some of them wedge-shaped and carved with fetching mermaids and randy little flute-playing fauns. The fourteenth-century frescoes, though badly faded, are also worth a look for their Giotto-esque naturalism.

Santissima Annunziata

Via Caudina • Opening times vary • Free

Sant'Agata's final church of note, **Santissima Annunziata** has been de-Baroqued and returned to its thirteenth-century Gothic elegance. A fine topiary garden and a graceful Renaissance portal greet the faithful, but the interior's fourteenth- and fifteenth-century frescoes are the main event. The *Last Judgement* is depicted on the entrance wall, the elect popping up perkily out of their tombs on Christ's right and the damned opposite, suffering graphically appropriate indignities, including a fornicator being hanged from a tree by his genitals and various bureaucratic types being roasted alive at their desks – each sinner explicitly labelled. In the apse, look for the archetypal story of St Nicholas the gift-giver (and original Santa Claus), who is seen tossing a bag of money in through a window so that the three impoverished sisters lying in bed won't be constrained to take up a life of prostitution.

ARRIVAL AND INFORMATION   SANT'AGATA DEI GOTI

By bus Three daily buses make the hour's journey here from Naples' Piazza Garibaldi. By car it's equidistant from Caserta and Benevento, just 15km north of the SS7 – the old Via Appia.

Tourist office Pro Loco, Largo Torricella (Mon & Thurs 8am–2pm & 4–7pm, Tues, Wed & Fri 8am–2pm; ☏ 0823 953 623, ⓦ prolocosantagatadeigoti.it). They offer guided tours as well as information.

ACCOMMODATION AND EATING

You should consider staying in Sant'Agata – it's magical after dark, and there's a couple of perfect accommodation choices, both of which serve great food, along with a couple of decent restaurants too.

Agriturismo Mustilli Piazza Trento 4 ☎ 0823 718 142, ⓦ mustilli.com. Set in a fine 17th-century palace, Palazzo Rainone, this place features a beautiful garden courtyard, a series of aristocratic rooms on the *piano nobile*, and spacious, traditional and comfortable guest rooms graced with family antiques. The family make their own wine, have a restaurant (meals about €30) and offer cooking courses. €80

A L'Antro di Alarico Vico Gioelli 11–13 ☎ 389 993 9883, ⓦ lantrodialarico.it. Carved out of the solid tufa rock on which the town sits, the interior of this restaurant offers an historic atmosphere. Look for *mela annurca* (see p.193), *pizzelle* and *frittelle*, as well as antipasti and pasta with truffles and wild herbs. Expect to spend about €30 for a full meal. Open daily except Mon for lunch and dinner.

Il Maniero dei Cesari Contrada Verroni (Le Pietre) ☎ 0823 716 213, ⓦ ilmanierodeicesari.com. About 3km from town, *Il Maniero dei Cesari* has a small pool, and rooms mix antique with modern furniture. The restaurant serves good traditional regional cuisine. Wed–Sun lunch and dinner. €80

La Cantina dei Briganti Via Parco 3 ☎ 0823 953 668, ⓦ lacantinadeibriganti.com. Near the Castello Ducale, this is a popular local restaurant that specializes in traditional dishes and meat. Great food and service. Open for dinner Mon–Sat and for lunch and dinner Sun.

Ristorante Zi' Paoluccio Via Roma 22 ☎ 329 989 1855. This centrally located wine bar has been here since 1927, serving aromatic local goat's and sheep's cheeses, pork sausages, *mostarda* (similar to chutney), and vegetables preserved in oil. These, with some good bread and potent local wine, easily make a full meal, all for about €20 a head. Open daily except Mon for lunch and dinner.

6

Benevento

The appealing and breezy ancient city of **BENEVENTO** is reachable in about an hour and a half from Naples by bus or train. An important Roman settlement, it was a key point on the Via Appia between Rome and Brindisi, and as such a thriving trading town. Founded in 278 BC, it was a far-flung outpost of ancient Rome, and even now the town has a remote air about it, circled by green forested hills, with the Apennines just in the distance. Its climate also ranks among Southern Italy's most extreme; the Romans originally called it Maleventum, in fact, for its notoriously bitter winter winds – an anomaly in this balmy region – but changed the name to Beneventum after a victorious battle here in 275 BC, when they decided it wasn't really such a bad place after all. The city centre was bombed in World War II, but it's been beautifully restored, and this bright, liveable town boasts several theatres and hosts a theatre festival around the end of summer. There's an occult connection too: spellbinding yellow liqueur, Strega ("witch"), which you see in bars all over Italy, is made in Benevento, making this the best place of all to take the plunge and try some.

Piazza IV Novembre

Benevento's main square, **Piazza IV Novembre**, is dominated by the **Rocca de' Rettori**, a fourteenth-century papal stronghold, now used as government offices (though its grounds stretch out behind as a lovely park, the **Villa Comunale**). An Egyptian obelisk, erected in 88 AD, adorns the square, and the San Michele chapel in the basilica of **San Bartolomeo** was designed by Raguzzini, who created Rome's lovely Piazza Sant'Ignazio. Most of the town's sights are within a ten-minute stroll of here.

Santa Sofia

A little way down Benevento's main street, **Corso Garibaldi**, stands a tower, engraved with maps showing the ancient independent states of which the city was once the capital. This is the erstwhile bell tower of the eighth-century church of **Santa Sofia**, which is worth a look for its recycled columns and other ancient remnants, as well as its part-circular and part six-pointed star floor-plan, reputed to reflect the esoteric harmonics of medieval spiritual alchemy.

Museo del Sannio

Corso Garibaldi 6 • Tues–Sun 9am–7pm • €4 • ☎ 0824 774 763

You have to pass through Santa Sofia's handsome twelfth-century cloister, whose Moorish arches are divided by beautifully carved Romanesque capitals, to reach the excellent **Museo Sannio**, which displays a first-rate selection of local Hellenistic and Roman finds, including exquisitely beautiful bas-reliefs, torsos, heads and other major fragments. The rarest pieces – in fact the largest such finds outside of Egypt – are the Egyptian artefacts, from a nearby temple to Isis; objects include various sphinxes, falcons, bulls, an effigy of Emperor Domitian as Pharaoh, two headless statues of priests of Isis and the granite head of the goddess herself. There are also very fine terracotta votive figurines from the fifth century BC, a sizeable collection of Greek vases and important finds from a Lombard necropolis of the sixth to eighth centuries. The museum's upper rooms house a modest array of sixteenth- to nineteenth-century paintings and furniture.

Arch of Trajan

Along Corso Garibaldi, to the right up Via Traiano, the **Arch of Trajan** (114–117 AD) is one of Italy's most important remnants from the Roman era, a marvellously preserved triumphal arch of glimmering Parian marble embellished with far more distinct images than Rome's arches; most of the refined carving is still very crisp, and you can get close enough to study its intricate bas-reliefs. Built to herald the entrance to Benevento from the Via Appia and to mark the start of the Via Traiana, which offered a shorter route to Brindisi, it glorifies the Emperor Trajan in various scenes of triumph, power and largesse. One frieze shows him being received into heaven by the gods themselves, and his adopted son and successor Hadrian being welcomed by the goddess Roma.

Duomo

The city's star-crossed **Duomo**, on Piazza Orsini, is an almost total reconstruction of a thirteenth-century Romanesque original, but a few cobbled-together fragments of the original Lombard structure now form the hotchpotch facade along with a celebrated set of twelfth-century Byzantine bronze doors that have been recently restored. Take a look, too, at the bell tower, with its line-up of Roman busts scavenged from local funerary sites, and the eighth-century crypt, which has thirteenth-century frescoes and hosts a small museum.

Teatro Romano

Piazza Ponzio Telesino • Mon–Sat 10am–1.30pm & 4.30–7.30pm • €2 • ⓦ teatroromanobenevento.it

Benevento has a shabby but picturesque medieval quarter, the **Triggio**, reached by following Via Carlo Torre down off to the left of Corso Garibaldi beyond the cathedral, where there's another ruined Roman arch and a substantial but indifferently maintained **Teatro Romano**, inaugurated in 126 AD. Built during the reign of Hadrian, it seated twenty thousand people in its heyday, and it's still an atmospheric sight, with views over the rolling green countryside of the province.

Hortus Conclusus

Via Pasquale Stanlislao Mancini 11 • Daily 9am–7.45pm • Free

One intriguing modern sight bears mentioning: the **Hortus Conclusus**, in the enclosed garden-courtyard of the convent of San Domenico in Piazza Guerrazzi, off Via Pellegrini, which offers a fantastically unexpected and witty sculptural installation by local artist Mimmo Paladino.

ARRIVAL AND INFORMATION

BENEVENTO

By train There are several trains every day to Benevento direct from Naples, and several more changing at Caserta; the station is about a half-hour walk from the sights, but frequent buses run from the station to the centre.

By bus Around 8 daily buses make the 90min trip from

Naples, dropping off in a car park below Benevento's centre, where you can also park if you're driving.

Tourist office Via Nicola Sala 31 ☎ 0824 319 911 (Mon–Fri 9am–1.30pm & 3–4pm).

ACCOMMODATION AND EATING

Benevento is emphatically not a tourist town, so finding accommodation can be a problem. There is only a handful of hotels; they're short on charm but functional, and even the best choices are not very expensive.

Il Tricorno Via Capitano Pasquale De Juliis 13 ☎ 0824 21 568. This simple trattoria, on the corner of Via Mario La Vipera, serves wonderful wood-fired pizzas from just €4, and has a superb antipasto buffet, in a convivial space painted Pompeiian red. Open daily except Sun for lunch and dinner.

Nunzia Via Annunziata 152 ☎ 0824 29 431. A basic,

friendly trattoria which serves excellent traditional fare at reasonable prices. You can easily eat your fill for €20–25. Mon–Sat for lunch and dinner.

Villa Traiano Viale dei Rettori 9 ☎ 0824 326 241, ⓦ hotel villatraiano.it. Maybe the town's best hotel, housed in a lovely *belle époque* building that offers plush guestrooms with marble bathrooms, a tranquil terrace garden and a bar. **€150**

Around Benevento

There are no compelling towns near Benevento, but the countryside is glorious, and one or two places repay a visit if you want to have a poke around. **Morcone**, about 30km to the north, is a beautiful place, its white houses spilling down a picturesque slope, while **Telese Terme**, the same distance west, is an old spa town with a small lake and the nearby Roman ruins of Telesia. A few kilometres north of here lie the famous majolica centres of **Cerreto Sannita** and **San Lorenzello**, which continue the eighteenth-century tradition of the famed Giustiniani family of ceramists, and host an antiques fair on the last weekend of each month. On the way, the imposing castle at **Castelvenere** is a worthwhile stop.

Further afield, the untamed limestone foothills of the Apennines afford excellent opportunities for **hiking**. Just 9km away from Pietraroja, the spectacular little hill-town of **Cusano Mutri** is the point of departure for a number of walks and treks into the **Parco del Matese**. One of the most popular is a moderate trek, three hours there and back, to the 28m waterfall known as the **Salto dell'Orso**, the "Bear's Leap", where one of the rewards is a swim in the pristine natural rock pool.

ACCOMMODATION AND EATING

AROUND BENEVENTO

Grand Hotel Telese Via Cerreto 1, Telese Terme ☎ 0824 940 500, ⓦ grandhoteltelese.it. If you want time to explore the area, try this truly luxurious turn-of-the-century hotel with full spa facilities. **€170**

Il Gelso delle Maitine Contrada Maitine Pesco Sannita ☎ 0824 981 157, ⓦ ilgelsodelle maitine.it. This agriturismo is a magical spot – not for the rooms which are quite basic, but for the falcons,

other birds and beautiful horses that share this idyllic location (the owner is a falconer), set in the scenic Benevento hills with Mts Taburno, Camposauro and Pentime as backdrop. You can go riding, swim in the pool, and it's a good lunch option too – Antonietta cooks delicious traditional country food served with local wines. Phone ahead for either rooms or for dining. **€150**

The Amalfi Coast

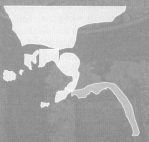

VIETRI CERAMICS

The Amalfi Coast

Occupying the southern side of the Sorrentine peninsula, the Amalfi Coast – Costiera Amalfitana – can lay claim to being Europe's most beautiful coastline, its corniche road winding around towering cliffs that slip almost sheer into the sea. You've seen it all before, of course, in countless films and car adverts, but nothing quite prepares you for the reality: the rocky outcrops topped by Saracen towers; the impossibly balanced umbrella pines; the tunnels cut through the rock; the green-speckled peninsulas stretching out like lizards as far as you can see; and the sea shimmering invitingly far below. The settlements here are triumphs of faith over reason, and you can't even see a lot of the buildings from the road, due to the fact that most of the villas cling limpet-like to the cliffs, often only accessible by way of hidden steps down from the road.

7

By car or bus it's an incredible ride (though it can get mighty congested in summer), while getting there by sea – easy and affordable with a wealth of coastal ferries – is a gentler experience, but an equally special one, taking in the precarious houses, decked with flowers, along the serpentine coast road, and the river valleys that cut through the mountainous cliffs, opening out at almost inaccessible beaches. The coast as a whole is inevitably rather developed, and the villas atop its precipitous slopes are some of the country's most sought-after; it's also home to some of the most aesthetically lovely hotels in Italy, and budget travellers should be aware that you certainly get what you pay for here. But if there is anywhere in the country that you might be tempted to blow your budget, this, most definitely, is it.

Of the main coastal targets, high-profile **Positano** gets most of the plaudits – undeniably picturesque, but these days it's almost entirely the province of high-end mass tourism, and somewhat the worse for it. Smaller resorts like **Praiano**, which haven't been entirely overrun, make more appealing options, as does **Amalfi** itself, with a hint of a life beyond tourism, and a fascinating old whitewashed centre that stretches up the valley from the sea. Amalfi also provides easy access to the more low-key seaside village of **Atrani** – one of the nicest places to stay on the coast – as well as the fabled village of **Ravello**, whose mountain-top villas and gardens occupy a space that feels "closer to the sky than the sea", in the words of the French writer André Gide.

GETTING AROUND   THE AMALFI COAST

The dream, of course, is to **drive** the coast road in a convertible – an exhilarating ride by any standards (see ⓦ spiderlifestyle.com for vintage car rental). Just be aware that whatever car you're driving, the sheer concentration required to negotiate the bends in the road can limit your enjoyment of the views, and that parking when you reach your destination can leave you a frazzled wreck at the end of the day – plus you'll usually pay a premium to keep your car at your hotel. For those without a car, navigating the Amalfi Coast by **bus** couldn't be easier, though summer traffic and an increase in tourists mean buses are often full to bursting. Travel by **ferry** is a more restful experience, and generally quicker too, but it is more expensive.

ATRANI

Highlights

❶ Sentiero degli Dei The Amalfi Coast's most celebrated walk, the "Path of the Gods" offers head-spinning views. **See p.210**

❷ Marina di Praia This little beach, a watersports hub with a cluster of good restaurants, is just one of down-to-earth Praiano's many charms. **See p.211**

❸ Marina di Conca Although reached by several hundred steps down from the road, this beach is one of the coast's best – and for much of the year is relatively uncrowded. **See p.214**

❹ Atrani Amalfi's tiny neighbour is an often-overlooked gem. **See p.217**

❺ Valle dei Mulini, Amalfi This wonderfully lush valley of now derelict paper mills is the starting point for some wonderful walks around the historic city. **See p.217**

❻ Villa Rufolo, Ravello These colourful gardens are brimming with history, with some of the most photogenic views anywhere in Italy – the perfect setting for a concert under the stars. **See p.221**

❼ Paestum One of Southern Italy's finest Hellenistic sights, full of brooding atmosphere. **See p.230**

HIGHLIGHTS ARE MARKED ON THE MAP ON PP.206–207

GETTING TO THE AMALFI COAST

Getting from Naples airport to the Amalfi Coast can be a time-consuming and expensive business: routes by public transport can be lengthy, and **private transfers** cost at least €120. Currently, one **shuttle service**, Positano Shuttle, runs hourly from Naples airport, train station and port to the coast, stopping to drop off at hotels along the way (Positano and Praiano/ Amalfi €35/40 per person; booking obligatory; ⓦ positanoshuttle.com).

If opting for public transport, the best route (if the timings fit with your flight arrival time) is to travel **via Salerno**. Two buses go from Naples airport to Salerno station: Buonotourist (2 daily Mon–Sat, currently at 9.30am and 1.30pm; 1hr 15min; ⓦ buonobus.it) and SITA (2 daily Mon–Fri, except in Aug, currently at 10.30am and 4pm; 1hr 15min; ⓦ sitasudtrasporti.it). From Salerno station it's a short walk to the port, where ferries serve Amalfi (35min) and Positano (1hr 10min): a scenic journey past a particularly rugged stretch of the Amalfi Coast.

Many people opt to travel **via Sorrento**, but if you're not breaking your journey in the town, this can be a long slog. Circumvesuviana trains from Naples (1hr 10min; ⓦ eavcampania.it) and Curreri buses from the airport (10 daily in high season; 1hr 15min; ⓦ curreriviaggi.it) run to Sorrento station, from where SITA buses travel to the Amalfi Coast (1hr 40min to Amalfi). Summer traffic on the coast road can make the journey feel interminable; in high season, Alicost run two ferries a day between Sorrento, Positano and Amalfi, a more relaxing experience than the bus.

7

BY BUS

SITA The big SITA buses travel frequently up and down the coast, stopping off at all the major resorts and linking them in turn with the major centres of Sorrento and Salerno. UnicoCostiera tickets cover unlimited bus journeys during a specified time period and cost €2.50 (45min), €3.80 (1hr 30min), €7.60 (24hr) or €18 (three days); the last two options also get you

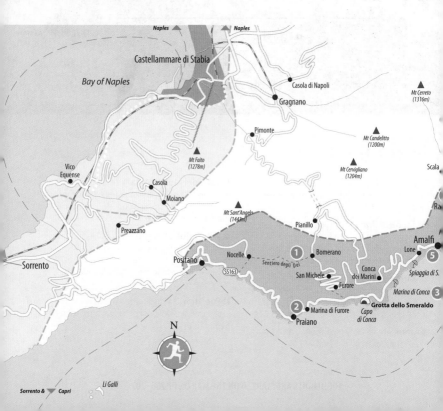

a free single trip on some of the City Sightseeing services (see p.138). For more information, see ⓦunicocampania.it; for timetables see ⓦsitasudtrasporti.it (Italian only).

City Sightseeing Touristy they may be, but the big red open-top buses that serve the main parts of the coast (April–Oct) can be a breath of fresh air after one too many journeys on an overcrowded SITA bus, though they only run roughly every hour, so in high summer queues are inevitable. Routes include Sorrento–Positano–Amalfi, Amalfi–Ravello and Amalfi–Minori–Maiori. For timetables and fares, see ⓦcitysightseeing.com.

BY FERRY

Alicost ☎089 871 483, ⓦalicost.it. Runs between Sorrento, Capri, Positano, Amalfi and Salerno.

Coop Sant'Andrea ☎089 873 190, ⓦcoopsantandrea.com. Stops at pretty much everywhere along the coast, from Capri to Salerno, taking in Sorrento, Positano, Amalfi, Minori and Maiori.

Gescab ☎089 234 892, ⓦgescab.it. Services from Naples to Positano via Capri and from Amalfi to Capri.

Travelmar ☎089 872 950, ⓦtravelmar.it. Services between Salerno, Amalfi and Positano.

Tickets and schedules To give you an idea of prices and journey times, Amalfi–Positano costs around €8 and takes 20–30min; Sorrento–Amalfi takes 50min–1hr and costs around €17, and Naples–Positano costs around €29 and takes 1hr 40min. For specific timings, see the daily newspaper *Il Mattino*, check with the local tourist offices or look up schedules online.

ON FOOT

The coast can also be enjoyably explored on foot. The mountains that sweep down to the sea are magnificent walking country, with some well-marked-out routes, and if you're up to scaling some pretty precipitous inclines, you get to see a different side to the coast, a world away from the often-crowded places on the shore. We've noted some circular routes in this chapter, from Positano and Amalfi (see p.210 & p.218); the extensive bus routes make it easy to pick and choose your starting point. Chapter 3 also has details of a walk you can do from the north side of the Sorrentine peninsula to the coast (see p.129).

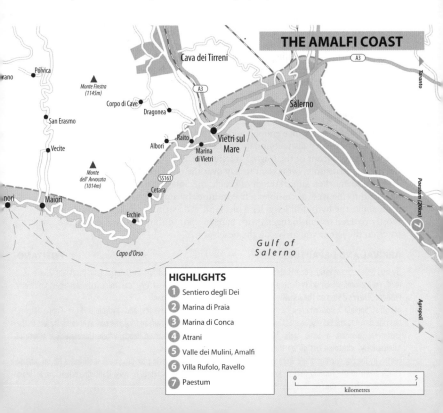

THE AMALFI COAST

Pólvica · Cava dei Tirreni · A3 · Toranto

Monte Finstra (1145m) · Corpo di Cave · Dragonea · Salerno

San Erasmo · Raito · Vietri sul Mare

Vecite · Albori · Marina di Vietri

Monte dell' Avvocata (1014m) · SS163 · Cetara

nori · Maiori · Erchie

Capo d'Orso · Gulf of Salerno

Paestum (30km)

Agropoli

HIGHLIGHTS
1. Sentiero degli Dei
2. Marina di Praia
3. Marina di Conca
4. Atrani
5. Valle dei Mulini, Amalfi
6. Villa Rufolo, Ravello
7. Paestum

0 · 5
kilometres

Positano

The first place that can really call itself a town on the coast, **POSITANO** was in the Middle Ages a commercial rival to the maritime powerhouse of Amalfi, but it proved to have far less staying power, and these days it is so completely consumed by the tourist trade that it can be a hard place to like in summer. It has a couple of decent beaches and a great many boutiques – the town has long specialized in clothes made from linen, georgette and cotton, as well as handmade shoes. But it is the spectacular setting – a jumble of pastel-coloured houses heaped up in a pyramid high above the water – that has inspired a thousand postcards and helped to make it a moneyed resort that runs a close second to Capri in the celebrity stakes. Since John Steinbeck wrote up the place in glowing terms back in 1953 – he called it "a dream place that isn't quite real when you are there and becomes beckoningly real after you have gone" – Positano has enjoyed a fame quite out of proportion to its tiny size. Franco Zeffirelli is just one of many famous names who have villas nearby, and the crowds that pack the beach here consider themselves a cut above your average sun-worshipper.

Santa Maria Assunta

Rampa Teglia • Daily 8am–noon & 4–8pm • Free • ⓦ chiesapositano.com

Positano's inordinately crowded centre is a mass of shops aimed at the tourist trade, and there's little in the way of sights apart from the church of **Santa Maria Assunta**, whose glittering majolica dome marks the centre of town. It harbours a Byzantine icon of the "Black Madonna" which, local legend has it, was stolen by Saracen pirates around 1000 AD. They were crossing the Mediterranean when a terrible storm blew up and the pirates heard a voice crying *"Posa! Posa!"* ("Put it down!"). The icon was unloaded at the nearest village, and the storm promptly calmed, because, it was believed, this was where it wished to remain. The village was renamed Positano after the Madonna's command.

The beaches

Positano's **beaches** are nice enough and not overly busy most of the time – though watch out for the jellyfish, abundant in these waters. The main stretch, the **Spiaggia Grande** right in front of the town, is reasonable, although you'll be sunbathing among the fishing boats unless you want to pay over the odds for the nicer area on the far left. There's also another, larger stretch of beach, the **Spiaggia del Fornillo**, around the headland to the west, accessible in five minutes by a pretty path that winds around from above the hydrofoil jetty. It's a pleasant, wide strip of sand and shingle but is mostly covered in sun-loungers, with barely a spot to throw a towel down; the small patch to the left as you arrive on the beach is free.

ARRIVAL AND DEPARTURE

POSITANO

By bus Buses stop at various points along the main coastal road, Via Marconi, which skirts the top of the old town of Positano. There's a stop on the Amalfi side of town (ask to get off at "Sponda"), from where it's a steep walk or a short bus ride down to the little square at the bottom end of Via Cristoforo Colombo, a 5min walk from the seafront. Alternatively, you could get off on the other side of the centre, by the *Bar Internazionale*, from where Viale Pasitea winds down to the Fornillo part of town. Open-top City Sightseeing buses run on a route between Sorrento,

Positano and Amalfi (hourly; tour takes 1hr 25min; €8; ☏ 081 877 4707, ⓦ sorrento.city-sightseeing.it); buy tickets on board.

By ferry Ferries and hydrofoils from Capri, Naples, Sorrento, Amalfi and Salerno pull in at the jetty just to the right of the main beach, where there are also plenty of ticket booths.

By car Arriving by car, you'll shell out a lot on garage space as parking is very limited; reckon on at least €20 a day.

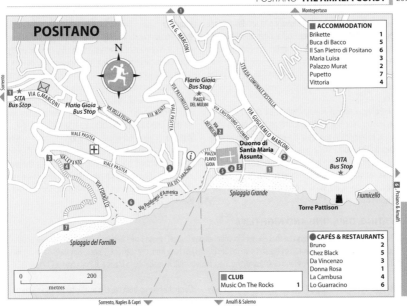

GETTING AROUND AND INFORMATION

By bus Flavio Gioia local buses (☎089 811 895, ⓦflaviogioia.com) link the two SITA stops every 30min and also run up to Montepertuso and Nocelle (for the Path of the Gods) and Praiano. You can buy tickets in *tabacchi* shops (€1.30) or on the bus (€1.70).

Boat rental Lucibello have a desk on the Spiaggia Grande and lots of different boats, rentable without skipper, from €35/hr (Easter–Oct). There are also excursions to the nearby attractions, such as Capri, the Grotta dello Smeraldo and the rest of the coast. Pedalos (€15/hr), canoes (€10/hr)

and paddleboards (€15/hr) are also available. Main office at Via del Brigantino 9, Positano (☎089 875 032, ⓦlucibello.it).

Scooter rental Positano Rent-a-Scooter, Via Pasitea 99 (☎089 812 2077, ⓦpositanorentascooter.it; rental from €60/day).

Tourist office There's a tourist office just back from the beach by the church steps at Via del Saracino 4 (June–Oct Mon–Sat 9am–7pm, Sun 9am–2pm; Nov–May Mon–Sat 9am–4pm; ☎089 875 067, ⓦaziendaturismopositano.it).

ACCOMMODATION

Accommodation in Positano tends to be pricey. Not surprisingly, it's cheaper to stay up in the newer neighbourhoods near the main road through town, or above Fornillo beach, than near the Spiaggia Grande. Blu Porter will transport luggage to and from your hotel for a fee (☎089 811 496).

Brikette Via Marconi 358 ☎hostelworld.com. The only hostel in town, a couple of minutes' walk from the bus stop on the west side of town along the coast road. It's friendly and clean, with stunning views, a cheap bar and free wi-fi. No kitchen facilities or lockers. Open year-round. Dorms €30, doubles €100

Buca di Bacco Via Rampa Teglia 4 ☎089 875 699, ⓦbucadibacco.it. Right on the seafront with its own patch of beach, this charming old-timer has gleaming tiled floors throughout, and the spacious, traditional-style rooms come with marble bathrooms. It's worth paying a little extra for one of the Superior rooms, which have a sea-view terrace. Closed Nov–March. €350

Il San Pietro di Positano Via Laurito 2 ☎089 812 080, ⓦilsanpietro.it. High on a promontory around 3km east of Positano proper, the *San Pietro* has a host of celebrity admirers, a range of individually designed rooms, beautiful public spaces that make the most of the all-round views, and a private beach and waterfront bar to which you're whisked by elevator. All this, plus a tennis court, and a Michelin-starred restaurant supplied by its own kitchen garden, makes this many people's idea of the ultimate five-star hotel. Closed Nov to mid-April. €690

Maria Luisa Via Fornillo 42 ☎089 875 023, ⓦpensionemarialuisa.com. Very friendly, and great value at almost half the price of the nearby *Vittoria*

– though you don't have the luxury of a lift down to the beach, and the climb up can be a killer. Breakfast isn't included, but there's a coffee machine and fridges, not to mention a lovely light breakfast room and terrace with great views. It's worth paying an extra €20 for one of the rooms with a spacious sea-view terrace. Closed Nov–March. **€75**

★**Palazzo Murat** Via dei Mulini 23 ☎089 875 177, ⓦpalazzomurat.it. Perhaps the nicest place to stay if you want to be right in the heart of things, just 2min from the beach. The rooms are a good size with most in a new extension, rather than in the old *palazzo* itself. Around half have sea views, if a little obscured by the church, and all have satellite TV, a/c, wi-fi, large bathrooms and balconies. Closed Nov–March. **€220**

Pupetto Via Fornillo · 37 ☎089 875 087, ⓦhotelpupetto.it. With its sister hotel, the *Vittoria*, to which it is connected by elevators, the *Pupetto* has pretty much colonized Fornillo beach. It has rooms with sea views – and some with large terraces – on the first and second floor, and ground-floor garden rooms that are a bit cheaper; all have TV and a/c, and are decently furnished. Prices include beach access, and there's a good restaurant too (half board €28/person). Closed Nov–March. **€160**

Vittoria Via Fornillo 19 ☎089 875 049 ⓦhotelvittoriapositano.com. Sister hotel to the *Pupetto* down below, the *Vittoria* makes a decent, slightly cheaper alternative. All rooms are simply and brightly furnished and have sea views and balconies, a/c and TV. Closed Nov–March. **€150**

EATING, DRINKING AND NIGHTLIFE

Positano's many **restaurants** can make a dent in your holiday budget; those listed below are the more reliable options. For **picnics**, there's an *alimentari* by the steps up to the church, just back from the seafront (Easter–Nov daily 8am–10pm). In summer boats run from Positano to *Africana*, the most famous club hereabouts, in Marina di Praia (see p.212).

Bruno Via C. Colombo 157 ☎089 875 392. Some way from the more touristy places near the beach, both in distance and in price. There are lovely views over the water at night, although you're basically sitting right on the road, and the food is good and well priced; main courses start at around €9, more for fish and seafood. Daily 12.30–11pm.

Chez Black Spiaggia Grande ☎089 875 036, ⓦchezblack .it. A long-established seafood restaurant, maybe a bit over-branded these days, but the food is unfalteringly good, and the location probably Positano's best. Lots of great seafood options – try the *paccheri* with cuttlefish and octopus – but it also does pizza, from around €10. Daily noon–11.30pm; closed Nov, Dec & last two weeks Jan & Feb.

★**Da Vincenzo** Via Pasitea 172–178 ☎089 875 128.

Worth the hike up from the centre, this family-run restaurant has a cosy cave-like interior and a few seats outside. The jovial service, lively atmosphere (it's usually packed with locals) and tasty food make for a memorable dining experience. Two courses with wine will set you back around €35 per person. Mon & Wed–Sun 12.30–2.45pm & 6.30–11pm.

Donna Rosa Via Montepertuso, 97–99 ☎089 811 806, ⓦdrpositano.com. Run by mother-and-daughter team Raffaella and Erika, *Donna Rosa* is a romantic restaurant that's a good bet for a special meal. The risotto (which changes daily) is always a highlight, as is the fresh fish. The food is pricey – a plate of pasta goes for up to €27 – but very tasty. It's 3km from Positano, but they'll pay for your taxi. Mon & Wed–Sun 11am–2pm & 5–11pm; closed Nov–Easter.

WALKS FROM POSITANO

As with everywhere on this coast, Positano offers plenty of opportunities for **walks**, though most involve a steep uphill slog to start off, unless you want to cheat and take the bus. One of the easiest circular walks from town is up to **Montepertuso** and along the cliff to the village of **Nocelle** for lunch, and then back down again – a walk that would take you 2–3 hours there and maybe half that coming back down, though any leg of the journey can be done by bus. Walking up from the centre of Positano, take the path to Via Cristoforo Colombo and then the steps up to the coast road and continue east along here as far as the bus stop, opposite which there's a path off to the left that begins the ascent. For a more serious hike, you can take the path east from Nocelle along the so-called **Sentiero degli Dei** ("Path of the Gods"). From Nocelle follow the path to **Colle la Serra**, a two-hour hike, and from there to **Bomerano**, a relatively easy one-hour walk. From here you could pick up the Agerola–Amalfi bus which descends down through the Furore gorge to the coast – a spectacular ride.

Some walkers prefer this hike **in reverse** – from Bomerano to Nocelle – as it affords lovely views along the coast towards Sorrento, and is also downhill. If you do the walk in this direction and are looking for lunch in Nocelle, head for *Ristorante Santa Croce*, Via Cappella 25 (☎089 811 260), for a restorative plate of pasta. In April and May, a music festival, "I Suoni degli Dei" (ⓦisuonideglidei.com), sees classical music concerts performed at various points along the route.

La Cambusa Piazza A. Vespucci 24 ☎089 875 432, ⓦlacambusapositano.com. One of the fancier options on the seafront, and unashamedly a tourist hangout, just back from the Spiaggia Grande on the left. But its fish and seafood options are pretty good, and it's a fine place to watch the Positano world go by. A full fish blowout here will set you back around €50 a head. Daily noon–10pm; closed Dec–March.

★**Lo Guarracino** Via Positanesi d'America 12 ☎089 875 794, ⓦloguarracino.net. For a restaurant that has perhaps the best views in town – you eat on a bright, flower-fringed terrace overlooking the sea and Fornillo beach – this place is relatively reasonably priced, at least by

Positano standards (pastas €10–20, mains €12–22), and does great food too. The antipasti and *primi* are great: try the *scialatello Guarracino* – pasta with seafood and cherry tomatoes – or the *linguini ai ricci di mare* (with sea urchins). There's also excellent wood-fired oven pizza (from €9). Daily noon–3.30pm & 7–11pm; closed Nov–March.

Music on the Rocks Via del Brigantino 19 ☎089 875 874, ⓦmusicontherocks.it. Just off the far end of the Spiaggia Grande, this bar-restaurant-club is central Positano's best place for a night out, with atmospheric lighting and a sleek bar and grotto-effect main room and dancefloor. Dazzling sea views and a predictably glitzy clientele. Daily from 7pm (DJ from 10.30pm). Closed Nov–Easter.

Praiano and around

7

Some 5km east of Positano, **PRAIANO** is much smaller and very much quieter than its more renowned neighbour. The town consists of two tiny centres: **Véttica Maggiore**, which is Praiano proper, scattered along the main road from Positano high above the sea; and **Marina di Praia**, squeezed into a cleft in the rock down at shore level, a couple of kilometres further along towards Amalfi. There's not much to either part of Praiano, but it is a more peaceful and authentic place to stay than Positano.

Although lacking in sights, there are a few decent places to **swim**. The closest are the swimming spots off rocks immediately below the village, most notably the **Spiaggia Gavitella**, which you can reach from the main road by taking the path from the *San Gennaro* restaurant or from the *Smeraldo* hotel; there's also the small patch of shingly beach at Marina di Praia, a watersports hub offering diving, kayaking and boat rental. A couple of restaurants and places offering rooms to rent border the beach, to which steps lead down from the main road by the Torre Asciola or a proper road with parking a little further along. Beyond Marina di Praia on the way to Amalfi you'll also find some decent, properly sandy spots (see p.214).

ARRIVAL AND INFORMATION

PRAIANO

By bus There are SITA buses roughly every 30–45min to Positano (15min), Amalfi (25min) and Sorrento (1hr 15min). Smaller Flavio Gioia buses link Praiano with Positano (10 daily; 15min; buy tickets before boarding), stopping both on the main coast road and in the upper

part of Praiano in Piazza San Luca.
By water taxi Water taxis from Amalfi or Positano cost €35/30 to Marina di Praia with La Sibilla (see below).
Tourist office Via Capriglione 116b (Mon–Sat 9am–1pm & 5–9pm).

GETTING AROUND AND ACTIVITIES

Boat rental La Sibilla, Marina di Praia (daily 8am–8pm; ☎089 874 365, ⓦlasibilla.org) organizes boat rental (from €50/hr excluding fuel) and excursions to the Amalfi Coast and Capri (from €60).
Scooter rental Mr Rent a Scooter, Via Capriglione 99, by the *Trattoria San Gennaro* (☎089 813 071; from €38/day).

Watersports Diving La Boa (☎089 813 034, ⓦlaboa .com) charge from €60, equipment included, for a 45min dive. Windsurf Praiano (☎339 483 5115, ⓦwindsurfpraiano.it) organize windsurfing (€100/4hr) and kayaking (from €40/hr). Both are based in Marina di Praia.

ACCOMMODATION

Casa Angelina Via Capriglione 147 ☎089 813 1333, ⓦcasaangelina.com. This modern boutique hotel has a lobby full of contemporary art and a selection of rooms decorated with stark white minimalism that range greatly in price from those with small balconies in the main building

to top-end suites down by the water. There's a restaurant, a smallish pool, a fitness centre and a lift that takes you part-way down to the beach. It's excellently done, if a little too self-consciously cool for its own good – with a ban on young kids (over-12s only). Closed Nov–Feb. **€335**

★Casa Privata Via Rezzola 41 ☎089 874 078, ⓦcasaprivata.it. A wonderfully secluded boutique hotel set amid luxuriant gardens, with a lovely saltwater pool set above the sea. The rooms are impeccably styled and furnished with antiques; those on the second floor are spacious and share a huge terrace looking out to sea. A private stretch of seafront completes the idyllic picture. Due to the number of steps though, you have to be reasonably fit to enjoy a stay here. Closed Nov–March. **€250**

★Locanda Costa Diva Via Roma 12 ☎089 813 076, ⓦhotelspraiano.com. Above Marina di Praia, this hotel spills down a lovely, leafy series of terraces from the road – 15 rooms, all with sea views, including a superior room with its own little pool, solarium and private garden (€210). There's a garden and a decent restaurant too (see below), so in theory you never have to leave its shady confines except to take the steps down to the beach at Marina di Praia nearby. Closed Nov–Feb. **€130**

Onda Verde Via Terramare 3 ☎089 874 143, ⓦondaverde.it. Perched on the cliff edge at Marina di Praia, just a 5min walk from the beach, and with 25 lovely rooms in a series of cliff-side villas. The spacious rooms are beautifully furnished and have traditional tiled floors. There's also an excellent restaurant with great views over the sea. Closed Nov–March. **€190**

EATING, DRINKING AND NIGHTLIFE

Africana Via Terramare 2, Marina di Praia; lift from the coast road or entrance at sea level ☎089 874 858, ⓦafricanafamousclub.com. The most spectacular place for a big night out hereabouts, tucked away in two big grottoes with a glass floor that looks down onto the rocks and sea below. Outside the main dance area, terraced seating overlooks the sea and lit-up rocks. Mid-April to mid-Sept daily 8pm–3/4am; mid-Sept to mid-Oct Fri & Sat only.

Locanda Costa Diva Via Roma 12 ☎089 813 076, ⓦhotelspraiano.it. Fresh fish is the order of the day at this relaxed restaurant, enhanced with herbs and vegetables grown in their own garden. Mains cost around €13; a typical dish is the traditional *totani e patate* (squid with potatoes). Food aside, this is a lovely place for a meal, with gorgeous terrace dining under a pergola heavy with lemons, with stunning views of the sea. Daily noon–4.50pm & 6–11.30pm.

★Petit Restaurant Bar Mare Via Marina di Praia 9 ☎089 874 326. This simple place by the beach at Marina di Praia is run by Salvatore, whose grandfather was a fisherman here; *mamma* Clelia presides over the kitchen. Stop by for home-made pastries in the morning, a plateful of saffron and seafood risotto for lunch (€20 for two) or a beachside *aperitivo* at sundown. Daily 7.30am–1am; closed Jan & Feb.

★Vivaro Via Caprigliione 156 ☎335 562 4805. In the capable hands of chef-sommelier-waiter Gennaro, this cosy little wine bar makes an atmospheric place for dinner. There's no menu – when you arrive you choose between meat and seafood, and Gennaro decides the rest. Expect to spend €30 per person, plus (strictly local) wine. It's tiny, so book ahead. Mon & Wed–Sun 6pm–midnight, opens 7pm in winter.

Furore

Shortly after Praiano you pass the **Furore gorge**, which gashes into the mountainside just above the coast road. Just below the bridge that crosses the beginning of the gorge, **Marina di Furore** is a small beach accessible by way of steps down from the bridge, with just a handful of fishermen's houses and a disused paper mill where the gorge cuts into the mountain. The beach is nice enough and is shady in the morning, only getting the full sun in mid-afternoon. There's a café-restaurant here, and even a local museum, the **Ecomuseo** (June–Sept: daily 9am–6pm; free), with a room dedicated to the celebrated Italian actress Anna Magnani, who had a house in Furore. Some of the steepest paths you'll encounter on the coast lead up from here to the scattered houses of the **village of Furore** (600m) above – a two-hour walk. If this doesn't appeal, do the walk in reverse by taking the Agerola bus from Amalfi; you can get off in the upper part of the village and walk down.

Grotta dello Smeraldo

Daily: April–Oct 9am–4pm; Nov–March 9am–3pm • €5 • Bus stop and car park at the top, from where you take the lift down to the grotto, which you then tour by boat; alternatively, Gruppo Battallieri d'Amalfi (ⓦ gruppobattellieriamalfi.com) runs boats from Amalfi, which leave you at grotto level (April–Oct hourly 9.40am–2.40pm; 1hr round-trip; €10 return, plus entrance fee)

About 4km out of Praiano, the **Grotta dello Smeraldo** is one of the most highly touted

natural features locally. Discovered by an Amalfi fisherman in 1932, the grotto is not unimpressive, but it's basically one huge chamber and it doesn't take long for the boatmen to exhaust their patter and whisk you around the main features – an underwater nativity scene and various statues that supposedly resemble famous people. The real draw, though, is the intense green of the water on one side, caused by the sun shining through the water to a depth of 16m, and the stalagmites and stalactites that drip from every surface.

Conca dei Marini and beyond

Just around the headland from the grotto, **CONCA DEI MARINI** has a slightly bigger stretch of beach than Praiano – **Marina di Conca**, accessible by way of three hundred or so steps after the *Belvedere Hotel* – worth the trek as it's a pretty and sheltered spot, and often relatively empty. The longer strip next door is the private preserve of the *Hotel Saraceno* up above. The house below the road past the next headland, a fairly modest white villa with green shutters and its own landing stage, used to belong to Sophia Loren, and is within swimming distance of the **Spiaggia di Santa Croce** a little further along – also reached by around four hundred steps from the roadside signpost. There's another small beach down below the hamlet of **Lone**, which is the last village you pass before the road starts to descend into the outskirts of Amalfi.

Amalfi and around

Set in a wide cleft in the cliffs, **AMALFI**, a mere 4km or so further east, is perhaps the highlight of the coast, and a good place to base yourself. It has been an established seaside resort since Edwardian times, when the British upper classes found the town a pleasant spot to spend their winters, but Amalfi's credentials actually go back much further: it was an independent republic during Byzantine times and a great naval power, with a population of some seventy thousand. The city's traders established outposts all over the Mediterranean, setting up the Order of the Knights of St John of Jerusalem in the eleventh century. Amalfi was finally vanquished by the Normans in 1131, and the town was devastated by an earthquake in 1343, but the odd remnant of its past glories remains, and there's a crumbly attractiveness to its whitewashed courtyards and alleys that makes it an appealing place for a wander.

THE REGATTA OF THE MARITIME REPUBLICS

It takes place only once every four years, but Amalfi's **Regatta of the Maritime Republics** is a boat race with much at stake, as the modern-day descendants of the four maritime city-states of Venice, Genova, Pisa and Amalfi pit their wits and strength against each other to be the fastest rowing team. The race alternates from city to city (it's next due to be held in Amalfi in 2016) – an event that excites huge local interest and involves a long build-up. Usually held on the first Sunday in June, it begins with a procession of four hundred people dressed in historic costume and representing episodes in each city's history. This starts in Atrani about 4.30pm before heading to Amalfi, where the so-called "regatta of the galleons" takes place at 6pm.

The **rules** are pretty exacting: the crews are composed of eight rowers and a helmsman, all of whom must be local men; each team's boat has to be built in the same way and measure and weigh exactly the same as the others – 11m long and precisely 760kg. The boats are decked out in traditional colours – blue in Amalfi's case, with the symbol of a winged horse; Genova's boat sports the cross of St George; Pisa's a red eagle; and Venice's the lion of St Mark. The course is 2km long, starting opposite the Santa Croce beach a little way west of the city and finishing in front of the specially erected grandstands in Amalfi's harbour not long after. Revellers fill the streets late into the evening, and the day concludes with a fireworks display – whatever the result.

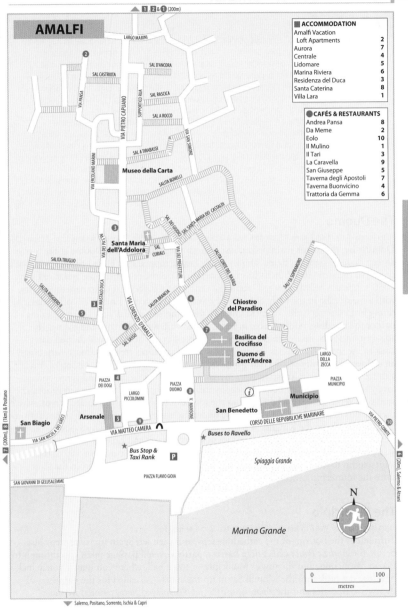

AMALFI

■ ACCOMMODATION	
Amalfi Vacation Loft Apartments	2
Aurora	7
Centrale	4
Lidomare	5
Marina Riviera	6
Residenza del Duca	3
Santa Caterina	8
Villa Lara	1

● CAFÉS & RESTAURANTS	
Andrea Pansa	8
Da Meme	2
Eolo	10
Il Mulino	1
Il Tari	3
La Caravella	9
San Giuseppe	5
Taverna degli Apostoli	7
Taverna Buonvicino	4
Trattoria da Gemma	6

Amalfi's immediate focus is the seafront, a humming, cheerfully vigorous strand given over to street stalls, a car park for the town's considerable tourist traffic, and a reasonably crowded beach, **Spiaggia Grande**, although as usual the best bits are pay areas only. Boats and buses drop off at the transport hub of Piazza Flavio Gioia, where you'll also find a taxi rank; from here all sights can be reached within around fifteen minutes.

> **AMALFI PAPER**
>
> The **Monte Lattari** or "Mountains of Milk" that rise up behind the coast here are so named for the colour the local water took on when mixed with cotton to make **paper** – an industry that goes back to the twelfth century in Amalfi, when the merchants of the maritime republic brought back the secrets of paper-making techniques from the Arabs. With a ready supply of fast-running water, Amalfi's location was ideally suited to the manufacture of paper, and it gained such a reputation for both quality and quantity that it was soon patronized by the court at Naples, and then by the Vatican and an international clientele.
>
> The industry thrived here for several hundred years, and only fell into decline in the late eighteenth century, when machinery began to replace the traditional techniques and made it hard for producers to remain competitive; by the mid-twentieth century very few mills remained. However, a few dedicated producers managed to stay in business, and nowadays a tiny industry in luxury and faux-antique paper survives; although inevitably focused on the tourist trade, it does provide an authentic connection with Amalfi's commercial past, as well as turning out exquisite notebooks, envelopes and writing paper of a quality you'd be hard pushed to find anywhere else.

7

The Duomo

Piazza Duomo • Daily: March 9.30am–5.15pm, April–June & Oct 9am–6.45pm, July–Sept 9am–7.45pm, Nov–Jan 6 10am–3.15pm • €3

Dominating the town's main piazza, just in from the seafront, is the **Duomo** at the top of a steep flight of steps, its tiered, almost gaudy facade topped by a glazed-tiled cupola that's typical of the area. The church's bronze doors came from Constantinople and date from 1066, while the heavily restored interior is a mixture of Saracen and Romanesque styles, with a major relic in the body of St Andrew buried in its crypt. Entrance is off to the left, through the cloister – the so-called **Chiostro del Paradiso** – actually the most appealing part of the building, oddly Arabic in feel with its whitewashed arches and palms. The adjacent **museum**, housed in the ancient, bare Basilica di Crocifisso which itself dates back to the sixth century, has various medieval and episcopal treasures, most intriguingly an eighteenth-century sedan chair from Macau, which was used by the bishop of Amalfi; a thirteenth-century mitre sewn with myriad seed pearls, gold panels and gems; and a lovely fourteenth-century bone and ebony inlaid box, made by the renowned Embriachi studio in Venice. Steps lead down from the museum to the heavily decorated **crypt**, where the remains of the Apostle St Andrew lie under the altar, brought here (minus head) from Constantinople by the Knights of Malta in 1204. The altar is topped by a giant bronze statue of the saint, and flanked by statues of saints Stefano and Lorenzo by Pietro Bernini – father of the better-known Gianlorenzo. A small receptacle is placed on top of the saint's coffin to catch a miraculous fluid that has supposedly emanated from the saint since the fourteenth century.

The Municipio

Piazza Municipio • Mon, Wed & Fri 9am–2pm, Tues & Thurs 9am–2pm & 4–6pm • Free

Turn left at the bottom of the cathedral steps, and then left again up some steps just before the *Andrea Pansa* café, and a narrow, partly covered passage takes you through to Piazza Municipio, and the town's **Municipio** or town hall, where you may if you're lucky be allowed a peek into the Morelli Salon up the stairs – so called for the paintings of the twelve Apostles and the *Apocalypse of St John* displayed here, painted by the nineteenth-century Neapolitan painter Domenico Morelli, and reproduced in mosaic on the facade of the cathedral.

The Arsenale

Largo Cesareo • Tues–Sun 10am–1pm & 4–7pm • €2 • ☏ 334 917 7814

Facing the waterfront square, the town's ancient, vaulted **Arsenale** is another reminder of the former military might of Amalfi. It was used to build the maritime republic's fleet and used to open right onto the sea; now it hosts temporary exhibitions and a small museum containing bits and pieces relating to Amalfi's history, including the costumes worn by the great and the good of the town for the Regatta of the Maritime Republics (see box, p.214), and the city banner, showing the emblems of Amalfi – the diagonal red strip and Maltese cross you see everywhere. Also here is the **Tavoliere Amalfitana**, the laws of the maritime republic, which were formulated during the town's eleventh-century heyday and remained in force for five hundred years.

Museo della Carta

Via delle Cartiere 23 • March–Oct daily 10am–6.30pm; Nov–Feb Tues–Sun 10am–3.30pm • €4 • ☎ 089 830 4561, 🖝 museodellacarta.it

At the top of Via Genova, a fifteen-minute walk from the main square, the **Museo della Carta** is housed in a paper mill that dates back to 1350 and claims to be the oldest in Europe. The valley beyond the museum is still known as the **Valle dei Mulini** (Valley of Mills), from the fact that it was once the heart of Amalfi's paper industry, with around fifteen functioning mills. This is the only one to survive, and it makes all of the high-spec paper you see on sale around town. Tours take in the tools of the trade and the original paper-making process and equipment, including that in use when the mill shut down in 1969. They still make paper here (clients include the Vatican) and tours usually include the chance to have a go yourself. There's also a shop selling paper products, calligraphy pens and other stationery. Afterwards, if you're feeling energetic, you could do a **walk** from here that takes you right up into the heart of the valley, past some of the remains of the mills which sit by the river in charming dereliction (see box, p.218).

The beaches

Amalfi is as good a place as any on the coast to spend time if you just want to laze on the **beach**, though it does get crowded during high season. The main town beach has a public sandy patch to the right, while the rest is shingly and covered in parasols. There are a few patches of beach and bathing spots around the marina, as well as the small stony triangle of Lido delle Sirene at the far end. There's also the beach at the next-door village of Atrani (see below) and in the opposite direction, where, about 1km out of town, 350 steps lead down to the Duoglio beach.

Atrani

A short walk around the headland (take the path off to the right just before the road tunnel and cut through the *Zaccaria* restaurant), **ATRANI** is to all intents and purposes an extension of Amalfi, and was indeed another part of the maritime republic, with a similarly styled church sporting another set of bronze doors from Constantinople, manufactured in 1086; it's here that the Regatta of the Maritime Republics (see box, p.214) begins every four years. It's a quiet place, with a pretty, almost entirely enclosed little square, Piazza Umberto, giving onto a smallish sandy beach. It's a little more developed than it once was, but is still gloriously peaceful compared to the bustle and crowds of Amalfi next door.

ARRIVAL AND DEPARTURE   **AMALFI AND AROUND**

By bus SITA buses from Positano, Ravello and Sorrento arrive at Piazza Flavio Gioia on the seafront. Buy tickets and check timetables at the Divina Costiera travel office, next to the bus stops (daily 8am–1pm & 2–8pm). From April to October open-top City Sightseeing buses run from Sorrento and Positano (see p.138), to Maiori and Minori (7 daily), and to Ravello (4 daily), for €4 for a single trip, or €10 for

four trips. As they only run every hour, it's worth joining the queue early.

Destinations Bomerano (for the Sentiero degli Dei; 3–11 daily; 40min); Cetara (every 1–2hr; 45min); Conca (Grotta dello Smeraldo; every 30min–1hr; 15min); Maiori (hourly; 20min); Minori (hourly; 15min); Positano (every 30min–1hr; 40min); Praiano (every 30min–1hr; 25min); Ravello (every 20min–1hr; 25min); Salerno (every 1–2hr; 1hr 15min); Sorrento (every 30min–1hr; 1hr 40min); Vietri sul Mare (every 1–2hr; 1hr).

By boat Ferries and hydrofoils for Salerno (Travelmar, 35min; Alicost, 50min), Sorrento (Alicost, 50min–1hr 15min), Positano (Travelmar and Alicost, 50min) and Capri (Alicost and Coop Sant'Andrea, 1hr 20min) arrive and leave at the landing stages in the harbour, right by the main bus terminal, as do the smaller boats to the Grotta dello Smeraldo and other points along the coast.

INFORMATION AND GETTING AROUND

Tourist office In a courtyard on the seafront next door to the post office (April–Oct Mon–Sat 8.30am–1pm & 2–6pm, Nov–March Mon–Sat 8am–1pm; ☎ 089 871 107, ⓦ amalfitouristoffice.it). Though not overburdened with information, it will provide you with a map of the town and answer basic questions.

By boat There are quite a few places touting boats by the hour, half-day and day down in the far corner of the harbour; try Amalfi Boats (☎ 333 362 5773, ⓦ amalfiboats.it).

By scooter or bike Scooters are available from Amalfi Rent a Scooter (ⓦ amalfirentascooter.com) from €50/day, bikes from €20/day.

ACCOMMODATION

Amalfi is a great base for the coast as a whole, with plenty of good places to splurge as well as a fair array of inexpensive options. You might also consider staying in neighbouring Atrani, which has a couple of excellent choices at both price extremes, or Agerola, a little way inland, which is the nearest place to camp.

AMALFI

Amalfi Vacation Loft Apartments Via Cardinale Marino del Giudice 38 ☎ 338 118 4219, ⓦ amalfivacation.it. These apartments are an excellent option for families, or those that want to self-cater: centrally located and beautifully furnished, with access to a large pool. There are equally good apartments available elsewhere along the coast; check the website. Minimum stay three nights. **€150**

Aurora Piazzale dei Prontini 7 ☎ 089 871 209, ⓦ aurora-hotel.it. Right in the corner of the harbour, a 5min walk from the centre of town, this hotel has bright rooms, some with sea-view terraces, and a spacious lounge and terrace at which to eat breakfast while looking out to sea. The hotel also owns apartments in the centre of town, available for three-night stays throughout the year. Closed Nov–March. Doubles **€200**, apartments **€130**

Centrale Largo Piccolomini 1 ☎ 089 872 608, ⓦ hotelcentraleamalfi.com. An excellent location, overlooking the Duomo, with 17 good-sized and pleasantly furnished rooms with TV and a/c. Breakfast is taken on the hotel's lovely roof terrace. Open all year. **€130**

Lidomare Via Piccolomini 9 ☎ 089 871 332, ⓦ lidomare.it. Tucked away off to the left of Piazza Duomo, this is the most characterful of Amalfi's cheapies, a beautiful, family-run ex-ducal palace, nicely old-fashioned and full of antiques. They're very proud of the fact that some of the rooms are equipped with hydromassage tubs, although some of the bathrooms are otherwise a bit grotty. In every other respect it's well worth the money you pay for a large double room, over half of which face the sea. Eat breakfast on the square or in the pretty breakfast room. Open all year. **€145**

A WALK TO THE TORRE DELLO ZIRO

A relatively easy **walk** from Amalfi (2hr 30min–3hr) is up the Valle dei Mulini to the village of **Pontone**, perched on a clifftop high above Amalfi, and then back down to the town, taking in, if you have the energy, the paths that loop around the headland that divides Amalfi and Atrani to the ruins of the **Torre dello Ziro**.

To start, follow Amalfi's main street to the top and take a right opposite the paper museum, about 50m past the *Bar della Valle*, and then a sharp left up a moderately steep flight of steps which soon level out to become the path that proceeds gently up the valley. After 1.5km or so it leaves the town behind and becomes unpaved, following the bubbling river past several derelict paper mills. The river alternates between waterfalls and rock pools, some of them deep enough for at least a cooling paddle. At the fourth mill, signalled by a wide arch, the path leads right, climbing out of the valley and up towards Pontone – some 1.5km away at the top. You should arrive at Pontone after around 1 hour 45 minutes. Leave Pontone's main piazza through the arch and bear right to the main road; cross over and follow the path underneath the church, round to the beginning of the promontory, from where you can either fork right back to Amalfi – a steep, 30-minute descent (not to be attempted in reverse) – or left up some zigzagging flights of steps that lead to the paths that loop around the overgrown outcrop of rock to the ruins of the Torre dello Ziro, where there are some precipitous views (allow at least an additional 30min).

★**Marina Riviera** Via Pantaleone Comite 19 ☏ 089 871 104, ⓦ marinariviera.it. Not a cheap option by any means, but not up there with Amalfi's most stratospheric places either. In a central location overlooking the beach, it's beautifully kept, bright and light. The 34 rooms are on the large side and have sea views, and it's family-run and friendly too. They also have a rooftop pool, and host the stylish *Eolo* restaurant (see below). Closed Nov to mid-April. **€350**

Residenza del Duca Via Mastalo II Duca 3 ☏ 089 873 6365, ⓦ residencedelduca.it. This tiny hotel is tucked away among the alleys and courtyards off to the left of Amalfi's main street – turn left just past *Trattoria Gemma*, then turn right and you're there. It's a steep climb, but worth it for the most tastefully furnished of Amalfi's *pensioni*, with several smart antique-style rooms, two of which have their own large terraces with loungers. All have bathrooms with hydromassage showers, satellite TVs and a/c. Closed Nov–April. **€120**

Santa Caterina Via Maura Comite 9 ☏ 089 871 012, ⓦ hotelsantacaterina.it. A kilometre west of town right on the coast road, this elegant villa with period furnishings is Amalfi's best hotel, and very much the celebrity choice, but also still family-owned and run. If money's no object, there's no better place: there are two top-notch restaurants (half-board €70) and a spectacular seawater pool and small spa, as well as rocks to swim from, all accessible by a lift which plummets down from the bougainvillea-wreathed terrace. Closed mid-Nov–Dec 19 & early Jan to end Feb. **€500**

Villa Lara Via delle Cartiere 1 ☏ 089 873 6358, ⓦ villalara.it. It's quite a climb to get up to this marvellously positioned B&B, making it feel wonderfully separate from the crowds and hubbub of central Amalfi, despite being just 5min walk away from the main street (and there's a lift in

any case). Some of the seven beautifully furnished rooms have their own terrace, and there's a comfortable lounge and communal terrace overlooking both the town and the sea beyond. Closed mid-Oct to Easter. **€150**

ATRANI

A'Scalinatella Piazza Umberto 1 ☏ 089 871 492, ⓦ hostelscalinatella.com. One of the cheapest places to stay on the entire coast, a friendly, family-run establishment that offers good-value hostel beds and private rooms in various buildings around town, some of them overlooking the main square. It's not a party hostel though, so you'll have to look elsewhere for entertainment after dark. Open all year. Dorms **€30**, doubles **€90**

Palazzo Ferraioli Via Campo 16 ☏ 089 872 652, ⓦ palazzoferraioli.it. Not that easy to find, among the whitewashed steps and passages off to the left of Atrani's main square. But it's worth the bother, as the coolly contemporary rooms of this ingeniously converted *palazzo* are a wonderful escape, and have some good views over the town and bay. Each room is decorated differently, but each follows a determinedly stylish and modern theme. There's a small spa, and a rooftop terrace with bar. Closed Nov to mid-April. **€170**

AGEROLA

Beata Solitudo Piazza Avitabile 4, ☏ 081 802 5048, ⓦ beatasolitudo.it. Up in the hills about 16km north of Amalfi, this is a great budget one-stop shop – a hostel-cum-hotel with a small campsite that also has a few bungalows. Regular buses to Amalfi stop right outside, and plenty of cafés and restaurants are nearby. One of the best budget choices in the area. Open all year. Camping **€9.50**, dorms **€15.50**, bungalows **€50**, doubles **€75**

7

EATING AND DRINKING

Inevitably, most of Amalfi's **restaurants** are aimed squarely at the tourist trade, but quality on the whole remains high. For picnic supplies, there's a Tardis-like **supermarket** on Piazza del Dogi (Mon–Sat 7.30am–1.30pm & 4.30–8pm).

AMALFI

Andrea Pansa Piazza Duomo 40 ⓦ pasticceriapansa.it. Right on the main square, this is *the* place to sit and drink coffee, with an unrivalled selection of cakes and pastries – try the candied sweets made with fruit brought from the Pansa family's nearby farm, or the tasty *sfogliatelle*, chocolate-coated almond biscuits and home-made chocolates. Daily 7.30am–1am; closes at 9.30pm and all day Tues in winter, and closed 2 weeks in Jan.

Da Meme Salita Marino Sebaste 8 ☏ 089 830 4549. You can eat in the vaulted interior of this former monastery, or outside among the passageways of old Amalfi. Lots of pasta choices, from €5.50, including non-seafood options, plus pizzas for €5 and even fish fairly cheaply priced at €9 upwards. Daily noon–4pm & 6.30–11.30pm.

★**Eolo** Via Pantaleone Comite 3 ☏ 089 871 241, ⓦ eoloamalfi.it. This restaurant aims to provide Amalfi's most refined dining experience, and with one room, overlooking the main beach, and a small outside terrace, it doesn't do badly – the ultimate romantic Amalfi night out, only spoilt by the schmaltzy background music. The seasonal menu is short, with a few pasta dishes (around €20) and 5–6 *secondi* (around €30) such as salt-encrusted fish and Neapolitan fish stew – but usually with a couple of vegetarian options too. Mon & Wed–Sun 12.30–2pm & 7–10.30pm; mid-June to mid-Sept dinner only; closed Nov–Easter.

Il Mulino Via della Cartiere 36 ☏ 089 872 223. At the top of the main street, a 10min walk from the Duomo, this is a cheery, family-run place that does good home-made pasta dishes and pizza too. Eat outside on the terrace, and enjoy their excellent *puttanesca* pasta, with tomatoes, olives and capers, for just €7, or with clams for €12. Pizzas too, from €6. Tues–Sun 1.30–4pm & 6.30pm–midnight; closed Nov–Feb.

Il Tari Via P. Capuano 9/11 ☎089 871 832, ⓦamalfiristorantetari.it. Right in the heart of town, but not as touristy as you might think, this long-established place has a large menu of antipasti, such as *involtini di peperoni* – peppers stuffed with olives, capers and *provola* cheese – as well as all the pasta classics, including a number of non-seafood varieties like *rigatoni con zucchine* for €8.50, *secondi* from €10 to €20, and cheap pizzas. There's a three-course menu for €20 too. Mon & Wed–Sun 11.30am–3pm & 6.30–10pm.

La Caravella Via Matteo Camera 12 ☎089 871 029, ⓦristorantelacaravella.it. One of the town's posher options for a night out, or when you're tired of the same old offerings everywhere else. They serve creative takes on traditional dishes, all put together with fresh local ingredients. The 4-course lunch tasting menu costs €50. Mon & Wed–Sun noon–2.30pm & 7–11pm.

San Giuseppe Salita Ruggiero II 4 ☎089 872 640. Left off the main street by *Trattoria da Gemma* and then right, this very simple restaurant puts a few tables out on a tiny courtyard and serves excellent pizzas and pretty much everything else at low prices – great value. Choose from *monti* or *mare* menus – 3 courses for €15 or €18 – or at lunchtime a pizza, drink and dessert costs just €10. Mon–Wed & Fri–Sun noon–3.30pm & 6.30–11.30pm.

Taverna degli Apostoli Supportivo Sant'Andrea 6 ☎089 872 991 or ☎334 258 2254. Because of its location next to the cathedral steps, most people assume this is just another tourist joint. But its relatively small menu chalked on the blackboard outside is a good indication that it's not. *Primi* €9–13, *secondi* €12–18. Tasty food and a warm welcome. Daily noon–3pm & 7pm–midnight; closed two months in winter.

★**Taverna Buonvicino** Largo S. Maria Maggiore 13 ☎089 873 6385, ⓦtavernabuonvicino.it. This place serves good, reasonably priced food from a menu that's a touch different to the competition. All the usual fish and pasta dishes are here, including a nice *spaghetti alle vongole* for €13 and excellent grilled lamb for €16. It's nice enough inside, but get an outside table if possible, to get the most out of this atmospheric little square. Daily noon–2.30pm & 6.15–10.15pm; closed Nov to mid-Dec, Jan & Feb.

Trattoria da Gemma Via Frá Gerardo Sasso 11 ☎089 871 345, ⓦtrattoriadagemma.com. A stalwart of the Amalfi restaurant scene, and still one of the best and most appealing places to eat in town. The small, carefully considered menu is strong on fish and seafood, with starters for around €16 and mains at around €25 (or push the boat out and order the excellent fish soup at €80 for two), and enjoyed on a lovely terrace overlooking the main street. Daily noon–3pm & 7–11pm; closed Nov–Jan.

ATRANI

A'Paranza Via Dragone 2 ☎089 871 840, ⓦristoranteparanza.com. On the road that leads inland from the main square, a friendly seafood trattoria with fabulous home-made pasta and a speciality of *zuppa di pesce*. Mon & Wed–Sun 12.30–3pm & 7–11pm.

Birecto Piazza Umberto I ☎089 871 017. The principal bar on the main square, this place hosts quite a scene, vying for the custom of young travellers from the *A'Scalinatella* hostel. Has reasonably priced drinks, decent pizzas and other food, plus free wi-fi. Daily 8am–midnight.

Le Arcate Largo Orlando Buonocore ☎089 871 367, ⓦlearcate.net. Right by the beach, hogging the best location in Atrani, *Le Arcate* serves pizza and seafood pasta dishes – try the pasta with shrimps and courgettes (€12), or with garlic, chilli and anchovies (€10). Tues–Sun 12.30–3.30pm & 7.30pm–midnight.

Ravello

The loveliest views of the coast can be had inland from Amalfi in **RAVELLO**: another of the Amalfi Coast's renowned beauty spots. The town was also an independent republic for a while, and for a time an outpost of the Amalfi city-state. Now it's little more than a large village, but its unrivalled location, spread across the top of one of the coast's mountains, 335m up, makes it more than worth the thirty-minute bus ride through the steeply cultivated terraces up from Amalfi. Wagner set part of *Parsifal*, one of his last operas, here; D.H. Lawrence wrote some of *Lady Chatterley's Lover* in town; it was the location for John Huston's 1953 film *Beat the Devil* (a languid movie in which the setting easily outshines the plot, written on location here by Truman Capote); and Gore Vidal is just one of the many celebrities who used to spend at least part of the year here. His former home, La Rondinaia or "swallow's nest", is one of the most spectacular villas on the entire coast (see p.221). But the great thing about Ravello is that it's so much quieter than the coast below, especially at night when the coaches have left. It's often a degree or so cooler too, which can be welcome during high summer. Ravello sprawls across quite a wide area, but its centre is indisputably Piazza Duomo, a large and rather featureless square edged by one or two cafés and focused on the **Duomo**. A few minutes south and east of the Duomo respectively, **Villa Rufolo** and **Villa Cimbrone** offer lush greenery and dazzling panoramas, their gardens making photogenic locations for the town's international festival (see box, p.223).

The Duomo

Piazza Duomo • Daily 9am–noon & 5–7pm, museum daily 9am–7pm • Church free, museum €3

Ravello's **Duomo** is a bright eleventh-century church, renovated in 1786, that's dedicated to Pantaleone, a fourth-century saint with miraculous blood like that of Naples' San Gennaro (see p.43). A pair of twelfth-century bronze doors, cast with 54 scenes of the Passion, lead to a richly ornamented interior, with two monumental marble thirteenth-century pulpits, both wonderfully adorned with intricate and glittering mosaics. The more elaborate of the two, to the right of the altar, the Gospel pulpit, dated 1272, sports dragons and birds on spiral columns supported by six roaring lions, and the coat of arms and the vivacious profiles of the Rufolo family, the donors, above the door, while on the left, the Epistle pulpit depicts *Jonah and the Whale*. The chapel to the left of the main altar is dedicated to St Pantaleone and holds a vial of his blood – a murky liquid that is said to become translucent every July 27, the day of his martyrdom; a door gives access to a passage behind the altar if you want to get a closer look. Downstairs in the crypt, the **museum** holds the superb bust of one Sigilgaita Rufolo and the embossed silver and wood reliquary of Saint Barbara, alongside a collection of highly decorative, fluid mosaic and marble reliefs from the thirteenth century.

Villa Rufolo

Piazza Duomo • Daily: April–Oct 9am–8pm; Nov–March 9am–5pm • €5; concerts €27.50 • ☎ 089 857 621, ⓦ villarufolo.it, ⓦ ravelloarts.org

Across the square from the Duomo, various leftovers of the **Villa Rufolo** lie scattered among lush gardens overlooking the precipitous coastline. The park is a spectacular venue for the open-air concerts of the Ravello Festival (see box, p.223). If the crowds – best avoided by coming early in the morning – put you off, turn left by the entrance and walk up the steps over the tunnel for the best (free) view over the shore, from where it's a pleasant stroll through the back end of Ravello to the main square.

LA RONDINAIA

The only place to rival the views from the Villa Cimbrone's belvedere is the former home of maverick US writer **Gore Vidal** (1925–2012), La Rondinaia or "swallow's nest", which was built by the former owner of the Villa Cimbrone for his second daughter in 1930 and juts out over the edge of the ocean in a spectacular location next door to the villa's gardens – as Vidal himself had it, "I don't live in Ravello, I live at La Rondinaia". A magnificent, six-floored property, only reachable on foot, Vidal bought the place in 1972 for around a quarter of a million dollars and sold it in 2006 for many times that amount when he became too infirm to negotiate its steps and balconies. During the thirty or so years he lived here Vidal entertained guests as diverse as Sting and Tennessee Williams, Erica Jong, Andy Warhol and the Clintons, to name just a few. The villa was bought some time ago by the group that owns the *Villa Maria* hotel and its future is currently uncertain. With its unique cachet – not to mention its stratospheric price tag – it's likely that it will end up as luxury accommodation of some kind; with any luck, though, the developers will preserve the Vidal connection, and make it somehow accessible to the public.

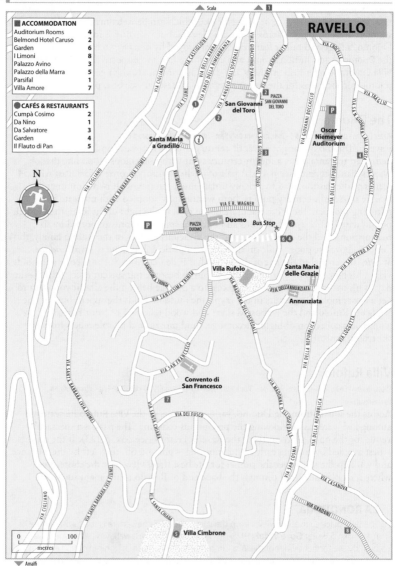

ACCOMMODATION

Auditorium Rooms	4
Belmond Hotel Caruso	2
Garden	6
I Limoni	8
Palazzo Avino	3
Palazzo della Marra	5
Parsifal	1
Villa Amore	7

CAFÉS & RESTAURANTS

Cumpà Cosimo	2
Da Nino	1
Da Salvatore	3
Garden	4
Il Flauto di Pan	5

Via San Giovanni del Toro

Outside Villa Rufolo a tunnel takes you through to the other side of Ravello's central ridge. Or you can walk across the footbridge to the end of the town's upper level, where **Via San Giovanni del Toro** is home to some of Ravello's most prestigious hotels, among them the unsurpassable *Belmond Hotel Caruso* (see p.224), and the pleasant gardens of the Principessa Piemontese, which replicate the views of the terrace of the luxury hotel, *Palazzo Avino*, below (see p.224). At the far end of the street, Via Richard Wagner leads down from some shady gardens to the main square, while a little further on, before the bridge, there's a house which put up

THE RAVELLO FESTIVAL

Ravello's **festival** has grown into quite an annual event, and these days it dominates the summer months, with performances all over town stretching from June to September (tickets from around €30, more for top international performers; ⓦ ravellofestival.com). Concentrating on classical music, dance, film and the visual arts, it makes the most of the town's settings – concerts under the stars at Villa Rufolo are particularly atmospheric – and attracts an increasingly high level of international talent. If your visit doesn't coincide with the festival, you can still catch a performance: classical music concerts are organized from April until October. The kiosk near the entrance/exit to the tunnel just before the main square has information and sells tickets.

both André Gide in 1902 and E.M. Forster in 1928; Gide was inspired to set his novel *L'Immoraliste* in Ravello, and Forster wrote his short story, *Story of a Panic*, while he was here.

Auditorium Oscar Niemeyer

On the far side of Ravello's Via della Repubblica, the **Auditorium Oscar Niemeyer** is an oddity in Ravello's otherwise mostly unchanged environment, a sleek, modern white wave below the crown of the hill that was designed by the prolific Brazilian architect Oscar Niemeyer, who was no less than 102 years old when it opened in 2009. It's not open for tours, but no one will stop you wandering down and peeking into its four hundred-seat main theatre space, which is the main venue for the Ravello Festival (see above) and more besides.

Villa Cimbrone

Via Santa Chiara 26 • Daily 9am–sunset • €7 • To organize a tour of the gardens call ☎ 089 857 459, ⓦ villacimbrone.com

Turn left out of Villa Rufolo and walk in the opposite direction through some of Ravello's most characteristic and peaceful streets and paths to reach the **Villa Cimbrone**, ten minutes away, whose formal gardens spread across the furthest tip of Ravello's ridge. It's a unique and ravishing spot: if Ravello itself sometimes feels removed from the rest of the coast, then here you can feel one step removed from the rest of Ravello, such is the sense of isolation. Most of the original buildings are given over to a smart hotel, but you can peep into the crumbly, flower-hung cloister as you go in, and the open crypt down the steps from here – perhaps the only crypt in the world with views over cliffs and open sea. But the **gardens** are entirely accessible, dotted with statues and leading down to what must be the most famous spot in Ravello – a belvedere, fittingly known as the "terrace of infinity", that looks down to Atrani and the sea. By the hotel is a pricey and smart **café** serving salads, sandwiches and ice creams with tables set out on the grass, from which you can enjoy the views of the Dragone valley below, but there are beetling views too from the balcony of the modest little snack bar hidden under the belvedere. Elsewhere in the gardens there are any number of corners to explore, and you could spend a good few hours here if you're in no hurry. Take in the viewpoints on the western side at the little Tempietto di Bacco and Poggio di Mercurio, wander through the rose garden near the entrance, and consider stopping for lunch at the hotel's lovely restaurant. Better yet, stay at the hotel to really soak up the unique atmosphere.

ARRIVAL AND INFORMATION   **RAVELLO**

By bus SITA buses run up to Ravello from Amalfi roughly every 30min (25min) from Piazza Flavio Gioia and drop off the other side of the tunnel from Piazza Duomo, at the top of Via della Repubblica. Open-top City Sightseeing buses also travel up from Amalfi (8 daily; €4 single trip or €10 day ticket, also valid on Amalfi–Maiori buses).

By car There are car parks just below the main square (€2.50/hr) and underneath the Auditorium Oscar Niemeyer (€2/hr).

By taxi Taxis stop just through the tunnel outside the *Garden* hotel, though be aware that taxis up here from Amalfi are around €35 one-way.

Tourist office Via Roma 18 bis, 2min from the main square (Mon–Sat: June–Aug 10am–7pm; Sept–May 9.30am–5pm; ☎ 089 857 096, ⓦ ravellotime.it).

ACCOMMODATION

It's worth staying overnight to experience Ravello's more tranquil side, after the day-trippers have left. It also has some of Southern Italy's finest – and priciest – **hotels** along Via San Giovanni del Toro, if you really want to splurge. But there are also some excellent budget options, and the tourist office has information on private **rooms**.

★ **Auditorium Rooms** Via Crocelle 23 ☎ 339 418 2233, ⓦ auditoriumrooms.com. Perfectly placed for a concert at the Auditorium, this two-room B&B is fast gaining a reputation as one of Ravello's best accommodation options (book well ahead). Each of the rooms has its own little terrace with stunning views; the bigger of the two can also be a triple, and boasts a shower with five-star views of the coast below. Open all year. **€130**

Belmond Hotel Caruso Piazza San Giovanni del Toro 2 ☎ 089 858 800, ⓦ belmond.com. Hogging Ravello's finest views from its clifftop perch, this beautifully restored hotel is one of the Amalfi Coast's best. The rooms – all frescoed ceilings and cool tiled floors – are discreetly stylish, but it's the infinity pool and beautiful grounds that really steal the show. The hotel puts on boat trips along the coast, which are free for guests – if you can bear to drag yourself away. Closed Nov–April. **€900**

Garden Via Boccaccio 4 ☎ 089 857 226, ⓦ hotelgardenravello.it. Just the other side of the tunnel from central Ravello, this small hotel and restaurant occupies a prime spot looking up the coast, and makes the most of it with its 10 rooms, all with dazzling sea views. The rooms aren't huge but they have small terraces and are neatly finished and well equipped, and there's free wi-fi throughout. The new swimming pool with lovely views is a bonus. Closed Dec–Feb. **€160**

I Limoni Via Gradoni 14 ☎ 089 858 275, ⓦ ravellobebilimoni.it. A bit of a hike down a series of very steep flights of steps way below the centre of Ravello, but its wonderfully peaceful location, garden and two lovely rooms make this B&B worth considering. Cash only. Closed Nov–Jan. **€110**

Palazzo Avino Via San Giovanni del Toro 28 ☎ 089 818 181, ⓦ palazzoavino.com. Housed in a converted medieval villa on the top ridge of Ravello, this five-star hotel has elegant rooms and public areas and attention to detail and service that you don't often find – as well as a pool with about as breathtaking a view as you could imagine. Rooms vary a lot in price, depending on the views. Closed mid-Oct to March. **€320**

Palazzo della Marra Via della Marra 3 ☎ 089 858 302, ⓦ palazzodellamarra.com. Just off the main square, this is one of the cheapest places to stay in central Ravello, with two simply furnished rooms (the antiques-furnished "Antica" is nicer) and a warm welcome. The common area with apartment-style facilities (fridge, toaster, washing machine) is useful. Open all year. **€80**

Parsifal Viale Gioacchino d'Anna 5 ☎ 089 857 144, ⓦ hotelparsifal.com. Dating from 1288 – it was originally a convent – the family-run *Parsifal* is an appealing mid-range option, with wonderful flower-filled terraces to rival any of the five-stars. The rooms are furnished in traditional style – go for one of the spacious deluxe rooms if you can – and there's a good restaurant; you can eat on a bijou terrace under the stars in summer. Open all year. **€130**

Villa Amore Via dei Fusco 5 ☎ 089 857 135, ⓦ villaamore.it. Down a short path off the main route between the centre of Ravello and the Villa Cimbrone, the rooms here are nothing special but some of them enjoy stunning views. The drawback is that you have to carry your luggage from the nearest car park a 10min walk away back on the main piazza – or pay for the hotel to do it for you. Closed Nov to mid-April. **€100**

EATING AND DRINKING

Ravello isn't overloaded with places to eat, and most of its **restaurants** are attached to hotels. Not surprisingly, the cheaper places are those without views, but whatever the location, you won't eat badly anywhere.

Cumpà Cosimo Via Roma 44/46 ☎ 089 857 156. This long-standing favourite serves tasty local food – home-made pasta, fish *fritti misti* – at moderate prices; reckon on €25–30 for a full meal with wine. It's firmly on the tourist map but it's still down-to-earth and Mamma Netta greets everyone warmly. No views or outside seating. Daily noon–3pm & 7.30–11pm; closed Mon Nov–Feb.

Da Nino Parco Della Rimembranza 35/37 ☎ 089 858

6249. A great family-run takeaway pizza place (with a few seats inside). Try the "Ravellese", topped with tomato, mozzarella, *pancetta*, onion and courgette flowers (€5). There are a few hot dishes on offer too. Daily noon–2.30pm & 7–10.30pm; closed Tues Oct–May.

Da Salvatore Via della Repubblica 2 ☎ 089 857 227, ⓦ salvatoreravello.com. In business for over fifty years, *Salvatore* has fantastic views from the restaurant and outside terrace, and a creative menu, with Campanian specialities like *ndunderi* (ricotta dumplings). *Primi* from €13, *secondi* around €18, and cheap pizzas at lunch; there's also a pizzeria downstairs, which does starters and pizzas only in the evenings. Tues–Sun 12.30–3pm & 7.15–10pm; closed Jan & Feb.

Garden Via Boccaccio 4 ☎089 857 226, ⓦhotelgardenravello.it. A nice simple menu at this hotel restaurant with just 5 *antipasti*, 5 *primi* and 4 *secondi* to choose from. It's not especially cheap, but the view over Minori and Maiori is one of Ravello's best, and the food is a cut above what you get elsewhere – try the octopus salad

– really good for €13 – or the pasta with mussels and potatoes for €12; main courses include fish soup and rack of lamb with potatoes (both €16). Daily 12.15–3pm & 7–10pm; closed Nov–Feb.

Il Flauto di Pan Via Santa Chiara 26 ☎089 857 459, ⓦvillacimbrone.com. The Michelin-starred restaurant of the *Villa Cimbrone* makes good use of its celebrated gardens, with home-grown ingredients going into its elegant Mediterranean cuisine, and scenic views from its terrace. Though undeniably a fine-dining experience, the portions are generous, so don't over-order. *Primi* around €22, *secondi* from €26. Daily 7.30–11pm.

Minori to Vietri sul Mare

The coast between Amalfi and Salerno is quite different from that further west – not as busy and less obviously wealthy, its settlements a mixture of down-to-earth resorts like **Minori**, **Maiori** and **Vietri**, and small, relatively undisturbed fishing villages like **Cetara** and **Erchie**. It's no less dramatic, though, the coast road only really straightening out as you come into Vietri, which signals the end of the Amalfi Coast.

Minori

There's not much to **MINORI**, a small town named after the Regina Minor River, which reaches the sea here – just a decent sandy beach fronting the main road, behind which there's a compact old centre. Minori's only real sight, right by the main road, is the **Villa Romana** (daily 8am–7pm; free), where you can see the remains of an originally two-storey Roman villa, most notably a frescoed and mosaicked *nymphaeum* and pool. There's a small display of finds from the villa and around – mostly the usual ceramic shards and some well-preserved patches of fresco.

The liveliest Minori gets is during September's **Gusta Minori** food festival (ⓦgustaminori.it), which sees stalls selling gourmet goodies lining the seafront promenade, and evening dance and music performances.

Maiori

Around the next headland from Minori, **MAIORI** sits at the mouth of the larger tributary of the same river – the Regina Maior – and it's this that is responsible for the town's largely modern and slightly characterless appearance: it was almost entirely destroyed by floods in 1952. Nowadays the river has been diverted under the main street, Corso Regina, a pedestrianized stretch that leads inland from the seafront. Maiori is a much larger and livelier town than Minori, and altogether a nicer place to stay, with several stretches of its long sandy beach not taken up by umbrellas and beach clubs.

Erchie

The coast from Maiori to Vietri is if anything more rugged and more sparsely populated than in the other direction towards Positano, though the road doesn't have the same number of dizzyingly high hairpins either. Beyond Maiori the first settlement of any kind is **ERCHIE**, a small village nestled in a pretty cove that grew up originally in the shadow of a Benedictine monastery. It's little more than a cluster of buildings – two or three restaurants, a grocer's and *tabacchi* and a handful of **rooms** to let – but the

beach is one of the coast's best. A reasonably wide stretch with fairly fine sand, it's more or less dominated by scruffy beachfront establishments that levy the usual charges for umbrellas and sun-loungers – but nonetheless it's quite a gem.

Cetara

CETARA, just beyond, is a busy and – for the Amalfi Coast – unpretentious and untouristed fishing village, straggling down its valley to a small port area and a slightly scrappy stone and shingle beach (and another small triangle of beach beyond the fishing port). The furthest eastern outpost of the Amalfi republic, it's twinned with Sète in France and is an equally fishy sort of place. In fact its name is based on an old word for "tuna net", although the fish they're known for landing here are anchovies, samples of which you can taste in its many restaurants – of which there are several located on and around the main drag. The annual **Sagra del Tonno** – a celebration of tuna and anchovies, with plenty of tasting opportunities – takes place in late July.

Vietri sul Mare

A few kilometres further down the coast from Cetara, **VIETRI SUL MARE** is a larger and more sprawling town than anywhere else along the Amalfi Coast, its eastern suburbs almost mingling with the port areas of Salerno, for which it is the closest major resort. Its wide sandy beaches are well used. The town is mostly known as a centre of the ceramics industry, in particular the brightly coloured Mediterranean pottery that you will have seen in every town along the coast.

Museo della Ceramica Vietrese

Villa Guariglia, Via Nuova Raito • Tues–Sun: June–Sept 9am–7pm, Oct–May 8am–4.25pm • Free • ☎ 089 211 835

Housed in a tower of the Villa Guariglia, and a few rooms of the villa itself, in the Raito quarter, high above Vietri proper, the **Museo della Ceramica Vietrese** has several floors of ceramics and other pieces by the colony of mainly German artists and ceramicists who have been attracted to Vietri and its surrounding area over the years – not just practical objects (though there are plenty of those), but figurative pieces too, from devotional works to decorated tiles.

Ceramica Artistica Solimene

Via Madonna degli Angeli 7 • Mon–Fri 9am–7.30pm, Sat 9.30am–1.30pm & 4–8pm, Sun 10am–1pm • Free • ☎ 089 210 243, ⓦ solimene.com

Housed in a vast Dalíesque edifice on the edge of Vietri's old centre, the **Ceramica Artistica Solimene** is the longest-established and best ceramics manufacturer in town, in business for more than a century. This is its factory shop, with a vast array of colourful pottery to sort through.

ARRIVAL AND INFORMATION

MINORI TO VIETRI SUL MARE

By bus Buses run between Amalfi and Salerno about every 30min–1hr, stopping at several spots in each town on the way. It takes 20min from Amalfi to Maiori, 45min from Amalfi to Cetara, 1hr from Amalfi to Vietri and a total of 1hr 15min from Amalfi to Salerno.

Tourist office Maiori's tourist office is on the main street in the Palazzo Mezzocapo at Corso Regina 73 (Mon–Sat 9am–1pm & 2–6pm; ☎ 089 877 452); Vietri's is at Piazza Matteotti (Mon–Sat 10am–1pm & 5–8pm; closes 1pm on Sat in winter; ☎ 089 211 285).

ACCOMMODATION

Cetus Via SS 163, Cetara ☎ 089 261 1388, ⓦ hotelcetus .com. Perched right by the road just outside Cetara, in the direction of Vietri, with steps leading down to a tiny private beach, *Cetus* is a good choice. It has clean,

modern rooms, as well as a restaurant and terrace with views round the bay to Salerno. Open all year. **€180**
Hotel Botanico San Lazzaro Via Lazzaro 25, Maiori ☎ 089 877 750, ⓦ botanicosanlazzaro.it. In a scenic

location, clinging to the cliffside in Maiori, and set in extensive botanical gardens (hence the name), this is a classy 5-star with beautiful views of the sea. The rooms are spacious and tastefully furnished, and there's a small spa and a restaurant too. Closed Nov to mid-April. **€330**

Palazzo Vingius Via San Giovanni 19, Minori ☎ 089 854 1646, ⓦ palazzovingius.it. This friendly hotel, reached by 120 steps, has spotlessly clean, spacious rooms

and marvellous views. A tasty breakfast is served on the sunny terrace, or on your own balcony. Open all year. **€100**

Santa Lucia Via Nazionale 44, Minori ☎ 089 877 142, ⓦ hotelsantalucia.it. Probably the nicest of the hotels that line the main road on the way into Minori from Amalfi, an old-fashioned sort of place, with nicely furnished rooms and a quaint bar-restaurant downstairs. Closed Nov to mid-March. **€130**

EATING AND DRINKING

Acqua Pazza Corso Garibaldi 38, Cetara ☎ 089 261 606. A stylish restaurant in the heart of Cetara, serving top-notch (and pricey) seafood; try their signature dish, pasta with *colatura di alici*, a home-made anchovy sauce. Tues–Sun 1–3pm & 8–11pm.

Il Giardiniello Corso Vittorio Emanuele 17, Minori ☎ 089 877 050, ⓦ ristorantegiardiniello.com. Just two minutes back from Minori's seafront, the covered garden here is a nice place to escape the heat and sit down to a seafood feast (fish soup €28). There's pizza at lunch and dinner, and a potent home-made orange liqueur to finish off your meal. Daily noon–3.15pm & 6.45pm–midnight; closed Wed Oct–March.

Ristorante 34 Da Lucia Via Scialli 38, Vietri Sul Mare

☎ 089 761 822. This friendly, family-run trattoria is always heaving with locals, who flock here for the well-priced seafood and home-made pasta. A full meal will set you back around €20 per person, including wine. Thurs–Sun 1–3pm & 7.30–11pm.

Torre Normanna Via Diego Tajani 4, Maiori ☎ 089 877 100, ⓦ torrenormanna.net. Housed in the bulky sixteenth-century tower on the main road at the far end of Maiori's bay, this is the town's best place to eat, and certainly the easiest to find. It's a smart fish restaurant (8-course tasting menu €95) in a beautiful dining room that makes the most of the curved and vaulted interior of the tower, not to mention the views over the sea. Daily noon–3.30pm & 7pm–midnight; closed Mon in winter.

7

Salerno

Capital of Campania's southernmost province, the lively port of **SALERNO** is much less chaotic than Naples and is well off most travellers' itineraries, giving it a pleasant, relaxed air. It has a good supply of cheap accommodation, which makes it a reasonable base for some of the closer Amalfi Coast resorts and for the ancient site of Paestum to the south; even if you're not staying you may find yourself passing through, as the quickest route from Naples airport to the Amalfi Coast is via Salerno (see box, p.206).

During medieval times the town's medical school was the most eminent in Europe; more recently, it was the site of the Allied landing of September 9, 1943 – which reduced much of the centre to rubble. A recent regeneration furnished Salerno with some cutting-edge modern architecture in the shape of Zaha Hadid's ferry terminal building, and the spruced-up, tree-lined seafront promenade is a pleasant place for a stroll. A world away from the crowds of Positano and Amalfi, the town is a low-key yet lively place, with plenty of nightlife and shops. The vibrant centre holds an appealingly ramshackle old medieval quarter, which starts at the far end of the pedestrianized main shopping drag of **Corso Vittorio Emanuele**, and has **Via dei Mercanti** as its spine.

Pinacoteca Provinciale di Salerno

Via dei Mercanti 63 • Tues–Sun 9am–7.45pm • Free • ☎ 089 258 3073

Housed in the seventeenth-century Palazzo Pinto, the **Pinacoteca Provinciale di Salerno** is basically half a dozen rooms, displaying some fairly missable paintings, but there are a few highlights, including some fifteenth-century altarpieces and a couple of works by Carlo Rosa and other followers of the Neapolitan Baroque artists. It is, however, the small collection of modern paintings and drawings of local scenes – of Salerno, Vietri and Maiori – that is most enjoyable.

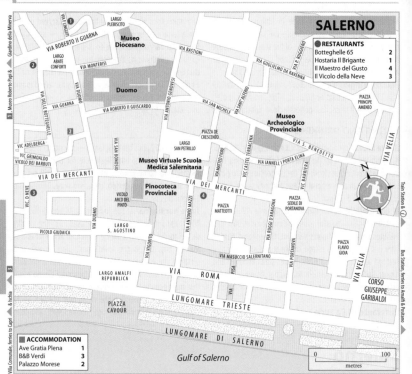

Museo Virtuale Scuola Medica Salernitana

Via dei Mercanti 74 • Tues & Wed 9.30am–1pm, Thurs–Sat 9.30am–1pm & 5–8pm, Sun 5–8pm • €3 • ☏ 089 257 6126

A museum without exhibits, **Museo Virtuale Scuola Medica Salernitana** is housed in an old church in the centre of town and recounts the history of the Salerno medical school – and indeed medieval medical practices in general – through a series of touch screens. The technology is fairly simple, with the texts of learned medieval physicians dramatically read (in Italian with English subtitles) with accompanying images.

The Duomo

Piazza Alfano 1 • Basilica Mon–Sat 8.30am–6.45pm, Sun 8.30am–1pm & 4–8pm; crypt Mon–Sat 9.30am–8pm, Sun 4–8pm • Free

The **Duomo** is Salerno's highlight, an enormous church built in 1076 by the Norman conqueror of Southern Italy, Robert Guiscard, and dedicated to St Matthew. Entrance is through a cool and shady courtyard, built with columns plundered from Paestum, and centring on a gently gurgling fountain set in an equally ancient bowl. In the heavily restored interior, the two elegant mosaic pulpits are the highlight, the one on the left dating from 1173, the other, with its matching Paschal candlesticks, a century later. Immediately behind there's more sumptuous mosaic work in the screens of the choir, as well as the quietly expressive fifteenth-century tomb of Margaret of Anjou, wife of Charles III of Durazzo, in the left aisle. To the left of the tomb, steps lead down to the polychrome marble **crypt**, which holds the body of St Matthew, brought here in the tenth century.

Museo Diocesano

Largo Plebiscito 12 • Mon, Tues & Thurs–Sun 8.30am–7.30pm • Free • ☎ 089 239 126

Next door to the cathedral, the main attraction at the **Museo Diocesano** is a set of 69 ivory panels depicting biblical scenes from a large eleventh-century altar-front – said to be the largest work of its kind in the world. They're amazing, minutely crafted pieces, showing everything from Creation to the Expulsion from Paradise to the Last Supper – a sort of biblical comic strip in ivory.

Museo Archeologico Provinciale

Via San Benedetto 28 • Tues–Sun 9am–7.30pm • €2 • ☎ 089 231 135, Ⓦ museoarcheologicosalerno.it

Five minutes' walk from the cathedral, the **Museo Archeologico Provinciale** occupies two floors of a restored Romanesque palace. It's full of local archeological finds, and has an array of terracotta heads and votive figurines, jewellery, lamps and household objects, from Etruscan as well as Roman times, but its most alluring piece is a sensual *Head of Apollo* upstairs, a Roman bronze fished from the Gulf of Salerno in the 1930s.

Museo Roberto Papi

Via Trotula de Ruggiero 23 • Thurs–Sat 9.30am–1pm & 6–8pm, Sun 9.30am–1pm • €3 • ☎ 089 253 190

The **Museo Roberto Papi** is two floors of eighteenth- and nineteenth-century surgical, gynaecological and dental instruments well displayed alongside mock-ups of dental surgeries, field hospitals and consulting rooms.

Giardino della Minerva

Via Ferrante Sanseverino 1 • March Tues–Fri 9am–1pm, Sat & Sun 9am–4pm; April & May Tues–Fri 10am–1pm & 5–8pm, Sat & Sun 10am–8pm; June–Aug Tues–Sun 10am–1pm & 5–8pm; Sept Tues–Fri 10am–1pm & 5pm–sunset, Sat & Sun 10am–sunset; Oct & Nov Tues–Fri 9am–1pm, Sat & Sun 9am–4pm; Dec–Feb Tues–Sun 9am–1pm • €3 • Ⓦ giardinodellaminerva.it

Perhaps Salerno's best – and most original – attraction is the **Giardino della Minerva** on Via Ferrante Sanseverino, a medicinal garden that was restored a decade ago to something like it would have been in the time of Matteo Silvatico, court physician to the king of Naples in the fourteenth century. Set across a series of terraces, laid out according to medieval medical principles and traversed by channels of tinkling water, it's a gloriously fragrant place, its shady terraces a wonderful retreat in summer – and there's even a café serving herbal tea to ensure you leave healthier than you arrived.

ARRIVAL AND INFORMATION   SALERNO

By train Salerno's train station lies at the southeastern end of the town centre on Piazza Vittorio Veneto, about a 10min walk from the old town. It has a left-luggage office – handy if you're just killing time before catching a ferry (Mon–Sat 9am–8pm; €2/hr).

By bus Buses run between Amalfi and Salerno about every 30min–1hr; the journey takes 1hr 15min. Buses generally pull up at the station; some also arrive and leave from Piazza della Concordia, down by the waterside nearby; buses from Naples use the SITA bus station at Corso Garibaldi 119.

By ferry Ferries and hydrofoils for the Amalfi Coast and Bay of Naples and elsewhere arrive in Piazza della Concordia, a 5min walk from the centre of town, and 10min from the train station. Some ferries, including those for Capri and Ischia, dock at the Molo Manfredi, west along the waterfront, near the Villa Comunale.

Tourist office At Via Lungomare Trieste 7–9, near the Villa Comunale (Mon–Sat 9am–1pm & 3–7pm; ☎ 089 231 432), and in the Galleria Capitol shopping centre on Corso Vittorio Emanuele (Mon–Fri 9am–1pm & 5–8pm, Sat 9am–1pm; ☎ 089 6629 5152).

ACCOMMODATION, EATING AND DRINKING

For pre-dinner drinks, head to Piazza Flavio Gioia, known to all as "La Rotonda", and the Villa Comunale, favourite hangouts of young *Salernitani,* with lots of bars and restaurants. The city's main drag, Via Roma, also sees a lively *passeggiata* in the early evening.

Ave Gratia Plena Via dei Canali ☎089 234 776, ⓦostellodisalerno.it. Housed in a former church and cloister complex, Salerno's official HI youth hostel is right in the centre of town and is a clean and welcoming place with a mixture of dorms and private rooms. There's a lovely central courtyard and wi-fi throughout. Open all year. Dorms €16, doubles €52

B&B Verdi Via Indipendenza, 5 ☎345 341 6372, ⓦbbverdi.it. A bijou, impeccably kept B&B with only three rooms, each en suite and with a balcony or small terrace. A simple breakfast is included, or it's an extra €5 for a more lavish affair with cheeses and cold meats. Open all year. €80

Botteghelle 65 Via Botteghelle 65 ☎389 262 5756, ⓦbotteghelle65.it. A great little *enoteca* selling all sorts of gourmet goodies; out back is a rustic dining room with mismatched furniture and hams hanging from the ceiling. Owner Pino Adinolfi is a cheesemaster and sommelier, and serves up tasty meat and cheese platters, and rice and pasta salads, for around €4 per plate. The food, wine and beer are local and delicious. Daily 9am–3.30pm & 6.30pm–midnight.

★**Hostaria Il Brigante** Via Fratelli Linguiti 4 ☎089 226 592. This great, old-fashioned *osteria* near the Duomo has been serving up hearty food at rock-bottom prices (*primi* around €6, *secondi* €7) for thirty years. Try the *sangiovannara*, which is always on the menu – pasta with mozzarella, aubergine, peppers and basil. Tues–Sun 1.30–2.30pm & 8.30–11pm.

Il Maestro del Gusto Vicolo Piantanova 7 ☎333 910 2296. This relatively new restaurant specializes in unusual dishes – such as *pennoni* pasta with shrimp, melon and smoked mozzarella – made using carefully chosen gourmet ingredients from all over the country. Mains €16–20. Mon–Thurs 7pm–midnight, Fri–Sun 12.30–2pm & 7pm–midnight.

Il Vicolo della Neve Vicolo della Neve 24 ☎089 225 705, ⓦvicolodellaneve.it. An attractively downbeat place serving great pizza and local specialities like *cotechino* sausage and broccoli. The *calzone* is particularly good. Pizzas go for €4 upwards, mains for about €10. Mon, Tues & Thurs–Sun 7pm–midnight.

★**Palazzo Morese** Largo Cassavecchia 4 ☎329 446 8710, ⓦpalazzomorese.it. In the heart of Salerno's old centre, just steps from the Duomo, this B&B is set in a historic *palazzo*. It offers three tastefully decorated and comfortable mini-apartments (no a/c), with kitchen facilities and a self-service breakfast. Open all year. €90

Paestum

About an hour's bus ride south of Salerno, the ancient site of **PAESTUM** spreads across a large area at the bottom end of the **Piana del Sele** – a wide, flat plain grazed by the buffalo that produce a good quantity of Southern Italy's mozzarella cheese. Paestum, or Poseidonia as it was known, was founded by Greeks from Sybaris in the sixth century BC, and later, in 273 BC, colonized by the Romans, who Latinized the name. But by the ninth century a combination of malaria and Saracen raids had decimated the population and left the buildings deserted and gradually overtaken by thick forest. The site was rediscovered by road-builders in the eighteenth century.

Beyond the site, the Paestum area is a gateway to the **Cilento**, Italy's second-largest national park, with an untamed beauty and low-key charm far removed from the gloss of the Amalfi Coast's resorts. It offers swathes of pristine sandy beach – popular with holidaying Italians in high summer – and two further points of interest, both UNESCO-protected: **Velia** (daily 8.45am–1hr before sunset; €3), the ruins of an ancient Greek colony, and the **Certosa di Padula** (Mon & Wed–Sun 9am–7pm; €4), a sprawling monastic complex founded in 1306, which boasts the world's biggest cloister.

The site

Via Magna Grecia 887 • Daily 8.45am–1hr before sunset • €6, €11 with museum; buy tickets at the museum • ☎ 0828 811 016, ⓦinfopaestum.it

Paestum is a dramatic, windswept place even now ("inexpressibly grand", Shelley called it), and is mostly unrecognizable ruins but with three golden-stoned **temples** that are among the best-preserved Doric temples in Europe. Of these, the Temple of Neptune, dating from about 450 BC, is the most complete, with only its roof and parts of the inner walls missing. The Basilica of Hera, built a century or so earlier, retains its double rows of columns, while the Temple of Ceres at the northern end of the site was used as a Christian church for a time. In between, the forum is little more than an open space, and the buildings around are mere foundations.

Museo Archeologico Nazionale di Paestum

Daily 8.45am–7.30pm; closed first and third Mon every month • €4, €11 with site

The splendid **museum**, across the road from the site, holds Greek and Roman finds from the site and around. There are many highlights, but the choicest include a set of weathered, archaic-period Greek metopes from another temple at the mouth of the Sele River, a few kilometres north, showing scenes of fighting and hunting, some stunning sixth-century bronze vases (*hydriae*), decorated with rams, lions and sphinxes, and, at the back of the museum, a selection of bronze helmets, breastplates and greaves. Near to these are some rare Greek tomb paintings, the best of which are from the Tomb of the Diver, graceful and expressively naturalistic pieces of work, including a diver in mid-plunge, said to represent the passage from life to death, and male lovers banqueting. Attractive fourth-century terracotta plates depict all sorts of comestibles, including fruits, sweets and cheese. The first floor, which is devoted to Roman finds, holds a marvellous collection of statues and reliefs, some very complete toga-ed figures, busts of Tiberius, Livia and others, a third-century statuette showing a baby in pointed hat with amulets, and a sarcophagus cover of a tenderly embracing couple.

ARRIVAL AND INFORMATION   PAESTUM

By train It's easy to see Paestum on a day-trip from Salerno. The quickest way to get there is by train (13 daily; 35–45min). The site is a 15min walk from the train station. You could also get off the train at Capaccio, slightly further from the ruins but a pleasant place for a wander. Gennaro di Giovanni, who runs a taxi service in the area (☎ 338 874 3105), can pick up from the station.

By bus Giuliano buses run from Salerno 9 times a day and take about 50min–1hr, dropping off outside Paestum station; buy your ticket before boarding. One bus a day (currently at 6.35am) goes from Paestum to Naples, dropping off at Salerno.

Tourist office Via Magna Grecia 887 (daily 9am–1pm & 3–5pm; ☎ 0828 811 016, ⓦ infopaestum.it), tucked away on a side street to the left of the museum. There's also an office in Paestum station (daily 9am–7pm; ☎ 0828 725 649).

ACCOMMODATION AND EATING

★ **Agriturismo Podere Rega** Via Porta Giustizia ☎ 0828 722 432, ⓦ podererega.it. This cosy, wood-beamed restaurant, impeccably run by husband-and-wife team Tiziana and Gerardo, is a stone's throw from the site. The food is elegant and delicious, and all ingredients are organic and local, with mozzarella served up many different ways. Two courses with wine will set you back €30–40 – pricey but worth it. There are four comfortable rooms too. **€100**

★ **Il Granaio dei Casabella** Via Tavernelle 84 ☎ 0828 781 014, ⓦ ilgranaiodeicasabella.com. An easy walk to the ruins – some rooms have a view of the temples – this rustic hotel has bags of home-spun charm. Breakfast is a feast of steaming cappuccinos and home-made pastries. The on-site restaurant serves simple dinners (half board €25/person). Open all year. **€80**

La Bottega del Gusto Via Magna Grecia 847 ☎ 333 408 4898. Right opposite the entrance to the ruins with a large terrace, this busy restaurant serves tasty over-stuffed sandwiches (€4.50) and tasting platters of cheese and cold meats (€10), and also has a *tavola calda* section with simple hot dishes. Daily 9.30am–10pm.

Oleandri Resort Via Poseidonia 177 ☎ 0828 851 876, ⓦ oleandriresort.com. Set 2km from the site, this four-star resort hotel set in parkland is a good option for families, with a large pool and a private beach. Accommodation in en-suite doubles or self-catering apartments is set around gardens, and there's a decent restaurant on site. Closed Nov–Easter. Doubles **€133**, apartments **€140**

Villa Rita Via Nettuno 9 ☎ 0828 811 081, ⓦ hotelvillarita.it. Pleasantly situated in relaxing gardens with a pool, just south of the archeological site. There's a restaurant, and bikes are available free of charge for guests to reach Paestum and nearby beaches. Closed mid-Nov to Feb. **€100**

7

ATLAS, MUSEO ARCHEOLOGICO NAZIONALE

Contexts

History

A comprehensive history of the Campania region would consist of a collection of more or less independent histories, as each of the major settlements has a complex story to tell. Instead, within a broad account of the evolution of the region, we have concentrated on the city that emerged as the dominant force – Naples – while background on the other major towns is given in the appropriate sections of the Guide. Naples' rich and varied history is ever-present on any tour of the city – in the street plan, the buildings, the art and in the Neapolitans themselves, whose anti-authoritarian streak and in-built fatalism is perhaps a natural consequence of centuries of outside influence and misrule.

The Greeks and Etruscans

The oldest settlement in the Bay of Naples, inhabited since about 2000 BC, is Ischia – then known as Pithekoussai. From the eighth to the fifth centuries BC, this area became an important part of Magna Graecia (Greater Greece), when a contingent of Greeks travelled here from Euboea to set up trading posts. In the eighth century, Ischia's rumbling volcanoes led them to found **Cumae** on the mainland, and it soon became the region's major city: a prosperous commercial centre whose legendary oracle, the Sibyl, was thought to be the mouthpiece of Apollo.

The Greeks dominated the region for centuries, and gradually spread out around the bay, in the seventh century BC building a city they called Parthenope on the hill of Monte Echia. As the Greeks cemented their power, the powerful **Etruscans** began to have designs on the settlements around the Bay of Naples, moving from their homeland in Tuscany to claim Capua as their southern capital in around 600 BC. The Etruscans twice invaded Cumae – in 524 BC and 474 BC – but were defeated on both occasions. Following the second attack, the Greeks created a colony called **Neapolis** or "New Town" on the lower ground below Parthenope to strengthen their hold on the region. The conflicts had served to sap the rivals' strength and resources, however, leaving them an easy target for the approaching Samnite hill tribes, who seized Capua in 424 BC and Cumae in 421 BC.

The Romans

The Samnites were soon usurped by the most powerful group to the north, the **Romans**, who moved into the area in the mid-fourth century BC, eventually taking Neapolis in 326 BC after a two-year battle. They quickly turned it into a colony of Rome, albeit one that remained at heart a Hellenistic city, highly regarded as a place of refinement and culture by the Romans. The city was attacked by – and resisted

2000 BC	8th century BC	600 BC	474 BC
Foundation of Pithekoussai on Ischia	Foundation of Cumae	Etruscans settle in Capua	Foundation of Neapolis by the Greeks

– Hannibal and his Carthaginian forces during the Second Punic War (218–201 BC), and during the Roman Civil War (88–82 BC) Sulla occupied the city on his way to take Rome from his rival Marius. Capua, too, became notorious as the centre of the slave revolt led by the renegade Spartacus in 73 BC.

Above all, though, Naples and its bay during this period were regarded as a pleasure resort for wealthy Romans, who flocked here to build villas and palaces by the sea for their leisure time and retirement. Virgil wrote much of his poetry in Naples, Pliny lived in a house on the bay, and Julius Caesar's father-in-law resided in the refined Villa dei Papiri. Stabiae, Baiae and Herculaneum became popular holiday resorts, while Tiberius famously relocated his administration to Capri in 26 AD until his death eleven years later. The largest town in the region, **Pompeii**, was a prosperous place, but was already in decline in 79 AD when Vesuvius erupted and buried it and the surrounding towns in volcanic ash.

The Byzantines and Normans

With the decline of the Roman Empire, the city was preyed upon by a myriad of invaders, first of which were the Ostrogoths who took the city in the mid-sixth century AD. They were, however, quickly dislodged by Byzantine forces under the general Belisarius, and the city changed hands several times until the Byzantines finally conquered the city in 553 after years of conflict. The following year it became a duchy ruled from Ravenna, during which time it prospered, its power increasing while that of Capua waned. It was only a matter of time until the city came under attack again, however; this time the aggressors were the Lombards from the north, and Saracens from the east. Shifting its allegiances between Rome and Constantinople, the city somehow managed to remain independent of all these marauding powers, maintaining a quasi-independence for around four hundred years.

To the south, Amalfi and the coast west as far as Positano (as well as Capri) and east as far as Cetara split from Naples in the seventh century and grew into a thriving commercial state in its own right, with its own currency and set of maritime laws, the **Tavola Amalfitana**. It continued to thrive into the tenth century, developing a rivalry with other mercantile city-states such as Pisa, Genoa and Venice, all of them vying for trade with the Byzantine empire to the east. However, in 1073 it fell prey to the **Normans**, who had already taken Capua eleven years earlier, and went on to take Naples in 1139. The Normans controlled a considerable swathe of the surrounding area, and the Norman Roger II proclaimed himself king of both Sicily and Naples. He ruled his subjects from Palermo, keeping them sweet by presiding over an economic boom and offering the restless barons and landowners land and privileges in return for cooperation.

The Hohenstaufen and Angevins

Despite the peace and prosperity of much of their rule, the Normans didn't remain in Naples for long, and like the rest of the region the city came under the rule of the **Hohenstaufen** dynasty in 1194, who stayed rather half-heartedly until 1269, when their last monarch, Conradin, just 14 years old, was beheaded in what is now Piazza del Mercato by the **Angevin** king, Charles I of Anjou.

326 BC	73 BC	79 AD	553 AD
Romans conquer Neapolis	Slave revolt led by Spartacus in Capua	Eruption of Vesuvius	Belisarius assumes control of Naples

Such was the unpopularity of the Hohenstaufen that the city welcomed its new ruler with open arms. Charles moved the capital of his Italian realm from Palermo to Naples, forming the **Kingdom of Naples** and establishing it as one of the great cities of Europe, a centre of culture and diplomacy. He also made his mark on the cityscape, building the Castel Nuovo in 1279, redeveloping the surrounding area and expanding the port. In spite of this, the reign of the Angevin kings was not entirely harmonious, and they took much more from the city than they gave back. Furthermore, Charles was distracted by the loss of Sicily to the Aragonese from Spain; his subsequent struggle to win it back led to a fierce naval battle just outside the city during which his son and heir, also called Charles, was taken prisoner. He was eventually released and a truce with the Aragonese agreed, after which a long period of peace was overseen by the Angevins' most enlightened ruler, Robert the Wise, who ascended to the throne in 1310 and made the city a fitting capital for the dynasty, building impressive monuments – Santa Chiara, San Lorenzo, the Duomo and Castel Sant'Elmo among them – attracting artists and craftsmen from all over Europe.

The Aragonese

The Angevins ruled Naples for the best part of two hundred years, while Sicily remained under Aragonese control, until 1422 when the **Aragonese** king Alfonso I took Naples and briefly unified the two kingdoms for the first time since the Normans. He handed over the reins to his son Ferdinand I, or Ferrante, on his death in 1458, who then passed them on to Alfonso II. In 1493, Charles VIII of France invaded but was soon forced out again by Ferdinand's grandson, Ferdinand II, or Ferrantino. After his premature death in 1496, the people wanted Ferdinand's widow Joan to take the crown, but his uncle Frederick was appointed instead – a move that angered both French and Spanish and led to the Franco-Spanish invasion of 1501. Faced with the loathing of his subjects, Frederick renounced the throne in favour of King Ferdinand of Spain, who consolidated the Spanish hold on the city – a hold which would last for around three hundred years.

The Spanish didn't particularly have the interests of Naples at heart, and King Ferdinand III appointed a series of viceroys to run the city, which they did with increasing brutality and punitive taxation, not to mention an upsurge in corruption among the ruling classes. In spite of this, it was a settled time during the city's history, and by the beginning of the seventeenth century Naples was the second-largest city in Europe, with a population of around three hundred thousand. Many of the city's residents were living in squalid conditions, however, and the swelling population meant that parts of the city had become dangerously overcrowded; in an attempt to raise standards of living, viceroy Don Pedro redeveloped the city on a grand scale, creating a new quarter, the Quartieri Spagnoli, to house the masses.

Sporadic uprisings against Spanish misrule culminated in the so-called **Masaniello revolt** of July 1647, when a popular insurrection against taxes on basic necessities such as fruit and vegetables broke out in Palermo and was quickly emulated in Naples, with riots and assassinations of major political and aristocratic figures that lasted for several days. The ringleader of the rebellion was a Neapolitan fisherman called Tommaso Aniello ("Masaniello"), who after a week was invited by the Spanish to sign a truce in

7th Century AD	1073	1139	1269
Amalfi becomes an independent city-state	Amalfi is conquered by the Normans	The Norman Roger II is proclaimed king of Naples	Charles of Anjou forms the Kingdom of the Two Sicilies

return for a prominent position in the governance of the city. Shortly after refusing the offer, he was assassinated while giving a speech, though his influence continued to be felt when later the same year a Neapolitan Republic was declared under the protection of the French. In spite of this, the Spanish were back by mid-1648, quickly restoring the city to order. Naples began to enjoy some degree of calm – at least until the devastating plague of 1656, which wiped out over half the urban population.

The Bourbons

Following the War of the Spanish Succession (1701–14), Naples was briefly ceded to the Austrians, before being taken, to general rejoicing, by **Charles of Bourbon** in 1734. Charles was a cultivated and judicious monarch and added greatly to the city's infrastructure, building the Teatro San Carlo, the Reggia at Caserta, the Palazzo Reale di Capodimonte and the Albergo dei Poveri, as well as renovating the Palazzo Reale and setting up the Biblioteca Nazionale. However, he abdicated to become king of Spain in 1759, and his eight-year-old son became **Ferdinand IV**, assisted at first by his trusted lawyer, Bernardo Tannucci, and later by his scheming queen, **Maria Carolina of Austria**. With an intellect far greater than that of her dim-witted husband, on the birth of her first son in 1777 Maria Carolina entered the Council of State – a clause in her marriage contract – and was able to take control. She swiftly orchestrated the downfall of Tannucci and replaced him with an English-born, anti-French aristocrat, John Acton – a disastrous alliance that led eventually to them abandoning Naples to the republican French and Napoleon in 1798.

The following year the French set up the so-called **Parthenopean Republic** – a semi-autonomous state within the Kingdom of Sicily – under the charge of Napoleon's brother Joseph. He was replaced two years later by Napoleon's sister Caroline and his brother-in-law Joachim Murat, who ruled precariously until 1815, when they were deposed by the British and the Austrians. The Bourbon Ferdinand IV was immediately restored to the throne as **Ferdinand I of the Two Sicilies**, ruling both Naples and Sicily – the first time the two kingdoms had been united for several hundred years.

The British in particular dealt out vicious reprisals against the republican rebels under Admiral Nelson, who was famously having an affair with Lady Hamilton, the wife of the British ambassador to Naples. Under continuing Bourbon rule, the city became one of the most densely populated in Europe, and one of the most iniquitous, with a reputation for poverty, violence and corruption. In spite of this, for the rest of Europe, Naples was the requisite final stop on the **Grand Tour**, a position it enjoyed not so much for its proximity to the major classical sites as for the ready availability of sex. The city was for a long time the prostitution capital of the continent, and its reputation drew people from far and wide, giving rise to the phrase – in the days when syphilis was rife – "see Naples and die".

Italian Unification

By the mid-nineteenth century Naples was a bastion of royalism in an increasingly republican world, and with the growing popularity of the Unification movement that was sweeping across the rest of Italy, it was only a matter of time before the Neapolitan

1282	1501	1600s	1647
Naples becomes an independent kingdom under the Angevins	Naples is ruled by the Spanish under King Ferdinand	Naples becomes the second-largest city in Europe	Masaniello uprising against Spanish rule

monarchs were deposed. Alarmed by the capture of Sicily by Unification forces in May 1860, Ferdinand II's son Francesco II agreed to a constitution, but it was too late. **Giuseppe Garibaldi** entered the city on September 7, receiving a hero's welcome, and on October 21, the people voted in overwhelming numbers to become part of a united Italy under the Savoy king **Vittorio Emanuele II**. It was the first time for centuries that the city had effectively governed itself, but it also signalled that Naples' glory days as a great European capital were over, as now Rome grew in importance. Naples entered a period of decline, culminating in a cholera epidemic in 1884 that devastated much of the city. In an attempt to clean up the city – now in a ruinous state – the worst of the slums were demolished, Corso Umberto I was bulldozed through the city centre, and a new residential district, Vomero, was constructed.

The twentieth century

The city continued its recovery during the early twentieth century: an airport was constructed in 1936, and infrastructure was improved with a network of railway and metro lines and funiculars. Naples was finding its place as a vital port in the new Italian kingdom, though this proved to be a disadvantage with the outbreak of **World War II**, during which the city was bombed more heavily than anywhere else in the country, leaving twenty thousand people dead. Fortunately, most of its architectural treasures escaped undamaged, although the church of Santa Chiara was destroyed by Allied bombs in 1943. During the so-called *Quattro Giornate di Napoli* ("Four Days of Naples") from September 27 to 30, 1943, fierce street battles led by local residents routed the Germans and paved the way for the Allied troops. When the Anglo-American forces entered the city, they found a population close to starvation and much of the city in ruins – a period brilliantly documented by Norman Lewis in his war memoir, *Naples '44* (see p.241).

There was little real improvement in the living standards of the average Neapolitan during the **postwar years**, with a very high percentage unemployed, and a disgraceful number still inhabiting the typically Neapolitan one-room *bassi* – little more than slums, letting in no light and housing many people in extremely overcrowded conditions, particularly in the Quartieri Spagnoli, widely held to be the most dangerous part of town. Although money poured into the city to rebuild its war-shattered infrastructure, the same period saw a rise in the power and influence of **organized crime**, with the Camorra creaming off a lot of the funds intended for reconstruction and diverting them into their own businesses. At the same time the Sicilian-American gangster, Lucky Luciano, arrived in Naples, having been deported from the US after helping with wartime intelligence operations in Italy.

The latter part of the century was no less bleak: in the late 1970s there was a cholera outbreak in part of the city, and in November 1980 the region suffered a massive **earthquake**, based in Irpinia but causing devastation across the whole area, leaving nearly three thousand dead and around one hundred thousand homeless. There was a huge relief effort, and a considerable amount of money was pledged to the recovery operation, not only by the Italian government but also from around the world. However, this proved just another business opportunity for the region's criminal gangs, and of around $40 billion donated it's thought that less than half went on genuine

1656	1734	1759	1777
Plague wipes out more than half the city's population	Charles of Bourbon becomes king of Naples and the city prospers	Eight-year-old Ferdinand assumes the throne	Maria Carolina of Austria takes control of the city

projects, while the rest went straight to the Camorra or into the hands of politicians in bribes. Naples and its surrounding area was also the recipient of much of the money that poured into the south under the national government's **Cassa per il Mezzogiorno** scheme to revive the Italian South, but again it's estimated that around a third of this was squandered due to corruption, with little benefit felt by local people.

The present day

Naples experienced a long-awaited upturn in its fortunes with the appointment of **Antonio Bassolino**, charismatic left-wing mayor of the city from 1993 until 2000, who made it his business to turn things around, fighting the corruption that was endemic in the city, and making his administration more transparent. Bassolino was confident

THE CAMORRA

Most people associate the mafia with Sicily, but Cosa Nostra is just one of a number of southern Italian criminal organizations, and whereas the power of the Sicilian mafia has declined in recent years, so the influence and prosperity of its sister network in Naples, the **Camorra**, has risen hugely.

The Camorra is different to the Sicilian mafia in its **structure**: rather than one umbrella group that maintains control over numerous families and sectarian interests, it is less centralized and more parochial, with families and wider clans controlling their own tight-knit districts all over the region. Today's Camorra is an ugly, brutal phenomenon that craves power at any cost, and even innocent bystanders are at risk when clan violence erupts, as it has frequently over the last decade. There have been some spectacularly indiscriminate territorial battles, and casual violence that's almost medieval in its brutality, mostly over control of the lucrative drugs trade in the northern suburbs of the city. The so-called Secondigliano war of 2004 ended with over one hundred deaths, and in 2006 a fight between prominent clans after the fall of the notorious Camorra clan led by Paulo di Lauro resulted in a dozen deaths in as many days. These wars have continued on and off ever since, and in 2012 led to the bloody and very public assassinations of prominent mobsters in both northern Naples and the seaside resort of Terracina, between Naples and Rome. It's perhaps no coincidence that Campania has the highest murder rate in Italy by some way, and one of the highest in the world.

SOME HISTORY

Organized crime in Naples is nothing new. The Camorra was at its height during the **nineteenth century**, until the Unification of Italy forced many of its members to flee to the US. The system then – and indeed right up until the 1980s – was mostly based on *pizzo*, the payment of protection money by businesses, and the illicit diversion of goods from Naples' port – even today less than half of the goods that come through the port of Naples pass through customs. The city centre was once the power base of the major families, and the main criminal activity was the black cigarette trade, which you could see on every street corner. This, however, has almost disappeared, and if there ever was an honourable tradition among Naples' thieves, it has pretty much evaporated.

THE CAMORRA TODAY

Estimates vary, but some reckon there are over five thousand *camorristi* living in Naples, divided between a hundred or so families, and their activities are so much part of life here

1799	1815	1860	1884	1940s
Napoleon forms the Parthenopean Republic	Bourbon rule is restored in a new Kingdom of the Two Sicilies	Naples joins the newly formed Kingdom of Italy	A cholera epidemic wipes out much of the city	Naples is heavily bombed during WWII

that supporting Naples' cultural strengths would boost local pride, and scores of neglected churches, museums and palaces were restored and are now regularly open; initiatives such as May's Maggio dei Monumenti festival, which sees buildings usually out of bounds to the public open their doors, are a further example of his influence. The city has also enjoyed a burst of creative activity from local filmmakers, songwriters, artists and playwrights. One of the prime movers in this aspect of Naples' resurgence is **Giuseppe Morra**, whose Fondazione Morra promotes all aspects of the arts in the city, such as its funding of the challenging Museo Nitsch and the annual Independent Film Show.

Bassolino's finest hour was perhaps the 1994 G7 summit, when world leaders met in a newly scrubbed Naples, at the request of Italian President Carlo Azeglio Ciampi. However, his efforts have been overshadowed by the fact that the real power in the area

that the network of organized criminal gangs is known collectively as *il sistema* or "the system". They have long been active in the poorer quarters of the city centre – Forcella, the Quartieri Spagnoli and La Sanità. But it's in the blighted **suburbs** mainly north of the city – Scampia, Secondigliano, Miano, Marigliano, and, further inland, around Caserta and Casal di Principe – that their newer power bases lie. With a third of the population officially unemployed, the local youth almost looks to the local *camorristi* as their careers advisors, and recent years have seen a rise in the Camorra's influence, and the bloodshed that goes with it. A handful of families lie at the centre of the network, and it's in these quarters that their presence is really felt. There's an unwelcoming air to these areas, and you'd be advised to stay away.

The Chinese too have begun to join forces with *il sistema*: most of Europe's vast Chinese imports enter Europe through the port of Naples, including a massive haul of illegal textiles which find their way into the garment business. Today the Camorra's main **commercial activities** are in high-quality designerwear, fake and otherwise; construction – they own the cement works and through contacts in local councils manage to land all the most lucrative contracts; drugs, which have brought the mob massive returns in recent years – Naples has Europe's highest ratio of drug dealers to inhabitants; arms dealing – Camorra clans supplied the Basque terrorist organization ETA at its height, and Serb irregulars during the Yugoslav wars of the 1990s; and perhaps most notoriously, waste disposal: the city was in the grip of a rubbish crisis in the summer of 2008 that has never really been resolved. There have also been reports of the mob infiltrating the profitable bakery industry – worth €600 million a year across the province – by selling cut-price bread, baked in toxic ovens, from underground bakeries.

Ex-Prime Minister Romano Prodi threatened to send in troops to bring the mob to heel, and his inability to get to grips with the problem was to a large extent responsible for his downfall in 2007. Berlusconi vowed to sort it out once and for all, sending five hundred troops to Campania at the end of 2008, but made little progress. Like most instances of racketeering in Italy, there's a widespread suspicion that the main Naples families have friends in very high places, but it's just possible that a determined national government with a clear mandate might be able to root out the key figures, as they have with the Cosa Nostra in Sicily – *if* they had local support. However, for the moment the Camorra march on regardless – still untouchable in a city that is naturally predisposed to mistrust the government, as well as too terrified of the potential consequences to revolt.

1943	1944	1980	1993	1994
Allied troops enter the devastated city	Vesuvius erupts	The city suffers a massive earthquake	Antonio Bassolino becomes mayor	G7 summit in Naples

is still in the hands of organized crime: much of the coastline west of the city – Bagnoli – was built with Camorra money and little that matters happens here without the nod of the larger families, who have consolidated their power bases around the city. Indeed it's clear that whatever Bassolino achieved – and it was undoubtedly a great deal – the Camorra is no closer to being eradicated than it ever was. If anything, it's more powerful than ever, having developed into Italy's most notorious and vicious organized crime network, ahead even of Sicily's Cosa Nostra.

The rubbish crises which peaked in 2008 and Roberto Saviano's book and film **Gomorrah** (and his exile from Naples) have only served to emphasize the city's plight, and where Naples goes from here is anybody's guess. Its mayor, Luigi de Magistris, a former prosecutor specializing in links between politicians and organized crime, has engendered a new optimism since his election in 2011, signing the city up to host major events like the Americas Cup, experimenting with closing parts of the centre to traffic, and making the odd arrest of high-level *camorristi*, such as Michele Zagaria of the Casalesi clan, who had been on the run for fifteen years, and Mario Riccio (head of the Amato-Pagano family), in 2014.

One thing is for sure: Naples is unique. But it could be so much better than it is – it has the location, the history, the culture and the monuments to compete with anywhere in Europe. However, the city will never be able to join Europe's mainstream as long as organized crime holds sway. For visitors, it's a vexed question. Because who, even among the city's critics, would ever want to change it?

2007	2008	2011	2013
Roberto Saviano documents the influence of the Camorra in every aspect of Neapolitan life	The first of the city's rubbish crises	Luigi de Magistris becomes mayor	Americas Cup takes place in Naples

Books and film

Listed below are a number of books on Naples and the Amalfi Coast region, and on Italy in general, that we think may enhance your trip; most should be readily available in bookshops or online. We've added ★ to indicate books that make especially good reading; titles currently out of print are marked o/p.

TRAVEL AND MEMOIRS

Thekla Clark *Wystan and Chester*. Written with ease and affection, this memoir of the author's postwar friendship with W.H. Auden and partner Chester Kallman is extremely readable, and paints a vivid picture of Ischia, and in particular Forío, in the 1950s.

Shirley Hazzard and Francis Steegmuller *The Ancient Shore*. A slim collection of reflections on a lifetime of visits to Naples by this literary American couple. Some good old black-and-white photos help to illustrate a lyrical and nostalgic text.

★Dan Hofstadter *Falling Palace*. Hofstadter's memoir of his time as a young man in Naples is a story of his love both for a local woman and also for the city, the peculiarities of which he documents with an intrepid and poetic fascination. One of the best and most revealing contemporary travelogues on the city currently in print.

★Norman Lewis *Naples '44*. Lewis was among the first of the Allied troops to move into Naples following the Italian surrender in World War II, and this is his diary of his experiences there. Part travelogue, part journalism, this is without question one of the finest accounts available both on the region and the war in Italy.

H.V. Morton *A Traveller in Southern Italy*. This charming memoir, written by an intrepid traveller and Italophile, is worth a look for its evocative descriptions of Naples circa 1969, as well as fascinating background on sites such as Paestum and Cumae, and entertaining insights into the Neapolitan persona.

★Axel Munthe *The Story of San Michele*. The oddly selective autobiography of a Swedish doctor to the rich and famous, documenting his discovery and conversion of the famous Anacapri villa he moved into in 1887 and the part he played in the Naples cholera epidemic of the 1880s. A great and very personal book, written with insight and humour.

Amanda Tabberer *My Amalfi Coast*. Above all, this is a sumptuous book of Amalfi Coast photographs, but it's also a guide and a memoir, with a personal perspective that really brings the region to life.

Robert Zweig *Return to Naples*. A recently published memoir of an American-Italian Jew who holidayed in Naples as a boy, and who returns to the city in middle age to dig up the truth about his family and the war. A personal history with lots of local colour.

HISTORY AND CURRENT AFFAIRS

Luigi Barzini *The Italians* (o/p). Long out of print but worth getting hold of as it's still a highly readable and relevant work on the Italian nation.

Tom Behan *See Naples and Die*. The definitive and most up-to-date work on the Camorra until Saviano came along, and still well worth reading if you're after some really comprehensive history and background.

Alex Butterworth and Ray Laurence *Pompeii: the Living City*. A dramatic and successful re-creation of the last generation of Pompeii, imagined from actual sources by a historian and dramatist, and as such a marvellously readable social history of imperial-era Rome.

Christopher Duggan *The Force of Destiny*. This history of Italy since Unification exposes the flaws in the notion of a unified Italy, particularly with regard to the political crises of the last twenty years.

Jordan Lancaster *In the Shadow of Vesuvius*. Subtitled "a cultural history of Naples", this is a treat for anyone who wants to dig a little deeper, and is an accessible and

revealing portrait of the city from the Greeks to the present day.

Valerio Lintner *A Traveller's History of Italy*. A brief history of the country, from the Etruscans right up to the present day. Well written and concise, and just the thing for the dilettante historian of the country.

Giuliano Procacci *History of the Italian People*. A comprehensive history of the peninsula, charting the development of Italy as a nation-state.

Peter Robb *Streetfight in Naples*. Robb lived in Naples for a while but his book concentrates not on the contemporary city but on the years of Spanish rule, when it was one of the largest cities in the world. He's most interested in the art of the time, in particular the fugitive Caravaggio and the artistic community he left in his wake. A slightly sprawling book, with more breathless enthusiasm than structure. Much like the city itself.

★Roberto Saviano *Gomorrah*. Saviano's exposé of the Neapolitan Camorra is the first to have dished the dirt on the most violent grouping of Italy's various organized criminal gangs, and he is currently in hiding because of it. At its heart, the book is a passionate protest against a problem that only seems to get worse, and it has also been made into a highly regarded film (see box below).

FOOD AND WINE

Carlo Capalbo *The Food and Wine Guide to Naples and Campania*. About as detailed a guide to the food, wine and produce of the region as anyone could ever want. Written with enthusiasm and authority,

---

NAPLES ON FILM

Naples' golden age of cinema is generally considered to be the postwar **neorealist** years, its most celebrated exponent the director **Vittorio De Sica**, who put a comic spin on the traditionally gritty genre. His *L'Oro di Napoli* ("The Gold of Naples"; 1954) is an appealing tribute to a city De Sica knew well. The director turned his attention to Naples again in the comedy *Ieri, Oggi, Domani* ("Yesterday, Today, Tomorrow"; 1963), in which Sophia Loren plays a dealer in black-market cigarettes who uses pregnancy as a means to keep out of jail.

Also in a comic vein, the films of the actor **Totò** (1898–1967), born in La Sanità, are some of Italy's most loved. His favourite role was that of a hustler, getting by on nothing but his wits – which may explain his iconic status in Naples. Totò's modern-day successor in many ways, **Massimo Troisi**, was another gifted comic actor, known for his jittery, melancholic screen persona. His most famous film, *Il Postino* (1994), set in Procida, was sadly his last; he died just after completing filming, at the age of just 41.

Film has played a crucial role in Naples' much-heralded modern-day renaissance, with directors such as **Antonio Capuano**, **Pappi Corsicato** and **Paolo Sorrentino** focusing on the less salubrious aspects of Neapolitan life. In 2008, the international release of the film based on Roberto Saviano's bestselling book *Gomorrah*, directed by **Matteo Garrone**, put Naples firmly in the spotlight, marking a return to neorealism – but without the comedy plots of old to sweeten the pill.

TOP TEN FILMS

Beat the Devil *John Huston, 1953.* An all-star cast stars in this comedy-thriller shot on location in Ravello and Atrani. Great performances from Humphrey Bogart, Gina Lollobrigida and Robert Morley work wonders with its somewhat creaky plot (written, incidentally, on a daily basis while on set), and turn it into a truly atmospheric film.

Gomorrah *Matteo Garrone, 2008.* Based on Roberto Saviano's ground-breaking bestseller (see above), this is as admirably candid and non-glamorous as the book. It portrays a Naples you're not likely to see on any visit – it's shot in the housing projects and wastelands north of the city and even uses locals as actors.

It Started in Naples *Melville Shavelson, 1960.* Clark Gable and local girl Sophia Loren star in this romantic comedy, which does indeed start in Naples but takes place mainly on Capri. Well acted and fun, with great shots of Capri especially.

The Life Aquatic *Wes Anderson, 2004.* This strangely deadpan and quirky comedy stars Bill Murray as a Cousteau-like underwater filmmaker having a midlife crisis against a backdrop of Naples and parts of the Amalfi Coast. Great shots of the theatre and main staircase of the Palazzo Reale, among other places.

Le Mani sulla Città *Francesco Rosi, 1963.* A political drama of corruption and property scams in Naples, starring Rod Steiger – perhaps the ultimate Naples film. The opening in particular has some impressive overhead shots of the city.

L'Oro di Napoli *Vittorio de Sica, 1954.* Local stars Sophia Loren and Totò star in this collection of six stories set in Naples, with memorable performances.

Il Postino *Michael Radford, 1994.* Procida's Chiaia beach, main waterfront and the post office were all used as locations in this life-enhancing film about the friendship between the Chilean poet Pablo Neruda and a simple Italian postman.

Star Wars 1: The Phantom Menace *George Lucas, 1999.* The royal palace at Caserta is a ready-made, larger-than-life setting for Queen Amidala's palace on Naboo in this *Star Wars* prequel. It also doubled as the Vatican in *Mission Impossible III*.

The Talented Mr Ripley *Anthony Minghella, 1999.* Many of the Italian locations in this film are in and around the area, most recognizably Naples' San Carlo opera house and the Castello Aragonese in Ischia.

Voyage to Italy *Roberto Rossellini, 1954.* An American couple travel to Naples for the first time and are pulled apart by the city's extremes. Lots of shots of Capri, Pompeii and Naples itself.

with details on producers, shops, restaurants and vineyards.

Marcella Hazan *The Classic Italian Cookbook*. A step-by-step guide that never compromises the spirit or authenticity of the recipes, Hazan draws her recipes from all over the peninsula, emphasizing the intrinsically regional nature of Italian food. The best Italian cookbook for novices.

Arturo Iengo *Cucina Napoletana*. A rare cookbook in English focusing on the food of Naples and Campania, and a great introduction to the recipes and ingredients of the region.

Accademia Italiana della Cucina *La Cucina*. Perhaps the widest selection of authentic Italian recipes you can find in one volume. A lovely lesson in the simplicity and diversity of Italian food, though perhaps not quite as practical as Marcella Hazan's book.

FICTION

Luciano de Crescenzo *Thus Spake Bellavista* (o/p). One of the few books by this Naples-focused author to be translated into English, this is a marvellous exploration of all the things that make the city unique.

Michael Dibdin *Cosi Fan Tutti*. The late author's Aurelio Zen is a classically eccentric loner detective, and his novels take place in an array of Italian locations – this is his Naples yarn.

Norman Douglas *South Wind*. This gloriously camp and largely autobiographical classic, published in 1917, follows the fortunes of the expat crowd on a thinly disguised Capri, where Douglas himself lived in exile following a prosecution for sexual molestation in the UK. An arch soap opera of disreputable sexual manners.

Elsa Ferrante *My Brilliant Friend*; *The Story of a New Name*; *Those Who Leave and Those Who Stay*. Ferrante's Neapolitan trilogy is set in the city from the 1950s through the 1970s, following the lives of two friends and chronicling the changes in the city itself during the same period. Great, gritty storytelling and vivid period detail from an author who has been described as the Italian Alice Munro.

Carol Goodman *The Night Villa*. Loosely based around the long-running excavations of the Villa dei Papiri in Ercolano, this is a scholarly, well-paced thriller, nicely written and very evocative of the city and region. Even if you never entirely accept the slightly preposterous storyline, it's an entertaining and eminently appropriate read for any trip to Naples.

Neil Griffiths *Betrayal in Naples*. An assured debut novel, this tightly wrought thriller follows a hopelessly out-of-his-depth hero through a city swathed in a corruption he doesn't remotely understand. A convincing take on Naples and a great holiday read.

★**Robert Harris** *Pompeii*. The days leading up to the eruption of Vesuvius and the destruction of Pompeii, Herculaneum and the surrounding area are skilfully re-created in Harris's dramatic novel. Told from the perspective of Pliny and a number of other characters, it does a good job of evoking the period in the Bay of Naples.

Patricia Highsmith *The Talented Mr Ripley*. This novel follows the fortunes of the eponymous hero through Italy, including Naples and Ischia, as he exchanges his own identity for that of the man he has murdered. Made into a stylish and evocative film in the 1990s (see box, p.242).

John Horne Burns *The Gallery*. This novel captures brilliantly the devastation of Naples after the Allied liberation of 1944, telling the stories of a number of different characters in the wartime city whose lives converge in the bombed-out Galleria Umberto I. A mixture of fiction and reportage, it pulls no punches, but is beautifully written and stands as a classic of postwar fiction about the city, by a little-known American writer who died tragically young.

Italian

It's relatively easy to master some of the basics of Italian. Speaking at least a little of the language, however tentatively, can mark you out from the masses in a country used to hordes of tourists, and your efforts will be rewarded by smiles and genuine surprise. If you already have a smattering of French or Spanish, which are extremely similar to Italian grammatically, you should have no trouble in picking up the basics of Italian. *The Rough Guide to Italian* phrasebook can help set you on the right road.

Pronunciation

Pronunciation is straightforward: all Italian words are stressed on the penultimate syllable unless an accent (´ or `) denotes otherwise, and words are usually enunciated with exaggerated, open-mouthed clarity.

The only difficulties you're likely to encounter are the few consonants that are different from English:

c before e or i is pronounced as in church, while **ch** before the same vowels is hard, as in cat.

sci or **sce** are pronounced as in sheet and shelter respectively.

The same goes with **g** – soft before e or i, as in geranium; hard before h, as in garlic.

gn has the ni sound of onion.

gl in Italian is softened to something like li in English, as in stallion.

h is not aspirated, as in honour.

When **speaking** to strangers, the third person is the polite form (ie lei instead of tu for "you"). It's also worth remembering that Italians don't use "please" and "thank you" half as much as we do: it's all implied in the tone, though, if in doubt, err on the polite side.

WORDS AND PHRASES

BASICS

good morning	buongiorno	no	no
good afternoon/evening	buonasera	please	per favore
goodnight	buonanotte	thank you (very much)	(molte/mille) grazie
hello/goodbye	ciao (informal)	you're welcome	prego
goodbye	arrivederci	all right/that's ok	va bene
yes	sì	how are you?	come stai/sta?
			(informal/formal)

NEAPOLITAN DIALECT

Even fluent Italian-speakers are taken aback when they arrive in Naples. Although everyone here speaks Italian, the local dialect sounds quite different to Italian. In fact, **Neapolitan** – *napoletano* in Italian, *nnapulitano* in dialect – was officially granted the status of a minority language in 2008, and variations of it are spoken across much of the Italian South, particularly in Calabria and Sicily. Although similar to Italian in many ways, with its roots in Latin, it has been influenced by the fact that until the eighth century Naples was a Hellenistic city in which everyone spoke Greek; and of course by the South's numerous foreign colonists. When spoken, it sounds like a more guttural, slightly harsher version of Italian. If you see the language written down, you'll notice the predominance of the letters "u" and "j" in many words, and the doubling of consonants. The masculine and feminine definite articles are "o" and "a" rather than "il" and "la"; plurals are "e" for both genders rather than "i" and "le"; Naples is Napule in dialect, Napoli in Italian.

I'm fine	bene
do you speak English?	parla Inglese?
I don't understand	non ho capito
I don't know	non lo so
excuse me	mi scusi
excuse me (in a crowd)	permesso
I'm sorry	mi dispiace
What's your name?	Come ti chiami/si chiama? (informal/ formal)
I'm here on holiday	Sono qui in vacanza
I'm English/Irish	Sono inglese/irlandese
Welsh/Scottish	gallese/scozzese
American	americano/a (m/f)
Australian	australiano/a (m/f)
Canadian	canadese
a New Zealander	neozelandese
wait a minute!	aspetta!
let's go!	andiamo!
here/there	qui/là
good/bad	buono/cattivo
big/small	grande/piccolo
cheap/expensive	economico/caro
early/late	presto/tardi
hot/cold	caldo/freddo
near/far	vicino/lontano
quickly/slowly	velocemente/lentamente

QUESTIONS

where?	dove?
where is/are ...?	dov'è/dove sono ...?
when?	quando?
what?	cosa?
what is it?	cos'è?
how much/many?	quanto/quanti?
why?	perché?
is it/is there ...?	c'è ...?
What time does it open/close?	A che ora apre/chiude?
What's it called in Italian?	Come si chiama in Italiano?

TRAVEL AND DIRECTIONS

Where is ...?	Dov'è ...?
How do I get to ...?	Per arrivare a ...?
Turn left/right	giri a sinistra/destra
Go straight on	vai sempre diritto
How far is it to ...?	Quant'è lontano a ...?
What time does the ... arrive/leave?	A che ora arriva/ parte ...?
bus	l'autobus
ferry	il traghetto
hydrofoil	l'aliscafo
train	il treno

How long does it take?	Quanto ci vuole?
Can you tell me when to get off?	Mi può dire dove scendere?
I'd like a ticket to ...	Vorrei un biglietto per ...
one-way	solo andata
return	andata e ritorno

SIGNS

entrance/exit	entrata/uscita
arrivals/departures	arrivi/partenze
free entrance	ingresso libero
gentlemen/ladies	signori/signore
wc	gabinetto/bagno
vacant/engaged	libero/occupato
no smoking	vietato fumare
open/closed	aperto/chiuso
closed for restoration	chiuso per restauro
closed for holidays	chiuso per ferie
pull/push	tirare/spingere
cash desk	cassa
out of order	guasto
ring the bell	suonare il campanello

RESTAURANTS

I'd like to reserve a table (for two)	Vorrei riservare una tavola (per due)
Can we sit outside?	Possiamo sederci fuori?
Can I order?	Posso ordinare?
I'm a vegetarian	Sono vegetariano/a (m/f)
Does it contain meat?	C'è carne dentro?
It's good	È buono
The bill, please	Il conto, per favore
Is service included?	Il servizio è incluso?
(set) menu	menù (fisso)
waiter/waitress	cameriere/a
knife	coltello
fork	forchetta
spoon	cucchiaio
plate	piatto

SHOPPING AND SERVICES

I'd like to buy ...	Vorrei comprare ...
How much does it cost/do they cost?	Quanto costa/costano?
It's too expensive	È troppo caro
with/without	con/senza
more/less	più/meno
enough, no more	basta
I'll take it	Lo/la prendo (m/f)
Do you take credit cards?	Accettate carte di credito?
bank	banca
money exchange	cambio
post office	posta

tourist office	ufficio di turismo	
shop	negozio	
supermarket	supermercato	
market	mercato	
ATM	Bancomat	

DAYS, TIMES AND MONTHS

What time is it?	Che ore sono?
It's (four) o'clock	Sono (le quattro)
today	oggi
tomorrow	domani
day after tomorrow	dopodomani
yesterday	ieri
now	adesso
later	più tardi
in the morning	di mattina
in the afternoon	nel pomeriggio
in the evening	di sera
Monday	lunedì
Tuesday	martedì
Wednesday	mercoledì
Thursday	giovedì
Friday	venerdì
Saturday	sabato
Sunday	domenica
January	gennaio
February	febbraio
March	marzo
April	aprile
May	maggio
June	giugno
July	luglio
August	agosto
September	settembre
October	ottobre
November	novembre
December	dicembre

NUMBERS

1	uno
2	due
3	tre
4	quattro
5	cinque
6	sei
7	sette
8	otto
9	nove
10	dieci
11	undici
12	dodici
13	tredici
14	quattordici
15	quindici
16	sedici
17	diciassette
18	diciotto
19	diciannove
20	venti, vinte
21	ventuno
22	ventidue
30	trenta
40	quaranta
50	cinquanta
60	sessanta
70	settanta
80	ottanta
90	novanta
100	cento
101	centuno
110	centodieci
200	duecento
500	cinquecento
1000	mille
5000	cinquemila

ITALIAN MENU READER

BASICS AND SNACKS

aceto	vinegar
aglio	garlic
biscotti	biscuits
burro	butter
caramelle	sweets
cioccolato	chocolate
formaggio	cheese
frittata	omelette
marmellata	jam
olio	oil
olive	olives
pane	bread
pepe	pepper
riso	rice
sale	salt
uova	eggs
yogurt	yoghurt
zucchero	sugar
zuppa	soup

PASTA

bucatini	thick, hollow spaghetti-type pasta
cannelloni	thick pasta tubes
capellini	thin noodles of pasta
conchiglie	seashell-shaped pasta, good for capturing thick sauces

farfalle	literally "butterflies", or bow ties
fettuccine	flat, ribbon-like egg noodles
fusilli	tight spirals of pasta
gnocchi	potato and pasta dumplings, often served *alla sorrentina*, or with tomato and basil sauce
lasagne	big rectangles of pasta, most commonly baked in the oven with white sauce and beef *ragù*
linguini	thin, flat noodles, often served with seafood
macaroni	small tubes of pasta
maltagliati	flat triangles of pasta, often used in soup
orecchiette	small ear-shaped pieces of pasta
paccheri	large tubes of pasta, common in the Naples region
pappardelle	thick flat egg noodles
pasta al forno	baked pasta, usually with minced meat, tomato and cheese
pasta e fagioli	soup with pasta and beans
penne	the most common tubes of pasta
ravioli	flat, square parcels of filled pasta
rigatoni	large, curved and ridged tubes of pasta – larger than *penne* but smaller than *paccheri*
scialatelli	thick, twisted ribbons of spaghetti-like pasta, common in Southern Italy
spaghetti	the most common pasta shape of all – long, thin, non-egg noodles
strozzapreti	twisted pasta tubes – literally "priest-stranglers"
tagliatelle	flat ribbons, slightly thinner than *fettuccine*
tonnarelli	another name for *bucatini*
tortellini/tortelloni	small and big rectangular parcels of filled pasta
tortiglioni	narrow *rigatoni*

PASTA SAUCE (SALSA)

aglio, olio e peperoncino	olive oil, garlic and chilli
amatriciana	cubed bacon and tomato
arrabbiata	("angry") spicy tomato with chillies
bolognese	meat
burro	butter
carbonara	cream, ham and beaten egg
funghi	mushroom
genovese	chunks of slow-cooked beef with onions
panna	cream
parmigiano	parmesan cheese
pesto	ground basil, garlic and pine nuts
pomodoro	tomato
puttanesca	("whorish") tomato, anchovy, olive oil and oregano
ragù	meat
vongole	clams

MEAT (CARNE)

agnello	lamb
bistecca	steak
carpaccio	slices of raw beef
cervello	brain, usually calves'
cinghiale	wild boar
coniglio	rabbit
costolette	cutlet, chop
fegato	liver
maiale	pork
manzo	beef
ossobuco	shin of veal
pancetta	bacon
pollo	chicken
polpette	meatballs
rognoni	kidneys
salsiccia	sausage
saltimbocca	veal with ham
spezzatino	stew
tacchino	turkey
trippa	tripe
vitello	veal

FISH (PESCE) AND SHELLFISH (CROSTACEI)

acciughe	anchovies
anguilla	eel
aragosta	lobster
baccalà	dried salted cod
calamari	squid
cefalo	grey mullet

cozze	mussels
dentice	sea bream
gamberetti	shrimps
gamberi	prawns
granchio	crab
merluzzo	cod
ostriche	oysters
pesce spada	swordfish
polpo	octopus
rospo	monkfish
sampiero	john dory
sarde	sardines
sogliola	sole
tonno	tuna
trota	trout
vongole	clams

VEGETABLES (CONTORNI) AND SALAD (INSALATA)

asparagi	asparagus
carciofi	artichokes
carciofini	artichoke hearts
cavolfiore	cauliflower
cavolo	cabbage
cipolla	onion
erbe aromatiche	herbs
fagioli	beans
fagiolini	green beans
finocchio	fennel
friarielli	a kind of broccoli popular in Naples
funghi	mushrooms
insalata verde/mista	green salad/mixed salad
lenticchie	lentils
melanzane	aubergine
patate	potatoes
peperoni	peppers
piselli	peas
pomodori	tomatoes
radicchio	red salad leaves
spinaci	spinach

COOKING TERMS

al dente	firm, not overcooked
al ferri	grilled without oil
al forno	baked
al sangue	rare
alla brace	barbecued
alla griglia	grilled
alla milanese	fried in egg and breadcrumbs
allo spiedo	on the spit
arrosto	roast
ben cotto	well done

bollito/lesso	boiled
cotto	cooked
crudo	raw
fritto	fried
in umido	stewed
pizzaiola	cooked with tomato sauce
ripieno	stuffed
stracotto	braised, stewed

CHEESE (FORMAGGIO)

burrata	soft, fresh cheese made from mozzarella and cream
dolcelatte	creamy blue cheese
fontina	northern Italian cheese, often used in cooking
gorgonzola	soft, strong, blue-veined cheese
mozzarella	(di bufala) soft white cheese, traditionally made from buffalo's milk
pecorino	strong, hard sheep's cheese
provola/provolone	smooth, round mild cheese, made from buffalo or sheep's milk; sometimes smoked
ricotta	soft, white sheep's cheese

DESSERTS (DOLCI), FRUIT (FRUTTA) AND NUTS (NOCI)

amaretti	macaroons
ananas	pineapple
anguria/coccomero	watermelon
arachidi	peanuts
arance	oranges
banane	bananas
cacchi	persimmons
ciliegie	cherries
crostata	pastry tart with jam or chocolate topping
fichi	figs
fichi d'india	prickly pears
fragole	strawberries
gelato	ice cream
limone	lemon
macedonia	fruit salad
mandorle	almonds
mele	apples
melone	melon
pere	pears
pesche	peaches
pinoli	pine nuts

pistacchio	pistachio nut	**granita**	iced drink with coffee
sfogliatella	a shell-shaped pastry		or fruit
	filled with ricotta, vanilla	**latte**	milk
	and candied fruit	**limonata**	lemonade
sorbetto	sorbet	**spremuta**	fresh fruit juice
torta	cake, tart	**spumante**	sparkling wine
uva	grapes	**succo**	concentrated fruit juice
zabaglione	dessert made with eggs,		with sugar
	sugar and marsala wine	**tè**	tea
zuppa inglese	trifle	**tonica**	tonic water
		vino	wine
DRINKS		**rosso**	red
acqua minerale	mineral water	**bianco**	white
aranciata	orangeade	**rosato**	rosé
bicchiere	glass	**secco**	dry
birra	beer	**dolce**	sweet
bottiglia	bottle	**litro**	litre
caffè	coffee	**mezzo**	half
caraffa	carafe	**quarto**	quarter
cioccolato caldo	hot chocolate	**salute!**	cheers!
ghiaccio	ice		

Glossary

agora square or marketplace in an ancient Greek city

ambo a kind of simple pulpit, popular in Italian medieval churches

apse semicircular recess at the altar (usually eastern) end of a church

architrave the lowest part of the entablature

atrium inner courtyard

baldachino a canopy on columns, usually placed over the altar in a church

basilica originally a Roman administrative building, adapted for early churches; distinguished by lack of transepts

belvedere a terrace or lookout point

caldarium the steam room of a Roman bath

campanile bell tower, sometimes detached, usually of a church

capital top of a column

cella sanctuary of a temple

chancel part of a church containing the altar

chiaroscuro the balance of light and shade in a painting, and the skill of the artist in depicting the contrast between the two

ciborium another word for baldachino, see above

cipollino an Italian marble with alternating white and green streaks

cornice the top section of a classical facade

cortile galleried courtyard or cloisters

cosmati work decorative mosaic work on marble, usually highly coloured, found in early Christian Italian churches, especially in Rome; derives from the surname Cosma, a common name among families of marble workers at the time

cryptoporticus underground passageway

Decumanus Superior the main street of a Roman town – the second cross-street was known as the Decumanus Inferior

entablature the section above the capital on a classical building, below the cornice

ex voto artefact designed in thanksgiving to a saint

fresco wall-painting technique in which the artist applies paint to wet plaster for a more permanent finish

lararium a shrine for holding the images of the household gods and similar relics in the houses of ancient Rome

loggia roofed gallery or balcony

metope a panel on the frieze of a Greek temple

Mithraism pre-Christian cult associated with the Persian god of light, who slew a bull and fertilized the world with its blood

nave central space in a church, usually flanked by aisles

nymphaeum An ancient Roman feature or monument dedicated to water nymphs, in the form of a small artificial grotto

palestra a public place in ancient Greece or Rome devoted to the training of wrestlers and other athletes

pantocrator usually refers to an image of Christ, portrayed with outstretched arms

peristyle a colonnade enclosing a court or building

piano nobile main floor of a *palazzo*, usually the first

polyptych painting on several joined wooden panels

portico covered entrance to a building, or porch

presepio/presepe Christmas crib

putti cherubs

reliquary receptacle for a saint's relics, usually bones; often highly decorated

sgraffito decorative technique whereby one layer of plaster is scratched to form a pattern

stucco plaster made from water, lime, sand and powdered marble, used for decorative work

thermae baths, usually elaborate buildings in Roman villas

triptych painting on three joined wooden panels

trompe l'oeil work of art that deceives the viewer by means of tricks with perspective

Small print and index

ABOUT THE AUTHOR

Martin Dunford is one of the founders and the former publisher of Rough Guides and has worked in travel publishing for 30 years. He is the author of more than ten guidebooks and also works as a freelance writer and as a publishing and digital consultant to the travel industry. He travels to Italy, in particular Rome and Naples, regularly, and when not on the road, he lives in Blackheath, London, with his wife and two daughters.

Acknowledgements

Martin Dunford: Thanks to Kathryn Lane for precise and patient editing, my writing colleague Natasha Foges, and to everyone at Rough Guides who helped to bring this third edition to fruition. Thanks also to Nicky Vonk, Federico Flippa, Irene Strametto, Manuela Barzan, Marianna Sarno, Nino Miniero, Chiara Cocurullo, Tina Tolomello and Stefania Gatta – and to everyone who wrote in with thoughts and suggestions.

Natasha Foges: Thanks to Alice Park at Rough Guides for the opportunity; Kathryn Lane for excellent editing; Harriet Foges for her company on the Amalfi Coast; Will Widén for handling the twists and turns (of the coast road and otherwise) with aplomb; and Joe, for making his return visit one to remember.

Readers' updates

Thanks to all the readers who have taken the time to write in with comments and suggestions (and apologies if we've inadvertently omitted or misspelt anyone's name):

Tony Foster, Matt Hodges, Sophie Howman, Nigel Kendall, Andrew Maywood, Cairon Pearson, Mark Preston, John White.

A ROUGH GUIDE TO ROUGH GUIDES

Published in 1982, the first Rough Guide – to Greece – was a student scheme that became a publishing phenomenon. Mark Ellingham, a recent graduate in English from Bristol University, had been travelling in Greece the previous summer and couldn't find the right guidebook. With a small group of friends he wrote his own guide, combining a highly contemporary, journalistic style with a thoroughly practical approach to travellers' needs.

The immediate success of the book spawned a series that rapidly covered dozens of destinations. And, in addition to impecunious backpackers, Rough Guides soon acquired a much broader readership that relished the guides' wit and inquisitiveness as much as their enthusiastic, critical approach and value-for-money ethos.

These days, Rough Guides include recommendations from budget to luxury and cover more than 120 destinations around the globe, as well as producing an ever-growing range of ebooks.

Visit **roughguides.com** to find all our latest books, read articles, get inspired and share travel tips with the Rough Guides community.

Rough Guide credits

Editor: Kathryn Lane
Layout: Anita Singh
Cartography: Rajesh Chhibber
Picture editor: Roger Mapp
Proofreader: Anita Sach
Managing editor: Natasha Foges
Assistant editor: Sharon Sonam
Production: Janis Griffith

Cover design: Nicole Newman, Roger Mapp, Anita Singh
Photographer: Karen Trist
Editorial assistant: Rebecca Hallett
Senior pre-press designer: Dan May
Programme manager: Gareth Lowe
Publisher: Joanna Kirby
Publishing director: Georgina Dee

Publishing information

This third edition published June 2015 by
Rough Guides Ltd,
80 Strand, London WC2R 0RL
11, Community Centre, Panchsheel Park,
New Delhi 110017, India
Distributed by Penguin Random House
Penguin Books Ltd,
80 Strand, London WC2R 0RL
Penguin Group (USA)
345 Hudson Street, NY 10014, USA
Penguin Group (Australia)
250 Camberwell Road, Camberwell,
Victoria 3124, Australia
Penguin Group (NZ)
67 Apollo Drive, Mairangi Bay, Auckland 1310,
New Zealand
Penguin Group (South Africa)
Block D, Rosebank Office Park, 181 Jan Smuts Avenue,
Parktown North, Gauteng, South Africa 2193
Rough Guides is represented in Canada by Tourmaline
Editions Inc. 662 King Street West, Suite 304, Toronto,
Ontario M5V 1M7
Printed in Singapore

Martin Dunford © June 2015
Maps © Rough Guides
No part of this book may be reproduced in any form
without permission from the publisher except for the
quotation of brief passages in reviews.
256pp includes index
A catalogue record for this book is available from the
British Library
ISBN: 978-0-24100-973-4
The publishers and authors have done their best to ensure
the accuracy and currency of all the information in **The
Rough Guide to Naples & the Amalfi Coast**, however,
they can accept no responsibility for any loss, injury, or
inconvenience sustained by any traveller as a result of
information or advice contained in the guide.
1 3 5 7 9 8 6 4 2

Help us update

We've gone to a lot of effort to ensure that the third edition
of **The Rough Guide to Naples & the Amalfi Coast** is
accurate and up-to-date. However, things change – places
get "discovered", opening hours are notoriously fickle,
restaurants and rooms raise prices or lower standards. If
you feel we've got it wrong or left something out, we'd like
to know, and if you can remember the address, the price,
the hours, the phone number, so much the better.

Please send your comments with the subject line
"**Rough Guide Naples & the Amalfi Coast Update**" to
✉ mail@uk.roughguides.com. We'll credit all contributions
and send a copy of the next edition (or any other Rough
Guide if you prefer) for the very best emails.
Find more travel information, connect with fellow
travellers and plan your trip on ⊕ roughguides.com.

Photo credits

Index

Maps are marked in grey

Map symbols

The symbols below are used on maps throughout the book

✈	Airport	◆	Place of interest	═══	Road	⋯⋯ Funicular
★	Bus/taxi stop	ⵜ	Church	▬▬	Motorway	▬ Wall
Ⓜ	Metro station	⊠	Gate/entrance	▬▬	Pedestrian road	▦ Building
✉	Post office	⋇	Viewpoint	– – –	Footpath	✝ Church
@	Internet access	♜	Tower	ⵜⵜⵜ	Steps	⬚ Park
ⓘ	Tourist office	⌒	Cave	— —	Ferry	⬚ Beach
✚	Hospital	ⵜ	Lighthouse	▬▬	Railway	⊞ Cemetery
Ⓟ	Parking	▲	Mountain peak			

Listings key

■   Accommodation

●   Restaurant/café/bar/pub

■   Club/music venue

●   Shop/market